Helping Children Grow Up in the 90's:
A Resource Book for Parents and Teachers

Compiled by

The National Association of School Psychologists

The National Association of School Psychologists
8455 Colesville Road, Suite 1000
Silver Spring, Maryland 20910

From NASP Publications Policy Handbook

The content of this document reflects the ideas and positions of
the author(s). The responsibility lies solely with the author(s)
and does not necessarily reflect the position or ideas of the
National Association of School Psychologists.

First Printing: 1992

HQ
769
.N27
1992

Published by:
  The National Association of School Psychologists
  8455 Colesville Road, Suite 1000
  Silver Spring, Maryland 20910

ISBN 0-932955-07-X

Printed in the United States of America

Contributing Authors

Edward M. Levinson and
  Lynne M. McKee
Indiana University of Pennsylvania
Indiana, PA

Robert G. Harrington
University of Kansas

J. H. Presbury and A. J. Benson
James Madison University

J. Fitch
Lyndon State College

E. P. Torrance
University of Georgia

Chuck McBride and Max McFarland
Nebraska Department of Education

David C. Canaday
Leavenworth County Cooperative
Leavenworth, Kansas

Marcia Shaffer
Steuben-Allegany Board of Cooperative
  Educational Services
Bath, New York

John J. DeFrancesco
Connecticut Department of Children and
  Youth Services

Cynthia M. Sheehan
Just Kids Early Childhood Learning Center
Middle Island, NY

Ellis P. Copeland
University of Northern Colorado

Hedy Teglasi
University of Maryland—College Park

Elaine Clark and William R. Jenson
University of Utah

Thomas J. Kehle
University of Connecticut

Marie Boultinghouse
Charlotte-Mecklenburg Schools
Charlotte, North Carolina

Doris Benson
California State University—Northridge

Kathryn C. Gerken
The University of Iowa

Mahlon B. Dalley
University of Northern Colorado

Susan M. Vess
University of Maine-Portland

Patrick H. Tolan
Institute of Juvenile Research
  Chicago, IL

John R. Hester
Francis Marion College
Florence, South Carolina

Teresa A. Hutchens
The University of Tennessee

Elizabeth Bard
Akron Public Schools Child
  Study Department

Theodore A. Ridder
Belding Area Schools
Michigan

Theo Lexmond
Soldotna, AK

Beth Deemer
Anne Arundel County Board of Education
Annapolis, Maryland

Clyde J. Johnson, Betty E. Gridley, and
  Shauna Gatten
Ball State University
Muncie, Indiana

William Strein
University of Maryland, College Park

Maribeth Gettinger
University of Wisconsin-Madison

Diane Kriger Wilen
Broward County, Florida Public Schools

Gail Epstein Mengel
Longmeadow, MA Public Schools

David W. Peterson and Janice Miller
Glen Ellyn, IL

Andrea Canter
Minneapolis Public Schools
Minneapolis, MN

Peg Dawson
Brentwood, NH

Karen Carey
Fresno State University
Fresno, CA

Joseph R. Irilli
Niles City Schools
Niles, Ohio

Cathy J. Carty
Youngstown City Schools
Youngstown, Ohio

George Batsche
University of South Florida

Benjamin Moore
Hammett School—The Baby Fold
Normal, Illinois

H. L. Janzen
University of Alberta

D. H. Saklofske
University of Saskatchewan

Susan G. Forman and Kathy L. Jackson
University of South Carolina
Columbia, South Carolina

Robert Diamond
University of Virginia Health
  Sciences Center

Joyce Krumbein Slater
Milford School System
Milford, Connecticut

James R. Deni
Appalachian State University
Boone, North Carolina

Linda C. Caterino
Arizona State University
Tempe, Arizona

William O. Hahn
Behavior Management Consultants
New Kensington, PA

Scott Poland
Cypress-Fairbanks ISD
Houston, Texas

Randi Walls
Youngstown Public Schools

Margaret K. Greer, Barbara L. Armstrong,
and Dianna L. Dean
Medical University of South Carolina
Charleston, SC

Linda M. Neiheiser
Strongsville, OH

Steven E. Curtis
Utah State University

Margaret L. Potter
Moorhead State University
Moorhead, Minnesota

Alex Thomas
Miami University
Oxford, OH

Sharon W. Royal and Howard M. Knoff
University of South Florida
Tampa

Steven I. Pfeiffer
Devereaux Foundation
Devon, PA

Nancy A. McKellar
Wichita State University

Deborah D. Waddell
Columbus, Ohio

Don Brunnquell
Minneapolis Children's Medical Center

Elaine Clark and Douglas Goldsmith
University of Utah

Charles P. Heath
Deer Valley Unified School District
Phoenix, Arizona

Sally Linton Burton
University of Idaho

Cindy Carlson
University of Texas at Austin
Austin, Texas

Susan Kupisch
Oak Grove, KY

Pia Rebello
Lynn Ellen Thompson
Mary Ann Parkinson
Bradford P. Underhill
Shirley Peffers
Nancy Conti
Sherri L. West
Bonnie Matthews
Martha E. Scherer
Andrea M. Mowatt
Jeanne Raschke
Erika Manz
Kim Robinson
Nancy Conti
Diane Van Dusen
Lorene Heuvelman

University of South Florida

Helping Children Grow Up in the 90's: A Resource Book for Parents and Teachers

Compiled by the National Association of School Psychologists

Table of Contents

Foreword.   xi

**Part I: Growing Up—Developmental Issues for Children
and Adolescents**

Career and Career Decision-Making.   3
Communicable Diseases.   7
Creativity.   11
Dependency.   15
Different Cultural Backgrounds.   19
Hearing.   21
Homosexuality.   25
Humor.   27
Language Development.   31
Maladaptive Habits.   35
Masturbation.   37
Nailbiting.   39
Obesity.   41
Perception of Time.   45
Prejudice.   47
Prematurity.   49
Religion.   51
Responsibility.   53
Sexual Interest.   57
Shyness.   59
Sleepwalking.   61
Stress.   63
Temperament.   65
Thumbsucking.   69

Part II: Growing Out—Getting Along with Peers and Others

Anger Control Problems 75
Assertiveness. 79
Competition 81
Peer Relations. 85
Self-Control 89

Part III: Parenting—Helping Children and Adolescents to Grow and Develop

Childcare. 95
Family Size. 99
Household Chores 103
Medication 105
Siblings. 107
Surviving the Holidays. 113
Television. 115
Temper Tantrums 119
Working Parents 123

Part IV: The Home-School Connection—Bridging the Gap

Attention Deficit Hyperactivity Disorder. 129
Cheating. 137
Gifted Children: Special Needs and Considerations 141
Giftedness. 145
Grades 147
Homework 151
Increasing Academic Learning Time. 153
Limited English Proficiency. 157
Organization. 161
Peer-Influenced Academic Interventions in the Classroom 163
Reading. 167
Retention 171
School Entry Decisions 175
Study Skills. 177

Part V: Helping Out—Emotional and Behavioral Problems with Children and Adolescents

Anorexia and Bulimia. 181
Anxiety 185
Bullying. 189
Delinquency. 195

Depression. 199
Drug Abuse. 203
Encopresis. 207
Enuresis. 209
Fears and Phobias. 211
Firesetting. 213
Head Injury. 215
Obsessive Compulsive Disorder 217
Physical Abuse. 221
Running Away. 225
Sexual Abuse. 227
Stealing. 231
Suicide 233
Suicide Intervention 235
Tourette Syndrome. 239

Part VI: Working it Out—Adapting to Life Crises and Changes

Adolescent HIV/AIDS. 245
Adopted Children 253
Asthma. 263
Cancer. 267
Chronic Illness. 271
Diasters—How to Respond. 273
Divorce. 285
Divorce—Access and Visitation Arrangements. 287
Dysfunctional Families. 291
Foster Homes 293
Holidays—Coping with Loss. 295
Hospitalization. 299
Moving. 303
Reactions to Death. 307
Seizures. 309
Siblings of the Handicapped. 313
Single-Parent Homes. 315
Stepfamilies. 319
Transition Planning for Handicapped Students. 323
War—Responding to Operation Desert Storm 329

Part VII: Fact Sheets

Adopted Children at School. 339
Attention Deficit Hyperactivity Disorder. 347
Bullying. 351
Divorce and Our Children. 359

Dropouts: Reasons and Responses.................................... 361
Early Childhood Primary Prevention Programs for Emotional and
       Behavioral Problems... 365
Grade Retention.. 373
Multicultural and Minority Issues................................... 377
Self-Esteem... 381
Sexual Abuse Prevention Programs................................. 385

Index... 399

Foreword and Acknowledgments

Today's children are significantly at-risk for both educational and social failure. According to the Children's Defense Fund (1990), "(t)he mounting crisis of our children and families is a rebuke to everything America professes to be. It also will bring America to its economic knees and increase violence and discord within this country unless we confront it" (pg. 3). As examples of the broad-based problems currently facing our children and families, this report highlights the devastating statistics regarding school drop out, child runaways, abuse and neglect, teenage parents, drug and alcohol abuse, children killed by guns, and the effects of poverty and homelessness on America's children (Children's Defense Fund, 1990, pgs. 3-5).

From an applied and practical perspective, the decade of the 1990s may turn out to be one of the most important relative to these educational and social needs. Starting with the 1982 National Academy of Sciences report (Heller, Holtzman, & Messick, 1982) addressing the fundamental problems that exist in the provision of services to handicapped and at-risk students, the 1983 *Nation at Risk* report of the National Commission on Excellence in Education, and finishing with the National Governors' Association educational summit in the Fall of 1989 to specify the nation's educational goals for the coming ten years and now, President Bush's America 2000 initiative, the commitment to rededicate ourselves to quality education and parenting has been sounded at national, state, and local levels.

In all of these reports and initiatives, a number of facts have been clearly reinforced: that

- Children spend the greatest amount of time in home and then school settings.

- Parent education and preventive services must be provided to meet the needs of disadvantaged, minority, and rural families whose children are at-risk.

- Teachers and parents must have high expectations for all children and must establish appropriate and collaborative learning objectives and goals.

- Approximately 12%, and perhaps as many as 25%, of all school-aged children will experience psychological problems that will necessitate mental health services during their school-aged years, and often these students' problems will never be fully identified or addressed.

- Most school initiatives appear to be focused on declining academic achievement rather than on efforts needed to meet the diverse, social *and* academic needs of all students.

- Schools must actively involve parents as an integral part of the socialization and educational process. Parent involvement is a necessary and critical process that ensures home-school consistency, reinforcement, and childhood success.

This resource book has been developed by over one hundred school psychologists, each an expert in his or her field, to address many of the areas that place children at-risk for educational and social failure. Organized in handouts and fact sheets, it is hoped that psychologists and other educators will photocopy different parts of this book and give them to parents, teachers, and other educators so that they can more broadly understand and address some of the situations and circumstances that children confront on the "road to growing up." In a small way, we hope that this resource book will make a difference in the lives of these children so that they can become the parents of a next generation that doesn't have to deal with as many of the problems as those described above.

As with any book of this magnitude, a great number of individuals have had a hand in its development and production. Gratefully acknowledged are the following people: all of the authors who spent the time to share their expertise for the benefit of our children, families, and schools; Alex Thomas, Jeff Grimes, and Deborah Waddell who initiated this project through the *Children's Needs: Psychological Perspectives* monograph and the *Communique* of the National Association of School Psychologists; the students at the University of South Florida School Psychology Program who added significantly to the breadth of the handouts in this book; Linda Murphy who spent many hours copyediting these handouts, ensuring that they were teacher- and parent-friendly; the National Headquarters staff at NASP (especially Margie Gibelman, Richard Yep, and Mary Beth King); and Jane Carey and her staff at Boyd Printing for their printing and production expertise in "getting the job done." To all of you, thank you for your dedication, goodwill, and commitment to excellence!!!

Howard M. Knoff, Ph.D.
Chair, Publications Board
National Association of School
Psychologists
February, 1992

Part-I

Growing Up—
Developmental Issues for Children
and Adolescents

NATIONAL
ASSOCIATION OF
SCHOOL
PSYCHOLOGISTS

Children and Career Decision-Making

Edward M. Levinson
Indiana University of Pennsylvania, Indiana, PA

Background—Work is an integral aspect of American life. Over the course of 45 working years, an individual spends as many as 94,000 hours on the job. Because work occupies such a large part of our lives, it has a major effect on how we feel about ourselves and our overall quality of life. The frequency with which people say "I am a(n) . . . (occupation)" indicates the extent to which our views about ourselves are influenced by the kind of work we do. Because work has such a significant effect on our lives, it is important to prepare children and adolescents to make decisions about the kind of work they will do. Ideally, we want to see children and adolescents decide upon and prepare for jobs in which they will both succeed and find happiness. Being able to choose such a job requires an understanding of oneself, an understanding of the world of work, and an ability to make effective decisions.

Development—The rate at which children and adolescents acquire the knowledge and skills necessary to make effective decisions about work varies. The following is a listing of the knowledge and skills required for effective career decision making and successful adjustment to work, and the general age range during which these are acquired.

Age Range	Knowledge and Skills
0–10 years	—Children begin to gain an understanding of their personal qualities.
	—Children begin to develop skills necessary for getting along with others.
	—Children begin to take pride in their accomplishments, and strive toward producing quality work.
	—Children begin acquiring information about different kinds of work via conversation, television, visits to work settings, and role playing (playing cowboy, astronaut, detective, etc.)
11–13 years	—Children begin to develop and recognize specific interests, and relate these interests to jobs.
	—Children begin to assume additional responsibilities and begin developing planning, problem-solving, and decision—making skills.
	—Children increase their knowledge of the work world.
13–14 years	—Young adolescents begin to recognize their abilities and values.
	—Young adolescents begin to understand that different jobs require different abilities and provide different rewards.
	—Young adolescents begin to assume responsibility for their own decisions and become aware of imminent academic choices and their relationship to post high school alternatives.

15–17 years	—Adolescents begin to identify and explore vocational options, and assume responsibility for career—related decisions.
	—Adolescents develop tentative career goals.
18–21 years	—Young adults decide on a career and acquire the education and training required for entry—level employment in the field.
22–24 years	—Adults acquire a job in their chosen field.

What Can I Do As A Parent? Your goal as a parent should be to assist your children in

1) gaining an understanding of themselves (that is, their abilities, interests, and values),

2) gaining an understanding of the world of work (that is, the nature of different jobs, and the requirements and rewards offered by these jobs), and

3) assuming responsibility for making their own decisions, and developing effective decision—making skills.

—**Increasing Self Understanding**—You can increase your children's understanding of themselves by simply talking to them. Tell them what they do well and what they need to improve on, and offer specific examples of accomplishments and tasks that they've had difficulty with as examples. Ask your children what they like to do and why, and offer your own views of their interests based upon what you see them enjoying. Encourage your children to respond to this feedback and to offer their own ideas about their strengths, limitations, and interests. Such discussions can be especially profitable following the completion of household chores or reviews of report cards, and also within the context of part—time jobs. Encourage others (friends, relatives, and teachers) to offer similar feedback to your children. Vocational testing by psychologists and counselors is another method by which self understanding can be increased.

—**Increasing Occupational Awareness**—You can increase your child's understanding of the world by simply talking about jobs. Discuss jobs you've had, the activities you performed in these jobs, the setting in which you worked, the education, and training that was required to obtain the job, and what a typical day was like. Encourage questions about jobs, and in response to questions you can't answer, work with the children on finding the answers (talk to a guidance counselor, look up information in the library, request information from business or professional organizations). Workers are all around us, so such conversations can occur virtually anytime and anywhere. It's especially helpful to initiate such discussions when on vacation, since you are likely to come into contact with jobs that may not be present in your community. When discussing jobs, try to remain neutral; try not to overly influence your children's opinions about different jobs. Encourage your children to join school clubs and to attend Career Fairs or Career Days at school.

—**Facilitating Effective Decision-Making**—You can facilitate effective decision making by reflecting on decisions that have already been made. Ask your children how and why they made a decision. Encourage them to think about aspects of the decision they may have overlooked. Ask them how they would go about making that same decision in the future (emphasize the process of decision making as much as the decision). Offer examples of good and bad decisions you've made, and discuss what made them good and bad. Evaluate the decisions made by others (friends, relatives, television characters, etc.). Give your children choices, and let them practice decision making. Encourage your children to recognize when certain decisions need to be made (i.e. what courses to take, what jobs to apply for, what college to go to, what field to major in, etc.), and to begin working on them early. Avoid making all decisions for your children; this encourages them to rely on you rather than themselves.

Resources

—**How To Help Your Child Choose A Career,** by L.B. Otto, Evans, Publisher, 1984. This book provides parents of high school children with information about post—high school alternatives, and includes a career explorations workbook and bibliography.

—**Careers: Exploration and Decision,** by J.L. Rettig, David Lake, Publisher, 1986. This book, written for high school students, guides students through the career decision making process.

—**Career World**—General Learning Corporation, Publisher. (P.O. Box 310, Highwood, IL 60040). This monthly magazine provides information on general career planning issues and different occupations.

Children and Communicable Disease

Robert G. Harrington
University of Kansas

Background—Sixty percent of the children who go to their doctors with health problems are diagnosed as having some form of infectious communicable disease. What all communicable diseases have in common is that they can be easily transmitted from one individual to another. Communicable diseases can take many seriously debilitating and even life-threatening forms such as polio or AIDS, but the "flu," the "common cold" and "sore throat" are the most common. When a communicable disease infects a child attending school, parents must decide whether to stay home with a sick child and skip work or go to work and try to find home care for a sick child. The discomfort and inconvenience of infectious communicable diseases in children can be sharply reduced when parents become involved in communicable disease prevention and control.

Development—How Disease Spreads and General Behavior Symptoms:

There are several reasons why children may be prone to catching diseases when they enter school.

First, they may become infected when they engage in contact play, share toys and use other school equipment in common such as desks, toilets and sinks.

Second, children's natural immunities are lower than those of adults.

Third, the increase in the number of human contacts in school heightens the probability of exposure to infection.

Viral or bacterial infections may be spread in several ways: through the water supply, contaminated food, animal waste, the air we breathe, and personal contact with a carrier of the virus.

A feeling of malaise may be the first sign that a child is suffering from an infectious disease and is often followed by listlessness, inability to concentrate, lack of drive, uneasiness, light-headedness, weakness, headache, and anorexia. Chronic illnesses may adversely affect the child's school performance and self-concept.

Four Broad Types of Communicable Diseases

1. Respiratory infections such as colds and flu are responsible for the greatest number of illnesses. Symptoms include colds, runny nose, coughing and sneezing. These infections become complicated when they lead to ear infections or lower respiratory infections. They are generally transmitted by secretions from the mouth or nose or through droplets coughed or sneezed into the air.

2. Certain infections resulting in diarrhea include viral enteritis, giardia, shigella, salmonella and hepatitis A. The infection is transmitted from fecal matter on the hands, food or other objects placed in the mouth.

3. Skin infections may be due to impetigo, ice, scabies, and ringworm and are generally transmitted through direct contact.

7

4. Viral rashes may result from chicken pox, measles, roseola, and mumps, are transmitted through oral and nasal secretions, and many are preventable through immunizations.

Treatment—Medical treatment usually is restricted to symptomatic relief. Fluid therapy may be used to control dehydration, and aspirin may be prescribed (except in case of "flu") to relieve aches and to reduce fever. There are few drugs that can be directly used to combat an infecting virus. Viral diseases are resistant to the usual forms of drug therapy now available such as penicillin and the other antibiotics.

Immunization is the most successful control over communicable diseases. Parents should be aware that for the vast majority of children vaccinations are safe, effective, and frequently free at their local health clinics.

Parents should also keep in mind that immunizations are required for admission to school and schools may bar students from attendance who have not been immunized or who might infect other students.

What Can I Do As A Parent?—

—Your child should be seen for medical check-ups on a regular basis.

—Immunization should be current and parents should keep a record to ensure booster shots are timely.

Table I shows the recommended schedule of immunizations.

Age of Child	Diptheria/ Tetanus	Polio	Measles	Child Diseases Mumps	Rubella	Hib
2 months	X	X				
3 months	X					
4 months	X	X				
15 months	X	X	X	X	X	
24 months**						X
4–6 years (kindergarten entry)	X	X				
14–16 years*	X					

* A booster of Tetanus—needed every 10 years unless there is a "contaminated wound" such as a puncture wound, animal bite or barnyard injury. If it has been more than 5 years since the last TD booster another booster is needed within 72 hours after such an injury.

** HIB can be given at 18-23 months for children who are thought to be at increased risk of disease, e.g., children attending day care.

—Don't send your child to school when he/she is sick.

—Report serious illnesses to the classroom teacher and school nurse within 24 hours so that other parents have the opportunity to take action.

—Handwashing after toileting, and before handling or eating foods is one of the most effective preventive measures. Liquid soaps are recommended.

—Food preparation areas should be kept clean and dry.

—Cleaning dishes in a dishwasher is more effective than handwashing dishes.

—Diapering areas should be disinfected and diapers properly disposed of.

—Have plenty of tissues, not handkerchiefs, readily available for nose-dripping and dispose of soiled tissues into covered containers.

— To avoid head lice, discourage children from sharing combs, brushes, hats, and other head gear and from hanging coats on top of each other.

— Food containing eggs, mayonnaise, or poultry should be refrigerated to reduce the chance of salmonellosis. Cook poultry well and refuse unpasteurized dairy products.

— Teach your child to cover his or her nose or mouth when he/she coughs or sneezes.

— Avoid dry, overheated rooms which can make respiratory passages more susceptible to infection.

— Wipe off doorknobs, shelves, and other furniture at children's level as well as toys which cannot be placed in the dishwasher at least once a week.

— Encourage children to get plenty of rest and fresh air and drink lots of fluids, especially those rich in Vitamin C.

Resources

— *For Medical Questions and Immunizations:* Your child's physician and office staff; nursing staff at your local hospital; local health department.

Books

— *Understanding Your Immune System* by E. Potts and M. Morra, 1986.
   This book is designed to help parents understand the immune system, how to strengthen immunity and why viruses and bacteria invade the body to cause communicable disease.

— *Dr. Spock's Baby and Child Care* by B. Spock and M. Rothenberg, 1985.
   This book contains useful ideas on how to manage certain childhood diseases until proper medical care is provided. Dr. Spock also shares some of his own clinical wisdom about how parents can cope when their children are sick.

— *Germs Make Me Sick: A Health Handbook For Kids* by P. Donahue and H. Cappellaro, 1975.
   This book is intended to be read by early elementary school age children and explains how germs make you sick and how good hygienic habits can prevent the spread of germs.

— *Preventing Illness in Infant/Toddler Daycare* by R. Highberger and M. Boynton in Young Children, 1983, 38, 3-8.
   This is a good overview of how parents can become involved in disease prevention in their child's preschool.

— *Sex, Drugs and AIDS* by Bradley Kesden, O.D.N. Publishers, 1987.
   This video tells adolescents what AIDS is, how it can and cannot be transmitted, provides peer support for modifying at-risk behavior and provides understanding for those who are infected with the AIDS virus.

NATIONAL ASSOCIATION OF SCHOOL PSYCHOLOGISTS

Children and Creativity

J. H. Presbury & A. J. Benson, *James Madison University*
J. Fitch, *Lyndon State College*
E. P. Torrance, *University of Georgia*

Background—Everybody is creative. Without creativity, we could not adapt to new situations or change the way we view the world. When people identify someone as "creative," then they mean something about the degree of creativity displayed. This **degree** of creativity depends upon the extent to which the ideas or results of the process are novel, valuable, differ from previous ideas or approaches, can be applied in other situations, and go beyond the commonplace. Such creative behavior is, by definition, unusual and unconventional. It has been said that just as low intelligence is stupidity, so is very low creativity ordinariness.

Not everyone will be delighted by the way a creative child thinks. No adult would wish for a child to be stupid, but they often pressure children to be ordinary.

Development—An active imagination is at the heart of creative thinking. For the young child, fact and fantasy, dreaming and waking, wish and reality, one's own view and "the truth" are all without clear distinction. This frame of mind is essential to remaining open to creative possibilities. But our "grown-up" society has strong feelings that children must fit in and be like everyone else. For example, it's okay for a two year old to develop imaginative and unusual uses for mother's saucepans (they can be hats, cars, anything), but later their use must be restricted to cooking and household tasks.

It is natural for young children to learn in creative ways-to learn by experimenting, manipulating objects, singing, dancing, story telling, making believe and the like. One of the first challenges to creative imaginings may be formal schooling. Teachers, and parents by this time, like conforming behaviors best-e.g., being courteous and obedient, following rules, handing work in on time, etc. Along about age 9 or 10, creative children often experience the "fourth-grade slump," marked by a significant reduction in creative production. The pressure to conform and be like others increases during adolescence and some creative children never recover from the "slump." They go on to be conventional and ordinary adults.

The, personality traits which some creative children develop are often viewed by others as strange or unproductive: (a) **Free Thinking.** Toying with ideas may appear undisciplined and lacking in goal orientation; (b) **Gullibility.** Creative children get excited about "half-baked" ideas and may not see the drawbacks or flaws that an adult would easily see; (c) **Humor.** Creative children find humor in ideas which adults consider to be very serious. This ability to question and see other perspectives may be interpreted as mocking and obnoxious; (d) **Daydreaming.** Creative children learn through fantasy and solve many of their problems through its use. Letting one's mind wander can help imagination to form new connections but may be seen as being inattentive or spacey; (e) **Aloneness.** Creative thinking develops from delicate, unformed ideas. Children need to be alone while their ideas emerge, but society's emphasis on togetherness makes this difficult; and (f) **Activity.** Ideas often come at times of "doing nothing." But once the idea comes, the creative child will become absorbed in the activity. This fluctuation, from what may seem to be laziness to over commitment to only one thing, is confusing and frustrating to others.

What Can I Do As A Parent?—

—**Set an example.** Honor your own childlike curiosity, enthusiasm, and "crazy" ideas. Keep yourself open to new experiences, share your own creative interests and take delight in the interests of your child. Give yourself a break-expect not to know all the "right" answers and accept less than perfection.

—**Examine your attitudes.** Children who feel loved and trusted gain the confidence to be different and the courage to create. Over-concern for societal convention or sex-role stereotypes may inhibit creativity. If you believe that "a good child is a modest child," the child may be ashamed of the strong need to show his or her creative products to others.

—**Encourage your child.** Encourage experimentation and exploration. Practice listening to your child without being judgmental. Edit, criticize, and question your child's ideas with great caution. Allow for and support your child in failure. Avoid "empty praise" for every production and show your enthusiasm when you really feel it!

—**Enrich the environment.** This does not mean that you must spend a lot of money. Children often ignore expensive toys in favor of the box in which they come. Unstructured play materials enable children to create their own ideas and encourage imagination. Old magazines, books, newspapers, games, old clothes, discarded jewelry can be precious treasures of unlimited possibilities. Take trips. Talk with people. Observe outloud and talk about the child's reactions. Provide experiences that stretch the imagination such as "pretend" situations, "1 wonder what would happen. . . . ?" discussions and making up stories. Daily rituals such as bedtime and mealtime can be opportunities for creative expression through conversation and storytelling.

—**Structure the environment.** While it may be true that creative children's uniqueness may cause problems, it is not true that all children with problems are creative. All children require a predictable household where limits are set on their behavior. Creative thinking may lead children to question rules and to violate standards. Rules should be as few as possible but must be clear and consistently applied with obvious consequences for misbehavior and not as a show of parental power. Creative children will need time just "to be" and some control over how they spend their time. Today's push on being constantly busy (i.e., all the child's time filled with lessons, after school activities, groups) interferes with creativity.

—**Watch TV.** And watch out for TV! TV can enhance visual imagry and imagination, and increase ones knowledge if used responsibly. However, creative people are not only consumers of the ideas of others, but producers of new ideas. Getting hooked on the passive consumption of any medium, like TV can block the productive energy of the creative child.

—**Encourage your child to record ideas.** Children love to paint and draw from a very early age. This is an excellent creative problem solving medium. Before they begin to write, they can dictate their ideas to adults or older children. Later you may encourage your child to keep a diary or journal.

—**Work with your child's school.** Most schools do not have programs especially designed for creative children. Help your school obtain volunteers and funding for programs in the creative arts such as dance, art, music, drama, etc. Keep a dialogue with your child's teacher so that he or she will interpret your child's behaviors in the light of possible creative ability. Advocate for your child but do not remain blind to the fact that creative children cause problems for the teacher. Anything you can do to relieve pressure on the teacher will benefit your child. Try-every so gently-to get school officials to honor divergent thinking and to reduce the stress on correct answers and proper form.

Teach your child about creative children. The creative process never runs smoothly and children get into "bad moods" when they are frustrated. Say it's okay to daydream, pretend, have imaginary friends, think things other people don't think, and not be interested in everything that interests other children. As one now successful author put it: "My elementary school experiences were awful . . . if (only) somebody had told me back then that I was 'creative' I would have had something to hold on to. All I knew was that I was different."

Of course, as a parent you cannot control all aspects of your child's creativity. You can follow the suggestions outlined above but your child will respond in his unique way. Your vision is unlikely to be your child's vision. However deep satisfaction can be gained from participating in unlocking your child's creative potential, kindling within the lifelong fire of artistic and intellectual enthusiasm.

Resources

—*The Gifted Child Today.* G./C./T. Publishing Co., P.O. Box 6448, Mobile, AL 36660-0448. The articles are readable and interesting. Included are activities in problem solving, poetry, and cartoons.

—Davis, G. A. (1981). *Creativity 15 Forever.* Badger Press, Cross Plains, WI. This is an easy to understand book which uses everyday examples to explain the creative process. It includes humorous and imaginative comments on the subject of creativity.

—Samples, B. (1976). *The Metaphoric Mind: A Celebration of Creative Consciousness.* Addison-Wesley Publishing Co., Reading, MA. A more technical book than Davis's, this is a good treatment of the differences between logical thinking, which currently leads to academic success, and metaphorical thinking, which is the starting point of creativity.

NATIONAL ASSOCIATION OF SCHOOL PSYCHOLOGISTS

Children and Dependency

Chuck McBride and Max McFarland
Nebraska Department of Education

Background—Dependency is often overlooked as a problem with children. Outwardly, it does not appear to be as serious as the problem posed by a child who is aggressive and hitting other children on the playground. However dependency can seriously interfere with a child's development of "thinking" skills and the confidence necessary to make decisions on his/her own. Dependency can also affect the child's ability to develop the social skills necessary to make friends and get along with classmates. For these reasons, dependent children often experience major problems in the classroom, with classmates on the playground, and when trying to socialize with other children around the home.

Development—Dependent behaviors are normal in children as they grow from birth to adulthood. For example, a baby is dependent upon the mother for feeding, a child depends on the father for transportation to school, and when sick he/she is dependent on the parents for health needs. It is when the child is able to do little on his/her own and becomes reliant upon others for such things as reading, making decisions, self-help skills, and so on, that dependency becomes reason for concern.

There are a number of reasons that dependency develops, and dependency may be seen any time from birth to adulthood. Parents and other family members encourage the development of dependency by doing such things as:

- Being overprotective—e.g., not letting the child play on the playground for fear of the child getting hurt.
- Discouraging independent decision-making skills—e.g., never letting the child choose his/her own clothing to wear because the parents do not feel he/she can coordinate the colors.
- Not giving the child responsibility—e.g., always cleaning the child's room and making his/her bed.
- Preventing social development—e.g., choosing friends, activities, and organizations for the child.
- Not allowing opportunities for problem solving—e.g., interceding if the child is arguing or fighting over a toy with a friend or sibling, the parent intercedes rather than allowing the child to work out his/her own solution.

Other factors that can cause dependency include guilt and health issues. For example, parents feel guilty about not spending enough time with the child because of work, and overcompensate by doing unnecessary things for the child when the child could do these things on his/her own. Health reasons may include such situations as the child having a broken leg and, during the healing process, being waited on as though he/she is totally helpless. Then when the child is recovered, the parents continue doing everything for him/her because they have become used to doing so, and the child has demanded it. The child may also "work" others (manipulation) to gain something for his/her own self, as in appearing not to be able to do a math problem, resulting in the problem being done for him/her.

Sometimes in addition to dependency, the child learns to be "helpless" because the development of independence has been hindered or prevented by adults, siblings, or peers. While parent intentions may be good, smothering the child ("smother love") only increases the dependency and the helplessness.

Helpless children do not appear to be interested in trying to do anything. They do not set goals for themselves and feel as though they have no control over certain situations. For example, the helpless child may feel that no matter how hard he/she studies he/she will still fail the history test; or, no matter how hard he/she tries, mom and dad will not be pleased. Consequently, the child wonders, "what's the use?" Because the child is failure oriented, he/she is afraid to try new activities or meet new friends. The helpless child feels it is safer to not try, rather than risk the chance of failing. So, the child relies more and more on others to do things for him/her.

Dependency may be more evident in one setting or situation than in others. Dependency may also occur with one particular person more than others. For example, the child may be more dependent around one parent within the home, than at school with his/her teacher.

There are a number of indicators to signal parents that there may be a dependancy problem. These indicators include:

Clinging to adults	Failure oriented
Immaturity	Difficulty making independent decisions
Prefering younger children	Poor self-concept
Withdrawing	Lack of self-confidence
Poor peer relations	Fear of making mistakes
Avoiding trying new things	Depression

What Can I Do As A Parent?—It may not be easy to "let loose of the apron strings" and stop doing things for your child. It may be very hard not to be overprotective, thus smothering the child's independent growth. Listed below are some suggestions when dealing with a dependent child.

—When a child has a health problem it is important to take care of his/her needs. However, let the child do what he/she is capable of doing. Do not pamper or baby the child unnecessarily. If a child has a broken arm, it does not mean that he/she cannot walk or talk. Align expectations accordingly.

—If the child is using the parent to get what he/she wants, it may become necessary to ignore these manipulative attempts. However the parent must encourage and praise the child for trying on his/her own. It is also important to remind other family members to encourage the child to try things on his/her own.

—Establish open lines of communication between and among all people involved with the child. This means between mom and dad, brothers and sisters, and between parents and teachers. Each should be aware of "do's and don'ts" when dealing with this problem. Each should know what the other is doing. Lack of communication will send mixed signals to the child and confuse him/her more.

—Consistency, routine, and follow-through are all necessary to be successful with a dependent child. All adults dealing with the child in the same way will be very helpful. If mom handles the child one way and dad another, the child will pick up on this very quickly and use one against the other. Also, once a plan of action has been determined, then follow-through on that plan is very important. Following through one time and not the next will cause the plan to fail.

Give the child lots of opportunities to try new things and meet new friends. Encourage the child to take part in activities and organizations. Be sure to let dependent children know you are proud of them for taking a chance and becoming involved. A hug and a kiss is a nice touch! Remember you cannot become independent if you are never given the chance to "try your wings."

It is important to set the child up for success. Do not ask nor expect the child to do something he/she is incapable of doing. Do not give him/her something to do that will be a failure from the onset. Failure will encourage the child not to try. After all, wouldn't you rather succeed than fail?

To encourage independent decision making, begin by giving the child the opportunity to select between two choices. For example, the parent may lay out two sets of clothing and let the child choose one. The parent needs to be comfortable with both choices and learn not to be critical of the child's selection. As time goes by, extend the choices. Be careful, however not to hurry and rush the process.

Children need to learn how to solve their own problems. Little by little allow your child to confront disagreement with friends at home and school. Try not to intercede for the child. This only hinders progress toward learning how to solve problems.

No matter how time consuming or painful it may be, it is very important to give the child responsibility around the home. Cleaning his/her room, making the bed, and emptying the garbage can all be valuable learning experiences that should not be overlooked. Of course the child should be praised for his/her efforts. Remember to praise the process of doing the job, not just the end result or how well it is done.

If you, the parent, feel as though you are the only one in the world dealing with this type of problem, seek out a parent support group. It helps to talk to other parents dealing with similar problems and to share ideas and strategies.

Let the child know that you care . . . that you support him/her. It will take a great deal of time and patience to increase a child's independence. One step at a time . . . gradually. The child's dependency problem did not develop overnight, nor will it disappear overnight. Remember, be patient, be supportive, and do not forget to encourage and praise the child.

Resources

—*The Basics of Encouragement*, by G. D. McKay. Communication and Motivation Training Institute, Inc., 1976.This booklet stresses encouragement and accepting children as they are. It also focuses on the positive aspects of the child and his/her strengths.

—*Living With Children*, by G. R. Patterson. Research Press, 1976. This book is intended to assist parents of normal and problem children in dealing with situations that arise within any family.

—*The Next Step* (Effective Parenting through Problem Solving), by D. Dinkmeyer & G. D. McKay. American Guidance Services, Inc., 1987. In this program, parents learn skills for understanding and dealing with children's behavior more effectively. Parents learn ways to build their own self-esteem as well as the child's. This program provides a video and video manual.

—*Solving Child Behavior Problems at Home and at School*, by E. A. Blechman. Research Press, 1985. This book answers specific questions that parents have about their child's behavior. The main purpose of this book is to provide practical and concrete advice to parents and families.

NATIONAL ASSOCIATION OF SCHOOL PSYCHOLOGISTS

Different Cultural Backgrounds

Pia Rebello
University of South Florida

Background—Culture refers to the habitual patterns of behavior that characterize a given group of people (Henderson, 1982). It varies in the ways people believe, act, and think. Norms and ideals act as major determinants and unifying forces in identifying different cultures. These norms, both material and abstract, involve the use of cultural symbols. Language, religion, social values, family roles, cuisine, and dress are examples of cultural symbols. These symbols determine patterns of behavior and provide a basis for interpreting the world. Thus, through these symbols, a person's understanding of the world is passed on to succeeding generations and the culture is continued.

Development—The American society at present comprises individuals from diverse ancestral history, language, and heritage. According to the National Center for Education, in 1980 there were approximately 5 million school-age children whose mother tongue was not English or who lived in homes in which languages other than English were spoken. The percentage of ethnic diversity in the American school-age population is ever increasing, and it is predicted that by the year 2000 this ethnically diverse population will double (Cardenas, 1980).

Many patterns of behavior that are thought to be normal or natural in one culture may not be thought so by other cultures, for example, the interpretation of emotional states by facial expressions. In a study by McAndrew (1986), it was found that the accurate identification of emotional facial expressions such as anger was affected by cultural background of the subjects. Peoples' stereotypical expectancies and interpretation of the world often direct their interpersonal interactions and thought patterns. For example, consider the interplay between gender and ethnicity. Hispanic men who do not express macho qualities and women who are not appropriately passive are subject to stressful evaluation by their peers (Either & Deaux, 1990). In a study by Hartman and Askounis (1989) it was noted that Asian-American students are extremely restrained in their expression of emotional sentiments. They perceive a revelation of personal problems and difficulties as a negative reflection on the entire family. Therefore, misunderstandings can often arise from cultural variations in verbal and nonverbal communication and can lead to dysfunctional relationships and alienation. Often cultural differences are a combination of ethnic differences and social class, locale (rural, urban, or suburban), and individualism. For example, a child from a poor communal subculture of group ownership may not view taking another child's crayons as stealing (West, 1986).

An individual's adjustment to a new cultural context is accompanied by the stresses of adopting the mainstream culture's values and retaining one's own identity (Suberri, 1987). Four adjustment patterns have been identified by English (1984): assimilation, traditionalism, transitionalism, and biculturalism.

What Can I Do as a Teacher?—The pluralistic nature of the American school system has stressed the need for teachers to take into consideration the social and cultural characteristics of their students as they plan and carry out their instructional programs. This poses problems for the teachers, because often little is known about interrelationship between the culturally determined student characteristics and the instructional process (Henderson, 1982). To help achieve this objective, teachers should:

(1) use information concerning the sociocultural characteristics of children and families as the basis for alternative possible explanations of problems of learning and adjustment;

(2) use assumptions concerning the cultural characteristics of minority children through discussion with parents and other community members;

(3) be aware of the relationship between the teacher's expectancies and student achievement and be sensitive to personal biases regarding minority students and their families; and

(4) be skillful in resolving differences in role expectations of teachers and parents, and in reaching a consensus concerning shared goals (Henderson, 1982).

Muniz and Chasnoff (1983) present a six-level conceptual model that teachers can use to promote understanding of another culture by building on their own values. The levels of this cultural awareness hierarchy consist of: (a) self-awareness: ability, cultural background, and experience; (b) professional skills; (c) understanding of factors that may affect behavior, such as the dynamics of poverty and empathy; (d) recognition and acceptance of one's own culture; (e) examination of factors specific to one's own country; and (f) understanding of the other culture. By following these steps teachers can enhance the efficacy of their instructional activities with students of different cultural backgrounds.

What Can I Do as a Parent?—An intelligent consideration of "effective parenting" in the present day society requires an understanding of cultural diversity in parenting goals, values, and behavior. Parenthood is a universal and highly variable aspect of human behavior, but human parents everywhere can be seen as sharing a common set of goals in their role as parents (Levine, 1980). The natural and institutional environments of human societies are so diverse that these goals must be realized differently in different places.

Parents raising children in the culturally diverse American society need: (a) information about the environments their children are likely to face; (b) contact and communication with the school, mental care workers, and other parents to share their concerns; and (c) a general understanding of the minority cultures and the dominant American culture. To help fulfill these needs, the parents must identify the resources that are already available and plan strategies to optimize their use. Recommended are: (a) initiating multicultural parenting groups, organized and conducted by the parents themselves; and (b) identification of programs that assess the emotional costs of child-rearing in a multicultural society and are sensitive to the cultural implications of child-rearing customs of different groups.

References

Cardenas, R. (1980). Parenting in a multicultural society. New York: Longman, Inc.

Either, K., & Deaux, K. (1990). Hispanics in Ivy: Assessing identity and perceived threat. [Special issue] Gender and ethnicity: Perspectives on dual status. *Sex Roles, 22*(7-8), 427-440.

English, R. A. (1984). The challenge for mental health: Minorities and their world views. The 2nd Annual Robert C. Sutherland Lecture. Austin: University of Texas. (ERIC Document Reproduction Service No. ED 255 796)

Hartman, J. S., & Askounis, A. C. (1989). Asian-American students: Are they really a "model minority"? *School Counselor, 37*(2), 109-112.

Henderson, R. W. (1982). Teacher relations with minority students and their families. Washington, DC: Office of Special Education and Rehabilitative Services. (ERIC Document Reproduction Service No. ED 249 213)

LeVine, R. A. (1980). A cross-cultural perspective on parenting. In M. D. Fantini & R. Cardenas (Eds.), *Parenting in a multicultural society* (pp. 17-26). New York: Longman, Inc.

McAndrew, F. T. (1986). A cross-cultural study of recognition thresholds for facial expressions of emotion. *Journal of Cross-Cultural Psychology, 17*(2), 211-224.

Muniz, P., & Chasnoff, R. (1983). The cultural awareness hierarchy: A model for promoting understanding. *Training and Development Journal, 37*(10), 24-27.

Suberri, K. C. (1987). Children and different cultural backgrounds. In A. Thomas & J. Grimes (Eds.), *Children's needs: Psychological Perspectives* (pp. 167-172). Washington, DC: National Association of School Psychologists.

West, B. (1986). Culture before ethnicity. *Childhood Education, 62*(3), 175-181.

Hearing

Lynn Ellen Thompson and Mary Ann Parkinson
University of South Florida

Background—Hearing affects all levels of a child's education including not only academic achievement but also social learning and interaction. A 1984 study of 60 students (ages 6-18) who each had unilateral hearing losses showed that one third of these students had failed at least one grade. In addition, 50% of the students either failed a grade or needed resource assistance during their education. "When a persistent mild-moderate hearing loss is recognized for the disabling condition that it is, hearing-impaired students represent the largest single population of school children requiring special education services" (Flexer, Wray, & Ireland, 1989). Furthermore, the ability to hear clearly is perhaps the most important factor influencing speech development. Not surprisingly, most studies suggest that, other things being equal, the more residual hearing one has, the more understandable his or her speech will be.

Hearing impairments can be diagnosed on a spectrum of hearing loss from mild to profound. The degree of hearing loss is measured in decibels (dB), which represents the ratio of the intensity of sound that is heard. For educational purposes, a mild hearing loss is a loss of 30 to 45 dB. A moderate hearing loss falls between 46 to 69 dB. Severe or profound losses range from 70 to 89dB and 90dB and greater, respectively. Recently there has been a tendency to restrict the classification of deafness to individuals whose hearing loss (of 90dB or greater) occurred prior to the acquisition of language.

Causes and Development—Hearing loss is the result of a breakdown of air conduction passageways in the outer, middle, and inner portions of the ear and the auditory nerve. The degree of hearing loss is determined by the extent of this breakdown. Some possible causes of infant hearing impairment include: heredity, maternal rubella (during the first trimester of pregnancy), mother-child blood incompatibility, meningitis, and prematurity. Left untreated for an extended period of time viral and bacterial infections, such as mumps and measles, may cause a hearing loss. Certain drugs and antibiotics have also been shown to cause hearing loss. Quinine and nicotine are among a number of drugs that can gain access to the inner ear through the bloodstream and affect hearing. The antibiotic streptomycin (used to treat tuberculosis) has also been linked to hearing losses.

Common causes of mild and fluctuating hearing losses include: otitis media or middle ear infections, allergies, inconsistent use of hearing aids, or poorly working hearing aids. Of these, otitis media is responsible for 60% of mild and fluctuating hearing losses in children under age 5.

When mild or fluctuating hearing losses go unnoticed or cause hearing impairment for a significant amount of time, young children may miss the contribution and importance of hearing for learning and communicating. Instead they rely more heavily on their other senses and gestures. This can lead to serious educational difficulties for children in regular education classrooms as children spend up to 45 % of their day in school listening. In fact, when asked, teachers reported that listening is the single most important skill for classroom success.

In noisy classrooms children with mild and fluctuating hearing losses have trouble hearing p, t, k, s, sh, th, and f, plural endings such as s and es, and final position fricatives such as th, s, sh, and lf. The omission of this information may not only make lessons difficult to follow but may also influence children's language development. These students may not speak as clearly as their age-mates; have difficulty with expressive vocabulary; have problems with cognition including small, abstract, or distant concepts; and respond inappropriately when interacting with others.

Hearing-impaired students may also experience difficulty with tasks requiring comprehension of verbal language or verbal language concepts such as reading. These students have difficulty in this area because learning to read is based upon speaking. Poor reading skills further limit their academic options and may lead to special education placement. Finally, it should be noted it has been hypothesized that mild and fluctuating hearing losses are associated with learning disabilities (Katz, 1978, p. 879). In a study conducted by Freeman and Parkins (1979) they found that 20% of learning-disabled and 9.5% of non-learning-disabled students had some form of middle-ear pathology. In a similar study researchers found that 38% of learning-disabled and only 16% of non-learning-disabled students had abnormal hearing thresholds (Bennett, Runska, & Sherman, 1980).

What Can I Do as a Parent?—Parents may find the following suggestions helpful when dealing with a child who has a mild and fluctuating hearing loss:

—Set responsibilities that show the child that he or she is a competent, productive, and valued member of the family (participation in family interactions and chores, for example).

—Be aware that certain periods during the child's education will be more difficult and require some adjustment. These periods may include 1st grade with the introduction of language arts and reading skills, 4th grade when an emphasis is placed on textbook information particularly for science and social studies, and junior high with its rotating class schedule, which forces the student to meet demands of a variety of teachers, students, and differing expectations.

—Be supportive and understanding during transitional periods. Set aside time to help the child with homework assignments.

—Designate a specific homework time every day.

—Be aware that grades may fall during junior high. Try not to emphasize the bad grades or associate them with lack of effort on the child's part.

—Be aware that children with mild and fluctuating hearing losses may need compensatory measures to counteract the loss of auditory information during otitis media episodes.

—Periodic use of a mild-gain hearing aid or an aggressive home stimulation program may be helpful.

What Can I Do as a Teacher?—The following guidelines may be helpful for dealing with children who have mild and fluctuating hearing losses in the classroom:

—Provide flexible seating arrangements for the student near the front of the room.

—Do not seat the student near a window, the glare from the window will make lipreading more difficult.

—Be sure to have the student's attention before speaking.

—When speaking, speak normally and do not use exaggerated lip movements.

—Ask the student to repeat back what was said to check for comprehension of directions.

—Arrange for a notetaker for the student.

—Understand that these students have a great deal of difficulty following class discussions because they have trouble locating the speaker. Rephrase what was said by other students.

—Be aware of the student's location relative to classroom activities and give the student permission to move closer to instructional activities without requesting permission to do so.

—Use "listen" as a cue word to alert the hearing-impaired student to attend auditorily to important classroom information.

— Decrease the length of assignments if the student is not able to complete classwork.
— If asked, agree to wear a wireless microphone for the hearing-impaired student's FM equipment (hearing aid). This will allow the student to hear your voice more clearly above background noises in the classroom.
— If necessary, provide tutoring or enlist the aid of another student for pre- and post-tutoring. Allow the student to preview new material before class, especially key vocabulary, concepts, and facts. After the lesson has been taught review with the student the important aspects of the lesson to ensure comprehension.

Resources

Parents and teachers may wish to contact the school psychologist or the following organizations for more information.

American Speech Language Hearing Association (ASHA), 10801 Rockville Pike, Rockville, MS 20852, (301) 879-5700 (TDD/Voice)

Better Hearing Institute (BHI), 1430 K Street, N.W., Washington, D.C. 20005, (202) 638-2848(TDD), (202) 638-7577, (800) 424-8576 Hearing Helpline

Listen Foundation, 2525 South Downing, Denver, CO 80210, (303) 778-5841

International Parents' Organization (IPO), 3417 Volta Place, N.W., Washington, DC 20007, (202) 337-5220 (TDD/Voice)

Parent to Parent, House Ear Institute, 256 South Lake Street, Los Angeles, CA 90057, (213) 483-4431, (213) 484-2642 (TTY)

Additional Resources

Ling, D. (1976). *Speech and the hearing-impaired child: Theory and practice.* Washington, DC: The Alexander Graham Bell Association for the Deaf.

Luterman, D. M. (1986). *Deafness in perspective.* San Diego: College Hill

Martin, F. N. (1986). *Introduction to audiology* (3rd ed.). Engelwood Cliffs, NJ: Prentice-Hall.

Moores, D. F. (1982). *Educating the deaf: Psychology. principles and practice* (2nd ed.). Boston: Houghton Mifflin Company.

References

Bennett, F. C., Runska, S. H., & Sherman, R. (1980). Middle ear effusion in learning disabled children. *Pediatrics, 66,* 254-260.

Flexer, C., Wray, D., & Ireland, J. (1989). Preferential seating is NOT enough: Issues in classroom management of hearing-impaired students. *Language, Speech and Hearing Services in the Schools, 20,* 11-21.

Freeman, B. A., & Parkins, C. (1979). The prevalence of middle ear disease among learning impaired children. *Clinical Pediatrics, 18,* 205-210.

Katz, J. (1978). The effects of conductive hearing loss on auditory functioning. *ASHA, 20,* 879-886.

Children and Homosexuality

David C. Canaday, School Psychology
Leavenworth County Cooperative, Leavenworth, Kansas

Background—Once shunned and ignored, the topic of homosexuality has generated public interest, and societal attitudes toward gays and lesbians have changed during the past generation. Although they remain targets of fear and hostility, gay men and women have been able to lead more comfortable and open lives. Until recently, however, the plight of gay and lesbian teenagers has been ignored. For adolescents, coming to grips with a personal identity has always been a major task. For the teen struggling with same-sex feelings, this task is especially difficult. Guilt, lack of information and support, alienation, and, loneliness are experienced by many gay and lesbian youth. Fortunately, more and more people are learning about adolescent homosexuality and are willing to help teens deal with this issue.

Development—The adolescent years are a time of exploration for the teenager in building a sense of "who I am." The formation of a personal identity takes many different pathways, including the sexual. Physical and psychosexual attraction toward others begins around ages 11 to 14 for most children. Many teens (research indicates anywhere from 5% to 50% of boys and somewhat fewer percentages of girls) experience homosexual emotions or activities during their adolescent years: Homosexual behavior among teenagers is relatively common. Many teens who have same-sex feelings and behaviors eventually lead heterosexual lives as adults. Some eventually lead gay lives. Most adult homosexuals do report having same-sex feelings as teenagers, and many gays first identify themselves as homosexual in their teen years.

But teenage sexual behavior does not necessarily predict adult sexual preference: not all adolescents who have homosexual experiences will become gay adults, nor will all teens who behave heterosexually grow up to be heterosexual.

Sexual orientation—the types of sexual emotions and behaviors a person has—is multifaceted. Surprisingly few people are either 100% homosexual or 100% heterosexual emotionally and behaviorally throughout their lives. Alfred Kinsey, the noted sex researcher in the 1950's, found that only 50% of the men in his sample had no homosexual feelings or behaviors—fully one-half of males have some degree of homosexual emotion or behavior, yet only 10% of males are more or less exclusively gay. Teens often have both opposite-sex and same-sex attractions, which are especially confusing to them. Adolescents who consider the possibility that they might be gay may debate the issue intensely within themselves for this reason. A skilled and nonbiased counselor or psychologist knowledgable about sexual orientation issues can be of great use in helping the adolescent sort out conflicting feelings.

Many theories abound as to the causes of homosexuality. None of them adequately explain why some people have same-sex attractions, and it is less important to search for a "cause" than it is to understand the gay or lesbian child as an individual. Part of this understanding means realizing that acceptance of one's self as gay is usually a difficult process, but a process which if successfully completed can enable the person to live a happy and productive life.

What Can I Do as a Parent? The idea that your son or daughter might be gay may shock, scare or anger you. These reactions, within limits, are normal, since you want only the best for your child and may believe that being gay hurts one's chances for happiness in life. But in thinking about your child's possible homosexuality, keep in mind these points:

- The gay feelings your child has are probably quite scary to him or her at this point. Feeling such as "I'm the only one who's like this," "There's nobody I can talk to about this," and "If people find out, they'll hate me" are all common for kids who have same-sex feelings. Dealing with uncontrollable drives that others label "queer" will be the most difficult task your child will ever face. Whatever your views on homosexuality, your son or daughter needs your love and support now more than at any other time.

- The process of exploring a sexual orientation, whether homosexual, heterosexual or bisexual, is one that teenagers have to accomplish themselves. Attempts by others to persuade or force individuals to change their sexual orientation are normally unsuccessful and often breed resentment. Although sexual behavior may change throughout a person's life, it is only that person who can be responsible for such change.

- Your child is not "choosing" to have homosexual feelings to "assert his/her independence" or to "get back at others." No one chooses one's sexual orientation; the only "choice" is whether to cope with or suppress sexual desires.

- Dealing with your own feelings about homosexuality and your teenager may be difficult. Seek out supportive resources, such as counselors, other parents or gays, etc. If possible, talk with other gay people to gain their insight. Family counseling is often useful as well.

- Be as open and honest as you can with your child. Communicate your concerns, but listen to your teenager's view as well. Try to be supportive regardless of the path your teenager takes. Realize that happiness and success in life are not dependent upon sexual preference.

Resources

—Parents and Friends of Lesbians and Gays (P-FLAG), P. O. Box 20308, Denver, CO 80220, (303) 321-2270. An excellent support group for parents, with local chapters in many cities.

—*Now That You Know: What Every Parent Should Know About Homosexuality,* by B. Fairchild and N. Hayward. 1979. Harcourt, Brace, Jovanovich. This book, written by two founders of P-FLAG, discusses parent's views of their children's homosexuality while giving information about homosexuality and issues surrounding it.

—*A Family Matter: A Parent's Guide to Homosexuality,* by Charles Silverstein. 1977. McGraw-Hill. This book illustrates experiences that parents and gay children commonly have together in dealing with homosexuality.

Humor

Bradford P. Underhill
University of South Florida

Background—Humor is powerful. It is a form of intellectual play that is founded on incongruity between what is predicted and what actually occurs. It can be a signal that something is wrong or it can be an expression of joy. It also allows children to deal with problems such as anxiety, pain, stress, death, and fear (Prerost, 1987).

Humor has been shown to be a behavior that facilitates social interactions and learning (Masten, 1986; Gorham & Christophel, 1990), and decreases stress and anxiety. It can function as a direct release and at other times as a signal that something is wrong through thinly veiled aggression, interference with needed exploration of serious subjects, or when it is lacking.

Humor has a dark side such as when it is used as a weapon to degrade or hurt. Sarcasm or jokes at another's expense may serve the giver towards some inappropriate goal. It can, however, be devastating to the recipient.

Humor, lastly, can function as a tool to ease another's pain, facilitate bonding, enhance leaning, or make it easier to deal with a difficult situation or topic.

Whenever approaching a problem involving inappropriate use of humor it is important to understand humor in its developmental context as well as the function it serves (Prerost, 1987).

Development—McGhee (1979) is one of the leading researchers of humor. He has identified four stages of development of humor that are strongly related to children's cognitive ability. Although ages are presented with the stages they are only approximates.

Stage 1 (ages 0-2)

Laughter at this stage may be a release following a build up of tension or anxiety. Humor on the other hand involves the ability to predict and see the incongruity of an event. Visual incongruities such as parents making faces, talking fruit, and using a shoe as a telephone are funny at this stage.

Stage 2 (ages 2-3)

Although there is overlap with Stage 1, in this stage **verbal** incongruities create humor. Children in this stage of development enjoy misnaming and progress to enjoying making up funny names.

Stage 3 (ages 3-7)

Stage 3 humor begins to emerge around 3 years of age and involves conceptual incongruity. An example of what is funny is role reversals. Visual incongruity is still the most impacting. Humor is found in things that violate the characteristics that define an object or class of objects. Also rhyming and repetition of words emerge. Parents may view this as regression or baby talk and need to be informed that this is progression and not regression.

Stage 4 (ages 7-adult)

The final stage, Stage 4, involves the development of logic and understanding of multiple meaning. The more developed the child's sense of logic the more they are able to understand more complex or abstract jokes.

Gender differences in the area of humor do not appear to develop until school age. At this point boys begin to initiate and engage in more silly rhyming and clowning than do girls. One possible explanation is the social acceptability of boys engaging in these more extroverted behaviors. These differences, however, appear to diminish during adolescence. When examining humorous behavior it is important to assess the roles it plays. One role is the release of tension or anxiety. Children and adolescents, when faced with stressful situations, can use humor to alleviate tension and develop a sense of mastery. The content of children's humor can often provide information as to the nature of their fears or concerns. One possible explanation for the behaviors of the class clown is inadequate coping skills to deal with pressures or excessive amounts of anxiety or tension from any number of sources. Thinly veiled attacks can be an indication of aggressive impulses not under the child's control if observed frequently. Shocking content may be a developmentally appropriate exploration of taboos and whether with preschoolers or with adolescents is an expression of individuality.

An additional role is evident when humor is used to deal with sensitive issues as an attempt at acceptance of one's real or perceived differences. An example is a handicapped child joking about their particular disability.

Peer acceptance is another role for the use of humor. Humor is a socially desirable characteristic when used in moderation and can be used to break the ice or increase social desirability. Excessive clowning or acting foolishly can be an intense desire for social acceptability and/or lack of alternative methods of achieving social goals.

What Can I Do as a Teacher?—Reasons for a healthy use of humor include: facilitation of socialization, release of tension, and instilling a sense of mastery. The context and content of the expression of humor of children and adolescents (taken in a developmental context) can provide a wealth of information for the development of hypotheses leading to effectively targeted interventions. Interventions for class clowns can include monitoring peers' reinforcement of the child's behavior, teaching social skills as an alternative to the clowning behavior, and use of self-control techniques for the child to monitor and decrease their own behavior. Sarcasm and or scapegoating can be dealt with by identifying the child's issues, contingencies for inappropriate behavior, and reinforcement for positive interactions with others. Additionally, anger control techniques can be effective.

What Can I Do as a Parent?—Although not pleasant to hear, it is important to realize that your preschooler's references to bodily functions or your adolescent's use of shocking language are to a certain degree developmentally appropriate. With the preschooler explain the inappropriateness of the content of their language but be open to listening to any concerns they may have. Adolescents may respond better to your expressing your dislike of their language but not making a battle of it.

Summary

The use of humor plays many roles. It is important to look at normative information, developmental levels, contextual settings, and the goal or function of the humor prior to developing interventions. Behaviors such as scapegoating, playing the class clown, or using shocking language can have many different antecedents, functions, or reinforcers at work which would necessitate different interventions. Knowledge of these issues will help develop effective interventions and enhance constructive parent and teacher interventions.

References

Gorham, J., & Christophel, D. M. (1990). The relationship of teachers' use of humor in the classroom to immediacy and student learning. *Communication Education, 39,* 46-62.

McGhee, P. (1979). *Humor: Its origin and development.* New York: Freeman.

Masten, A. S. (1986). Humor and competence in school-aged children. *Child Development, 57,* 461-473.

Prerost, F. J. (1987). Children and humor. In A. Thomas & J. Grimes (Eds.), *Children's needs: Psychological Perspectives* (pp. 305-311). Washington, DC: NASP.

Language Development

Lynn Ellen Thompson
University of South Florida

Background—The ability to use and understand language is important for academic and social success in the classroom. Language influences a child's ability to understand the material being presented during class and his/her ability to interact successfully with peers. Language has been defined as "an organized set of symbolic relationships, mutually agreed upon by a speech community to represent experience and facilitate communication" (Kretschmer & Kretschmer, 1978, p. I). Young children must master rules of syntax, semantics, and pragmatics. These components govern the way individuals order words in a sentence, ascribe meaning to words, and use language in a social manner.

A portion of the school-aged population experience delayed or disordered language development. Estimates of speech or language disorders range from 2-4% to as high as 15-20% of the school-aged population.

Development—As an infant matures he or she is prepared for language development in many ways. By interacting and playing games with parents (such as peek-a-boo) the infant learns to take turns. Parents actively try to interpret their infants' movements and vocalizations and will respond as if the baby had taken a conversational turn. In this manner the infant is shaped and rewarded for engaging in interaction with others. By pointing to or holding a toy infants will determine conversational topics, again providing the foundation for language. Motherese also influenced infants' language development. Motherese has been defined as the speech pattern of a mother as she interacts with her infant. It contains an emphasis on the here and now, and uses a restricted vocabulary. Frequent repetitions, paraphrasing, and simple well-formed sentences are used. In addition, a slow rate of speech is used with pauses between utterances and after content words.

For normal language learners, at approximately 18 months there is a rapid increase in the number of words learned. This is also the period when two word combinations emerge. The child is learning to use language as a social tool to get the attention of others, request actions, greet others, and to protest and comment on events or objects. However, this phase may not emerge for delayed language learners until as late as 40 months.

As language development progresses children learn to use prepositions (on, by) plurals, past tense of both regular and irregular verbs, present progressive verb form (-ing), and contraction rules. For normal language learners these skills typically appear between 27 and 34 months.

Between 30 to 34 months children begin to master syntactical rules. These rules govern the use of "and" to link more than one thought in a sentence. The use of because, but, so, and if also typically appear during this period.

Causes—It is difficult to pinpoint one specific cause of delays in the acquisition of language. However, the literature does suggest that a directive adult communication style in which the adult uses many commands, directions, and instructions is associated with a slower rate of language development (Nelson, 1973). In addition, language disorders may be associated with another handicapping condition which is influencing the child's ability to acquire language skills at the same rate as his or her peers.

Parents who notice that their child is slow to develop language skills may also consider consulting an audiologist for an evaluation of the child's hearing abilities.

What Can I Do as a Parent?—The following suggestions may be helpful for parents who feel that their child is having difficulty with language-based tasks in school, or is delayed in language skills relative to his or her peers:

—Use labeling, when conversing with the child use natural opportunities to increase their vocabulary by providing them with the names of objects, places, or people.

—Consistently use short, simple sentences.

—Make conversation meaningful for the child by focusing on topics in the here and now which are relevant to the child.

—Keep sentences focused on concrete objects or topics.

—Reward the child for interaction with others.

—Try to avoid the use of sarcasm, ambiguous statements such as "pretty good," and words with multiple meanings such as "hand me the stapler."

—Keep directions or instructions simple. For example, say "shut the door" instead of "can't you shut the door?" to avoid confusion.

—Play games with the child where he or she has information that the listener needs. Help the child to express the information clearly and in an organized manner.

—Have the child repeat directions or instructions to check for understanding of the message.

What Can I Do as a Teacher?—In addition to the suggestions for parents listed above, teachers may consider assisting the student with the following classroom and study skills:

—Academic organization, or the ability to break short- and long-term assignments down into smaller steps.

—Budgeting of time for completion of assignments, both in class and homework.

—Organizing a binder with sections for each subject and assignment sheets in the front of each section on which to record assignments.

—Text analysis skills, for example, reading a passage and then restating the main idea in the child's own words.

—Reading of headings and subheadings of a text book and using the information to provide clues about content to follow.

—Note-taking using mapping, outlining, or pictographs containing words and pictures.

—Mnemonic and memory strategies such as chunking, self-recitation, and visual imagery.

—Problem-solving skills in which the child is taught to identify the problem, analyze the problem, predict outcomes, make a decision, and then critique the decision made may also be helpful.

—Reading books and stories may also provide an opportunity to read with the child and assist him or her to interpret phrases and central ideas in the text that he or she might otherwise have missed.

—Ask comprehension questions when reading to check the child's literal and inferential understanding of the story.

—Involve the child in whole-class instruction and discussions by asking for comments or opinions from him or her. Encourage him or her to ask questions.

Postscript—If the guidelines above are not sufficient, contact your school psychologist for information or organizations in your area.

Resources

Blennerhassett, L. (1987). Children and language development. In A. Thomas & J. Grimes (Eds.), *Children's needs: Psychological perspectives* (pp. 316-325). Washington, DC: The National Association of School Psychologists.

Blue, C. M. (1981). Types of utterances to avoid when speaking to language-delayed children. *Language, Speech and Hearing Services in Schools, 12,* 120-123.

Buttrill, J., Niizawa, J., Biemer, C., Takahashi, C., & Hearn, S. (1989). Serving the language learning disabled adolescent: A strategies based model. *Language, Speech and Hearing Services in Schools, 20,* 185-203.

Norris, J. A. (1989). Providing language remediation in the classroom: An integrated language-to-reading instruction method. Language, Speech and Hearing Services in Schools, 20, 205-218.

References

Kretschmer, R., & Kretschmer, L. (1978). *Language development and intervention with the hearing impaired* (pp. 1-30). Baltimore: University Park Press.

Nelson, K. (1973). Structure and strategy in learning to talk. *Monographs of the Society for Research in Child Development, 38,* 2.

Maladaptive Habits

Shirley Peffers
University of South Florida

Background—The problems caused by maladaptive habits in children may range on a continuum from minor discomfort and irritation among significant others to significant social and physical problems for the child. Some common maladaptive habits include fingernail biting, thumbsucking/fingersucking, hair pulling, self-destructive oral habits, tics, and bruxism [nonfunctional clenching and grinding of the teeth] (Pray & Kramer, 1987). These behaviors are classified as maladaptive or problematic depending on their frequency, severity, and duration. In general, the habits worsen when the child is stressed. Typically, the school psychologist will become involved when the dysfunctional behavior is causing physical disorders, social difficulties, or embarrassment (Pray & Kramer. 1987).

Research indicates that interventions for maladaptive habits have two primary purposes: (1) stopping the habit to prevent further damage to affected body areas, and (2) teaching the child to deal with stress in more adaptive ways (Pray & Kramer, 1987). Presently, habit reversal [HR] (Azrin & Nunn. 1973, 1977 cited in Pray & Kramer, 1987) seems to be the most effective treatment available for a number of maladaptive habits.

Development—Of the behaviors listed above, only thumbsucking and transient tic disorder are considered developmentally normal behaviors (Pray & Kramer, 1987). Thumbsucking is the most common behavior, and typically stops by age 4. Thumbsucking generally appears between the 4th and 10th month of infancy and peaks between the 3rd and 4th year of childhood (Jensen, Kehle, & Clark, 1987). Approximately 10% of children in the age range of 6 to 11 years are thumbsuckers. After age 12, the percentage drops to between 2-5%. Before the age of 4, the severity of the habit and dental complications should be considered prior to deciding whether an intervention is necessary (Pray & Kramer, 1987).

The American Psychiatric Association [APA] (1980) indicated that from 12% to 24% of school children have a history of tics. "A mild transient tic disorder is common in childhood and systematic treatment is usually unnecessary" (Pray & Kramer, 1987). Tics usually disappear after several months, but may last as little as one month or as long as a year. The most common transient tic is the eye blink or other facial tic (Pray & Kramer, 1987).

Nail biting, bruxism, and self-destructive oral habits are considered normal or abnormal depending on chronicity and the physical problems caused by the habit (Pray & Kramer, 1987). Hair pulling or trichotillomania is abnormal at any age and should be considered for possible intervention efforts (Pray & Kramer, 1987).

Causes—There could be many causes of these maladaptive habits, but in general, they are considered stress-related disorders. Azrin and Nunn (1973, 1977 cited in Pray & Kramer, 1987) state that the habits begin as low-frequency behaviors that gradually increase in frequency, intensity, and duration over months and years. Often individuals are unaware of the high-frequency behavior and become habituated to the pain or injury caused by the behavior (Azrin & Nunn, 1973, 1977 cited in Pray & Kramer, 1987). The maladaptive habits are not considered to be symptoms of emotional or mental disturbance.

What Can I Do as a Parent?—Caretakers and the referred child must be the primary change agents if change is to occur and be maintained (Pray & Kramer, 1987). A detailed history of the child's habit is necessary to design an effective treatment plan. It is important to determine the motivation of the child and the significant others for treating the disorder (Pray & Kramer, 1987). It will be necessary to collect data on habit occurrences for several days (Alessi & Kaye, 1983, p. 61 cited in Pray & Kramer, 1987).

Habit reversal (HR) is the most effective treatment for maladaptive habits. "However, HR is a self-management program that is effective only for children capable of managing their own treatment with supervision from caretakers" (Pray & Kramer, 1987). Brief descriptions of the HR procedures are listed below (Pray et al., 1986 cited in Pray & Kramer, 1987):

1. Inconvenience Review — What are the problems caused by the habit?
2. Awareness Training — Notice when the habit occurs. Self-awareness can be increased by performing the habit slowly and deliberately in front of a mirror while describing the habit aloud.
3. Habit-Promoting Situations — Identify the situations in which the habit is likely to occur and be prepared to use a competing behavior.
4. Competing Reaction — Learn a behavior that is incompatible with the behavior. For example, for fingernail biting, have the child grasp other objects.
5. Corrective and Preventive Reaction — After learning the competing reaction, use it to interrupt or prevent the maladaptive habit.
6. Associated Behavior — Identify the behavior that precedes the behavior and use the competing reaction to stop this behavior.
7. Relaxation Training — Learn to handle stressful situations.
8. Social Support — Parents/teachers will want to maintain a high ratio of positive statements and reminder statements.
9. Practice — Practice the competing reaction.
10. Records — Keep a daily record of the frequency of the habit to chart progress.

Parents will wish to identify the environmental stressors related to the habit and will need to help the child manage these stressors. Additionally, they will need the assistance of their school psychologist, guidance counselor, or other mental health professional in designing and implementing the intervention. It is important to ensure consistency of the treatment plan across school and home settings.

Resources

The school psychologist, school guidance counselor, or other mental health professionals may be very helpful in providing information about the child and any necessary treatment plan. Additionally, the family physician or other professionals will also be helpful.

References

American Psychiatric Association. (1980). *Diagnostic and statistical manual of mental disorders (3rd ed.)*. Washington, DC: Author.

Pray, B., & Kramer, J. J. (1987). Children and maladaptive habits. In A. Thomas & J. Grimes (Eds.), *Children's needs: Psychological perspectives* (pp. 343-351). Washington, DC: National Association of School Psychologists.

Jensen, W. R., Kehle, T. J., & Clark. E. (1987). Children and thumbsucking. In A. Thomas & J. Grimes (Eds.), *Children's needs: Psychological perspectives* (pp. 643-650). Washington, DC: National Association of School Psychologists.

NATIONAL ASSOCIATION OF SCHOOL PSYCHOLOGISTS

Children and Masturbation

Marcia Shaffer
Steuben-Allegany Board of Cooperative Educational Services, Bath, New York

Background—For hundreds of years, masturbation (i.e., manipulating one's genitals for sexual pleasure) has been regarded as a dirty, evil act. This attitude, based largely on widespread religious stories, has led to the belief that masturbation causes such dread conditions as blindness and insanity. Because it is an emotion-laden subject; because so many generations have had the ingrained idea that masturbation is bad, adults may be uneasy, guilty, and even struck dumb when it occurs. To avoid temptation, even tiny babies are taught to keep their hands away from their "private parts.' By the time they go to school, most children have learned that masturbation gets them severe scolding or physical punishment.

Development—Masturbation is a normal form of sexual release for human beings of all ages. It is to be expected in small babies who quite naturally explore their entire bodies. It occurs often in four year-olds and often again at adolescence. Masturbation,however frequent, does not lead to insanity, blindness, loss of one's pens, or any terrible disease.

What Can I Do as a Parent?—Even if your own parents have made you believe that masturbation is an act of public shame and private guilt, you don't want your child to be as uneasy about it as you are. Try not to become agitated if you see his hands at his genitals; and remember that the myths are untrue. You may not like to see him masturbate, but it won't hurt him.

The child who masturbates in school is likely to be teased, ridiculed, and/or reprimanded. To save him humiliation, teach your child that it is ill-mannered to touch his genitals in public.

Be sure that your child's body is clean, and that his underwear is clean and loose.

Uncomfortable bodies and clothing may lead to behavior which looks like masturbation and upsets teachers, who are as susceptible to the myths as anyone else.

Very few school-age children engage in masturbation in front of other people. If a teacher reports to you that your child is masturbating regularly, take the complaint seriously. Check with your doctor to be sure there is no physical cause, such as a genitourinary infection. If there is no physical cause, consult your school psychologist or a similarly trained professional person. There may be emotional problems which require your youngster to seek the comfort of masturbation.

Resources

The following books are as suitable for teachers, school administrators, and pupil personnel staff as for parents.

Calderone, M. S. and Johnson, E. W. (1981). *The Family Book about Sexuality*. New York: Harper and Row. This covers almost every conceivable aspect of sexual functioning in a dignified style. It includes sex information for the handicapped and sexual conditions which have legal implications. It deals thoughtfully with the emotional side of sexuality.

Gordon, S. (1975). *Let's Make Sex a Household Word*. New York: John Day. Like all of Dr. Gordon's publications, this one is honest. It is addressed to parents, and discusses topics of concern for children of preschool age through adolescence. There is an excellent bibliography.

Gordon S. and Gordon J. (1983). *Raising a Child Conservatively in a Sexually Permissive World*. New York: Simon and Schuster. Dr. Gordon's customary courage, compassion and comprehensibility are here supported by his wife's social work philosophy. "The book places more than the usual emphasis on social relationships and "sexual integrity." It provides a fine bibliography listed by topics.

Johnson, C. B. and Johnson, E. W. (1970). *Love and Sex and Growing Up*. Philadelphia: Lippincott. This volume presents sexual information in a gentle, direct way. It makes clear the Johnson viewpoint, which is that sexual information should be available to young people, but that they should feel free to embrace old-fashioned morality if they so choose.

Children and Nailbiting

John J. DeFrancesco
Connecticut Department of Children and Youth Services

Background—Nailbiting is a behavior that has confused parents, researchers, and practitioners for years. There is confusion regarding the meaning and severity of the behavior, whether the behavior can or should be treated, and what treatment or intervention, if necessary, is most effective. It is one of the most frequent and persistent behaviors among children and adolescents. The behavior typically does not manifest itself before the age of 4. Between the ages of 4 and 6 approximately 38% of all children bite their nails. By the age of 10, this increases to 60%. Nailbiting behavior peaks at age 13 for males, when 62% of males bit their nails, and for females at age 11, when 51% engage in the behavior. As the nailbiter enters adulthood, the incidence stabilizes at about 10-20%. Nailbiting is a behavior that will sometimes go unnoticed; however, it can cause social embarrassment, parental concerns and anxiety, dental problems and infections and it can indicate underlying emotional problems. Generally, it is a behavior that should not be ignored once it becomes persistent and severe.

Development—During the course of what is considered normal development, most children will engage in some form of nailbiting. The behavior is evident in males and females of all ages, social backgrounds and levels of functioning. It has been termed an "everyday problem of the everyday child." While mild cases of nailbiting may cause some concerns among parents, most children will outgrow the behavior. Moderate and severe cases of nailbiting, however, can be considered developmentally inappropriate and require investigation and treatment. The possibility of underlying emotional difficulties in children with severe and moderate cases of nailbiting is great. It is generally agreed upon that nailbiting is a response to stress and is indicative of internal tension and anxiety. Children typically exhibit the behavior at stressful moments, for example, waiting to be called upon in class, being teased on the playground, listening to their parents argue, or having to go home to an abusive family situation. Medical/dental issues should also be addressed in these cases because the nailbiting can cause finger infections and dental problems. In short, moderate and severe nailbiting must be scrutinized, not only as a means of treating the behavior, but because it can be indicative of other difficulties, that can affect the development of the child.

What Can I Do as a Parent?—Nailbiting is a behavior that, in most cases, is first noticed by parents. It is so prevalent, however, that most parents dismiss it as a behavior that every child engages in and will soon outgrow. In many instances, particularly in cases of mild, infrequent nailbiting, this is considered the best and most effective way to deal with the behavior.

- When parents or teachers begin to notice that the behavior is persistent and/or severe, however, there is reason for concern, particularly if the nails are sore and bleeding and/or infections develop. In this situation it is often prudent to consult a physician if bleeding or infection is evident. Unfortunately, after the medical condition is treated, many parents will not seek further assistance. It is only after parents realize that the behavior will continue (perhaps with accompanying soreness and/or bleeding) that they will seek the assistance of a psychologist.

- Since nailbiting is generally seen as a response to stress it becomes important to identify and

39

reduce the stress and anxiety in the child's life. The psychologist can assist the parents in this area. Identifying external and internal causes of stress can be accomplished by obtaining information from parents, teachers, testing, rating scales and behavioral checklists. Developmental, medical, academic and family information should be obtained. The parent, child and teacher can be asked to indicate the situation in which the nailbiting occurs. Once the source(s) of stress is identified the parents, along with the psychologist, must develop strategies to relieve/reduce the stress in the child's life. For example, if parental expectations are too high and producing high levels of stress they should be encouraged to decrease their expectations; if the child feels rejected because of the arrival of a new sibling, vigorous attempts should be made to involve the child in more family activities.

- Developing strategies to reduce stress may require considerable efforts by psychologists, parents and teachers and may be a time consuming process. In the interim, it may be necessary to immediately decrease the overt behavior, particularly if the nailbiting is severe. Parents, again with the assistance of the psychologist, can implement a behavioral procedure called the habit reversal technique. In this technique, children practice physical movements that are not compatible with nailbiting such as grasping or clenching reaction. Children are also taught to be aware of each time they engage in the nailbiting behavior and to be aware of situations in which it is likely to occur. The child should be reinforced for not engaging in the behavior. The habit reversal technique has been the most successful behavioral treatment for this behavior.

- Some behavioral techniques, however, have the reputation of not producing long term effects. Because of this it is necessary to combine behavioral treatment (habit reversal) with stress reduction strategies. This will produce both long and short term results. The source of stress that is causing the behavior not just the observable behavior is eliminated. While the psychologist may have to initially assist parents in both of these processes, most parents will be able to go it alone once they are acquainted with the strategies.

- Since nailbiting has been found, in certain situations, to cause dental problems, parents should inform the child's dentist of the behavior. This can be done at regular check-ups.

Resources

—*Habit Control in a Day*—by N.H. Azrin and R.D. Nunn. Simon & Shuster, 1977. A self-help book based on the habit reversal method. Instructions on how to use the method are outlined.
—*Nailbiting and Cuticle Biting*, Kicking the habit-by D.C. Perkins and F.M. Perkins. Self Control Press. A manual designed to help individuals control nailbiting behavior using behavioral techniques.
—*Children Under Stress*—by L. Chandler. Charles C. Thomas Publisher. A book that describes how emotional and behavioral reactions develop from internal and external sources of stress. Strategies for parents, teachers and psychologists to use to relieve/reduce stress are provided.

Obesity

Nancy Conti
University of South Florida

Background—Weight problems can range from being overweight, which is considered 10% above ideal or normal weight, mildly obese at 20% to 30% above ideal, obese at 30% or more above normal, and morbid obesity at 100% or more above ideal weight. If using a weight/height index, weight falling above the 95th percentile is most frequently considered obese (Kirschenbaum, Johnson, & Stalonas, 1987). Currently in the United States the number of obese children and adolescents ranges from approximately 20% to 25% (Brone & Fisher, 1988; Kirschenbaum et al., 1987), and overall estimates range from 15% to 50%, the wide range being due to differing criteria (Brone & Fisher, 1988).

It is suggested that obese children and adolescents are likely to become obese adults, and it is estimated that they have an 80% chance of becoming obese adults (Brone & Fisher, 1988; Hammer, 1975; Blackburn & Bristrian, 1975). If the excess weight is not lost prior to adulthood, there is a 28 to 1 chance that the obese child or adolescent will be a thin adult (Kirschenbaum et al., 1987).

The physical side effects associated with obesity include increased chances for diabetes, high blood pressure, hyperlipidemia, kidney stones, and musculoskeletal disorders in adulthood (Brone & Fisher, 1988; Graves, Meyers, & Clark, 1988; Knittle & Ginsberg-Fellner, 1975). Social-emotional side effects of childhood and adolescent obesity include the potential for rejection by peers and lowered self-esteem (Bruch, 1975; Graves et al., 1988; Kirshenbaum, et al., 1987; Sidbury & Schwartz, 1975). Obesity is also suggested to be associated with greater levels of psychological problems (Graves et al., 1988; Kirschenbaum et al., 1987). Graves, Meyers, and Clark (1988) further suggest that although obesity is difficult for both boys and girls, emotionally, the impact is greater for girls. Overweight and obese children and adolescents are likely to face discrimination and be stereotyped as "lazy, stupid, and weak." Discrimination is more likely to occur against girls and women than boys and men (Bruch, 1975; Kirschenbaum et al., 1987) and girls are more likely than boys to be obese (Brone & Fisher, 1988).

Development—Obese children and adolescents most often have obese or overweight parents (Epstein, Valoski, Wing, Perkins, Fernstrom, Marks, & McCurley,1989). The causes of obesity have been associated with numerous factors, which can be separated into the categories of physiology or biology and the environment. Physiology focuses on a genetic predisposition as a contributing factor in obesity, whereas the environment can be divided further into the areas of: family interactions, food and exercise, and emotionality (Brone & Fisher, 1988; Epstein et al., 1989; Knittle & Ginsberg-Fellner, 1975).

It has been suggested that obese children and adolescents are genetically predisposed to being overweight, but that a predisposition is not a sufficient or necessary condition to becoming an obese child/adolescent (Brone & Fisher, 1988; Collipp, 1975a; Epstein et al., 1989). Fat cells in the human body replicate in response to intake of food most frequently during infancy and to a lesser degree in childhood. The number of fat cells is determined partly by genetics and partly by eating habits, but regardless of changes in eating habits, the number of fat cells will not decrease. Therefore, an overfed baby who develops an excessive number of fat cells will never be able to eliminate the excess. It is the size of the fat cells that is the focus of weight reduction (Brone & Fisher, 1988; Collipp, 1975; Knittle & Ginsberg-Fellner, 1975).

The environmental factors that may affect weight include family interactions, food and exercise, and emotionality. Family factors such as parents maintaining a strict eating schedule for infants may lead the child to use external cues, such as time of day, for hunger rather than internal cues. Obese children are often inaccurate in judging their own hunger. Modeling inappropriate eating and exercising habits and using food as rewards for the child's behavior are also habits that may adversely affect the child/adolescent. They may lead the child/adolescent to prefer and maintain inappropriate eating habits and again affect the child's ability to accurately judge their hunger (Brone & Fisher, 1988; Bruch, 1975).

The food and exercise factor is the interaction between food intake and amount of exercise. Obese children and adolescents are often, but not always, found to overeat, be less active, or a combination of the two (Collipp, 1975a; Kirschenbaum et al., 1987). The factor of emotionality has been typically linked to adolescence. It is suggested that some adolescents eat to deal with stress and feelings of inadequacy, as well as use it as a tool for revenge against peers or parents (Brone & Fisher, 1988; Kornhaber & Kornhaber, 1975).

What Can Parents Do?—Research supports the role of parents in positively or negatively affecting child weight (Brone & Fisher, 1988; Bruch, 1975; Epstein et al., 1989; Knittle & Ginsberg-Fellner, 1975). Parents can deal with the problem of obesity in a preventative fashion or treat the problem after it has occurred. For prevention in those children who are genetically predisposed to obesity, parents can speak to their pediatrician for the most appropriate feeding habits and schedules for their children, model appropriate habits by modifying their own eating and exercising habits, and reinforce appropriate eating habits in their children. Also, parents of obese children and adolescents have been found to be highly protective and/or rigid with their children. This behavior is suggested to facilitate obesity by leading children to feel insecure and as though they are powerless to make changes in their lives (Bruch, 1975; Davidson, 1975; Epstein et al., 1989; Sidbury & Schwartz, 1975).

Treatment components that been successful in addressing obesity include behavior modification/ therapy, increased exercise, modification of eating habits (Kirschenbaum et al., 1987), support groups (such as Weight Watchers) (Brone & Fisher, 1988), and parent problem solving (Graves et al., 1988). The type of treatment and its success will depend on the needs and abilities of the child and family. Treatments that are not recommended for children and adolescents include drug therapy (Brone & Fisher, 1988; Grollman, 1975) and surgical intervention (Blackburn & Bristrian, 1975; Brone & Fisher, 1988).

What Can Schools Do?—Schools have been identified as vehicles for effecting and supporting change in children and adolescents due to their consistent interaction with children and families. Schools have therefore been suggested to be potential sites for the prevention and treatment of obesity. Schools can be involved in educating children to appropriate eating and exercising habits, and monitoring food intake and physical activity. School intervention can be comprehensive and include the family system (Bolocofsky, 1987; Collipp, 1975b).

Resources

If further information is desired concerning the prevention of obesity in children and adolescents, your pediatrician can provide you with the information necessary. The nurse at your child's school can also provide you with additional information on childhood obesity and types of interventions available at your school or district.

References

Blackburn, G. L., & Bristrian, B. R. (1975). Surgical techniques in the treatment of adolescent obesity. In P. J. Collipp (Ed.), *Childhood obesity* (pp. 117-130). Acton, MA: Publishing Sciences Group.

Bolocofsky, D. N. (1987). Children and obesity. In A. Thomas & J. Grimes (Eds.), *Children's needs: Psychological perspectives* (pp. 390-395). Washington, DC: National Association of School Psychologists.

Brone, R. J., & Fisher, C. B. (1988). Determinants of adolescent obesity: A comparison with anorexia nervosa. *Adolescence, 23,* 155-168.

Bruch, H. (1975). The importance of overweight. In P. J. Collipp (Ed.), *Childhood obesity* (pp. 75-82). Acton, MA: Publishing Sciences Group.

Collipp, P. J. (1975a). Differential diagnosis of childhood obesity. In P. J. Collipp (Ed.), *Childhood obesity* (pp. 25-42).Acton, MA: Publishing Sciences Group.

Collipp, P. J. (1975b). Obesity program in public schools. In P. J. Collipp (Ed.), *Childhood obesity* (pp. 43-54). Acton, MA: Publishing Sciences Group.

Davidson, M. (1975). Nutritional individualization—A necessary approach to feeding children with our current information. In P. J. Collipp (Ed.), *Childhood obesity* (pp. 55-64). Acton, MA: Publishing Sciences Group.

Epstein, L. H., Valoski, A., Wing, R. R., Perkins, K. A., Fernstrom, M., Marks, B., & McCurley, J. (1989). Perception of eating and exercise in children as a function of child and parent weight status. *Appetite, 12,* 105-118.

Graves, T., Meyers, A. W., & Clark, L. (1988). An evaluation of parental problem-solving training in the behavioral treatment of childhood obesity. *Journal of Consulting and Clinical Psychology, 56,* 246-250.

Grollman, A. (1975). Drug therapy of obesity in children. In P. J. Collipp (Ed.), *Childhood obesity* (pp. 83-96). Acton, MA: Publishing Sciences Group.

Hammer, S. L. (1975). Obesity: Early identification and treatment. In P. J. Collipp (Ed.), *Childhood obesity* (pp. 15-24). Acton, MA: Publishing Sciences Group.

Kirschenbaum, D. S., Johnson, W. G., & Stalonas, P. M. (1987). *Treating childhood and adolescent obesity.* New York: Pergamon Press.

Knittle, J., & Ginsberg-Fellner, F. (1975). Can obesity be prevented? In P. J. Collipp (Ed.), *Childhood obesity* (pp. 1-14). Acton, MA: Publishing Sciences Group.

Kornhaber, G. L., & Kornhaber, E. (1975). Obesity in adolescents: Contributing psychopathological factors and their treatment. In P. J. Collipp (Ed.), *Childhood obesity* (pp. 109-116). Acton, MA: Publishing Sciences Group.

Sidbury, J. B., & Schwartz, R. P. (1975). A program for weight reduction in children. In P. J. Collipp (Ed.), *Childhood obesity* (pp. 65-74). Acton, MA: Publishing Sciences Group.

Perception of Time

Sherri L. West
University of South Florida

Background—Many aspects of the adult world revolve around time. Parents often give children time lines to complete chores or homework in an effort to provide more structure and order to their child's life. When the youngster does not respond to this type of structure, the parent may interpret this as defiance. However, time is a very abstract concept and is not viewed in the same manner by a child as by an adult.

Development—Piaget (1969) discovered that children progress through different developmental stages. During the first of these stages, sensorimotor (birth to 2 years), time is measured by the sequence of events as it relates to the child himself. It is based on specific, concrete observable actions. For example, lunch to a 2-year-old child may mean the meal after breakfast. If given a snack a few hours after breakfast, the child may say "lunch." Similarly, when using time in their language, it usually reflects here and now, not the past or future (Cattoche, 1987). Although many preschool and kindergarten teachers attempt to teach time by having children look at the big hand and the little hand, it is merely an exercise. A child using a digital display watch might explain at four o'clock that an adult needs to tell him when it is five o'clock, because his clock only has a number four (Gormly & Brodzinsky, 1989).

Concepts such as dates and times are not understood until about age 8, the concrete-operational level of development. At this age, children may confuse time with measures of distance and velocity. When observing a race, for example, car A which arrived 1/2 second before car B would be considered the fastest, even though car B traveled twice the distance. Children who are developmentally delayed may need more time to develop the perception of time.

What Can I Do As a Parent—As previously mentioned, your efforts to structure your child's life by providing adult-like time frames may not be a realistic expectation for your young child. Instead, translate these time factors into language they can easily understand.

—A simple kitchen egg timer can be used to set time limits for children. Instead of saying you must go to bed at 8:00 p.m., explain that when the alarm rings, it will be time to go to bed.

—Establish a routine where everyday events occur at approximately the same time (i.e., lunch, dinner, bedtime, nap time, etc.) so the child can predict when the events are going to happen.

—Discuss the day's events prompting a recall of the order in which the day progressed, while relating them to the time of day (i.e., morning, afternoon, evening, etc.).

—When disciplining a child using time-out, remember 3-4 minutes will get your point across, to a preschool child more than 4 minutes is an eternity.

—Timers can also be set for completing homework. Ask the child to work on their homework until the alarm sounds. At that time you could review together how many problems were completed, the correctness, and estimate how much time would actually be needed each night to complete the work. This will also give you and your child a positive time to interact.

Resources

Berk, L. (1989). *Child development*. Needham Heights: MA: Allyn & Bacon, A Division of Simon & Schuster.
Berger, K. (1980). *The developing person*. New York: Worth Publishers, Inc.
Craig, G. (1989). *Human development*. Englewood Cliffs, NJ: Prentice-Hall, Inc.

References

Cattoche, R. J. (1987). Children and the perception of time. In A. Thomas and J. Grimes (Eds.), *Children's needs: A psychological perspective* (pp. 412-418). Washington, DC: National Association of School Psychologists.
Gormly, A., & Brodzinsky, D. (1989). *Lifespan human development*. Fort Worth: Holt, Rinehart and Winston, Inc.
Piaget, J. (1969). *The child's conception of time*. New York: Basic Books.

Prejudice

Pia Rebello
University of South Florida

Background—Prejudice refers to an organized predisposition to respond in an unfavorable manner towards people from different ethnic, religious, and racial background because of their ethnic, religious, and racial affiliation (Aboud, 1988). Thus, the most salient characteristic of prejudice is its negative quality. The three important components of prejudice are (a) an unfavorable evaluation of a person, (b) elicited by their group affiliation, and (c) based on an underlying organized predisposition. Research has shown that racial prejudice in school-aged children is related to the child's race, interracial contact, sex, intelligence, and self-concept. The results of a study by Moore, Hauck, and Deene (1984) indicated that White children appeared to be more prejudiced than Black children in situations requiring prolonged interracial interaction, however, no difference was noted in circumstances involving minimal intimate social relationships for short periods of time. Females were generally less prejudiced than males, and Black males of low prejudice were more intelligent, more external, and less anxious than Black males of higher prejudice.

Development—The most popular theory of prejudice is the Social-Reflection Theory. It states that prejudice reflects the differential values given to different groups in a stratified society and that children's attitudes reflect their parent's values. The Authoritarian Theory of prejudice explains negative attitudes in terms of states internal to the child rather than social ones. The Social-Cognitive Developmental Theories claim that prejudice is inevitable in young children because of their cognitive limitations. The prejudice seen in children at one developmental stage is qualitatively different from the prejudice seen in children at another age. This is so because it arises out of a different understanding of the social world.

Prejudice appears to develop naturally in children according to their developmental stage and their psychological needs (Walton, 1987). It begins as differences are distinguished and become translated into specific prejudiced beliefs, feelings, and behavior, or not, as the child and culture interact. According to Katz (1982), sex and racial differences are distinguishable in both Black and White children by ages 3 and 4. By middle-school, the differences are well noted and many children show negative affect about these differences. In adolescents the developmental drive for identity fosters same group preferences and rejection of outsiders (Bettelheim & Janowitz, 1964).

Causes—The research on social stratification indicates that ethnic heterogeneity does not itself produce prejudice. There must be a history of ethnic status differences or current status differences in the community. It also indicates that a child's socioeconomic status is not strongly related to prejudice (Aboud, 1984). Authoritarian child-rearing practices do not directly enhance prejudice in children, except sometimes in adolescent boys. The need for approval may account for prejudice in young children. Major determinants of prejudice are social values of the parents, and the extent of exposure to other ethnic and racial groups.

What Can I Do as a Teacher?—Teachers play a major role in advocating the values of multiculturalism and combating prejudice in the development of children. Their daily lesson plans should include societal problem-solving models that teach children to recognize inequality and prejudice in society and strive for change. According to Lynch (1988), teachers' strategies should be holistic, comprehensive in scope and sequence, and involve the total school environment. They should also make maximum use of the resources and skills of the local community. Teaching strategies for prejudice reduction should include components of cognitive development and affective and behavioral interactions. The teacher should strive to create a democratic classroom by desegregating the students. Instruction should be impartial, keeping different learning styles in perspective. The focus of the learning activities should be to include the development of decision making and societal change. Teachers can use multiracial teaching materials that present racial minority groups in a favorable and realistic fashion. Research indicates that visual material such as pictures and films greatly enhance attempts to change racial attitudes (Banks, 1982).

What Can I Do as a Parent?—Parents must be vigilant and take a conscious stand to reduce prejudice in their children. Parents should address the issues regarding differences in society and stress that these differences are natural and desirable. When the need arises they should talk to their children about the reality of an imperfect society, the forms of injustice that exist, and ways to deal with them. At the same time children should learn that aggressive and antisocial delinquent behavior will not result in the desired goals. Instead, in the face of racial pressures children should learn to be tolerant and show compassion for other human beings. Parents belonging to minority groups should keep in mind the stresses and strains children go through in their daily interactions. They should set realistic goals for their children and give them an opportunity to develop a sense of personal identity and self-esteem.

Finally, it is not enough for parents just to express racial acceptance in words, their actions must reflect their statements (Clark, 1963).

References

Aboud, F. (1988). *Children and prejudice*. New York: Basil Blackwell Inc.

Banks, J. A. (1982, February). *Reducing prejudice in students: Theory, research, and strategies*. Paper presented at Kamloops Spring Institute for Teacher Education Lecture Series, Burnaby, British Columbia.

Bettelheim, B., & Janowitz, M. (1964). *Social change and prejudice including dynamics of prejudice*. Glenclove, NY: Free Press.

Clark, K. B. (1963). *Prejudice and your child* (2nd ed.). Boston: Beacon.

Katz, P. (1982). *Development of children's awareness and intergroup attitudes* (Report No. BBB18183). Washington, DC: NIE. (ERIC Document Reproduction Service No. ED 207 675)

Lynch, J. (1988, April). *Pedagogical strategies to reduce prejudice: Towards middle range theories*. Paper presented at the annual meeting of the American Educational Research Association, New Orleans, LA.

Moore, J. W., Hauck, W. E., & Deene, T. C. (1984). Racial prejudice, interracial contact, and personality variables. *Journal of Experimental Education, 52*(3), 168-173.

Walton, J. R. (1987). Children and prejudice. In A. Thomas & J. Grimes (Eds.), *Children's needs: Psychological perspectives* (pp. 434-441). Washington, DC: National Association of School Psychologists.

NATIONAL
ASSOCIATION OF
SCHOOL
PSYCHOLOGISTS

Prematurity

Sherri L. West
University of South Florida

Background—In the past, "premature" was the label given to infants who were not as well developed at birth as normal babies. However, there are essentially two very different types of premature infants. **Preterm** infants are babies born prior to the 37th week of the full gestational period (42 weeks). The second type, termed **small for gestational age or low birth weight,** are those infants who were carried the full 9 months, but failed to gain sufficient weight (less than 2,500 grams or 5 1/2 pounds). Each type of premature infant is at-risk for developmental problems (Berk, 1989).

Development—The medical technology of today gives premature infants a better chance than those born only a decade ago. These improvements are helping to reduce some of the developmental consequences these infants may experience in the future. Developmental differences between premature infants and their normal term counterparts may diminish over the first few years of life. This will depend, however, on the severity of complications at birth (i.e., lungs fully inflated, etc.). Developmental milestones should be measured according to the child's gestational age rather than their birth date. To calculate this date, subtract the number of weeks the baby was premature from the chronological age (Pound, 1987). Therefore, a 10-week-old premature infant born at 32 weeks will more closely resemble a newborn full-term infant. Parents can then follow standard developmental charts for infant and toddler development using the corrected age.

The Causes of Prematurity—It is estimated that the cause of approximately 50% of all premature births is unknown (Harrison, 1983). Therefore, many parents are both unaware and unprepared when a premature birth occurs. Researchers do know that various factors seem to be associated with premature births. Mothers who possess some of the following factors are at a higher risk of experiencing a premature birth than mothers who do not possess these factors (Redshaw, Rivers, & Rosenblatt, 1985).

Factors Associated with Preterm Delivery

—previous preterm birth

—multiple pregnancy

—teenage pregnancy (under age 17)

—becoming pregnant within 3 months of giving birth

—previous termination of pregnancy

—low maternal weight

—maternal short stature

—poor maternal nutrition

—poor weight gain in pregnancy

—heart disease

—infection of the urinary tract in pregnancy (cystitis)

—major illness or operation during pregnancy

—separation of the placenta

—single or unsupported parent; divorced

—low socioeconomic status of baby's mother

—heavy smoking by mother

—alcoholism in mother

—drug addiction of mother

—long stressful journeys

(Redshaw et al., 1985)

What Can I Do as a Parent?—After the baby is born, a hospital stay is usually necessary. While the baby is in the hospital, isolettes are often used to regulate the baby's body temperature, as well as to provide a protective environment in which to grow. However, parents will probably not be able to hold their premature infant right away and this can cause distress for both parents and infant. Therefore, it is extremely important for parents to visit their infant regularly and take every opportunity to stroke, massage, or rock the infant for tactile stimulation. Providing both visual and auditory stimulation is also necessary. This enrichment can be accomplished by using mobiles and pictures for visual simulation Friedman & Sigman, 1981). Simply talking and/or singing to your baby will provide the auditory stimulation necessary. Some hospitals request that mothers tape record themselves reading a story to the infant, as this can calm the infant when in distress and the parents are unable to be there. Studies have shown that infants provided with such stimulation gained weight and improved their motoric ability and visual alertness (Schaefer, Hatcher, & Bargelow, 1980). Though the infant is very fragile and surrounded by medical equipment, the infant's need for love and affection is just as critical for improved health. Parents should become familiar with parent groups and infant stimulation programs in their area. Most medical centers, hospitals, and mental health agencies will be able to provide you with this information.

References

Berk, L. (1989). *Child development*. Needham Heights: MA: Allyn & Bacon, A Division of Simon & Schuster.

Friedman, L., & Sigman, M. (1981). *Preterm birth and psychological development*. New York: Academic Press Harrison, H. (1983). The premature baby book. New York: St. Martin's.

Pound, J. E. (1987). Children and Prematurity. In A. Thomas & J. Grimes (Eds.), *Children's needs: Psychological perspectives* (pp. 441-451). Washington, DC: National Association of School Psychologists.

Redshaw, M., Rivers, R., & Rosenblatt, D. (1985). *Born too early: Special care for your preterm baby*. New York: Oxford University Press.

Schaefer, M., Hatcher, R. P., & Barglow, P. D. (1980). Prematurity and infant stimulation: A review of research. *Child Psychiatry and Human Development, 80,* 195-198.

NATIONAL
ASSOCIATION OF
SCHOOL
PSYCHOLOGISTS

Religion

Mary Ann Parkinson
University of South Florida

Background—A variety of religious beliefs are acknowledged and practiced in the United States today. The predominant religious groups include Roman Catholics, Protestants, Eastern Churches, Jews, Old Catholic, Polish National Catholic, Armenian Churches, and Buddhist Churches of America (Williams, 1969).

Protestantism entails a diversity of families or faiths. the most common of these faiths in the United States are Lutheran, Presbyterian, Episcopal, Congregational, Baptist-Christian (Discipline), and Methodist (Williams, 1969). The term "Protestant" originally referred to a protest made against the political discouragement of certain religious beliefs in the early 1500s. However, the meaning of this faith's name is not to be confused. Although the verb "protest" traditionally has a negative connotation, the noun "Protestant" still describes a person who has a positive faith in religion. For a detailed description of Protestantism and other religious faiths, the reader is referred to Williams (1969).

Development—A child's initial religious beliefs typically are modeled after those of the parents. Religious customs such as going to church or synagogue, attending youth meetings, and saying bedtime prayers serve as the foundation for establishing a personal religious faith. Children's religious beliefs and perceptions of a higher power or God develop and change as they get older. The development of religious practices, values, and beliefs may have a strong impact on a child's social and emotional development as well.

Nye and Carlson (1984) proposed that a child's development of religious beliefs and religious thinking can be differentiated in three major stages relative to age. Children from the ages of 3 to 6 years may enter the "fairy-tale stage" of religious thinking. At these ages, the concept of God may be analogous to a cartoon hero who stands for good and justice and who comes to your rescue just before destruction. The "realistic stage" may emerge between the ages of 7 and 12, when the child begins more fully to understand the concept of God that is taught in the child's environment. The final stage, termed the "individualistic stage," may be reached between the ages of 13 and 18. During this developmental phase, the adolescent may strive toward a more personal relationship with God. Ownership of the responsibility for the religious practices, values, and beliefs may also be learned.

Children's development of the concept of God also may be compatible with Piaget's stages of cognitive development (Nye & Carlson, 1984). Younger children of 5 or 6 years of age may describe God in more concrete terms than do older children. Adolescents may be more likely to describe God in terms of deity and omnipotence.

As children approach adolescence, their perception of God may change to meet their individual psychological needs. God as visions of strength and beauty may change to worries of fear and obedience as the challenges of life become more difficult (Elkind, 1971). However, the association of God with love and goodness typically remains constant throughout childhood and adolescence.

Certain beliefs relative to religious practices also may change over time. For example, the belief that prayer produces immediate results may decline with age (Elkind, 1971). Children under the age of 7 may tend to believe in the immediacy of answers from God (the hero in the cartoon). As children get older,

51

they may begin to feel more satisfied with their communication with God (developing a more realistic perception). Approaching the ages of 12 or 13, adolescent prayers that are seemingly unanswered may be attributed to a consequence of selfish or materialistic requests (individualizing beliefs or owning actions). Later in adolescence, these consequences may be explained as "God knows best."

What Can I Do As A Teacher?—As a teacher, you naturally acknowledge and respect the individual differences of your students. In terms of religion, the following guidelines might be helpful:

—Investigate and understand the values, beliefs, and religious practices of the families of your students. This knowledge may facilitate the establishment of rapport and interventions with the children. It also may serve to avoid offending a student or parent. For example, a compliment to a girl of Amish faith would be inappropriate because of the religious perception toward vanity or personal pride. Another example may be retaining a student of Jehovah's Witness faith from holiday and birthday celebrations.

—Be aware of divorced parents who may not want the noncustodial parent contacted for certain religious reasons.

—Contact appropriate support personnel (e.g., school guidance counselor or school psychologist) when a student appears depressed or suicidal. These thoughts may be exacerbated when a student perceives rejection by the family for committing a designated sin.

—When your religious affiliation differs from that of a student or parent, consider maintaining a neutral attitude when issues of religion are discussed.

—Be particularly aware of your students' environment in communities where fewer common religious beliefs are practiced.

References

Elkind, D. (1971). The development of religious understanding in children and adolescents. In M. Strommen (Ed.), *Research on religious development: A comprehensive handbook* (pp. 673–674). New York: Hawthorn Books.

Nye, W. C., & Carlson, J. S. (1984). The development of the concept of God in children. *Journal of Genetic Psychology 145,* 137–142.

Williams, J. P. (1969). *What Americans believe and how they worship* (pp. 1–14; 94–151). New York: Harper & Row.

NATIONAL
ASSOCIATION OF
SCHOOL
PSYCHOLOGISTS

Children and Responsibility

By Cynthia M. Sheehan
Just Kids Early Childhood Learning Center, Middle Island, NY

Background—Society today places a high priority on "responsibility in children. However, with the conflicting advice offered in books, magazines, and newspaper columns parents may feel confused as to exactly what a responsible child is, and what, if anything, can be done to encourage responsibility in children.

Responsibility can be thought of as respect for the rights of others and personal accountability for one's actions. Responsible children use their own resources, confidence, and judgment to make decisions, act independently, consider the effect their actions have on others and meet their own needs without interfering with the rights of others.

Development—It is necessary to differentiate between typical childish behavior and truly irresponsible actions. All children, at times, engage in silly, selfish and irresponsible behaviors. In order to determine if a real problem exists, the following guidelines should be considered in evaluating a child's general behavior:

How often is this a problem? Does the concerning behavior predominate the child's actions, or is there only an occasional lapse in responsibility? To what degree is the irresponsible behavior upsetting the home routine or interfering with classroom structure? Most school age children forget an assignment once in a while, but a daily or weekly problem could signal trouble in accepting work responsibilities. Every adolescent occasionally ignores an assigned chore; but a parent is appropriately concerned if the garbage is rarely taken out, or the lawn is never mowed. Does the behavior change when these concerns are brought to the child's attention? If a child's lack of attention to rules or assignments is the subject of frequent complaints from teachers, friends, or parents the situation warrants further investigation.

Does the child have an opportunity to be responsible? Children can only demonstrate responsible behavior if they are given the chance. Parents must be willing to allow children the freedom to make choices, demonstrate judgment, and learn from their mistakes. Does the child have an opportunity to contribute to the running of the household, remember belongings, structure time, plan activities, demonstrate preferences in clothing and food?

Are expectations appropriate? The natural progression of children's intellectual, physical, and emotional growth allows for increasing acceptance of responsibility. It is very important that the expectations placed on children match their abilities. Are situational demands within the child's capabilities? Have expectations been communicated clearly? Following are some examples of tasks most children can accept at a given age:

Preschooler

—can usually clean up toys with some direction or assistance
—should be expected to sit and play independently for short periods of time
—can often select clothes and dress themselves with a little verbal or physical assistance

—can begin to help with household chores such as setting the table, picking up soiled clothes, etc.

—follow safety rules with occasional reminders

Early school age

—can often follow rules of group games

—can express anger without hitting most of the time

—remembers to attend to personal belongings (brings home gloves, books, etc.) with little reminding

—does simple chores independently (clears table, puts belongings away)

—can care for hygiene and dressing needs

Intermediate school age

—can complete assignments independently

—can organize personal time to fit in homework, play time, etc.

—helps with household chores on a daily basis

—respects personal property of others

Adolescents

—can evaluate and respond when extra help is needed around the house

—follows curfew rules, lets parent know change in plans, etc.

—developing sexual responsibility and respects personal rights of others

—developing increased awareness of long-term life planning, career exploration

What Can I Do as a Parent?

• Model appropriate, responsible behavior: Set an example of respect for self and others —-be on time for appointments, return extra change to a cashier, finish necessary chores before relaxing, speak respectfully to children, handle anger appropriately.

• Communicate effectively: Expectations and rules should be stated clearly and positively to children. The reason for rules should be given so children develop an awareness of their helpfulness and the respect they gain when acting responsibly.

• Allow children to set goals, make choices, and solve problems: Children need experience in being responsible decision-makers. Involve them in setting household maintenance goals and chores. These can be displayed in a chart or contract. Encourage children's responsible participation in family meetings by presenting them with acceptable choices in food and clothing selection, time management, television offerings, room decoration, free-time activities, and vacation choices.

• Allow for natural and logical consequences: Children who do not act responsibly should experience the effect of their actions. If homework is not done, a television show may be missed so the assignment can be completed before bed. If toys are not put away, they may be taken until the child can care for them better. Adolescents not helping with laundry chores may find no clean clothes to wear to a party. Children unwilling to help with cooking and cleaning may find dinner will be late and favorite activities will be missed to allow them time to clean dishes. A child dawdling each morning may miss the bus and have to walk to school or be driven in late and expected to make up missed work.

Resources

Crary, E. (1979). *Without spanking or spoiling: A practical approach to toddler and preschool guidance.* Seattle: Parenting Press. This brief handbook is helpful in the practical uses of communication skills, problem solving and encouraging responsible behavior in young children.

Dinkmeyer, D. and McKay, G. (1973). *Raising a responsible child.* New York: Simon and Schuster. This is a useful blend of practical and theoretical information on how to provide concrete opportunities for children to demonstrate responsible behavior.

Dinkmeyer, D. and McKay, G. (1982). *The parent's handbook: Systematic training for effective parenting.* Circle Pines, MN: American Guidance Service. This is a systematic presentation of child management skills. Readings, charts, and exercises allow parents to explore behavioral interventions and attitude changes designed to encourage responsible behavior in children.

Dreikurs, R. and Soltz, V. (1964). *Children the challenge.* New York: Hawthorn/Dutton. A philosophy of child rearing that emphasizes mutual respect and social adequacy is discussed. A focus on the goals of children's behavior and parental responses that stimulate independence provides information that is useful for practical application in the family.

Oppenheim, J., Boegehold, B., and Brenner, B. (1984). *Raising a confident child.* New York: Pantheon. This presents an explicit overview of sequential development in children that is useful in forming appropriate expectations.

NATIONAL ASSOCIATION OF SCHOOL PSYCHOLOGISTS

Sexual Interest

Bonnie Matthews
University of South Florida

Background—Humans are sexual beings. Yes, even from birth, our physical development includes sexual components. This development is normal and necessary. According to many experts, including Tharinger (1987), a child's sexual development, from the moment of birth, is influenced by factors in their environment such as parents, family members, peers, and the media. We all develop sexually, but whether we do so with comfortable, healthy feelings about our sexuality or uncomfortable feelings about our sexuality depends heavily on the interactions we have, as children, with these factors.

It is not only common, but important, for parents to wonder about how they can best address sexual topics with their children. Parents often ask questions such as what do I tell my children when they ask where babies come from or ask, "what is that?" when pointing to a genital on a person or an animal. Recognizing that sexuality is a basic part of human personality and that people have numerous questions and thoughts about this topic, it makes sense to help children of all ages develop a healthy concept of human sexuality. In order to determine if your child is developing normally in relation to sexuality, it is important to understand what is normal for children and what is not normal.

Development—Tharinger (1987) divided sexual development for children into three stages: infancy, early childhood, and middle to late childhood. During infancy, children start learning about their bodies. They naturally find that it feels good to touch certain parts. In fact, research has shown (Bernstein, 1978) that babies who received the best maternal care during the first year of life all began to masturbate by their first birthday. Masturbation provides very necessary learning about one's body, what it's like and how it works (Bruess & Greenberg, 1988).

During early childhood, children are acquiring language. They seek labels for sexual feelings, functions, and organs. They often want to know where babies come from and how birth occurs. When they enter school, children often encounter jokes containing sexual content. Some genital exhibitionism is common and normal among 3- to 4-year-olds, generally indicating pride in one's own body.

In middle to late childhood, secretive sexual play conducted out of the sight of adults occurs between same-sex and opposite-sex peers. This is normal if it occurs between children of similar ages, is cooperative, and is limited to a few episodes (Tharinger, 1987). It is also normal for children to begin talking more about members of the opposite sex and showing some desire to be around them.

What is not normal:

—Excessive/compulsive self-stimulation or exhibitionism. Gadpaille (1975) defines a compulsive activity as one that occurs "so repetitively and incessantly as to interfere with other normal activities or interactions." This may be a symptom of some type of emotional distress.

—Coercive and aggressive sexual behavior.

—Detailed and age-inappropriate understanding of adult sexual behavior. This may be a symptom of sexual abuse or the child may have witnessed an explicit television show.

—Engaging in sex play with other children who are not similar in age. If the exploration is with an older child or is aggressive it is sexual abuse, not play/exploration.

What Can I Do As A Parent?

—Be approachable to your child. Let the child know he/she can ask you questions about sexuality that will be answered in a warm and sincere manner.

—Be honest with your child. Provide them with the answer to their question with the amount of detail they seem able to understand. Research shows children well educated in this area are more sexually responsible in their teen years.

—If your child is masturbating or exhibiting himself in a public place or at an inappropriate time, explain that the behavior is not appropriate in that setting and explain that a private place like his/her bedroom is a more appropriate place.

In determining if abnormal sexual interest is present and is a problem to be addressed, you as a parent should consider the following questions:

—Are there signs of sexual interest that are not typical for my child's age?

—What are the signs of the problem and how do they affect my child's personal, social, and academic performance?

—Are there unusual circumstances that might contribute to the problem that may change or be changed within the immediate future?

—Is the sexual interest only a sign of a more serious problem that my child is experiencing?

—Is my child's behavior essentially normal, but people in his/her environment are having difficulty being tolerant of the behavior?

Finally, if you do suspect that your child has such a problem, DO NOT assume it will just "go away," because you may end up not recognizing a potentially serious problem.

Resources

If the above questions and suggestions do not provide you with the help you need, it may be that the child's sexual behavior is a sign of a larger problem that needs to be addressed. In these cases, the school psychologist or counselor may be very helpful in providing you with information about your child as well as helping to obtain counseling or similar services. Your family physician, local mental health centers, ministers, or other professionals may be helpful in understanding the problem and providing you with help.

References

Bernstein, A. C. (1978). *The flight of the stork*. New York: Dell.

Bruess, C. E., & Greenberg, J. S. (1988). *Sexuality education*. New York: Macmillan.

Gadpaille, W. J. (1975). *The cycles of sex*. New York: Scribner.

Tharinger, D. J. (Ed.). (1987). *Children's needs: Psychological perspectives*. Washington, DC: The National Association Of School Psychologists.

Shyness

Martha E. Scherer
University of South Florida

Background—Most people have felt shy at some time or in some situation. As many as 25% of high school and college students report having been shy most of their lives (Schwartz & Johnson, 1985). Excessive shyness, however, reduces both the amount and quality of social interactions a child has with others and results in lowered peer acceptance and fewer opportunities to acquire social skills. It is not clear why some children are bashful and withdrawing whereas others tend to be more outgoing. Several factors may be involved, including genetics, temperament, anxiety, and lack of social skills.

Development—Some degree of shyness in children is to be expected and is part of the child's normal development (Berk, 1989). A fairly high percentage of preschoolers are described as bashful and avoiding contact with others (Schwartz & Johnson, 1985). Between 30% and 50% of school-age children report feeling shy (Peterson, 1987). When shyness is experienced by the child in many or most situations over an extended period of time, interventions to help the child interact more appropriately are called for. Chronic and severe shyness can have a negative impact on social, emotional, and academic development. Shy children often have poor self-concept, feelings of failure, and make negative self-statements. The anxiety that accompanies shyness impairs memory and concentration and may keep children from asking for needed help in school.

What Can I Do as a Parent?—It will be important for your child to learn ways to reduce his or her anxiety in social situations. If the child does not possess the social skills needed to interact with others, it may be necessary to teach social skills directly. The child also needs to learn to feel better about himself or herself as a person. There are many ways to accomplish these goals.

Make sure your child knows that they are loved and valued regardless of their behavior or performance. Talk with your child about their experiences and help them to evaluate those experiences in nonjudgemental ways that allow them to feel good about themselves. Many times children judge themselves much more harshly than we realize and blame themselves for situations and events they cannot control.

As a parent, you can give your child more independence and opportunities to demonstrate responsibility. Successful handling of independence and responsibility will help to foster an improved self-image. A child's image of himself or herself is built on a foundation of many small experiences. The more of those that demonstrate to the child that they possess the capability to succeed, the better the resulting self-image will be.

Parents can seek out and provide activities that will allow the child to experience success in social environments. Structured group activities or small groups of one or two other children may facilitate success for the shy child. Parents can discuss, rehearse, and role-play activities with children such as introducing oneself, asking a peer to play, or joining a group of children who are playing a game. If the child is involved in a social-skills training program, parents can reinforce targeted social skills and provide opportunities for rehearsal of skills.

If your child is severely shy and inhibited in most situations, the best course of action may include seeking professional help, either through the school, local mental health agency, or your family physician. Severe shyness affects many aspects of the child's life and should not be left unaddressed.

What Can I Do as a Teacher?—Shy children may be easily overlooked in a busy classroom because they do not present classroom management problems and usually comply with instructions. Teachers need to be sensitive to the needs of shy children and facilitate their interaction with others and their participation in the class. Because shy children are often characterized by anxiety, it is best to avoid drawing attention to them or putting them in situations that will require that they be the center of attention. Structured interactions and small group activities may best facilitate participation by shy students. When children are to work on projects in small groups, the teacher should form the groups rather than allowing students to group themselves. Teachers can take this opportunity to pair shy youngsters with socially competent students who will serve as models for them.

Teachers need to avoid reinforcing shy behavior, to be sensitive to the needs of shy children but to refrain from giving the shy child special attention or privileges. When shy children interact appropriately, that is the behavior that should be reinforced. There is a natural tendency to either ignore or be overly protective of shy children, but neither of these responses benefits the child. Shy children should be encouraged to interact, provided with opportunities to interact in small, structured settings, and reinforced for interacting. Direct social-skills training and contingency management procedures have been found to produce positive results and may be beneficial for the entire class.

References

Berk, L. (1989). *Child development*. Boston: Allyn & Bacon.

Peterson, D. W. (1987). Children and shyness. In A. Thomas & J. Grimes (Eds.), *Children's needs: Psychological perspectives* (pp. 542-547). Washington, DC: The National Association of School Psychologists.

Schwartz, S., & Johnson, J. H. (1985). *Psychopathology of childhood* (2nd ed.). New York: Pergamon Press.

Children and Sleepwalking

John J. DeFrancesco
Connecticut Department of Children and Youth Services

Background—Sleep disorders are fairly common occurrences during childhood. These disorders include night terrors, nightmares, sleep talking, difficulty in falling asleep, restless sleep, and sleepwalking. The prevalence of sleepwalking in the general population ranges from 2 to 5 percent. Prevalence estimates in children indicate that approximately 15 percent of all children have at least one episode of sleepwalking before the age of 15. The occurrence of the behavior in a child is usually a frightening experience for parents. The child will typically rise out of bed, move about the house exhibiting fairly good motor coordination, and perhaps engage in activities such as eating, drinking, or urinating. Many times the child will walk toward the parent's bedroom. An episode of sleepwalking will occur within three hours of falling asleep and last for about 10 minutes. The child will have no awareness of the activity when he awakens and the episode generally ends without trauma.

Since the child is able to move about, however, and open doors and windows, there have been situations when sleepwalkers have been seriously injured. The behavior, in certain situations, is also indicative of underlying psychological difficulties that the child may be experiencing. Generally, it is a behavior that should not be ignored, particularly if it is recurrent.

The causes of the behavior have been linked to psychological, genetic and physiological factors. Children who are under extreme stress, experiencing separation anxiety and/or feelings of insecurity may be prone to sleepwalking. In fact, children and adolescents who are sleepwalkers usually report a significant stressful life event that occured before sleepwalking behavior began, such as the death of a parent, divorce, birth of sibling, or school failure. Further approximately 80 to 90 percent of sleepwalkers have a relative (usually a parent) who is also a sleepwalker. Abnormal EEG's have been indicated in some cases of sleepwalking and brain tumors have been found in a small number of cases.

What Can I Do as a Parent?

- The occurrence of the behavior is always alarming to parents. If the behavior is infrequent, however there is little reason for concern. In this situation the behavior should be considered innocuous and not indicative of severe emotional problems. Parents should be informed that children generally outgrow the behavior.

- When parents begin to notice that the behavior is frequent and intense (e.g., more than one episode per night) there is reason for concern. In this situation, it is often prudent to consult a physician to determine if the cause(s) of the behavior is physiological in nature. There is evidence that epileptic seizures and febrile illness can produce behavior similar to sleepwalking.

- If physiological factors can be ruled out it may be necessary to determine if the behavior is psychogenic in origin. A psychologist should be consulted to determine if the behavior is resulting from stress/separation issues or other emotional concerns. This can be accomplished by obtaining information from parents, teachers, testing and behavior checklists. Developmental academic and family information should be obtained. Information such as sleep history, age of onset, family history of sleepwalking, and the occurrence of any recent stressful life event is essential. Once the source of stress has been identified, strategies to reduce the stress and subsequently the behavior can be developed. For example, the child who experiences the divorce of his parents may develop separation anxiety and feelings of insecurity that may manifest itself in sleepwalking behavior. In this situation, it may be necessary for both parents to reaffirm their affection/loyalty to the child, to spend increasing amounts of quality time with the child, and to include the child in as many family types of activities as possible.

- Counseling to assist parents in coping with the behavior and developing stress reduction strategies is sometimes necessary. Counseling with the childhood sleepwalker is seldom effective; however, some success has been shown with the adult sleepwalker.

- Since there is a possibility of injury during sleepwalking, it is essential for parents to protect their children from harm. Windows and outside doors should have special latches. The child should sleep on the ground floor if possible; if this is not possible, then gates should be installed at stairways. Dangerous objects should not be accessible to the child.

- Medications such as antidepressants are sometimes used in treating children with frequent and intense episodes but the behavior tends to increase in frequency when the medication is discontinued. Generally, this is not recommended for children.

- There is no benefit in waking the sleepwalker during an episode. They will not awaken easily, will be somewhat confused, and will usually have no memory of what has transpired. It is better to simply watch and ensure that an accident does not occur.

Resources

American Medical Association (1984). *Straight-Talk, No Nonsense Guide to Better Sleep.* Random House. The general nature of sleep is discussed along with the various disorders of sleep including sleepwalking. Some treatment strategies are addressed.

Bawkin, H. & Bawkin, R. (1972). *Behavior Disorders in Children.* An older but comprehensive test on behavior disorders. The book contains a chapter on Problems of Habit and Training which outline sleepwalking and other childhood habits and disorders.

Orr, W., Altshuler K. Z. and Stahl, M. L. (1982). *Managing Sleep Complaints.* Year Book Medical Publishers. A fairly inclusive text that describes the various sleep disorders including sleepwalking. Treatment strategies are also discussed.

Children and Stress

Ellis P. Copeland
University of Northern Colorado

Background—To ask a child about stress would probably have no useful result as the term is unfamiliar to the average child. Adolescents often use the term, but do they know what it is? To the child, stress may be the result of an event or events which leave them feeling bad or upset. The adolescent tends to think of stress as the demands of life; demands which often come from teachers and parents. Technically, these demands are called *stressors* and our response to a demand is called *stress.*

Stress can be a pleasant experience yet is often perceived and reacted to as a "distressful" one. For both children and adolescents, life stress has been related to the occurrence and duration of medical problems, mental and emotional disorders, and delinquent behavior. Research further shows that:

- the effects of stress vary from one person to another and each person may develop unique symptoms or individual styles of handling stress;
- some environments (e.g., homes, schools, etc.) are more stressful than others;
- constitutional factors, including gender, play a significant role in how stress is perceived and handled;
- stress is cumulative and progressive, and improved resources and coping patterns are often necessary to reduce ill effects; and
- stress appraisal and coping capabilities increase with age and cognitive development.

Development—Stress is normal. Dr. Hans Selye, a pioneer in stress research, noted that the human body progresses through three stages when forced to react to a stressor. The first stage is the alarm stage (think of the alarm clock ringing in the morning) when heart rate and breathing increase and the body prepares to "fight or flight" or react to the stressor. Resistance is the second stage when the body attempts to return to normal functioning. When the stress does not diminish, and/or the child doesn't adapt or can't adapt, the stage of exhaustion begins the process. The results, however, need not be harmful.

For any child, a major stressor such as the death of a parent, parents' divorcing, child abuse and/or neglect, or poverty is difficult to handle. Various stress studies have looked at preschoolers through adolescents and the results have indicated that the younger children are less adaptive; thus, the stress often results in stress overload which can result in a medical or emotional problem. For the adolescent, the above events continue to be seen as major stressors yet their ability to assess an event and their ability to cope has increased with age.

In addition to major stressors, daily or common events can also be seen as distressful to children and adolescents. And each level has its own unique set of identified stressor events. Perhaps the most interesting finding for six- to eleven-year-olds is the lack of agreement between the parent's view of what is stressful and the events their children found stressful. The two groups agreed that a parent's death would be most stressful. However, the children place a fear of going blind as second on their list, followed by fearing upset over possible events at school. Being rejected or humiliated by wetting their pants in class, being sent to the principal's office, failing or being kept back a grade were troubling and tended to underscore their importance to the child's emerging sense of self.

For the preadolescent to early adolescent ("tween"—ages 11 to 15 years), school-related variables are again given the greatest emphasis. Hassles with parents and siblings are noted, but concerns about school performance and peer relations are more widespread stressors. Adolescents define major stressors as exams, career choice, sexuality, peer pressure to try alcohol/drugs, and "hassles" of cumulative events.

What Can I Do as a Parent?—*Don't assume* that you know what is stressful to your son or daughter. Remember the discrepancy between what we may consider stressful and what your child may be seeing as stressful. A son or daughter getting their driver's license and beginning to drive may be distressful to you, yet liberating for your son or daughter.

- *Do Listen!* Listen to the way your child assesses a stressful event. Children can often blow an event out of proportion. Being late to school does not make a "bad" child; however, the child may think he/she is bad at the time of the event. Discuss the event with the child and make comparisons to other prior occurrences. Show the child that the event was important, yet the one event did not make them a good or bad person. Listening to your child, discussing and comparing will help your child see the recent stressful event as more benign.

- *Remember* that school life and peer relations are extremely important. A child who is adjusting well at home may be having problems adjusting to the pressures of school and peers. Help the child to see the positive events that are taking place at school and to identify new resources to better adjust to school/peer pressures.

- *Encourage* opportunities for connectedness. Sports especially intramurals, can be an opportunity to find positive peer relationships. Community and church/synagogue activities can also greatly enhance social competence and self esteem. Most schools have a variety of clubs and activities. Call the principal or school counselor and have a list of activities and clubs sent home. Discuss them with your child.

- *Facilitate* new and adaptive coping behaviors. A tween's primary coping strategy is indirect and inactive. Most tweens cope by retreating to listen to music or watch TV. However, tweens also value making their own decisions, developing friendships, and working hard to achieve a goal. Encourage these more direct and active choices before detrimental ones such as taking drugs, drinking, and running away become primary choices.

Resources

Arent, R. P. (1984). *Stress and Your Child.* Englewood Cliffs, NJ: Prentice-Hall, Inc. Good overview of child stress and adolescent stress with a discussion of parenting skills and child management.

Charlesworth, E. A. & Nathan, R. G. (1984). *Stress Management: A Comprehensive Guide to 'Wellness.* New York: Ballantine Books. A comprehensive self-help book probably more for the parent, yet a less distressed parent helps the child.

Kersey, K. (1985). *Helping Your Child Handle Stress.* Washington, D. C.: Acropolis. Encourages the parent to help the child to build coping skills as the child becomes a better manager of his/her life.

Stroebel, E., Stroebel, C. F. & Holland, M. (1980). *Kiddie QR: A choice for children.* Wethersfield, CT. Provides relaxation materials for children especially those with medical or handicapping problems.

NATIONAL
ASSOCIATION OF
SCHOOL
PSYCHOLOGISTS

Children and Temperament

Hedy Teglasi
University of Maryland-College Park

Background—Temperament refers to a basic style in how a person approaches and responds to people and situations. Every child has a personal set of temperamental characteristics. These are evident at an early age. Temperament belongs to the child and resists change. However, the expression of the temperament is modified by interaction with other people and by events in the child's life.

Development—As children develop, their temperament become apparent. Their temperament can be described by examining the three clusters of characteristics described below.

- **Emotional Reactivity**—Children may vary in their mood. Some children show more joyful, friendly emotions while others tend to express worry, anger, or fear. The amount of stimulation needed to bring out an emotional response is determined by the sensitivity level of the child. Children differ in the intensity with which they customarily express emotion. A highly intense child may scream with anger in the same situation which would cause a low intense child merely to grumble or frown.

- **Coping**—Children try to maintain a level of stimulation which is comfortable and allows them to cope most efficiently with their experiences. Maintaining this comfortable level of stimulation is accomplished by approaching or avoiding unfamiliar situations. Children vary in their tendency to approach or avoid new situations. Overstimulation is prevented by withdrawing from threatening situations. On the other hand, stimulation can be increased by exploring and by approaching new people and challenging situations. Children differ in their ability to handle new and different situations which they cannot avoid. Some children take a long time to get used to unfamiliar situations or changes in routine; others adapt more easily.

- **Task Orientation**—Three temperament aspects are related to how easily children stick with ongoing tasks. These are:

Distractibility—Distractibility is the degree to which sights and sounds around children interfere with ongoing activity. Noises in a classroom are a good example of something which bothers some children and not others. A highly distractible child is greatly influenced by environmental sights and sounds and seems to be captured by the strongest stimulus present (e.g., the T.V).

Persistence—Persistence is the continuation of an activity even when there are other possible activities or requests to stop an ongoing activity. Another name for it is attention span. A persistent child will return to a task even after an interruption. Sometimes a highly persistent child may protest when a parent requests a change in activity.

Activity Level—Activity level is the amount of physical activity displayed by a child. Some children are very active and seem to run from one activity to another without stopping. Other children are more content with quiet activities. Children with a high activity level often also are very distractible and have a low level of persistence. These children have difficulty sitting still and concentrating in the classroom. Often, underachievers have this combination of high distractibility, low persistence, and high activity level.

It is incorrect to assume that children who are at the extreme ends of one or more of the temperamental characteristics described above are not normal. However, some children are at greater risk of developing emotional problems because the expectations of parents, teachers, and peers do not match their temperamental tendencies. These children are often described as difficult because those who care for the child find him/her difficult to manage. As a result the caretakers are frequently frustrated or angry. Such a child senses that others disapprove of his/her behavior. However, the child typically cannot change the behavior even with great efforts. When the characteristics of the child do not match the expectations of others, problems may arise in the child's development.

What Can I Do As A Parent?—It is very important to offer support to a child with behavior problems that are due to temperament. It is also important to change the consequences which the child experiences when the child is displaying behavior that is primarily manipulative. In managing a child with a difficult temperament, the goal is not to accept all of the youngster's behaviors but to reduce or eliminate the adverse impact of temperament. Goals for parents who are trying to change the behavior of a child with a difficult temperament might include:

- Minimizing demands or expectations that are substantially at odds with the child's temperament.
- Enforcing schedules and activities that will alleviate the undesirable effects of the child's temperament.
- Encouraging the child to learn self-understanding and ways of coping with temperamental difficulties.

The following techniques are suggested for accomplishing the above goals:

Structure—Despite detailed explanations of what is expected, some children cannot monitor their own behavior without supervision and guidance. For example, they have difficulty remembering to bring school books home and working independently. Positive methods of helping the child are more effective than constantly reprimanding the child for irresponsibility. It is beneficial to supervise the behavior of a distractible child by giving him/her frequent (but gentle) reminders, helping to organize homework, making lists with the child, and praising success.

Prevention—Understanding the child's temperament and anticipating the situations in which difficulties will arise can help parents avoid confrontations and minimize conflict. An active, distractible child may expend so much effort struggling to pay attention in school that parents may wish to ease up on their expectations at home. Also, a persistent child who finds it difficult to stop an activity abruptly may be given a few minutes notice so he/she can gradually terminate the ongoing activity. Changes in routine for a child who adapts poorly can be planned to allow time for adjustment.

Preparation—When parents cannot modify the environment or their demands to suit the child's needs, they can help prepare the child for upcoming stressful events. Children who adapt poorly do not like surprises and welcome being able to anticipate changes of routine. Such children benefit from being told of upcoming events such as what will happen on a trip or when company will arrive. Parents and children may even act out events such as an anticipated visit to the doctor's office.

Teaching coping skills and self-understanding—When children are old enough, discussion about their sensitivities may be helpful. Parents can label the child's emotional reactions with a non-judgmental attitude and convey understanding. Eventually, children can learn to label their own emotional reactions and verbalize their needs.

Acceptance—Parents may feel that it is their duty to attempt to change a child's irritating behavior. However, there is little that can be done to change negative mood or intense emotional expression.

In fact, it is damaging to require a child to "cheer up" because such requests convey the feeling that the child's natural mood is unacceptable. Children whose innate tendencies are constantly challenged may not develop positive self-esteem and in the long run may have more difficulties coping with their own problematic temperamental characteristics.

Building relationships—Parents are human so irritations caused by some temperamental traits are inevitable. Sometimes it takes a great deal of patience and perseverance to promote a solid relationship with a difficult child. Yet, criticism and hostility should not pervade the relationship. Parents can try to make the best of situations that are pleasant. Enjoyable activities in which a child's temperament is an asset should be planned. Parents can be alert for situations that bring out the best in a child. Building a positive relationship between parent and child helps to manage the difficult temperamental qualities while solidifying the bonds between parent and child.

Resources

The following two books help parents understand their child's temperament and offer useful suggestions:

Chess, S., & Thomas, A. (1987). *Knowing your child: Authoritative guide for today's parents.* New York: Basic Books.

Turecki, S., & Tonner L. (1985) *The difficult child:* New York: Bantam Books.

NATIONAL
ASSOCIATION OF
SCHOOL
PSYCHOLOGISTS

Children and Thumbsucking

Elaine Clark and William R. Jenson, *University of Utah*
Thomas J. Kehle, *University of Connecticut*

Background—Thumbsucking is a common but disturbing habit. Rough estimates place the number of children who thumb or fingersuck at approximately 40 million. Thumbsucking has been with us for a long time, and will undoubtedly continue to be a problem. There are frequent examples in both paintings and sculptures of early Renaissance children with a finger or thumb in their mouths, a symbolic representation of feelings of safety and tranquility. It was not until the end of the 19th century that thumbsucking was viewed as a problematic behavior with serious side effects. Contemporary thought, however, is benign in contrast to that of the early centuries. Parents are encouraged to be more tolerant of a young child's thumbsucking, and to interfere less. Nonetheless, questions still exist for many parents about the possible harmful side effects and what can be done to eliminate thumbsucking.

Development—Thumbsucking generally appears between the fourth and tenth month of infancy and peaks between the third and fourth year of childhood. It appears to be a developmental phenomenon which decreases in frequency as children get older. It has been estimated that nearly 50 percent of two- and three-year-olds, and 40 percent of four-year-olds suck their thumbs. The percentage drops significantly after age six, with about 10 percent of children in the age range of six to eleven years being thumbsuckers. After age twelve, the percentage again drops to less than two to five percent, depending on the age. Although thumbsucking does not appear to be a symptom of major behavioral or psychological problems in childhood, social censure and embarrassment by peers can result if children continue to suck their thumbs into middle childhood in public places such as classrooms. Dental problems are also a concern. While heredity is an important variable in the development of sound dental structures, the incidence of malocclusion is higher in chronic thumbsuckers. For example, the incidence of dental problems at age twelve is essentially equal in children who never sucked their thumbs and in children who quit the habit before age six; whereas among children whose habit of thumbsucking has extended into middle childhood, there is a higher probability of developing dental problems. Other medical problems include local infections on the thumb due to sores and multiple ulcers on the tongue.

What Can I Do as a Parent?—Some parents are reluctant to try and stop their child from thumbsucking, worrying that some other problematic behavior will take its place. Typically, just the opposite occurs. However, before intervening, it is important for parents to answer a few questions about their child's thumbsucking behavior. For instance, how old is the child? Unless the behavior is severe and damaging a program should not be started before four years of age. How long has thumbsucking been a problem and what is its current frequency? Was the onset correlated with any specific traumatic event such as a divorce or serious illness? Does it interfere with the child's adjustment; in other words, is he or she ridiculed by other children? What has been tried in the past to stop it? At what times, day or night, and in what situations (i.e., stress or boredom) does it occur? And is there any known event that immediately precedes the thumbsucking behavior? The following case of Jason will hopefully clarify why some of these questions are relevant.

Jason was a four-year-old boy who chronically sucked his thumb. The family dentist suggested that it was beginning to cause dental problems. Jason's parents were concerned that the sucking was a way

69

to manage stress and that stopping the thumbsucking might produce a negative psychological reaction. After carefully observing Jason for several days, they discovered that he most frequently sucked his thumb in front of the television and when sleepy. Instead of stressful situations, he thumbsucked in less stimulating or boring circumstances. it was also noted that he always picked up his blanket "Silky" and rubbed it between his fingers just before putting his thumb in his mouth. Instead of directly intervening with the thumbsucking, the parents decided to develop a contract with Jason to give up Silky. It was thought that if they could stop the blanket-holding behavior which preceded the thumbsucking, they might be able to stop the thumbsucking. At first, Jason refused the contract. However, after looking at a number of toy catalogs Jason changed his mind and announced that he would trade Silky for a $40 Star Wars toy. Jason never again sucked his thumb. Apparently rubbing the blanket between his fingers set the occasion for thumbsucking; therefore, by removing the blanket, the thumbsucking was eliminated.

In some circumstances, it may be necessary to *reinforce the child if thumbsucking does not occur* for a certain period of time. For example, a child is given a penny for each minute that he does not have his thumb in his mouth. Slowly the time for not sucking the thumb is increased until only periodic spot checks are made. In addition, a star can be placed on a chart if the child had a perfect day or night of no thumbsucking. The star chart could stipulate that the child earn a more highly valued reward after a certain number of stars are collected. Since it is impossible to observe the child night and day, some parents use what is called the Behavioral Seal. The seal is essentially a square piece of masking tape with a hole in the middle. Under the tape is litmus paper that shows through the hole. The seal is fixed to the child's thumbnail. Thumbsucking turns the paper blue, while other substances turn it different colors. If your child is old enough, and sufficiently motivated, you may prefer to have them self-record the frequency of thumbsucking. The very act of writing down the incident disrupts the behavioral chain that leads to sucking and can significantly reduce thumbsucking, while helping them gain initial mastery over a difficult habit.

If reinforcement of non-thumbsucking behavior is not effective, parents may wish to try a *response cost* method. This is more punishing in that something (e.g., toys or television time) is taken away from a child when the thumbsucking occurs. *Time out* can also be used. With this method, a child is placed in a boring environment, such as a chair or corner of the room, when he or she sucks the thumb. Both response cost and time out procedures have been successfully to reduce thumbsucking. For example, cartoons can be turned off for five minutes or a toy taken away for a brief time when the child sucks his or her thumb. Care must be taken, however, that a child not lose everything; in other words, go in the "hole". Neither would you want to place a child in a time out environment that is so boring that it may result in an increase in thumbsucking behavior due to lack of stimulation.

Bad-tasting substances like "Don't" or a combination of cayenne pepper extract and citric acid have been painted on thumbs to deter sucking. This, however, has been shown to be only marginally effective. Since it has the negative side effect of getting into a child's eye if the eye is rubbed after thumbsucking—such as while sleeping or when crying, bad-tasting substances should be used with caution, and in combination with other techniques such as the positive reinforcement of non-thumbsucking behavior or time-outs.

Response blocking is a form of punishment or mild restraint, such as placing a thick cotton glove on a child's hand or bandaging the thumb. It is more effective, however, for night-time thumbsucking.

Overcorrection is a procedure in which a child is required to repeat a behavior many times following an instance of misbehavior. For example, a child may be required to brush his or her teeth for two minutes with Listerine mouthwash for each instance of thumbsucking. The advantage to this procedure is that the repeated behavior, tooth brushing, may help the child learn to brush his or her teeth better. The procedure can also be used in a variety of settings where thumbsucking may occur. Unfortunately, it requires supervision of an adult, and this can be time-consuming.

Perhaps the most effective technique for reducing thumbsucking is the *habit-reversal* method. This includes: (1) having the child list all the problems created by thumbsucking; (2) having the child act out thumbsucking, particularly the events that precede it; (3) having the child make a fist in which the fingers grip the thumb — this is done for one to three minutes as a corrective measure in instances of thumbsucking or when any of the preceding behaviors occur; and (4) giving the child social reinforcement such as praise, for not sucking and making progress with the program.

The use of *hypnosis* may be a promising technique since children seem to enjoy the use of imagery. This procedure, however, requires the assistance of a well-trained professional. Parents are encouraged to contact their school psychologist for further information about the possibility of hypnosis, as well as information regarding the other procedures discussed here.

Resource

Azrin, N. H. and Nunn, R. G. (1977). *Habit control: Stuttering, nail biting, and other nervous habits.* Simon and Schuster. This is a how-to-do-it book geared for parents and professionals. The basic step-by-step procedures outlined in the book are designed for habits in general; however, they can be effectively applied to thumbsucking in children.

Part II

Growing Out—
Getting Along with Peers and Others

Anger Control Problems

Andrea M. Mowatt
University of South Florida

Background—How do we define anger? Anger is a social emotion, involving some type of conflict between people (Bowers, 1987), and because it allows people to identify and resolve sources of conflict, it is considered to be a normal part of our social interactions. More specifically, Novaco (1985) defines anger as a stress response that has three response components: cognitive, physiological, and behavioral. The cognitive component is characterized by a person's perceptions and interpretations of a social situation. The physical component of anger may involve an increase in both adrenaline flow and muscle tension. Behaviorally, anger is frequently seen in tantrum behaviors, yelling, hitting, and kicking. Children with anger control problems fall into two different categories: (a) those with a behavioral excess (anger is too intense, too frequent, or both), or (b) those with a behavioral deficit (an inability to express anger). Because anger can serve as a constructive force in relationships, children who are unable to express their anger in ways that facilitate conflict resolution are considered to have anger problems (Bowers, 1987).

Development—Behavioral manifestations of anger change from flailing arms and kicking legs in infancy to temper tantrums at 18 months, and finally, to verbal expressions of anger as a child's language skills develop (Gesell, Ilg, Ames, & Bullis, 1977). Tantrums usually appear during the second year, reach a peak by age 3, and are decreasing by age 4 (Bowers, 1991). How anger is expressed is learned by watching, listening to, or interacting with others and varies across and within cultures (Bowers, 1987).

Because aggressive children are most often referred because of their behavior problems, the focus of the interventions offered below will deal with children who have excessive anger. Aggressive behavior, defined as the set of interpersonal actions that consist of verbal and physical behaviors that are destructive or injurious to others or to objects, is displayed by most children (Bandura, 1973; Lochman, 1984). Aggression poses a problem when it is exceptionally severe, frequent, and/or chronic (Lochman, White, & Wayland, 1991). Children who display a wide range of different kinds of aggressive, antisocial behavior, and who are highly antisocial in multiple settings are at greatest risk for aggression problems in adulthood (Loeber & Schmaling, 1985), and for negative outcomes such as criminality, personality disorder, and substance abuse (Robins, 1978; Kandel, 1982; Lochman, 1990).

Causes—Feindler (1991) indicates that faulty perceptions, biases, beliefs, self-control deficits, and high states of emotional and physiological arousal contribute to the aggressive child's response to provocation. Aggressive youths generate fewer effective solutions and fewer potential consequences in hypothetical problem-solving situations (Asarnow & Callan, 1985), and display irrational, illogical, and distorted social information processing (Kendall, 1989).

What Should I Do as a Parent/Teacher?—The first step is to define and assess the situation. The following areas of investigation are suggested:

(1) What is the severity of the problem (frequency, intensity, duration, pervasiveness)?

(2) What factors may be causing the anger (e.g., academic frustration, grieving, illness, abuse, problems with peers, parental divorce)?

(3) What happens after the child/adolescent has an outburst?

(4) What skills and attitudes do the child, family, and school bring to the intervention process?

An observation of specific behaviors used by the child and his/her peer group in the setting in which the problem behavior occurs is an important component of the assessment process. This allows a direct comparison of the child's behavior with his/her peer group. Recording the frequency, duration, and intensity of anger outbursts can provide further information. In addition, it may be beneficial to record descriptions of: (a) how the anger is manifested (e.g., hitting, yelling, threatening), (b) the setting in which the behavior occurs (e.g., time of day, location, type of activity), and (c) the events that occur before (stressors that provoke anger) and after the anger outburst (the consequences). Finally, normative measures (Feindler & Fremouw, 1983), interviews (students, parents, and teachers), and an examination of self-monitoring and self-evaluation data (Feindler & Fremouw, 1983) often provide valuable information to the person(s) investigating the situation.

Once the problem has been defined, the following approaches are recommended:

(1) Try to keep your composure; it is important to appear approachable, empathetic, calm, and understanding (Bowers, 1987);

(2) Try to model the appropriate use of anger in situations where anger can be used to facilitate conflict resolution;

(3) Praise children when they are not angry (Bowers, 1987);

(4) Suggest that the explosive child temporarily leave the room to regain composure (Bowers, 1987);

(5) If further treatment is necessary, the following interventions have been suggested by Bower (1987):

   (a) Stress-inoculation training, a procedure that allows the child/adolescent to acquire coping skills, including adaptive self-statements and relaxation. This three step process involves cognitive preparation, skills acquisition, and applied practice.

   (b) Behavior modification strategies such as response cost, mediated essay, behavioral contracting, and direct reinforcement of alternative behavior (DRA) are often useful with nonverbal or noncompliant children; and

   (c) Social skills training, which systematically teaches and reinforces behaviors that enhance social competence, can reduce the child's/adolescent's need to rely on anger for problem resolution.

Feindler (1991) suggests that there are five basic components of anger control training: "(1) arousal reduction, (2) cognitive change, (3) behavioral skills development, (4) moral reasoning development, and (5) appropriate anger expression." Feindler also suggests that there are a number of strategies that can be used to enhance the maintenance and generalization of anger control training techniques. For example, Feindler and her colleagues (i.e., Feindler, Marriott, & Iwata, 1984) have recommended the use of **group anger control training programs** over individual anger control training programs. They suggest that the role-played scenarios of conflict and the provocation that occur in the group training experience are more like the "real world" experiences that occur when the therapy session is over. **Incorporating strategies to enhance self-management** (self-observation, self-recording, self-reinforcement, and self-punishment) **and self-efficacy** (belief that the treatment will be effective and that the child can actually implement the skills) also seem to be imperative. In addition, the **use of contingency management** (e.g., cues in the environment, goal-setting intervention, and homework assignments), **and the inclusion of additional change agents** (e.g., staff members, parents, church youth groups, peer trainers, self-help groups) are believed to increase the effectiveness of the training.

Resources

Goldstein, A. P., Glick, B., Zimmerman, D., & Reiner, S. (1987). *Aggression replacement training: A comprehensive intervention for the actinq-out delinquent*. Champaign, IL: Research Press.

Kendall, P. C. (Ed). (1991). *Child and adolescent therapy* (pp. 25-97). New York: Guilford Press.

Southern, S., & Smith, R. L. (1980). Managing stress and anxiety in the classroom. *Catalyst for Change, 10*, 4-7.

Tavris, C. (1982). *Anger: The misunderstood emotion*. New York: Simon & Schuster.

References

Asarnow, J. L., & Callan, J. W. (1985). Boys with peer adjustment problems: Social cognitive processes. *Journal of Consulting and Clinical Psychology, 53*(1), 80-87.

Bandura, A. (1973). *Aggression: A social learning analysis*. Englewood Cliffs, NJ: Prentice-Hall.

Bowers, R. C. (1987). Children and anger. In A. Thomas & J. Grimes (Eds.), *Children's needs: Psychological perspectives* (pp. 31-36). Washington, DC: NASP.

Feindler, E. L. (1991). Cognitive strategies in anger control interventions for children and adolescents. In P. C. Kendall (Ed.), *Child and adolescent therapy* (pp. 66-97). New York: Guilford Press.

Feindler, E. L., & Fremouw, W. J. (1983). Stress inoculation training for adolescent anger problems. In D. Meichenbaum & M. E. Jaremko (Eds.), *Stress reduction and prevention* (pp. 451-485). New York: Plenum.

Feindler , E. L., Marriott, S. A., & Iwata, M. (1984). Group anger control training for junior high school delinquents. *Cognitive Therapy and Research, 8*(3), 299-311.

Gesell, A., Ilg, F. L., Ames, L. B., & Bullis, G. E. (1977). *The child from five to ten* (rev. ed.). New York: Harper & Row.

Kandel, D. B. (1982). Epidemiological and psychosocial perspectives in adolescent drug abuse. *Journal of the American Academy of Child Psychiatry, 21*, 328-347.

Kendall, P. C. (1989). *Stop and think workbook*. (Available from the author, 238 Meeting House Lane, Merion Station, PA 19066)

Lochman, J. E. (1984). Psychological characteristics and assessment of aggressive adolescents. In C. R. Keith (Ed.), *The aggressive adolescent: Clinical perspectives* (pp. 17-62). New York: Free Press.

Lochman, J. E. (1990). Modification of childhood aggression. In M. Hersen, R. Eisler, & P. M. Miller (Eds.), *Progress in behavior modification* (Vol. 25). Newbury Park, CA: Sage.

Lochman, J. E., White, K. J., & Wayland, K. K. (1991). Cognitive-behavioral assessment and treatment with aggressive children. In P. C. Kendall (Ed.), *Child and adolescent therapy* (pp. 25-65). New York: Guilford Press.

Loeber, R., & Schmaling, K. B. (1985). Empirical evidence for overt and covert patterns of antisocial conduct problems: A meta analysis. *Journal of Abnormal Child Psychology, 13*, 337-352.

Novaco, R. W. (1985). Anger and its therapeutic regulation. In M. A. Chesney & R. H. Rosenman (Eds.), *Anger and hostility in cardiovascular and behavioral disorders*. New York: Hemisphere Publishing Corp.

Robins, L. N. (1978). Sturdy childhood predictors of adult antisocial behavior: Replications from longitudinal studies. *Psychological Medicine, 8*, 611-622.

NATIONAL
ASSOCIATION OF
SCHOOL
PSYCHOLOGISTS

Children and Assertiveness

Marie Boultinghouse
Charlotte-Mecklenburg Schools, Charlotte, North Carolina

Background—Assertiveness is a manner of self-expression by which children stand up for themselves without violating the rights of others. Children who behave assertively are able to honestly and directly express their feelings and opinions while at the same time showing respect for others and accepting responsibility for their own behavior.

Parents are often concerned because their children use too little or too much of certain kinds of behaviors. Concerns may center around children's lack of peer acceptance, shyness which results in their being unable to speak up in class, their inability to say "no" and make it stick, and their inability to live up to high standards or their expectation of future failure which results in lack of motivation. These problems can be minimized by teaching children skills they don't learn automatically. Assertive behavior can be taught, practiced, and used in everyday life.

Development—Children begin to assert themselves at the moment of birth; thus begins a lifelong attempt to deal with people and events in their environment. The way children learn to express themselves is influenced by what they observe from family, friends, and people at school. Peer influence becomes increasingly more powerful as children get older.

Problems may result from children's failure to learn more than one way of expressing themselves. When children learn a particular behavior they sometimes get "stuck" and can't get unstuck without assistance. Poor peer relationships may be traced to children's bullying or their failure to stand up for themselves. Conflict with parents and teachers may result from children's learning only one way of responding or their need for the attention-getting value of inappropriate behavior.

Children may be unable to properly speak up for themselves because of lack of self-esteem, anger toward themselves, and guilt. They may be unable to measure up to standards set by significant adults, their own unrealistic expectations and their ability to make reasonable social/academic efforts result in failure. Their inability to say "no" when appropriate may result from their inability to decide when it makes sense to do so, overwhelming need for peer acceptance, fear of the consequences of doing so, or lack of skills to do otherwise.

Normal assertiveness is self-expression which is satisfying and does not result in intolerable conflict with peers and authority figures such as parents and teachers.

What Can I Do As A Parent?—You can meet with your child's school psychologist in order to discuss your concerns. The psychologist may be able to provide ideas about things you can do at home in order to help your child become more assertive and find alternative ways to handle problems. The psychologist may also be able to provide you with first-hand information on your child's in-school behavior.

You can help your child to look at his/her behavior, the outcome of the behavior, and how your child feels about the behavior and outcome. You can help the child decide whether another way of dealing with the problem might be more appropriate. A good way of encouraging this is by encouraging your child to keep a journal in which to record situations in which he/she becomes involved, the outcome of the behavior, and whether another way of handling the problems makes sense. You might provide a physical means for him/her to express feelings by providing non-hardening clay with which to "model" feelings about situation-specific behavior.

You can help your child learn self-acceptance by calling attention to his/her positive attributes, discouraging unrealistic expectations of self and others, accepting limitations that cannot be changed, and rewarding the child's attempts to try new approaches to problem-solving.

You can encourage your child to discuss his/her problems with you. You can provide oral feedback by: (a) describing rather than labeling behaviors you are concerned about, (b) being objective rather than evaluative, (c) being specific rather than general about your concerns, and (d) requesting his/her reaction to your comments. This is an example: "John, I understand that you hit Susie, Susie told the teacher and you were kept after school. I am disappointed. How do you feel about this?"

You can avoid teaching the child behaviors which will result in conflicts in other environments. To teach a child to engage in physical fighting is to risk encouraging behavior which will result in difficulty in school where fighting is not allowed. You might wish to consider the potential consequences of ways you teach your child to handle school or community problems.

You can teach your child how to stop name-calling. This involves teaching your child to remain calm ("shut your eyes, count to 10 slowly, breathe deeply, and exhale slowly"), maintain eye contact with the name-caller and try to think of ways to eliminate the name-caller's fun. Other ways include continuing to ignore the name-calling, shrugging one's shoulders while looking at the name-caller smiling while remaining calm, and agreeing with the portion of the statement which may be true; for example, "Yes, and I'm sorry I'll probably never be Mr. America." These incidents and their outcomes can be added to child's daily journal.

You can teach your child to say "no" and make it stick by providing practice with statements such as: "No, I choose not to take Jane's toy" without excuse for not doing so and while remaining calm and continuing eye contact with the other person. The child should not provide excuses or explanations at this time.

You may encourage the child to complete assigned tasks quickly and satisfactorily by using assertive techniques such as: "I know that you're hungry; your dinner will be waiting for you after you take out the trash." You may delay doing a favor for the child until the child's tasks are completed by statements such as "I know that you want to go to the party. I will be ready to take you as soon as you finish the dishes." If your child persists, you may continue: "I realize it may be difficult for you to understand, but I won't take you to the party until the dishes are finished." You are thus able to be forceful while remaining assertive and calm, at the same time enforcing the child's acceptance of responsibility and its consequences.

Resources

—*How to Discipline Without Feeling Guilty: Assertive Relationships with Children*, by M. Silberman and S. Wheelan. Hawthorn Books (division of Elsevier-Dutton), 1980. This book gives specific examples of the kind of behavior and discusses parental rights, needs, and responsibilities.

—*My Very Own Book About Me!* by Lutheran Social Services of Washington, 1982. This children's coloring/activity book was prepared for use by both parents and teachers and includes a guide for its use. It uses an assertive approach to help a child protect himself/herself from sexual abuse.

—*The Assertive Woman*, by S. Phelps and N. Austin. Impact Publishers, Inc., 1975. Easily-read resource for both males and females contains much information despite its entertaining format. This book provides practical examples by which one can choose and work toward changing one's own behavior.

NATIONAL
ASSOCIATION OF
SCHOOL
PSYCHOLOGISTS

Children and Competition

By Doris Benson
California State University-Northridge

Background—In our society children will learn to be competitive naturally. Because of its pervasive existence, competition will affect the development of our children in either positive or negative ways. At best, it can facilitate the development of skills, self-discipline, and physical, mental, and social growth. At worst, it has been related to rivalry in siblings, often of a violent nature. For instance, one study found that in families where siblings aged 3-17 lived, 82% had taken violent action against a sibling in the previous year. In competitive children's sports, 1 out of 3 kids under the age of 15, or 17 million, sustain injury serious enough to warrant medical attention. In school, competition can lead to failure, dropping out, and anti-social behaviors. Less dramatic, though more common, is its impact on the self-concept. It encourages our children to rely on external sources for self-validation and esteem. Though some professionals believe all competition is harmful, other stress the importance of putting it in proper perspective. Though the debate continues, it is clear that the effects of competition on the individual child will depend on personality characteristics, social context, and the structure of the activities or situations at hand.

Development—During the preschool years, ages 3-5, children typically refuse to share objects, toys or places, and will also strive against a peer or sibling for the attention of adults. Yet, during this period of development, children are motivated primarily by the desire to attain an object or goal. Because they are characteristically self-centered, they tend not to focus on "beating" or gaining victory over another.

Older children, age 6-10 years, exhibit similar competitive behaviors. They differ, however, in their primary focus which is to outperform their peers. During this time social comparisons are more often made, and children judge the outcome of the events in self-evaluative terms. Now the results begin to have more serious consequences and implications for the child's self-concept.

Primary and secondary school-age children generally engage in competitive events on their own initiative. Their spontaneous contests are characterized by formal rules, structure, and allowance for a winner. The decision making and power are shared and everyone participates in his or her own way. Within this structure there does not seem to be any fear or loss of love or esteem due to failure to win. Negative self-evaluations are minimized and children acquire skills, receive feedback, and develop confidence in a safe and less judgmental context. This is in contrast to adult structured contests where the emphasis is typically on abilities, skills, and winning instead of belonging, participation, and fun. The importance of participation for the child is highlighted by a survey of youth football players which found that 72% of the children indicated they would rather play regularly on a losing team than sit on the bench of a winning team.

Inappropriate or excessive competition can be detrimental to all children. There are a number of indications which signal the negative impact of competition, and warrant parental attention. Some of the more prominent are as follows:

—preoccupation with the competitive activity and neglect of others.

—development of superiority and/or narcissistic attitudes or behaviors.

—self-worth becomes linked to talents and contests won.

—winning becomes more important than how the game is played.

—the activity is no longer fun, enthusiasm wanes, and concentration is lowered.

—the focus is more on feelings than strategies.

—there are somatic complaints before or after events or feigning illness.

Certain children are especially vulnerable to the effects of competition, and should thus be monitored closely during such activities. Events should be carefully structured for them; preferably they would be best encouraged towards more cooperative pursuits. Among such children are those that manifest the following attitudes and behaviors:

—low self-esteem and confidence.

—chronic or situational anxiety.

—non-assertiveness, shyness, or underachievement.

—avoidance of contests of any kind (excluding those who do so for cultural or religious reasons.)

What Can I Do As A Parent?—All children will benefit from an emphasis on cooperation and events that are fun, encourage growth, skill, participation, and belonging. Towards this end parents can teach children about the destructive aspects of competition, advocate for cooperative activities, and present children with appropriate resources and strategies that foster more cooperative behaviors. More specifically, parents can

—monitor formal sports and school contests to insure the child's well being takes precedence over winning.

—provide positive role models and guidance during competitive activities.

—avoid using children for vicarious victories.

—avoid language that reinforces competitive attitudes.

There are particular concerns for various age groups:

Preschoolers: Parents should consider the following do's and don'ts:

—Do be patient and accepting of self-centered behaviors.

—Do demonstrate appropriate sharing and cooperative behaviors.

—Do avoid lengthy explanations of why cooperation is necessary.

—Do not expect them to be empathic.

—Do allow time for adjustment to infant sibling and to share and care where possible.

School-age Children:

—Do allow them to structure their own contests.

—Do avoid comparisons with siblings, classmates, yourselves as children.

—Do not make love or approval dependent on winning.

—Do allow them to quit or participate in competitive events without any form of pressure, rejection, or humiliation.

—Do not remain silent or avoid child after a loss, nor blame or punish.

—Do empathize and encourage child to understand and accept loss, and learn from it.

—Do seek professional consultation if negative reactions are lasting or extreme.

Resources

—*No Contest-The Case Against Competition* by Alfie Kohn.Houghton Mifflin, Publisher, 1986. This work promotes the view that all competition is unhealthy. It does suggest alternatives and resources for cooperative methods.

—*The Second Cooperative Sports and Games Book* by Terry Orlick. Pantheon, Publisher, 1982. A wealth of materials to help parents and educators promote more creative cooperative contests.

—*International Association for the Study of Cooperation in Ed. (IASCE).* C/O Center for Teaching and Learning. University of N. Dakota, Grand Forks, N.D. 58202. The center disseminates information to promote cooperative education. Useful for parents as a resource to gain understanding and assist schools moving in this direction.

—*Focus on interscholastic Sports and the Middle School* by K.C. McEwin. E. Lansing: Michigan State University, Michigan Assn. of Middle School Educators, 1981. Gives the parent a clear presentation of the controversy surrounding interscholastic sports below the high school level. Sets forth the express advantages and disadvantages.

NATIONAL
ASSOCIATION OF
SCHOOL
PSYCHOLOGISTS

Children and Peer Relations

Kathryn C. Gerken
The University of Iowa

Background—Friends play an important role in shaping children's social skills and their sense of identity. Although the definitions and the expectations of friendships change with age and under different environments, almost everyone agrees that friends accept and support one another, enjoy one another, confide in one another, trust one another, and have a mutual understanding of one another. No matter what the age or environment is, most children face two problems when developing friendships: 1) learning to relate in a way that is acceptable to their peers in current circumstances, and 2) learning the skills of friendship that will be needed later in life.

Development—There are two major views about how children develop peer relations and/or friendships. One view is that the children work out for themselves what social relations are all about on the basis of their encounter with others. As children attempt to cooperate with one another, they learn to appreciate the capabilities, desires, and values of others. The other view is that children learn to relate to others because of the behavior of their adult caretakers (parents, teachers). The children are either directly rewarded or punished for certain behaviors or they observe the adults using certain behaviors.

The following is a brief overview of the major changes that occur in peer relations from infancy to adolescence:

First year	—Children look at each other, touch, and reach; but social contacts occur infrequently.
Second year	—Interaction increases, children are both positive and negative toward each other.
Preschool years (age 3-5 years)	—More positive and negative social interactions. Preschool children still spend considerable amounts of time by themselves or in noninteractive contact with other children.
	—Five-year-olds often work with another child.
	—Some groups are formed.
	—Overall increase in contact with peers.
Middle childhood (age 6-12 years)	—Recognition of differences in peers.
	—Increase in effectiveness of communication skills.
	—Decrease in overall aggression.
Early adolescence	—Highest level of conformity appears in the 11-13 year age range-gradual decrease in susceptibility to group pressure from then on.
	—Unisexual groups.
Adolescence	—Conformity affected by status in peer group and by self-blame.

—Adolescents seek friends who share their values and understand their questions.

Terms such as likeable, popular, unpopular, friendly, rejected, and neglected are used to describe children's status with others. What causes these differences in children's relations? The conclusions of several studies are that:

- children are liked and become popular when they are cooperative and friendly in their interactions, and are disliked and rejected when they are aggressive or disruptive in their peer interactions.
- children are neither liked nor disliked when they rarely interact with peers.
- rejected and neglected children are often unsuccessful when they try to join a group of peers already engaged in an interaction.
- the social environment influences the children's status.
- children's status may be increased following social training.

Children are at a social advantage if they are intelligent, achieve well in school work, and athletics, possess an attractive face and body, come from a middle or upper class family, have an ordinary name and do not have any physical, emotional, or learning disabilities. Not all children have these advantages, yet they can have positive relations with peers. Even minor changes in appearance, a child's name, or in the environment have had positive results for children.

What Can I Do As A Parent?—Having friends is a developmental "advantage" but it may not be easy for some children to make and keep friends. As a parent, you do influence your child's peer relations by choosing a neighborhood, school, and adult associates. Look around you and ask yourself some important questions. If you can control the environment, are you doing it? Are there children in the neighborhood? Can your child walk to school? Have you arranged social contacts for your child? Have you coached your child in social relations and skills and/or provided a good model of social relationships? Does your child have a home base to come to for support?

You need to recognize both positive and negative influences of friendship and deal with them. There are times when you must step in to remove a child from a negative friendship or group, but usually you will be needed to help children understand friendship and peer breakups and separations. Parents need to provide security and support. Too much emphasis on friendship can result in rejection, stereotyping, cruelty, jealousy, and resentment if the desired friends are not obtained, and some students may learn negative behaviors in order to keep friends.

At home, in school, and in other environments, there is a need to provide opportunities for both unique personal development and for conforming, cooperative effort. Rewards can be given for including others rather than excluding them, and for cooperative and tolerant behavior rather than competition and intolerance.

Resources

—*Teaching Social Skills to Children*—by G. Cartledge & J. F. Milburn, Eds., Pergamon Press, 1980. This book has an extensive appendix of resource materials (games, audiovisuals, books, dramatic play materials, pictorial and display materials, and kits to aid in teaching children social skills.

—*The Book Finder*—Vol. 3, by S. S. Dryer, American Guidance Services, 1985. This is an annotated guide to literature that deals with the needs and problems of children ages 2-15. Evaluative statements are made about each book listed and the general reading level is given for each book. One can find appropriate books for children about friends and friendship.

—*The Socially Competent Child*—by A. Gurian and R. Formanek, Houghton Mifflin, 1983. This book provides an overview of social development and suggestions are made for parents to help their children through the "normal" and "troubled" times.

—*Helping Kids Make Friends*—by S. H. Stocking, D. Arezzo, & S. Leavitt, Argus Communications, 1980. The book provides specific training steps and samples of training skills that may be needed to make friends.

—*Children's Friendships*—by Z. Rubin, Harvard University Press, 1980. The author uses everyday language to review the research in children's friendship development. He presents many samples of real children's conceptions about friendships and offers practical suggestions to parents.

—*A Kid's Guide to Making Friends*—by J. Wilt, Word, Inc., 1978. This is a book appropriate for 8-12 year-old readers. Humorous situations and illustrations are used to teach children how to make friends.

Self-Control

Lynn Ellen Thompson and Mary Ann Parkinson
University of South Florida

Background—Most adults have little difficulty identifying children who have poor self-control. They tend to be disruptive, impulsive, interrupt others who are speaking, and are disorganized and off-task most of the time. However, when teachers and parents are asked to identify the characteristics associated with self-control that they would like to see their children or students exhibit, little agreement is found (Boren, Weir, & Benegar, 1987).

Self-control has been defined as "specific skills or sets of behavior needed in order to maintain goal-directed behavior" (Rosenbaum & Baker, 1984). There are two aspects of this definition that have promise for parents and educators. First, behaviors are observable and if we can see it we can change it. Second, children's environments can be modified to increase the probability of new, or desired, behavior occurring.

Development—The development of self-control can be broken into four stages according to Mischel and Mischel (1983). However, these stages will occur at different age levels, because they vary and are influenced by a child's motivation, the environment, and the adults in that environment.

The first stage occurs when children begin to decrease their dependence on adults and explore their environment in an increasingly independent manner, typically during the preschool years. During this phase of development the child is typically distractible, tends to daydream, and needs adult modeling of problem-solving strategies. Adults should provide modeling of desired behaviors. opportunities for practice of the behavior by the child, and rewards for successive approximations of the behavior. Through this process the child becomes aware of daily routines and mimics taught behaviors and routines.

The second stage in the development of self-control requires children to remember routines when directed by an adult and delay impulsive behaviors until the completion of the routine. Children in this stage are beginning to develop problem-solving and organizational skills, although they still require adult prompting. Parents and teachers should provide opportunity for children to practice these skills and consistently reward good behavior. At the end of this stage children should have mastered daily routines and begin to predict adult expectations and appropriate behavior.

During the third stage, children initiate daily routines without prompting by adults, are organized and able to work independently, and are capable of delaying impulsive or off-task behavior. Adults must still evaluate problem-solving strategies selected by the child and provide consistent feedback for desirable and undesirable behavior. During this time, children begin to internalize and understand adult expectations. The fourth and final stage in the development of self-control begins when the child is able to internalize the behaviors expected of him/her and transfers those behaviors across situations. The child is also capable of determining whether his/her behavior was appropriate in a given situation. The role of the adult in this phase of development is to provide the child with guidance and encouragement as he or she learns.

Causes of Lack of Self-Control—Just as self-control may be defined in many ways, dependent upon the situation and the expectations associated with it, the causes for the lack of self-control are also varied. Researchers agree that the causes for lack of self-control in children are many.

One possible cause for off-task or impulsive behavior in children is attention deficit disorder. Attention Deficit Disorder (ADD) impairs a child's ability to concentrate on a task or item for as long as would be expected for a child of his/her age group (Rosenbaum & Drabman, 1979).

Another possible factor is lack of consistency in the child's environment. Children must be taught the skills necessary to exhibit self-control. Parents and teachers must be consistent in their behavioral expectations. It is confusing to a child, who is trying to learn rules for appropriate behavior, when it is acceptable to perform a behavior on one occasion and not on another.

Withdrawn or dependent children, although usually not a problem in the classroom, may fail to develop the skills necessary for independent decision making. These children may appear unmotivated when presented with a challenge or something new.

What Can I Do As A Parent?—The following suggestions may be helpful for parents of children who tend to be impulsive or distractible:

—Be consistent, if a behavior is unacceptable then it should be unacceptable all of the time. Do not allow the child to behave in unacceptable ways if you are busy or tired as it will only hurt in the long run.

—If your child has done something wrong try to explain to him/her why the action was wrong and what the expectations for his/her behavior are in that situation.

—Provide the child with a plan for problem solving to ensure that she or he has the skills to determine for himself or herself whether a behavior is appropriate.

—Model appropriate behavior for your children and, if necessary, verbalize your thoughts to help your child understand what you are telling yourself as you make decisions.

—Provide consistent praise and rewards for appropriate behavior.

—Focus on positive behaviors and rewards for those behaviors rather than punishment for undesirable behavior.

What Can I Do As A Teacher?—The following suggestions may be useful for teachers who have impulsive or distractible students in their classrooms:

—Make sure classroom rules are posted and understood by the students

—Be consistent in your enforcement of the rules.

—Help the student to name behavior, choose alternative solutions, and plan and take relevant consequences (Verble, 1985).

—Be patient and always explain to the student what he or she has done wrong and what the acceptable behavior in that situation would be (Chrystal, 1988).

—Model the acceptable behavior for the student and have him/her practice the behavior.

—Provide feedback on the correctness of the response and, if necessary, practice again.

—Provide the student with praise for acceptable behavior.

—Make use of the other students in your class by rewarding the class for appropriate behavior from all students. The students who are able to self-control will pressure those who are not and with time impulsive students will learn to control their own behavior.

—Token economies, or point systems, which state very specifically which behaviors will be rewarded and which behaviors will result in a fine have been shown to be effective in increasing self-controlling behavior in impulsive students (Anderson, Fodor, & Alpert, 1976).

—In any intervention used it is important to teach the impulsive student to evaluate his/her performance, self-evaluation will allow the student to modify unacceptable responses. It is also very important to ensure the generalization of training to other settings (Epstein & Goss, 1978).

—Communicate with home by using a daily note to let parents know how the child behaved in school during the day. One method that has been effective is a small sheet with three faces, one smiling face, one flat face, and one frowning face. You can simply highlight the appropriate face for a good, fair, or bad day. Ongoing communication between home and school is very important so that all of those involved with the child can be consistent and aware of progress or setbacks.

Resources

If classwide interventions are not successful, or problems at home persist, contact your school psychologist for more individual intervention strategies.

References

Anderson, L., Fodor, I., & Alpert, M. (1976) . A comparison of methods for training self-control. *Behavior Therapy, 7,* 649-658.

Boren, R., Weir, L., & Benegar, C. (1987). Children and self-control. In A. Thomas & J. Grimes (Eds.), *Children's needs: Psychological perspectives* (pp. 515-521). Washington, DC: The National Association of School Psychologists.

Chrystal, C. A. (1988). Teacher management and helping style: How can we develop student self-control? *Focus on Exceptional Children, 21,* 9-14.

Epstein, R., & Goss, C. (1978). A self-control procedure for the maintenance of nondisruptive behavior in an elementary school child. *Behavior Therapy, 9,* 109-117.

Mischel, H., & Mischel, W. (1983). The development of children's knowledge of self-control strategies. *Child Development, 54,* 603-619.

Rosenbaum, M., & Baker, E. (1984). Self-control behavior in hyperactive and nonhyperactive children. *Journal of Abnormal Child Psychology, 12,* 303-318.

Rosenbaum, M., & Drabman, R. (1979). Self-control training in the classroom: A review and critique. *Journal of Applied Behavior Analysis, 12,* 467-485.

Verble, M. (1985). How to encourage self-discipline. *Learning, 14,* 40-42.

Part III

Parenting—
Helping Children to Grow and Develop

Children and Childcare

Mahlon B. Dailey and Susan M. Vess
University of Northern Colorado

Background—Almost half of all mothers of children under age 5 years of age work. There are approximately 8 million preschool children with working mothers. The search for quality SUPERVISED childcare is a constant source of concern for many parents. Another type of childcare is SELFCARE or "latchkey." At least 5 million "latchkey" children take care of themselves before and after school while their parents work.

There are many childcare choices. Listed below are five with characteristics, advantages, and disadvantages.

Childcare Options

Characteristics	Advantages	Disadvantages

1. In-home care
Preferred for infants and
  toddlers
Adult-oriented
Familiar setting
One-to-one adult-to-child ratio
	Fewer morning "hassles"
	Fewer problems of illness
	Sitter often does housecleaning
	  and cooking.
		Costly
		Some loss of privacy
		Hidden expenses (food and utilities)
		Less social contact with other
		  children

2. Family daycare
Home-like features
Limit usually 5-6 children
May or may not be licensed
	Least costly of daycare options
	Exposure to other children
	Extended family, caring adult,
	  homey feeling
		Illness may be problem
		Taking child out in bad weather if
		  unlicensed, parents are
		  responsible for seeing that
		  house is safe and not
		  over-crowded

3. Relatives
Half of working mothers use this
  arrangement
In child's home or relative's
  home
Generally not licensed
	Familiar home setting
	Familiar adult
	May be least costly
		Family disagreements may arise
		Disadvantages same as in-home
		  care and family daycare

4. Daycare centers
School-like setting
Nursery school usually included
  but part-time
Adult-to-child ratios based upon
  state and federal standards
Licensed
	Usually trained staff
	Usually opened long hours
	Planned activities
	Educational materials
	Toys usually safe and
	  age-appropriate
	Must meet safety standards
		Nonhome, institutional environment
		Exposure to other illnesses
		Limited provisions for illness
		High turnover in staff
		May not accept children under
		  2 years

5. Selfcare (latchkey)
Children left alone because of
  economic restraints or
  when responsible
	No cost
	May foster sense of
	  responsibility
		Child is alone without supervision

Development—Here are some facts on daycare raised children versus children raised at home.

- **Physical Development**—For children from poor families, daycare improves motor development, increases height and weight, and makes illness and physical problems less likely. No differences are found for families that already provide opportunities for physical activities. Daycare children even in the best of homes and in the best daycare centers catch flu, rashes, colds, and coughs more often than children cared for by their mothers.

- **Intellectual Development**—Over the first several years, intellectual development is faster for daycare children; however, home-reared middle-class children soon catch up when they start school. Socially disadvantaged children without daycare never catch up intellectually.

- **Emotional Development**—Children who have daycare experiences of poor quality and with many different caregivers seem to have more short and long-term emotional difficulties. However if childcare is of good quality and stable, emotional problems are unlikely to develop.

- **Social Development**—Daycare children are generally more outgoing, helpful, and cooperative and are less timid and fearful than children raised at home. They are also generally louder more boisterous, competitive, and aggressive than those raised at home. Daycare appears to increase both positive and negative social development.

Self-care or latchkey children average about 2-3 hours daily without direct adult supervision. Latchkey children seldom complain about this situation and few parents express a desire to discontinue self-care. In fact, 90-95% of parents claim self-care has advantages-development of responsibility, independence, and survival skills. But parents also have lingering concerns about leaving children unsupervised such as fears of accidents and death, too much television, poor nutrition, sexual acting out and victimization from peers, siblings, and other adults, and poor family relationships. For the most part, these fears have not been shown to occur in carefully planned and monitored self-care experiences. Although self-care is not harmful to most children, latchkey children can experience feelings of loneliness, fear boredom, and resentment.

What Can I Do As A Parent?—When searching for "quality" childcare, parents should ask three questions of the caregiver: (1) "How many children will there will be in my child's group or class?" the fewer the better; (2) "How many children do you take care of?" the fewer the better; and (3) "What training and experience do you have?" the more the better.

Here are some suggestions to help children adjust to a new childcare setting:

- Spend time at the childcare place so that the child understands that both of you can share and enjoy this place.

- When you are ready to go, briefly tell your child that you are leaving, have a short goodbye ritual, promise to return later and make a prompt departure.

- Tell the staff and caregiver about the child's family and homelike so that the caregiver can talk to the child about home and neighborhood experiences.

- Bring items from home such as a toy, blanket, some possession of the mother or father or a favorite game.

- Post pictures of the family and parents on locker or cubbyhole.

- Explain to the child why parents work and why the child is in daycare. Keep the explanation simple.

To help children adjust better to self-care "latchkey" situations keep in mind the following points:

- Latchkey children do well when the parent-child relationship is one of cooperation and mutual confidence.

- Parents SHOULD NOT have self-care for children who are too young or immature for their age.

- Parents need to provide a visibly safe home-strong doors and windows, locks that keep the house safe, large or yappy dogs, and fences.
- The parent and child need to be familiar with the neighborhood. One or more neighbors whom the child knows and trusts should be available for emergencies or questions.
- Children should have ready access to parents by phone. Schedule a daily check-in phone time in which the child can tell about the events of the day or complain if necessary.
- Role-play emergency situations such as calling the fire department and police, answering the door and phone, and knowing safe from dangerous physical symptoms.
- Using housework to fill and account for time fosters resentment-limit household work to what's reasonable.

Resources

- *The Day Care Book: A Guide For Working Parents*—by G. Mitchell, Stein and Day, 1979. A single mother's search for daycare for her two children provides advice in choosing childcare with a look, listen, smell and touch approach.
- A Parent's Guide To Day Care—Gryphon House, 1981. A pamphlet for parents who are choosing daycare with helpful checklists and guidelines.
- *Going to Day Care*—by F. R. Rogers, Putman Publications, 1985. A child's and parents' book with photographs and age-appropriate script depicting both a daycare center and a family daycare facility.
- *Alone After School*—by H. Swan and V. Houston. Prentice-Hall. 1985. This easy-to-read and easy-to-use workbook was developed to encourage parents and children to discuss and make self-care decisions together.

NATIONAL ASSOCIATION OF SCHOOL PSYCHOLOGISTS

Children and Family Size

Patrick H. Tolan
DePaul University

Background—It is commonly believed that the once-common large family is disappearing and that the national average of two children is true for all families. However large families (more than four children) still make up about 14 percent of our population. With the present levels of divorce and remarriage, this number is probably even higher. In addition, about 20 percent of families have only one child. As research has shown that family size can affect academic and social behavior how it relates is important to understand. Apparently, family size can affect intellectual and personality development, with children from larger families faring more poorly and the single child faring better than average. However these differences mean little in understanding a specific child and it is misleading to assume a large family size is bad and a small family size advantageous. Family size effects vary depending on the family circumstances, resources, and values.

What is known is that family size accompanies different effects: some of which are desirable, some of which are not. Behavior problems are not more likely in large or less likely in small than in average sized families; but if a child has trouble, those from large families are more likely to have learning problems and social inhibition problems while children from smaller families are more likely to have aggression problems. Children from larger families are more outgoing but have lower self concept, less emotional expressiveness, and more difficulties with their parents. On the positive side, children from large families are likely to be more cooperative, altruistic, and responsible to others. Children from single-child families tend to be less outgoing and more self-centered than children from larger families. For example, one study found they were chosen less frequently as playmates by peers than other children. However as adults, although continuing to be less socially oriented, they were more successful occupationally. Beyond these general effects, it is probably more useful to understand the important characteristics that go with different family sizes than concluding one is good and the other is bad. Each size results in different concerns and ways of operating as a family.

Development

Single Child Family—The single child lacks siblings and because of this, his/her parents may be less absorbed by their jobs as parents than in other families. Often these parents have less time and economic demands on them than other parents, so they can devote more of both to the child. Another result is that the child may be included more in adult conversation and expected to fit in with adults. They may be included in many decisions usually reserved for parents in other families. The lack of opportunity to play with and learn from siblings can limit the single child's understanding of sharing, compromising, and other social skills important in school and for friendships. Thus, the problems that can result are parents becoming too invested in the child's school achievement or the child seeming spoiled and unable to share with others at the school. However, most single children make adequate to above average adjustment to school. The extra parental attention and involvement can increase confidence and independence. Similarly, a lack of siblings may result in earlier and more extensive peer engagement.

The Large Family—Large families tend to be more complex than smaller families because the needs of many people must always be considered. Along with the normal relationships of parent-child, husband-wife, and brother-sister, there are multiple sibling subgroupings, and each child may be grouped with different siblings depending on what family concern is important at the moment. Because of this, relationships shift; and who you feel closest to, who listens to you, who takes your side, and your status within the family can shift regularly. Family members are valued more for their contributions to the overall good than individual achievement, and members may feel more bound to their family than those from smaller families. This attitude may clash with the individualistic values held by peers and schools. Economic resources can be sparse, or must be spread further so that personal possession often becomes a luxury. Sharing is strongly emphasized. Similarly, privacy is emphasized less in large families. Rules become important for managing everyone's interests. Thus, privileges, responsibilities, and discipline are determined by rules rather than by individual actions or abilities. As a byproduct of the reoriented family organization, discipline will be communicated less by verbal reasoning and more by expectations for compliance and responsibility to others. Also, the sibling group is often the most central and influential part of the family (more than parents at times). There may also be less need and interest in outside peer relations and interests. Often older children help extensively in raising the younger ones, with parents acting as managers by directing older siblings in responsibilities for younger children. Younger siblings are likely to have several parental figures and may have little opportunity to develop responsibility and self-care skills. This can put them in strong conflict with the value placed on responsibility by these families. Also, younger siblings will often lag behind the rest of the family in developmental interests, feeling out of sync with others.

Depending on where in the birth order a child is born, large family members have risks for different types of problems. Older children may have difficulty finding time for outside peer and school interests because of the demands of family responsibilities. A more equitable sharing of these responsibilities may be needed to promote an adaptive balance between home, school, and peer interests. The last born groups of siblings in large families are most likely to develop problems. The parents are often exhausted by the time the younger children are born and ready to move to the "post-parental" stage. The youngest children may feel a need to stay and keep the parents from facing this next step or they may lack the independence and self-care skills to move outside the family. In elementary years they may have limited interest in making friends. In high school they may show little initiative towards academic and vocational planning. They may need help to develop independence-oriented skills or remove themselves from the parents' marital concerns.

What Can I Do as a Parent?—It is important to remember that family size is just one characteristic of families that can affect your child's adjustment, and it is probably not the most important one. However awareness of the family size effect described above can aid your understanding or problems that arise. In addition, school personnel may not be aware of these family size effects and you may need to bring them to their attention.

Beyond this use of information, there are several other possible actions you can take, depending on your family size and extent of problems. If you have a single child, you can try to make sure he/she is not involved in adult decisions before he/she is ready and that opportunities for time with children their own age and other ages are provided. If your family is large, and your concern is about one of the older children, you can act to ensure that they do not have so much family responsibility that they cannot develop outside interests or pay sufficient attention to schoolwork. If your concern is with the last-born children, increasing their responsibility for self-care, school work, or chores around the house can help. One of the older siblings can be asked to monitor the younger child's progress and to teach him/her to meet the responsibilities (but not do for him/her). You may want to consult with your child's teacher or the school psychologist to coordinate between school and home to accomplish your goals. If, despite such efforts, progress does not occur meeting with a family therapist to understand the issues of the family size affecting your family and then making needed adjustments is suggested.

Resources

Calladine, C. and Calladine, A. (1985). *Raising Siblings.* New York: Delacorte. This book provides some good advice and direction for parents to manage sibling problems, including those that come up often in large families.

Shyer M. (1985). *Here I Am, an Only Child.* New York: Scribners. This book talks about the problems and benefits of being a single child, from the child's view.

Contact your School Psychologists or Community Health Center for more specific information and direct intervention.

Children and Household Chores

John R. Hester
Francis Marion College, Florence, South Carolina

Background—Research indicates that approximately 90% of the families in the United States require children to regularly perform some chore. Why would parents want to assign chores that they could more easily do themselves? Basically there are three reasons: (1) to teach children responsibility and helping (2) children need to know how to perform certain jobs such as cooking, laundry, car maintenance, etc. (3) parents need help. Certainly with more parents than ever employed outside the home, there is a need in many families for children to share household responsibilities. However, most parents state that teaching of responsibility is their primary goal in assigning chores.

Development—Some general age guidelines for assigned chores are:

Age	Chores
Preschool (3-5 years)	pick-up toys, dress self, make their bed, put away clean clothes.
Elementary School (6-11 years)	simple food preparation (make sandwiches), clearing and setting table, empty garbage, wash car.
Secondary School (12-18 years)	cook meals, laundry, repairs to house and car.

Generally, as children get older they should move from chores that center on taking care of themselves, to chores that help the family, and finally to a real sharing of the work load. If a child complains about, or is slow in finishing a chore, the job **might** be too difficult. Parents should watch the child perform the chore to measure the chore's level of difficulty. On the other hand, a child expressing anger at someone assisting him/her with the chore, complaining about a chore being "baby work," or volunteering for older children's jobs, may be an indication the child is ready for more advanced work.

What Can I Do As A Parent?—Do not feel guilty about assigning chores to your children. Chores are very useful in teaching responsibility and the value of helping others. Even at an early age it is important for children to see that, just like everyone else, they have a work role in the family.

In initially choosing work for your child: (1) select only one or two chores, (2) choose something that is simple to do, (3) find a chore the child can do every day. The goal is for them to establish a habit of being responsible. As children reach school-age allow some choice of jobs. Allowing some choice will decrease complaining and refusal.

Feel free to assign chores such as food preparation, laundry, and housecleaning to boys, and jobs such as mowing the lawn, car maintenance and pet care to girls. Why is it desirable to have a variety of chores for each sex? First, there is fairness involved. Research indicates that adolescent girls in many families spend much more time on chores than boys, unless there is some sharing of the laundry, food preparation, and housecleaning chores. Second, all children need to learn the skills involved in food preparation, car maintenance, etc., in order to become independent adults who can function on their own. Third, having children who can perform different chores provides parents with a flexible group of workers who can be assigned to a variety of jobs as the family's needs change.

Place a chart in a prominent place such as the refrigerator door or the child's bedroom door and list: each child's name, the chores to be completed, and space for the days of the week. Let the child mark the chart that he/she has finished that chore for the day. Such a chart acts as a constant reminder of work to be completed and allows the child to supervise and reward his/her own work.

Chores should be completed by a set time every day. While there will be some exceptions, generally right before or after the evening meal is a good time. Children should have some free time when they come home from school.

Most parents use chores to teach their children responsibility and the value of helping their family. Therefore rewards for doing chores will occasionally be necessary, but should not be over-emphasized. Start with small, simple rewards such as the chart system mentioned previously (a star for completion of a chore), combined with praise from the parent ("Good, you have picked up your toys" or "I like the way you mowed the lawn.") Verbal praise from a parent that specifically mentions the chore can be powerful. Another simple procedure is to require the child to first do their chores, and then be allowed to do something they enjoy such as watch TV stay up 15 minutes later etc.

Many families like to give an allowance for the completion of chores. The advantage of such a system is it can teach the value of earned money, and the child can be required to buy small items from his/her money and/or save a portion. Be careful that the responsibility message is not lost in doing chores for money. With the giving of any reward the parent must emphasize how everyone in the family has household responsibilities, and how the child's work supports the family. Such a message can be expressed by the parent saying something such as: "The family depends on you to take the garbage out every day. The house will be clean for all of us."

If not overdone, rewards given consistently and **only** when a chore is completed, can be very useful.

Adults act as examples of behavior that children often imitate. The old adage "Do as I say not as I do" does not seem to work very well with children. Parents who share in household responsibilities without complaining and "putting off" the chore are more likely to have children who do the same. At the same time, parents who rarely help or constantly complain and dawdle when they do chores are more likely to have children who do the same.

Finally, as you assign chores be sure you understand and can carefully explain to the child:

—(1) Specifically what chores are to be done.

—(2) When the chore should be done.

—(3) What rewards, if any, will be received.

—(4) The value of the chore to the family and the child.

Remember, start with simple chores that can be easily completed. Be patient and expect some initially less than perfect work. Assign chores to all children based on age, ability, and other time limits such as homework, sports and part-time jobs.

Resources

—*Teaching Children Responsibility*—by L. Eyre & Eyre. Ballentine Books, 1985. This inexpensive book covers many topics on responsibility and offers some clever suggestions as to how to encourage chore completion.
—*Parents are Teachers: A Child Management Program*—by W. Becker. Research Press, 1971. Parents will find this book is a classic in outlining child management techniques that can be applied to chores and any number of other discipline topics.
—*Let's Talk About Being Lazy*—by J. Berry. Peter Pan Industries, 1982. A book that the children can read themselves or parents can read to them. The book emphasizes the value of chores.

Children and Medication

Teresa A. Hutchens
The University of Georgia

Background — There are literally thousands of medications available in the United States. Many are prescribed to children and adolescents as part of a comprehensive treatment program for physical illness, health maintenance (as in chronic conditions), and positive behavioral effects. Because of the many different medications and the many different conditions for which they are prescribed, it is important to consider the effects of each drug individually. Parents are in the best position to obtain information about medication from the child's physician; however, parents must be aware of the need to ask questions and to read the literature available with each medicine. All have the potential to affect a child's health and behavior not only as expected in treatment, but also as secondary effects or allergic reactions. Even doctor-prescribed medication can have unforeseen effects. It is, therefore, of great importance that all adult caretakers, both parents and teachers, consider the potential physical and behavioral effects for any given drug.

Medications are most often labeled by the manufacturer's trade name and a generic name. When a medication is usually effective in treating a particular illness or condition, it is said to be "indicated" or considered potentially appropriate for that condition. In the presence of other medications or physical conditions for which the drug would NOT be recommended, it is said to be "contraindicated."

The intended effect of a drug is to improve the specific condition for which it is prescribed, called the "direct effect." In contrast, "side effects" are not intended, but are secondary to use of the medicine. Any of the effects may be physical or behavioral, but side effects are less predictable. Changes in behavior or activity level may be observed, as well as physical effects, such as headache, nausea, or drowsiness. For example, diphenhydramine, available as Benadryl, is frequently prescribed for its antihistamine properties for colds and allergies in childhood. Side effects may vary; drowsiness or an increase in activity level may be observed. Tetracycline, an antibiotic, is prescribed frequently for acne in late adolescence; nausea is a common side effect of the drug. Parents should be aware that there is usually a range of side effects for each medication; they vary with the type of medication and are reported by physicians and drug manufacturers based on estimates of frequency. This information is helpful to provide guidelines for observation.

Development — A number of factors determine the degree to which effects are predictable; a primary factor is the age of the child. Although in adults, medication effects are fairly predictable, children have a much more variable response. Common concerns include long-term effects of the drug on growth patterns and developing tissue. Medications which affect behavior and cognitive functioning appear to produce qualitative difference in children, such as the tendency for stimulant medication to decrease motor activity for those under age 10. Individual variability plays an important role in medications' effects; children should be observed for unique reactions, developed on an individual basis. Observations by parents and teachers are needed to determine each child's particular response to each medication for optimal safety and effectiveness.

Currently, debate thrives over the use of medication for intended changes in behavior such as the use of stimulants with "hyperactive" children. As with most other medications, its effectiveness is variable, having been confirmed for some children and negated for others. It is very important for parents and teachers to note that medication given for specific behavioral concerns may be only one part of a comprehensive treatment program. While medication may enhance a child's immediate performance, there is frequently a more basic program of counseling or behavior management which is necessary for best and long-lasting results.

What Can I Do as a Parent?—Many medications taken by School-aged children may produce changes in behavior both in classroom behavior and academic performance. It is, therefore, important for parents to inform school personnel of the medicines each child has taken and for what condition, such as with seizure disorders. Parents should attempt to observe the child while on the medication; in this way, allergic reactions, unforeseen side effects, and changes in behavior can be determined. School personnel should also be informed of these observations so that they may be more able to deal effectively with the child.

Children are not usually attentive, responsible, or consistent enough to be in control of their own medication. Schools often have a specific administrative policy to control medicines which are required to be given during the course of the school day; however it is vital that parents be aware of the necessity of supervision and control of children's medications in the home. Safety, as well as effectiveness are important considerations that must be stressed.

Guidelines for Parental Supervision

- Know your child's medication. Learn the generic and trade names, as well as the intended effect of use.
- Administer the medication exactly as directed. "More" does not mean "better." Dosage is determined for your child's height and weight; changing it can be less effective and dangerous.
- Ask your doctor what side effects you can expect. Observe your child after medication and consult the physician in the event of anything unexpected.
- Avoid mixing medications even those sold over-the-counter unless directed by your doctor. Even non-Prescription medicines are drugs and warrant caution.
- Store medicines out of the reach of children. Never store more than one medicine in the same container. It is usually best for parents to control access to a child's medication.
- Discard unused medicines. They can lose effectiveness and/or become dangerous if too old.
- Supervise your child's medications even when used over long-term treatment. Children may not be responsible enough to maintain a regular schedule and may not remember details, such as dosage.
- Inform your child's teachers or other school personnel when medication has been given. Include type, expected effects, and dosage, in the event such information will be needed.
- Know school policy regarding medications at school. Discuss the rules with your child and assist in their enforcement.
- Consult your doctor if unexpected side effects or allergic reactions are observed.

Resources

Barnhart, E.R. (Ed) (annual). *Physicians' desk reference.* Ordell, NJ: Medical Economics Co. This is a Professional reference which includes the manufacturers' information about intended use, contraindiction, side effects, etc. Those with a medical or related background would find it most helpful.

Benovicz, R.J. (1983). *Non-prescription drugs and their side effects.* New York: Putnam. "Over-the-counter" medications are reviews with guidelines and contraindications for treatment in self-medication.

Gadow, K.D. (1986). *Children on medication*, 1, 2. San Diego, CA: College-Hill Press. This is a two-volume set devoted to understanding medications in the educational setting. Specific attention is given to categories of Special education Placement, seizures, etc., and behavioral effects of medications.

Siblings

Jeanne Raschke
University of South Florida

Background—Eighty percent of all children living in the United States have siblings (Dunn, 1985). On the one hand, children growing up together in a family may be drawn close together by common background, inherited similarities or complimentary differences, and by companionship through positive social interactions. On the other hand, children growing up together in a family may experience rivalry and resentment. Brothers and sisters may exhibit individual differences which conflict, not only between and among each other, but between parents as well. Chess and Thomas (1984) propose that when there is dissonance or a "poor fit" between temperamental dispositions and environmental demands, then the outcome is maladaptive relationships between family members. Clearly, early relationships differ among siblings and these early relationships play a paramount role in the development of children's sociocognitive skills (Foster, 1987).

Research suggests that many variables impact sibling relationships including divorce (Knoff, 1987), single-parent families (Carlson, 1987), stepfamilies (Kupisch, 1987), adoption (Hughes, 1987), family size (Tolan & McGuire, 1987), birth order (Hodapp & Hodapp, 1987), and cultural backgrounds (Suberri, 1987). Over the last several decades rapid changes in family life have challenged family stability (Berk, 1989). A decrease in family size due to a decline in birth rates, increasing family mobility, a rise in single-parent homes, and increasing participation in the labor force by mothers with children of all ages have impacted modern family functioning (Berk, 1989). Despite shrinking family size and changing lifestyles, the two-child family is still very common in the United States, accounting for 42% of families who have children (Berk, 1989).

Research in sibling relationships has received little attention until recently. The focus remained on mother-child relationships. However, current research has begun to examine the developmental processes which occur in sibling relationships (Foster, 1987; Dunn, 1983). Several theories have emerged, which focus on the developmental influences of sibling relationships within intact families. It should be noted that most of this research has focused on White, middle-class, intact families, which ignore the above mentioned variables. However, this research indicates that siblings exert important influences on development, both directly through interpersonal relationships with one another, and indirectly, through the reactions of parents toward siblings (Chess & Thomas, 1984; Berk, 1989).

Development—The literature cites several important behavior patterns which have been observed in the firstborn child following the birth of a second child. In a longitudinal study of the early development of relationships between siblings, Dunn and Kendrick (1982) conducted parent interviews of 40 preschoolers from a point late in the mother's pregnancy of a second child through the infancy of the younger child. Home visits were also conducted and observations were made. Results showed that there was a decrease in maternal involvement with the firstborn child immediately after the birth of the second infant. As a result, the older child began to display significant behavior changes indicative of jealousy (e.g., deliberate acts of noncompliance, disobedience). These behaviors were exhibited most often during the times the mother was preoccupied with caring for the new infant. However, other important behavioral changes were also observed in the older child. Positive social approaches and expressions of love, concern, and affection were also observed. As the infant began to interact significantly with others (about 9 months of age), the siblings had established social patterns which included sharing, imitating, and affectionate responses.

Nadelman and Begun (1982) observed several noteworthy behavior patterns in the firstborn child following the birth of a sibling. The reactions of the firstborn were characterized by ambivalence, with alternating reactions of interest versus resentment. Firstborns less than 40 months old were also more likely to display regressive behaviors, exhibiting clinging behavior toward the mother. Dunn (1985) reported that the disturbances in the firstborn's behavior generally disappeared within 2 to 3 months. However, firstborns who previously exhibited "difficult temperament characteristics" were most likely to have the most behavioral outbursts and take longer to adjust to the new sibling.

Dunn (1985) found that many positive behavioral changes also occurred, especially among preschoolers, upon the birth of the second child. She observed preschoolers willing to participate in care-giving activities. These youngsters could actually anticipate their younger sibling's needs and subsequently adequately engage in caregiving and modeling for the siblings. As the firstborns approach preschool and second borns become toddlers, other patterns of interaction have been observed. Studies during this period indicate that many prosocial behaviors occur, including cooperation, helping, sharing, and affection (Pepler, Corter, & Abramovitch, 1982). Aggressive and imitative behaviors, both positive and negative, also occur during this time. Pepler et al. (1982) found that preschool-aged older siblings exhibited more antagonistic behavior than their younger siblings. Males were apt to demonstrate more verbal and physical aggression with same-sex siblings than older females with same-sex siblings. Older sisters were found to initiate more prosocial behaviors. These researchers also found no effect for the size of age interval between siblings. In contrast, White (1985) observed that siblings spaced less than 3 years apart exhibited a higher frequency of antagonistic behaviors.

Substantial individual differences in the quality of relationships established by firstborns with their siblings remain stable over the early childhood years (Berk, 1989). Research has also found that children who tend to have poor sibling relationships later develop poor peer relationships. This suggests that social skills deficits may be involved. However, sibling relationships are also affected by the behavior of the mother toward the firstborn during this time (Dunn, 1985). Dunn found that when the mother talked to the firstborn about the infant as a person—as someone having needs similar to their own—then the relationship between the siblings was likely to remain positive. Dunn and Kendrick (1982) found that when mothers were positive and playful in their style of interaction, older children responded with feelings of rivalry. In contrast, among firstborns who had experienced tense relationships with the mother previously, or with mothers who were depressed after the birth of the second infant, warm and caring relationships developed. This suggests that environmental stress, due to parental behavior, actually encouraged successful relationships between siblings.

During middle childhood, when children are developing talents and outside interests, parental comparisons of each child's abilities and accomplishments occur frequently. Research suggests that the child who gets less parental attention or more disapproval is likely to express resentment or jealousy toward a sibling who receives more preferential treatment (Bryant & Crockenberg, 1980). Self-report studies (Sutton-Smith & Rosenberg, 1970) reveal that preadolescents consistently rated the firstborn as having more power, being more "bossy," and having more control over second borns and the second borns as having more submissive behaviors. Social comparisons are a source of conflict for all siblings during the middle childhood years and the tendency for siblings to strive to be different from each other may reduce sibling rivalry (Berk, 1989). Despite the potential for sibling rivalry at this age, many preadolescent youngsters rely on siblings as important sources of social support (Berk, 1989). Furman and Buhrmester (1985) found four distinct factors within sibling relationships in a factor-analytic study conducted with self-report data from preadolescents. These included warmth/closeness, relative status/power, conflict, and rivalry. It was found that the feelings of warmth and closeness were more prevalent in same-sex dyads than in mixed-sex dyads.

Research on the development of relationships between siblings during adolescence is sparse

(Foster, 1987). Siblings provide companionship, comfort, modeling, and teaching throughout adolescence and early adulthood (Bryant, 1982). Secure relationships often exist between brothers and sisters of large families (Bossard & Boll, 1956).

In summary, research suggests that sibling relationships offer a context in which children learn and practice a wide range of social skills which include caring, conflict resolution, and control of hostile feeling (Berk, 1989). In general, later born children are more popular with age-mates than firstborn children (Miller & Maruyama, 1976). More research is needed to better understand how experiences with siblings influences social relationships outside the family.

What Can I Do As A Parent?—What kinds of interventions should be directed toward a problem involving sibling interactions? Other than the behavior and temperaments of the siblings themselves, it is important to identify how children's developing social, emotional, and cognitive competencies are influenced by the quality of their interactions with their parents. Dunn (1983) has indicated that sibling interactions can be significantly influenced, both positively and negatively, by the mother. Baumrind (1967) gathered information on child-rearing practices by making home visits. She observed two broad dimensions of parent-child interactions which emerged from her observations. The first is child-centeredness. Some parents may establish high standards of expectations and insist that their children meet their demands. Other parents are highly acceptive of their children and their differences and allow "give and take" within their relationships.

Berk (1989) has summed up the basic differences in how parents go about the task of socialization within the family. She identifies four types of parents. The authoritative parent demonstrates a demanding and controlling style. However, even though this parent has high expectations, he/she is nurturant, patient, and sensitive to individual differences. The authoritarian parent is also demanding and controlling, but this parent places a high value on conformity and obedience. This type of parent may be highly punitive and intolerant of individual differences. The permissive parent is nurturant, communicative, and accepting, but lacks authority and seldom imposes controls of any kind. The uninvolved parent is not demanding, but is usually indifferent. This parent is not committed to the role of caretaker and often demonstrates behaviors that involve neglect or detachment. Overall, research indicates that authoritative parents have socially active, responsible, and cognitively competent children, whereas parents who rely on the other three styles have youngsters who develop less optimally (Berk, 1989). As suggested by Berk (1989), sibling conflict may be reduced if parents set clear rules, provide structure and problem-solving opportunities for individual children, and encourage input into family decision making. By using a rational, democratic approach to child rearing, the rights of parents and siblings are recognized and respected.

Much of the current literature on sibling relationships focuses on sibling rivalry. Dunn's research has suggested that the reduction of mother's attention toward the firstborn is often the cause of disobedience and noncompliance among these children. Actions by the mother to alleviate this situation which were successful included the provision of materials to the firstborn before infant caregiving (e.g., books, puzzles), talking to the firstborn about the infant's needs, and allowing the firstborn to assist in caregiving activities (Dunn, 1985).

Felson (1983) suggests that fighting among siblings may be due to conflicts over property, uneven division of chores, or poor mood. As suggested by Felson and by Berk (1989), family systems may need to be assessed to address parenting style, rules, consequences, and even distribution of chores. In addition, parents may need to assess their attributions or feelings toward individual children's achievements, and personality strengths and weaknesses.

Interventions that focus on the needs of individual children rather than on sibling conflict stress that parents recognize and appreciate the unique qualities of each of their offspring (Dobson, 1978). One of the effective interventions used is for each parent to spend "quality time" interacting on an individual basis with each child in the family.

Finally, a parent's own mental health and well-being affects each family member. It is imperative

109

that each parent assess individual stressors in an effort to reduce stress within the family environment and optimize family relationships.

What Can I Do As A Teacher?—As noted previously, most research on the developmental aspects of sibling relationships has focused on White, middle-class, intact families. Thus it is essential that interventions need to assess situations involving non-White families, families in lower socioeconomic groups, single-parent families, families with handicapped individuals, step-families, families of working mothers, and families of siblings by adoption. Professionals especially need to be familiar with family system dynamics (Foster, 1987).

Batsche (1991) has advocated for the assessment and remediation of social skills deficits among behaviorally disordered children. Social skills deficits may indeed be involved in poor sibling relationships as well. Millman and Schaefer (1982) have advocated for the use of group rewards and penalties to reduce antagonistic behavior among siblings. They advise parents to offer all siblings rewards contingent on cooperation between siblings. Teachers may need to conduct parent training in basic behavior modification principles.

Summary—Despite changes in the American family, research suggests that the two-child family is still very common in the United States. The consequences of growing up with brothers and sisters has received little research attention. However, recent research suggests that siblings exert important influences on one another as well as on the entire family. The quality of the sibling relationship itself has implications for childhood socialization and development. Past research has focused on sibling rivalry, but recent research indicates that relationships between siblings are positive. The older sibling has been found to be the dominant one in the relationship and the younger sibling has been found to be more submissive. Interventions which tend to be successful in improving sibling relationships have involved modifying parenting styles, particularly in the mother. Clearly, more research is needed to establish causal connections between children's sibling relationships and their social development with peers.

References

Batsche, G. (1991). *Social skills training: Interventions III*. Tampa, FL: University of South Florida.

Baumrind, D. (1967). Child care practices anteceding three patterns of preschool behavior. *Genetic Psychology Monographs, 75,* 43-88.

Berk, L. (1989). *Child Development*. Boston: Allyn & Bacon.

Bossard, J. H. S., & Boll, E. S. (1956). *The large family system*. Philadelphia: University of Pennsylvania Press.

Bryant, B. K. (1982). Sibling relationships in middle childhood. In M. E. Lamb & B. Sutton-Smith (Eds.), *Sibling relationships: Their nature and significance across the lifespan* (pp. 87-121). Hillsdale, NJ: Erlbaum.

Bryant, B. K., & Crockenberg, S. B. (1980). Correlates and dimensions of prosocial behavior: A study of female siblings with their mothers. *Child Development, 51,* 529-544.

Carlson, C. (1987). Single-parent homes. In A. Thomas & J. Grimes (Eds.), *Children's needs: Psychological perspectives* (pp. 560-569). Washington, DC: NASP.

Chess, S., & Thomas, A. (1984). *Origins and evolution of behavior disorders*. New York: Brunner/Mazel.

Dobson, J. (1978). *The strong-willed child*. Wheaton, IL: Tyndale House.

Dunn, J. (1983). Sibling relationships in early childhood. Child Development, 54, 787-811.

Dunn, J. (1985). *Sisters and brothers*. Cambridge, MA: Harvard University Press.

Dunn, J., & Kendrick, C. (1982). *Siblings: Love, envy, and understanding*. Cambridge, MA: Harvard University Press.

Felson, R. B. (1983). Aggression and violence between siblings. *Social Psychology Quarterly, 46,* 271-285.

Foster, B. (1987). Siblings. In A. Thomas & J. Grimes (Eds.), Children's needs: *Psychological perspectives* (pp. 548-554). Washington, DC: NASP.

Furman, W., & Buhrmester, D. (1985). Children's perceptions of the qualities of sibling relationships. *Child Development, 54,* 448-461.

Hodapp, A. F., & Hodapp, J. B. (1987). Birth order. In A. Thomas & J. Grimes (Eds.), *Children's needs: Psychological perspectives* (pp. 61-66). Washington, DC: NASP.

Hughes, C. (1987). Adoption. In A. Thomas & J. Grimes (Eds.), *Children's needs: Psychological perspectives* (pp. 9-19). Washington, DC: NASP.

Knoff, H. M. (1987). Divorce. In A. Thomas & J. Grimes (Eds.), *Children's needs: Psychological perspectives* (pp. 173-181). Washington, DC: NASP.

Kupisch, S. (1987). Stepfamilies. In A. Thomas & J. Grimes (Eds.), *Children's needs: Psychological perspectives* (pp. 578-585). Washington, DC: NASP.

Millman, H., & Schaefer, C. (1982). *How to help children with common problems.* New York: Plenum.

Miller, N., & Maruyama, G. (1976). Ordinal position and peer popularity. *Journal of Personality and Social Psychology, 33,* 123-131.

Nadelman, L., & Begun, A. (1982). The effect of the newborn on the older sibling: Mother's questionnaires. In M. E. Lamb & B. Sutton-Smith (Eds.), *Sibling relationships: Their nature and significance across the lifespan* (pp. 13-37). Hillsdale, NJ: Erlbaum.

Pepler, D., Corter, C., & Abramovitch, R. (1982). Social relations among children: Comparison of sibling and peer interaction. In K. H. Rubin & H. S. Ross (Eds.), *Peer relationships and social skills in childhood* (pp. 209-227). New York: Springer-Verlag.

Suberri, K. C. (1987). Different cultural backgrounds. In A. Thomas & J. Grimes (Eds.), *Children's needs: Psychological perspectives* (pp. 167-172). Washington, DC: NASP.

Sutton-Smith, B., & Rosenberg, B. G. (1970). *The sibling.* New York: Holt, Rinehart & Winston.

Tolan, P. H., & McGuire, D. (1987). Family size. In A. Thomas & J. Grimes (Eds.), *Children's needs: Psychological perspectives* (pp. 202-209). Washington, DC: NASP.

White, B. L. (1985). *The first three years of life.* Englewood Cliffs, NJ: Prentice-Hall.

NATIONAL ASSOCIATION OF SCHOOL PSYCHOLOGISTS

Children and Holidays:
A Holiday Survivor's Guide
Parent Handout

Akron Public Schools Child Study Department
Public Relations Committee, E. Bard, Ph.D. Chief Psychologist

Background Information—The holiday season is rapidly approaching along with good times, good food, and all too often, a good bit of STRESS. A season full of goodness and much merriment can become one of increased tension, accompanied by headaches, heartburn, and STRESS.

What Can I Do As A Parent?—There is not enough time to handle the hectic demands of the season. The normal day contains many tasks which seem to fill all our waking hours. The usual state of exhaustion which results in nodding off at 10:00 p.m. now becomes a day-long state. There are too many things for a person to do in a 24-hour period and this is precisely the point! A way to decrease STRESS is to use your time wisely.

- Make a list of all the things you need to do, find a quiet spot and go over it carefully.
- Prioritize the items and eliminate activities which you feel are not necessary. By carefully examining your priorities and being realistic in regard to the constraints, a more manageable list will emerge.
- In order to maintain a sense of accomplishment, cross out items as activities are completed.
- Depending on your schedule and the number of expectations, a fresh list may be compiled each day.
- Share your list with others so that family support systems can be enhanced and communication shared.
- Remember to plan time for yourself!

Another source of holiday STRESS is money. The holiday spirit is usually caught by all of us and a good bit of "impulse" buying occurs. Stores "help" us by deferring bills until February! Added to this is the increased amount of entertaining and the gala New Year's festivities. Both of these stretch the budget to its limits and can cause or add to our level of holiday STRESS.

- Only use deferred billing if you feel this payment plan fits your future budget.
- When possible, arm yourself with a list of specific items prior to entering the store. This will cut down on impulse buying.
- If impulse buying is a big problem for your family, use only cash and leave the credit cards at home.
- Reflect on the true meaning of the holidays and keep within your budget. An open discussion of finances with older children often can help.

- Let members of the family know the amount you have set aside for holiday purposes and ask them to keep their requests reasonable.
- Younger children may be disappointed by not finding the exact thing they want. If you decide it was not worth the money, stick to your decision.
- Children are tremendously resilient and their disappointment will pass if a specific present is not delivered.

A third source of holiday STRESS is **relatives.** During the holiday season, too much unwanted family togetherness enhanced by extended family members often leads to tension and hard feelings. When grandparents, parents, and other siblings arrive on the scene, adults may tend to feel displaced and repressed feelings associated with hostility, favoritism, and past perceived injustices may emerge.

- Try to limit the amount of time spent with family members who tend to agitate or cause ill feelings.
- When family gatherings are inevitable, conversation should be steered around unpleasant topics or past confrontations.
- Maintain a pleasant, cooperative, approachable facade even though this does not reflect your true feelings. Time will pass quickly and those around you will benefit from a positive effort made toward diminishing conflicts with relatives.
- If young children are involved in family gatherings, specific activities or play material should be available for entertainment. Children cannot be expected to sit quietly and listen to adult conversation.
- If guests are expected to extend their visit with overnight accommodations in your home, an attempt should be made to provide as much privacy as possible to your guests in order to diminish conflicts that arise from close living quarters.

A fourth source of holiday STRESS is children. Before you say, "Bah! Humbug to you," rest assured that the holidays are a wonderful time for children. As adults, the holidays are often filled with childhood memories. However children can become stressors for a number of reasons. First, the school schedule which helped to regulate their days has ceased. At school, children know when it is time to eat, play, do math, sing, etc. This schedule makes the day predictable and we all enjoy predictability. But the holidays become unpredictable times for children. Parents will be trying to cram more activities into their own schedules and children can become upset about this "perceived neglect." With this may come increased temper tantrums, and even a statement or two about a parent's lack of caring about them. Parents can quickly develop a case of the holiday hollers.

- Try to keep a schedule for your children. Let them know the day's itinerary.
- Be sure to allot an apropriate amount of time for rest during your child's schedule as had been maintained during the school year.
- When at all possible, reserve a specific portion of the day to schedule a quiet time with your children in enjoyable activities such as reading, discussing upcoming events, jigsaw puzzles, monopoly, or other family related games.

NATIONAL ASSOCIATION OF SCHOOL PSYCHOLOGISTS

Children and Television

Theodore A. Ridder
Belding Area Schools, Michigan

Background—Both the Surgeon General and the National Institute of Mental Health have cautioned us about the influences of television. Recommendations by researchers for controls on programming for children are opposed by the television industry; and the generations of citizens now in their twenties and thirties, parents of today, have no memory of a childhood without television. Meanwhile, children spend as much as 30 hours a week watching television. By the time they graduate from high school most have spent 12,000 hours with the school and 18,000 hours with the TV.

Development—Studies have demonstrated that watching violence on television can increase children's aggressive behavior. This seems most likely if the children consider the program realistic and if they want to be like the violent character. The television industry often uses production methods such as "cutting away" to spare viewers the really gory results of the violent acts. This is called "sterilizing" the violence. Some research suggests it is even worse than unsterilized violence because children see no bad results and don't learn to fear strong violence or feel uncomfortable when they see it. Using weak, unimportant strangers as victims is part of "sterilizing." It prevents children from experiencing the action from the victim's point of view.

The production methods which television uses are called formal features. Some of these formal features, such as short segment length, rapid action sequences, non-human voices, and special effects, are clearly able to hold children's attention better than the familiar voice of a classroom teacher. Children who grow up constantly entertained by these exciting, rapid-paced programs may find listening to a teacher simply too much effort. They may also find that if they pay attention in school only part of the time, the way they do to television, they completely lose track of what's being presented. Formal features may be more important than content or message in other ways. For example, the increased aggressive behavior and hyperactivity associated with viewing some programs may simply result from heightened arousal caused by the frantic pace.

TV is not a drug, but it does give instant pleasure and requires little effort from the viewer. Television allows children to escape boredom without thinking, talking with adults, or developing complex interests such as reading, studying, or playing complicated games.

Television functions as a "window on the world" for small children. Even as they get older, however, they do not necessarily make a clear distinction between true stories and fiction or between actors and the characters they play. Their ideas about life are shaped by the version of reality they see on TV. Watching life on TV can mislead children about the amount of crime, violence, and family conflict that is normal; the kinds of lifestyles, jobs, and income easily available; and the chances for constant excitement in life. Television programming creates impressions about the very pace of life. Only Mr. Rogers shows children how long real life events take from start to finish. Other shows cut out the boring parts. Trials on crime dramas are sometimes over in less time than it takes Mr. Rogers to change his shoes. The message underlying some television shows also impacts children, suggesting that uncontrolled aggression isn't really such a bad reaction.

What can I Do as a Parent?—Limit the amount of television children watch. It will take courage to do so. It may require parents to set an example and to find baby sitters who will do the same. It makes sense to require children to pay, from their allowance, for the privilege of watching television. It teaches them that television is entertainment, that entertainment costs money, and that free TV is not a constitutional right.

- Eliminate unplanned and incidental viewing. Allowing children to simply turn on the TV and search for something to watch insures that they will not find a more active or creative way to deal with boredom. Watching television while doing other activities may teach a subtle habit of not fully attending to anything. Watching television while doing homework may help to develop a superficial and disinterested approach to education.

- Specific programs can be stopped by simply charging a very high fee to watch them. Parents need to watch these shows and discuss them with children. Some high action, violent programs with gross distortion of reality and anti-social role modeling are easy to recognize; and most children will have a difficult time arguing that they get anything positive from watching them. But parents will need to learn what questions to ask to get at the impact of other shows. Which character are you most like? Do policemen really live like the ones on Miami Vice? Do cars always explode when they crash? Was Rambo justified in killing all those people? Where do the characters who never seem to work get all their money? Do people really make major personality changes in a few days? If children have never thought about such matters, they need to be helped to do so. Research suggests that they accept more on television as realistic than they should. Attention to the gross inaccuracy of much TV programming may diminish children's enjoyment of it. More importantly, such discussion can help parents to recognize the areas where children are learning wrong or undesirable beliefs, values, and behaviors. Parents must not assume that they can unteach what has been taught by a TV program simply by telling children to ignore the message. Parents will have to listen carefully to children, apply the TV messages in real life situations, and return to the themes repeatedly if they wish to prevail.

- Eliminate cartoons and high action shows for pre-schoolers. Preschoolers whose play themes involve specific references to cartoons, certain superheroes, and action-detective characters are more likely to be aggressive. It is not difficult to see how a child who wants to be the Incredible Hulk might have problems in kindergarten. Watching children will usually reveal which programs contribute to what parents often refer to as "hyperness."

- Encourage children to watch programs that require attention and that teach pro-social lessons. Viewing programs such as Nova, Wild America, and Wonder Works with children provides a chance to praise careful attention to fairly complicated material. It is ridiculous to reward children for paying careful attention to a show such as St. Elsewhere or Hill Street Blues because the programs jump back and forth between several plots with constant high-energy, action sequences to prevent anyone from losing interest. No real concentration is necessary.

- Help children to develop interests, hobbies, and pastimes that are more constructive and less passive than watching television.

- Try to change the nature of television for children. Action for Children's Television is a citizens action group that has organized in an effort to improve the quality of programming for children. Their address is 20 University Road, Cambridge, MA 02138.

Resources

—*T.V. On/Off: Better Family Uses of Television*, by E. DeFranco. Goodyear Publisher. 1980. This is a very practical book written on an easy reading level. It could be of considerable help to a family attempting to reduce or gain better control of viewing within the home.

—*The ACT Guide to Children's Television: Or How to Treat T.V. with TLC*, by E. Kaye, Beacon

Press, Publisher. 1979. This work could be helpful to parents who want to learn how to more effectively mediate the impact of television on their children.

—*T.V. Tips for Parents*, from Corporation for Public Broadcasting, 1111 16th St., N.W. Washington, D.C. 20036. 1987. Free pamphlet giving practical tips for parents that encourages positive use of television.

NATIONAL ASSOCIATION OF SCHOOL PSYCHOLOGISTS

Children and Temper Tantrums

Theo Lexmond
Barry Intermediate School District, Hastings, Michigan

Background—One of the most unsettling periods in a child's life, and certainly one of the most unnerving periods for parents, is the stage of development often referred to as "the terrible twos." The behavior that makes "the terrible twos" so terrible for many toddlers and their parents is the arrival of temper tantrums. Many children develop some form of temper tantrum behavior during their toddler years. Though two-year-olds seem to be especially prone to temper tantrums, tantrum behavior characteristic of "the terrible twos" may occur in children of any age.

Temper tantrums can include relatively mild behaviors such as pouting, whining, crying, and name calling. They can also include more disruptive behaviors such as screaming, kicking, punching, scratching and biting, and even self-injurious behaviors like head banging and holding one's breath to the point of fainting.

For most young children, the development of tantrums is only a temporary stopping point along the path of learning how to cope with frustration. For others, temper tantrums become a block to further emotional growth and development. The difference between tantrum behavior that is a step toward maturity and tantrum behavior that becomes a block to further growth lies in the way parents and caretakers deal with their youngster's tantrums.

Development—*Why do many children display temper tantrums in the course of normal development?*

The world is an exciting place for toddlers. Their ability to crawl, and later to walk, allows them to reach and explore any area they can see. Toddlers are constantly getting into things that their parents would prefer they left alone. In addition to their improved ability to move around and explore things, toddlers also grow rapidly in their ability to understand and use words. The growth of their vocabulary allows them to express their needs and to understand simple commands. The combination of these two factors, increased ability to move around and increased understanding of words, leads to an event that toddlers find very frustrating: the introduction of verbal rule training by their parents.

Verbal rule training is the flood of necessary do's and don'ts that parents shower upon their toddlers in order to protect them from harm and to keep them out of mischief. "Don't touch!" "Don't go in there!" "Don't hit!" "Don't cry!" "Do eat your carrots.' "Do be quiet." "Do put that away." "Do be good." These are just a few examples of the many commands that toddlers face each day.

Though infants learn to talk instead of gurgling and babbling, they never give up smiling, laughing, frowning or crying as ways of communicating how they feel. Crying or screaming by a two or three-year-old communicates frustration in a way with which the youngster is familiar. The experience of verbal rule training can be very frustrating to toddlers. In response to this frustration toddlers will often revert to screaming and crying to proclaim to the world that they are "fed-up." An occasional outburst of screaming or crying by a two or three-year-old child is not an uncommon or worrisome occurrence. A child of this age finds it hard to accept brief frustrations and putting these frustrations into words is an equally difficult task.

If a period of tantrum behavior is normal for many children, how do I tell the difference between "normal" tantrums and tantrum behavior that I should be worried about?

The best way to answer this question is to take a close look at your child's tantrum behavior and the behavior of you and your family when tantrums occur. Do any of these things happen in your family?

—Your child has tantrums in many settings, not just at home.

—Your child has tantrums regardless of who in the family is caring for the youngster.

—Your child is having more and more tantrums each day as time goes on.

—Your child's tantrums are becoming more severe as time goes on.

—Your child hurts him or herself or tries to hurt others during tantrums.

—Your child receives extra attention from family members when a tantrum occurs. For example, when your child has a tantrum someone hugs or holds the child, or perhaps someone scolds or lectures the child.

—Members of your family try to stop your child's tantrums by giving the youngster what he or she wants.

—Members of your family avoid taking a tantrum-prone child grocery shopping, to church, to visit friends or relatives, out to eat, etc., because they are afraid the child will tantrum in those settings.

—You find it hard to get someone to babysit your tantrum-prone child.

If one or more of the items above describe the experience your family is having, your child may be developing a severe tantrum problem.

A severe tantrum problem is characterized by tantrum behavior that has become goal directed. When children first develop tantrums, they use crying and screaming as a way of expressing frustration. Tantrums start out as a way for children to communicate that they are "fed up" with the limits placed upon them. If children learn, however that having tantrums can gain them extra attention from their family or can allow them to do things they would not otherwise be allowed to do, their tantrums will come to serve a different purpose. No longer will they use tantrums simply as a means of expressing frustration. Instead, such children will use tantrums as a tool for obtaining more attention and getting to do more things. Their tantrums will become goal directed.

Family members and other caretakers cause tantrums to become goal directed, usually without realizing they are doing so. If a child, for example, cries and screams because he desires a toy that is currently out of reach, hugging and rocking the child until he is calm will soothe the youngster for the moment, but will encourage him to cry and scream in the future when something else he wants is out of reach. Even though he/she was not given the toy as a result of his tantrums, he/she received a great deal of special attention. By repeating this pattern over and over again, family members may actually teach a child to have tantrums as a way of obtaining something he or she wants. This is not to say that children should never be soothed when they are upset. The key point to remember is that children should not be allowed to use tantrums as a way of getting special treatment from those around them.

What Can I Do As A Parent?—Whether tantrum behaviors are just beginning to develop in your child, or tantrums have become a long standing problem, there are actions you and members of your family can take to help your child gain control over tantrum behavior.

Some guidelines for dealing with tantrum behaviors when they first begin to develop.

—Rule out the possibility that tantrums are being caused by a factor other than general frustration with verbal rule training. Some factors which may cause or contribute to tantrums include teething, the presence of seizure activity, the side effects of some medications, or a sudden emotional loss such as the death or long absence of a parent. In the vast majority of cases, tantrums are the result of frustration encountered in daily living. If a specific cause, such as one of those mentioned above is suspected, you should have your child evaluated by an appropriate health care professional.

120

—Do not allow your child to receive extra attention from family members as a result of having a tantrum.

—Do not allow your child to obtain things he or she would not otherwise be allowed to obtain as a result of having a tantrum.

—Do not scold or spank your child for having a tantrum. Scolding or spanking is likely to reinforce tantrum behavior and cause it to get worse.

—Tantrums are not an appropriate way of asking for a desired object. Even if the object is something your child would normally be allowed to have, do not allow the child to obtain it by having a tantrum. Provide the object only when the child is calm and has asked for it in an appropriate fashion, considering the child's age.

—Do not ignore your child when the youngster is being good because you are afraid of "setting the child off" and causing a tantrum to occur. Pay extra attention to your child when he or she is behaving appropriately and is not having a tantrum.

Some guidelines for dealing with tantrum behavior that has become a serious, long standing problem.

—If tantrum behaviors have become a severe problem for your child, arrange to visit with a child care professional such as a school psychologist or clinical child psychologist. A trained child care professional can help you develop a program that will deal with the specific circumstances of your child's situation. Tantrum behaviors that are deeply entrenched do not yield to "quick fix" solutions. A professional child care worker can help you to develop a comprehensive plan for dealing with severe tantrum behavior and can demonstrate the special skills you will need in order to help your child get tantrums under control. There are effective techniques available for dealing with tantrums that occur at home, in school, in public places such as grocery stores and restaurants, and for dealing with bedtime tantrums as well.

—As mentioned earlier, you should not scold or spank your child for having a tantrum. Scolding or spanking is likely to reinforce tantrum behavior and cause it to get worse.

—Try to pay extra attention to your child when he or she is not having tantrums. By making yourself available when your child is behaving well, you teach your child that special attention can be gained by a means other than having tantrums.

Resources

—*Living With Children*—by G. R. Patterson. Research Press, Publisher, 1976. Chapter 14 of Patterson's book provides a model of a simple program for dealing with tantrums occurring in the home.

—*Living With a Brother or Sister With Special Needs: A Book for Sibs*—by D. J. Meyer, P. F. Vadasy and R. R. Fewell. University of Washington Press, Publisher 1985. This resource book, written for children of late elementary school age and older has a section devoted specifically to the questions children have regarding the role they must play in dealing with the behavior problems of a brother or sister.

—*Tantrums, Jealousy and the Fears of Children*—by L. Barrow, A. H. & A. W. Reed, Publisher 1968. This booklet in Barrow's series on child psychology provides a brief discussion of temper tantrum development in young children and includes descriptions by parents of tantrum problems they have dealt with in their own families.

NATIONAL ASSOCIATION OF SCHOOL PSYCHOLOGISTS

Children and Working Parents

Beth Deemer
Anne Arundel County Board of Education
Annapolis, Maryland

Background—In more than half of American families, there are two parents and both work, or there is a single parent and that parent works. Working parents are faced with decisions and compromises. A new mother may need to return to work shortly after a baby is born; parents must ask children to be more responsible about household chores; a husband and wife may drift apart as they argue about housework and their time for each other disappears. A strong family will share chores, manage time effectively, balance guilt with realistic expectations, and nurture the relationships which are important to a healthy family.

Development—Here are broad guidelines regarding child care:

0–4 months	• a good time to be at home with a new baby, to form attachments and new parenting skills.
7–8 months	• may not be a good time to place a child with new caregiver due to fear of strangers.
9–10 months	• may be a good age for change of caregiver as sitting and crawling are developed.
12–16 months	• may be a poor time for a change if fear of strangers is present.
18–24 months	• may be a good time for starting day care.

Here are broad guidelines for giving responsibility to children:

3 years	• undress completely, dress with help, empty wastebaskets, fold small laundry, clear silverware and plastic from table.
4 years	• all the above, pick up clutter, put away clean clothes.
5–6 years	• all the above, set the table, put away clean dishes, dust, feed and care for pet.
7 years	• all the above, clean sinks and tub, empty garbage, sweep walks, clean inside of car, fix cereal and sandwiches.
8 and up	• all the above, laundry and simple cooking.

What Can I Do As A Parent?

Parents and Children

1. Time is as important as money. It should be discussed and budgeted, just like an allowance. For one week, keep a written log of the ways in which time is spent.

2. Identify time consumers such as television, drinking, managing clutter, and taking care of possessions ("toys" like boats and animals). Make decisions about cutting out some time consumers.

3. Set a goal to make a regular time for meeting with each child alone. This could be done by letting that child stay up later than the others one night a week. During this special time, turn off the television and take the phone off the hook. This is a time to listen, not lecture, to share experiences and opinions.

4. When a child wants to add an activity or commitment to his schedule, talk it over carefully. Discuss why the child wants to do the activity, when and how much time it will take, what other activities will have to be stopped, and how it will affect the rest of the family.

5. Identify the times that cause trouble. (Mornings are often the worst.) Establish a routine which begins with choosing clothes and finding books the night before. In the morning, set rules like 'no television' and 'breakfast before 7:30.' The result of missing the bus is walking all or part of the way to school.

Parent to Parent

1. At a neutral time, make a list of household chores. Decide how much work could be done by paid help and hire someone to do it. Otherwise, divide the work equally and be prepared to lower some standards for housekeeping and meals. Accept a less-than-perfect job.

2. Examine time commitments and drop the activities which are not contributing to the health of the family and the marriage.

3. Plan ahead for "dates" or time alone to be together privately, without the distractions of television, phone, and other interruptions.

4. Think about the reasons for marriage and having a family.

5. When guilt and stress seem overwhelming, get counseling from a mental health center, a minister, or a licensed professional.

Parents and the Work Setting

1. Look at your involvement in work in terms of the time spent both working and thinking about work.

2. List the importance (in order) of work, spouse or significant other, and children. When work appears as the top priority, think about the reasons for that.

3. Analyze time at work according to what is controlled by others, and what is self-controlled. Identify the time-consuming activities at work which may be reduced by better organization: telephone, interruptions, meetings, and overcommitment.

4. Explore job options which permit greater flexibility: delegation, job sharing, part-time work, flexible hours, and work at home.

Handling the Guilt—Guilt is a reaction to the necessary compromises made by working parents; every working parent feels guilty at some time. Unless you have broken the law or committed some immoral act, guilt is the result of a personal evaluation of your performance as a spouse, parent, or employee. Guilt can be a motivator; it can help parents try to improve uncomfortable situations. Keep in mind these points.

1. There are no perfect families, no perfect parents, and no perfect children.

2. There is no research to support the notion that children are automatically better off with a full time mother in the home.

3. Working is often not a matter of choice.

4. Doing all your child's chores and giving in to your child's demands or wants is NOT the way to handle guilt.

5. When families have cluttered houses and fast food meals, it is the mother who assumes the most guilt. This guilt comes from the traditional idea that women must keep the house clean and cook the food. Women who handle this guilt do it by recognizing that no one can be everything and do everything. If the husband and children don't feel guilty or uncomfortable with clutter and restaurant food, then the guilt felt by the mother is self-imposed.

Resources

—*Working and caring*—by T. B. Brazelton. Addison-Wesley, 1985. Dr. Brazelton, a pediatrician, presents a realistic and objective approach to working and parenting. Chapters of particular value cover returning to work and managing time.

—*Practical parenting tips for the school-age years*—by V. Lansky. Bantam Books. 1985. Of special interest to working parents are the areas addressing responsibility for children and help for mothers returning to work. Single parents and blended families are included in a special section.

—*Perfect parenting and other myths*—by F. Main. CompCare Publications. 1986. The author's problem-solving chapters are valuable, humorous, and realistic. Discussions on building quality time and parent-to-parent relationships are especially useful.

—*Getting organized*—by S. Winston. Warner Books. 1978. Time management and household organization are two key elements of this guide to gaining control over disorder. The chapters addressing shared work and organization for children are excellent starting points for families committed to change.

Part IV

The Home-School Connection—
Bridging the Gap

Attention Deficit Hyperactivity Disorder (ADHD)
Parent Handouts

Debby Waddell
Columbus, Ohio

Background—ADHD children are more active, less attentive, and more impulsive than most other children of their age. In the past, ADHD has been called ADD (Attention Deficit Disorder) and hyperactivity. About 3% of children exhibit ADHD. More boys are diagnosed than girls.

Characteristics of ADHD include fidgeting or squirming, having difficulty remaining seated, being easily distracted, having difficulty waiting to take a turn, having a short attention span, shifting from one uncompleted activity to another talking excessively, interrupting others, and engaging in physically dangerous activities without thinking of consequences.

Sometimes children are not hyperactive, but are distractible and have a short attention span. This condition is more subtle but can interfere with functioning. It is called Undifferentiated Attention Deficit Disorder.

Developments—ADHD begins at an early age and is displayed in a wide variety of situations. Many children exhibit some characteristics of ADHD at times, but the ADHD child's difficulties are extreme and regularly interfere with day to day activities. The difficulties are typically most apparent in structured settings such as school. As a result, many ADHD children are not identified until they enter school. In some settings, ADHD children may be able to pay attention quite well. These include fast moving TV shows, video games, and novel situations.

ADHD is a chronic disorder which lasts through childhood and often into adulthood. While some characteristics may seem less extreme as the child gets older, ADHD students may experience other behavior and social-emotional disorders later in life.

Children with ADHD also may exhibit learning difficulties. Testing by the school's evaluation team may be appropriate if a child is having significant learning problems.

No one knows what causes ADHD. Differences in brain structure and functioning and heredity are being studied. However, it is very unusual to find treatable neurological difficulties as the cause of ADHD. Claims that allergies to foods or additives or vitamin deficiencies are responsible for ADHD have not been supported by research and special diets do not typically result in drastic or long-lasting changes in an ADHD child's behavior.

Often ADHD is treated with medication. Not every ADHD child needs medication, but medication can be very effective in controlling some of the behaviors associated with ADHD. The most commonly used medications for ADHD are Ritalin and Cylert. These are known as stimulant drugs, and although it may seem like the last thing an ADHD child needs is stimulation, these medications reduce some of the undesirable characteristics of ADHD. With appropriate use, stimulant medications are reported to be safe and to have few side-effects.

What can I do as a parent?

Don't expect to find a quick, easy remedy for ADHD.

- Diets, megavitamins or the elimination of fluorescent lighting have not been found to be effective treatments.
- When medication is administered for ADHD, the child will not be without any difficulties as soon as pills are taken.

Do expect ADHD to be chronic and help others in your child's life realize and adjust for this.

- Meet with your child's teacher to share information about medication and about strategies which have been effective in the past.
- Help relatives, close friends, Sunday school teachers, and parents of playmates understand your child's special needs.
- Share ways you have found to be most successful in managing your child's behavior with babysitters and other caretakers.
- Be prepared for the chronic nature of ADHD. Expect that behavior management techniques will be needed on a continuing basis.
- Help your child learn appropriate skills. Expect that you may need to teach your child the social skills that other children learn without specific instruction.

Do seek advice from professionals.

The **school psychologist** assigned to your child's school is a good place to start. The school psychologist may:

- Work with you and your child's teacher to help your child in the classroom.
- Work with you in designing behavior management programs for home or help you locate other professionals who can provide assistance.
- Help to determine the specific nature of learning difficulties by doing an indepth evaluation.

Consultation with your child's **physician** will be necessary if medication is being considered.

- Have specific examples of your concerns and bring school records or other related information to your appointment.
- Expect that you and your child's teachers may be asked to complete behavior checklists or observe your child for changes in behavior. This helps to ensure that your child is receiving the proper dosage of an appropriate medication.
- Consult your physician immediately if your child begins taking medication or begins an increased dose of medication and you notice drastic and undesirable changes in behavior.
- Do not increase your child's dosage without consulting your physician.
- Keep regularly scheduled appointments with your child's physician so that medication can be appropriately monitored.
- Remember that medication alone does not teach a child new behaviors, and instruction will be necessary to teach your child new behaviors.

Do accept your child's limitations and set appropriate expectations for your child.

- Make alternative arrangements rather than putting your child in a situation (e.g. church, synagogue) where he/she is expected to sit for long periods.
- Plan playtimes which incorporate physical activity. Your child's difficulties will be much less

apparent if he/she is playing outside with friends rather than playing in a small room with puzzles or games.

- Plan to supervise your ADHD child more closely than brothers and sisters who do not exhibit ADHD. Because ADHD children often take risks without considering consequences, it is important that they be regularly supervised.
- Try not to let your child become overly tired. Self-control breaks down when children are fatigued. Regular bedtimes can help you avoid serious evening difficulties.
- Try to distinguish between times when your child refuses to do something and behavior that is the result of ADHD (your child can't do something). These behaviors need to be treated differently. Behaviors that a child can't do require teaching or compensating for not being able to do that thing. Behaviors that a child won't do require discipline such as setting specific rules, rewarding appropriate behavior and removing a privilege or sitting in a chair for inappropriate behavior.

Do provide structure and teach strategies for organization.

- Give short, clear firm, and specific directions to your child. A child who has difficulty paying attention may have forgotten the first thing you said before you finish saying the second or third thing.
- Help your child learn strategies for coping with short attention span. For instance, if your child has difficulty remembering directions, make a list. As ADHD children grow, they learn to make their own lists and check off items as they are completed.
- Praise your child for jobs well done. Avoid falling into the criticism trap where all you are doing is correcting your child. Find small things to praise and make a point of doing this often.
- Try to establish regular household routines and let your child know your expectations for mealtime homework time, and bedtime, etc.

Resources

Parent support groups can be found in many locations. The national headquarters of Children with Attention Deficit Disorders (CHADD) may have information on a group near your home. CHADD can be reached at Suite 185, 1859 North Pine Island Road, Plantation, FL 33322.

Bever S. (1982) *Building a child's self image: A guide for parents.* The Minnesota Association for Children and Adults with Learning Disabilities, 821 University Avenue, 494 North, St. Paul, MN 55105.

Canter L., & Canter M. *Assertive discipline for parents.* (1988) New York: Harper & Row.

Goldstein, S., & Goldstein, M. (1989) *A parents' guide to attention deficit hyperactivity disorder in children.* Available from The Neurology, Learning and Behavior Center 670 East 3900 South, Suite 100, Salt Lake City, Utah 84107.

Patterson, G. (1975) *Families.* Champaign, IL: Research Press.

Smith, J.M., & Smith, D.E.P. (1978) *Child management.* Bellvue, WA: Edmark Associates.

NATIONAL ASSOCIATION OF SCHOOL PSYCHOLOGISTS

Attention Deficit Hyperactivity Disorder (ADHD)
Teacher Handout

Debby Waddell
Columbus, Ohio

Background—ADHD children are more active, less attentive, and more impulsive than most other children of their age. In the past, ADHD has been called ADD (Attention Deficit Disorder) and hyperactivity. About 3% of children exhibit ADHD. More boys are diagnosed than girls.

Characteristics of ADHD include fidgeting or squirming, having difficulty remaining seated, being easily distracted, having difficulty waiting to take a turn, having a short attention span, shifting from one uncompleted activity to another talking excessively, interrupting others, and engaging in physically dangerous activities without thinking of consequences.

Sometimes children are not hyperactive but are distractible and have a short attention span. This condition is more subtle but can interfere with functioning. It is called Undifferentiated Attention Deficit Disorder. Attention Deficit Hyperactivity Disorder is:

Development: ADHD begins during the developmental period-before the age of seven. Often parents describe their ADHD child as having been very active as a baby and toddler, always running and climbing, and usually needing constant adult supervision and much parental energy.

Chronic: ADHD persists throughout childhood and often into adolescence and adulthood. While some characteristics may seem less extreme as the child gets older ADHD students may experience behavioral and social-emotional disorders later in life.

Pervasive: ADHD is displayed in a wide variety of situations. The difficulties are typically most apparent in structured settings such as school. On the other hand, ADHD children may be able to pay attention quite well in some situations. These include fast moving TV shows, video games, and novel situations.

Many children may exhibit some characteristics of ADHD at one time or another but the ADHD child's difficulties in these areas are extreme and regularly interfere with day to day activities. Behavior management strategies which are sufficient for most children are not sufficient for ADHD children.

Children with ADHD also may exhibit learning difficulties. If severe enough, ADHD children may need a multifactored evaluation and special education services.

No one knows what causes ADHD.Differences in brain structure and function and heredity are being studied. However it is very unusual to find treatable neurological difficulties as the cause of ADHD. Claims that allergies to foods or additives or vitamin deficiencies are responsible for ADHD have not been supported by research, and special diets do not typically result in drastic or long-lasting changes in an ADHD child's behavior.

Often ADHD is treated with medication. Not every ADHD child needs medication, but medication can be very effective in controlling some of the behaviors associated with ADHD. The most commonly used medications for ADHD are Ritalin and Cylert. These are thought to act on the attentional system by assisting the child in organizing and dealing with incoming information rather than being overwhelmed by it. With appropriate use, stimulant medications are reported to be safe and to have few side effects.

What can I do as a teacher?

Approach the ADHD child with an understanding of the underlying condition.

- Be aware of the child's limitations. This can help to reduce your frustrations in dealing with the ADHD child.

- Try to distinguish between behavior that is non-compliant (the child refuses to do something) and behavior that is the result of ADHD (the child can't do something). Treat these behaviors differently. Behaviors that a child can't do require instruction or development of a strategy for compensation. Behavior that is noncompliant requires disciplinary techniques designed to teach compliance and eliminate non-compliance, such as setting specific rules, reinforcing compliance, and removing a privilege or points for non-compliance.

- Interpret group test results cautiously. This child may have rushed through the test, answered impulsively, or have been distracted and not completed the test. Therefore, results may not be useful for determining skill levels for the ADHD child.

- Remember that medication is not a panacea. An ADHD child who has been placed on medication typically has strikingly improved behavior but often will not have acquired the same skills as other children. Extra instruction may be necessary.

- Take advantage of the energy and spontaneity of the ADHD child to help eliminate potential difficulties. For instance, when planning for a class play, the ADHD child may be quite successful at acting out the role of the wind which whooshes across the stage and may be quite frustrated (and frustrating to you and classmates) if cast as the father who stands quietly and observes before saying his one line.

- Provide for close supervision during unstructured times like recess to help control risk-taking and eliminate potential injuries.

Work with parents and other professionals.

- Ask parents for information about strategies which have been tried with their child in the past.

- Help parents locate resources for dealing with the manifestations of ADHD outside of school such as training in child management skills.

- Involve parents in using management strategies such as daily checklists or assignment sheets to help with behavior and assignment completion.

- Use in-school resources. The school psychologist may be willing to observe the ADHD child to assist you in identifying specific behaviors or times when interventions would be helpful. Techniques which the school psychologist may be able to assist with include the think aloud program or verbal self-monitoring.

- Refer the ADHD child who is displaying significant academic or behavior difficulties for a multi-factored evaluation.

- Monitor changes in the child's behavior. If the ADHD student is taking medication, work with the parents and physicians in completing behavior checklists or keeping logs or behaviors to help ensure that medication is providing optimal benefits.

Expect ADHD to be an on-going condition and plan for this chronicity. Behavior management strategies are likely to be necessary on an on-going basis throughout the elementary grades and often in middle school and high school. Strategies for elementary students require the teacher as manager. As the child gets older, he/she will need help in learning self-management strategies.

Ideas for Elementary Students Include:

- Special seating near you or slightly apart from classmates may help reduce effects of distractibility.
- Provision of short assignments, or longer assignments broken down into shorter segments, may increase task completion.
- Pairing assignments with a checklist on the child's desk on which he/she can check off completed tasks may help with assignment completion. After showing the child how to make the checklist, provide blank checklists for the child to fill it out each day.
- Extra reinforcement will probably be needed if the ADHD child is to learn and continue to follow classroom rules. Developing rule-governed behavior requires frequent reinforcement and clear statements of what behavior is being reinforced. Response cost strategies have proved to be effective with many ADHD children. Such strategies involve giving points for appropriate behaviors and having the child pay a fine (in points) for inappropriate behaviors. Response cost systems work best when the rules are very specific.
- Organization is particularly difficult for many ADHD children. Try using a checklist of what to take home from school each night. Divided notebooks can be useful if the student understands how to use them. Assist with organization of desk or locker space.

Ideas for Secondary Students Include:

- Since organization often continues to be a problem, assist this student with organizational strategies. For example, help the student learn how to use a divided notebook for different subject areas and check periodically to ensure that this system is being used.
- Have the student purchase a small assignment book and use it daily.
- Help the student learn to make and use checklists. For example, when several assignments need to be completed, have the student list them and check them off as they are completed. Similarly, a checklist of what to take home or bring back to school can be used.
- Plan long-term projects with the student using a calendar with specific dates on which tasks are to be completed. Check back periodically to see how the student is progressing.

Resources

Barkley, R. (1981) *Hyperactive children: A handbook for diagnosis and treatment.* New York: Guilford Press.

Camp, B., & Bash, M. (1981) *Think aloud* (Primary & Grade 1-2, 3-4, 5-6). Champaign, IL: Research Press

Goldstein, S., & Goldstein, M. (1989) *A teacher's guide: Attention-deficit hyperactivity disorder in children.* Available from the Neurology, Learning and Behavior Center 670 East 3900 South, Suite 100, Salt Lake City, Utah 84107.

Kendall, P. (1988) *Stop and think workbook.* Available from the author at 238 Meeting House Lane, Merion Station, PA 19066.

Taylor J. (1983) *The hyperactive child and the family.* New York: Dodd, Mead and Co.

NATIONAL
ASSOCIATION OF
SCHOOL
PSYCHOLOGISTS

Cheating

Bradford P. Underhill
University of South Florida

Background—Cheating is the use of fraudulent deception for the purpose of obtaining higher grades or scores. Not only is the deception of the teacher a consequence but also the public is deceived by believing the obtained scores to accurately reflect that student's ability and/or performance. Cheating includes copying, permitting others to copy, plagiarizing, ghostwriting, and using crib sheets. Estimates suggest that 40-50% of students have cheated at one time during their academic careers (Murphy, 1987).

Although one may be tempted to associate cheating with lower SES, Calabrese and Cochran (1990) have found that White males who attended private schools were more likely to cheat than students at a large urban school.

Development—Several causes of cheating have been identified. Personality characteristics that have been identified with higher rates of cheating include feelings of alienation, unfavorable comparisons between self and external competence standards, fear of failure, higher need for approval, and a preference for immediate gratification (Sinha & Singh, 1989). Environmental influences include parent and social pressure, economic pressure for low SES, school norms, and school pressure, meaningfulness of the curriculum, authoritarian teaching style, and work that is too easy or difficult.

Putting Cheating in Perspective—It is important to examine cheating behavior in its context prior to developing interventions. The forces in the environment that may be allowing the behavior to occur or setting it up as an escape or avoidance paradigm are also important to consider. These would include insufficient barriers within the classroom or testing situation, and no consequences for cheating. Children who might not otherwise cheat may engage in the behavior due to an excessively stressful situation or lack of external restraints. Additionally, the forces that may be in effect that reinforce or maintain the behavior need to be included in an assessment. When exploring the student characteristics that facilitate cheating behavior, perspectives provided by Kohlberg's stages of moral reasoning or that of the social learning theorists may yield hypotheses that can be verified and that can guide interventions. The moral reasoning approach assumes that cognitions prior to the behavior of cheating justify or guide the behavior. Social learning theorists on the other hand suggest that the behavior be viewed in the context of the situation in which the behavior occurs as well as the person's tendencies or their internal set of rules. This internal set of rules, which is a function of the history of reinforcement of the learned or modeled behavior, interacts with the perceived demands of the situation, peer group norms, and/or emotional arousal. As for emotional arousal, cheating behavior has been found to be influenced by emotional states such as anger, fear, guilt, and shame (Dienstbier & Hunter, 1971).

What Can I Do as a Teacher?—Primary prevention efforts could focus on restructuring the classroom to make cheating less possible by creating physical and emotional barriers. Physical barriers would include greater security of test materials and monitoring of tests and paper development. Emotional barriers would include moral discussions and group exercises. Educational programs can focus on the ramifications of cheating for the students and others. Positive reinforcement of honest behavior along with strategies for students to help themselves develop self-control would go a long way towards preventing cheating. Following the occurrence of cheating behavior there are several strategies that can be used. These interventions need an assessment of the factors that influence cheating including environmental factors of: stress, peer pressure and family pressure, and the child's moral development.

The first step is not to overreact. For a first time occurrence, explore how the child views his or her behavior. Nucci (1984) suggests that if the behavior is viewed by the student as immoral that it would be best to pursue interventions focusing on the morality of the behavior. If the student views the cheating as a violation of social conventions, a focus on the deviancy of the behavior is recommended.

Punishment needs to be used with discretion. Punishment alone provides no learning mechanism for future situations. Paradoxically, it can actually increase arousal and increase the likelihood of a repeat of the cheating behavior in future situations. Additionally the severity of the punishment can cause the child to focus on the punishment rather than the behavior.

What Can I Do as a Parent?—Again, do not overreact. Explore with your child why they felt the need to cheat. Discuss morality and the impact that cheating has on others. As an alternative to cheating, look at ways of helping your child enhance their study skills or increase effectiveness of their study time. Examine your and/or their pressure for grades. If you choose to punish your child, make the punishment fit the crime. One possibility includes overcorrection by having your child write a paper on the subject area on which she/he cheated.

Summary

When cheating occurs it is important to assess the behavior in the context in which it occurs to develop verifiable hypotheses that can lead to effective interventions. It is important to not only decrease the behavior but to build effective barriers both internally and externally. Careful assessment of the classroom, family, peers, and the student can lead to interventions that provide effective barriers and alternative behaviors for the future.

Resources

If the above suggestions do not seem to meet your needs, additional information and some specific interventions can be found in the following sources:

Murphy, J. P. (1987). Children and cheating. In A. Thomas & J.Grimes (Eds.), *Children's needs: Psychological perspectives* (pp. 305-311. Washington, DC: NASP.

Stokes, T. F., & Osnes, P. G. (1991). Honesty, lying, and cheating: Their elaboration and management. In G. Stoner, M. R. Shinn, & H. M. Walker (Eds.), *Interventions for achievement and behavior problems* (pp. 617-631). Silver Springs, MD: NASP.

Additional help can be obtained in your child's school from the school psychologist or guidance counselor. Private and public resources outside the school include your family physician, local community mental health service centers, minister, or other private practice professionals.

References

Calabrese, R. L., & Cochran, J. T. (1990). The relationship of alienation to cheating among a sample of American adolescents. *Journal of Research and Development in Education, 23*(2), 65-71.

Dienstbier, R. A., & Hunter, P. O. (1971). Cheating as a function of the labeling of natural arousal. *Journal of Personality and Social Psychology, 17,* 208-213 .

Murphy, J. P. (1987). Children and cheating. In A. Thomas & J. Grimes (Eds.), *Children's needs: Psychological perspectives* (pp. 305-311). Washington, DC: NASP.

Nucci, L. (1984). Evaluating teachers as social agents: Students' ratings of domain appropriate and domain inappropriate teacher responses to transgressions. *American Education Research, 21,* 367-378.

Sinha, S. P., & Singh, M. (1989). Some personality correlates of cheating behavior. *Indian Journal of Current Psychological Research, 4*(1), 48-51.

Stokes, T. F., & Osnes, P. G. (1991). Honesty, lying, and cheating: Their elaboration and management. In G. Stoner, M. R. Shinn, & H. M. Walker (Eds.), *Interventions for achievement and behavior problems* (pp. 617-631). Silver Springs, MD: NASP.

Gifted Children:
Special Needs and Considerations

Clyde J. Johnson and Betty E. Gridley
Ball State University, Muncie, Indiana

"Gifted" applies to many children if not to all. The term describes creativity, excellence in a traditional school subject, or an ability to press oneself eloquently at a young age. Many times the developed skill is overshadowed by the pressure of growing up or by physical or social disabilities. Regardless of the situation, abilities can be identified and encouraged with or without formal gifted programs.

Students often overlooked

- **Learning disabled gifted students.** These students have abilities that go unnoticed because of poor performance or failure in areas outside of their strengths.
- **Students with physical, neurological, and communication problems.** Attempts to evaluate and compensate for obvious problems distracts from developing advanced abilities.
- **Minorities and females.** Mixed messages and misunderstanding of cultural differences limits the expression and detection of developed skills that are not traditionally believed to reflect intelligence.
- **Young children.** Standardized testing is unreliable at young ages. Alternative sources for information can be gathered from the parent for instance.
- **Children with behavior problems.** Boredom, frustration, "daydreaming," are considered signs of a 'difficult' child. However, this may also indicate a need for specialized instruction.

Identification

Standardized testing and group evaluations limit the type of abilities that are measured and may introduce testing error. Skills not traditionally believed to indicate giftedness, such as musical or spatial abilities, may be overlooked. Use of an initial screening, evaluation of information from various sources, and individual case evaluations seems to be a proper three phase process for identifying gifted children. Scant resources may limit the use of all three phases. Compensation can be made by using some of the following sources:

- Examination of group scores.
- Nomination by teacher parents and peers.
- Past accomplishment evaluations: For example: poems, paintings, test performance.
- Creativity and achievement tests.
- Outstanding ratings for future potential.

Programming

The decision of how to deliver what service is made within the limits of the school's resources. A good match is attempted for the particular needs of the student. Most schools use a combination of the following two formats:

- The child remains in the classroom. Instruction occurs with children of the same age.
- The child is 'pulled-out' of the classroom and is taught with children having comparable talents.

Regardless of the instructional format, the services provided may be a combination of the following types:

- Accelerated instruction beginning early with more material being presented. For example, 2nd graders would be given 4th grade material.
- Information would be presented in a broader scope. This differs from offering information at a quicker pace in that an area of interest is explored in greater depth.

If formal programming is not available, a careful match between students' learning styles and presentation styles could still be adopted.

- A student bored with repetitious exercises may excel with material presented at a quicker pace.
- Students that become engrossed in a topic, found occasionally daydreaming, may benefit from a broader more enriched area of study.

Regardless of the format or instruction style, the gifted child's attention and sense of accomplishment can be increased by providing an enriched environment. Allowing the child to pursue his or her own interests provides the opportunity to explore areas in science, mathematics, and language. Providing materials in these areas along with organized adult guidance will encourage development of learning habits and the confidence to use them.

Socioemotional concerns

- Gifted children often are aware that their abilities make them different. Adult support and attention can alleviate some of these alienated feelings.
- Adults should keep expectations for the child at a reasonable level. The child may be gifted, however, other skills, such as fine motor control will develop at a normal rate. These skills may seem to lag other abilities.
- As children reach the age where conformity and group membership are important, their talents and interests will conflict with these pressures. Again, adult support would be helpful for understanding and acceptance to take place.
- Gifted children may have difficulty understanding some of society's double standards. Their moral sense is well-developed and may conflict with hypocrisy and other social contradictions. This may become problematic for the child.
- Adults must be careful not to become themselves envious of the student's abilities.
- Some helpful traits for the adult to practice when working with a gifted child are: to be intelligent; have a good sense of humor; be patient; try to be aware of differences between people; try to communicate effectively; be flexible; be firm and be organized.

Resources

Freeman, J. (1985). *The psychology of gifted children.* New York: Wiley. An edited book with several chapters exploring the most overlooked gifted, including sensory handicapped, culturally different, and females.

Gridley, B.E. (1987). Children and giftedness. In J. Grimes & A. Thomas (Eds.), *Children's needs: Psychological perspectives* (pp. 234-241). Kent, OH: National Association of School Psychologists. Two practical summary sources for information about gifted children.

McCluskey, K.W. & Walker K.D. (1986). *The doubtful gift: Strategies for educating the gifted child in the regular classroom.* Kingston, Canada: Ronald P. Frye. A very readable and concise guide including definitions, identification, and programming.

Renzulli, J.S. (Ed.). (1986). *Systems and models for developing programs for gifted and talented.* Mansfield Center CT: Creative Learning Press. Fifteen different models for programming for gifted students are described. Rationale, practical applications, and research and evaluation are included for all models.

Children and Giftedness

Betty E. Gridley and Shauna Gatten
Ball State University
Muncie, Indiana

Background—Interest in the development of gifted potential has historically taken a back seat to concern for children with problems. The number of truly gifted individuals may be fairly limited (2% or less of the population). The stereotype seems to be that parents consider all their children as "gifted," and parents do sometimes misjudge their children's capabilities. This may result from too little knowledge about normal development in children, and or the desire that their children will be more successful than they have been. In fact, many parents are just as concerned about having a "gifted" child as a handicapped one.

Who Are These Children? Early definitions narrowly focused on exceptional intellectual ability (i.e., high 1.0.) alone. The current trend, however, has moved toward a multidimensional view of giftedness which includes elements of creativity and special talents.

Early identification of gifted children has been found to be important as the preschool years are thought to represent a sensitive period for development. Enriched experiences play a substantial role in determining the extent to which early promise of superior ability becomes reality.

How Can I Tell as a Parent? Parents of gifted children are often initially alerted to their child's exceptional abilities by noticing that they start to do almost everything earlier than other children. Characteristics which may indicate such potential include.

1. CURIOSITY. Persistent curiosity; "bug" you with a lot of questions; more logical and searching questions; keen observational skills; desire to learn rapidly.

2. MEMORY. Good memory; retention of an extraordinary quantity and variety of information; broad changing spectrum of interests.

3. HIGHER-ORDER THINKING SKILLS. Ability to find and solve problems; understanding of complex concepts; ability to perceive relationships; ability to work with abstractions and to generalize; generate original ideas and solutions; strong critical thinking skills and self-criticism.

4. LANGUAGE. High level of language development; early, accurate use of advanced vocabulary; ability to reproduce stories and events with great detail at an early age.

5. PRECOCIOUSNESS. Precocity in physical and intellectual development such as early walking, talking, or reading; advanced expression of interest or talent in a specific area such as music.

6. ATTENTION AND CONCENTRATION. Longer attention span and ability to concentrate for longer periods than normal for child's age; persistent goal directed behavior; periods of intense concentration.

7. SOCIAL MATURITY. Tendency to prefer companionship of older children and adults; ability to converse intelligently with older children and adults; social maturity above that expected for age.

8. SENSE OF HUMOR. Keen sense of humor; often more insightful than peers; able to see subtle humor in a situation.

Potential Problems for Gifted Children. Gifted children often face a unique set of problems as a

145

result of their giftedness. While not all gifted children will experience such difficulties, it is important for parents to be aware of areas where the potential for problems exists.

1. Gifted children often feel "different" from their peers which can lead to feelings of isolation, loneliness and inadequate social interactions.

2. Gifted children and adolescents frequently place unrealistic pressures on themselves to perform. They may develop problems in accepting their own shortcomings as well as in experiencing unrealistic reactions to failure.

3. Parents often place undue emphasis on intellectual achievement and do not allow enough time for play.

4. Parental expectations range from putting extreme pressure on these children to succeed to an attitude that "they can get it on their own.

5. Problems can develop when parents expect the child's emotional development to keep pace with his/her intellectual development.

6. Often sibling and peer relations become strained and rivalries develop because the gifted child is singled out for attention.

How can I help?

1. Parents of gifted children are encouraged to provide appropriate opportunities for intellectual growth without accompanying pressures for success.

2. It is equally important for parents to allow their children to be children and permit time for unstructured activities.

3. Parents need to help children to understand that while they are unique in their giftedness, all children are unique in some way.

4. Parents can promote healthy attitudes in accepting failures as a normal part of growing up.

Resources

Clark B. (1979). *Growing Up Gifted.* Los Angeles: Merrill. The author provides strategies for developing and integrating the cognitive, intuitive, emotional and physical aspects of the gifted child. This is one of the most comprehensive books in the field.

Colangelo, N. & Dettman, D. F. (1985). A review of research on parents and families of gifted children. *Exceptional Children,* 5(1), 20-27 The authors discuss problems parents often create and provide useful parenting ideas.

Ehrlich, V. E. (1982). *Gifted Children.* New Jersey: Prentice-Hall. This book contains many facts that parents of the gifted should know before their child enters the classroom for the first time.

Schwartz, L. L. (1981). Are you a gifted parent of a gifted child? *Gifted Child Quarterly.* 25(1), 31-35. This is a comprehensive discussion of the skills needed and usual hazards involved in raising a gifted child. Excellent for parents.

Webb, J. T., Meckstroth, E. A., & Tolan, S. (1982). *Guiding the Gifted Child.* Columbus, Ohio: Ohio Publishing. The authors cover problems (i.e., stress, depression, underachievement) the gifted often encounter and answer many tough questions.

NATIONAL
ASSOCIATION OF
SCHOOL
PSYCHOLOGISTS

Children and Grades

(This handout is based on the work of several individuals. Primary among them is William Strein, D.Ed., University of Maryland, College Park.]

Background—Like it or not, all parents, teachers, and children have to deal with grades, especially with the traditional A, B, C, D, F system. Many children and parents attach primary importance to grades and are less concerned with teachers' written comments or checklist of strengths and weaknesses.

Grading is a controversial topic. Some experts believe that traditional letter grades breed competition among students, inevitably creating "winners" and "losers." Others fear that grades cause students to be overly dependent on the evaluation of teachers, resulting in decreased self-initiative and creativity. However, still other experts believe that grades motivate children to do well and that they provide a succinct evaluation of students' progress. Actually, research suggests that grades have different effects on different children. Many high-achieving children are motivated by grades and actually like school more when grades are given. However, many low-achieving children are not motivated by the threat of a low grade or by trying to get a high grade-a task which may seem insurmountable. For these children, grades may be more of a burden than a help.

It is helpful to understand what grades are and what they are not. Like test scores, grades are NOT an absolute measurement of a child's skills or knowledge. Rather, grades represent the teacher's professional judgment about the quality of the child's work in a particular subject area. Teachers usually base grades on a combination of factors. Also grades are relative, and teachers assign grades in relation to their own standards and the standards of the school in which they teach. Consequently, children's grades depend partly on the teacher that they have and the school that they attend. To fully understand the child's grades, you need to know what grading system a particular teacher uses. Grades may indicate several things: (1) mastery of a specific set of skills or knowledge, (2) improvement, (3) effort, or (4) ranking of a student's performance relative to other children.

Development—Many people wonder whether grades in elementary or high school relate to anything important beyond the school years. In research, little or no relationship is found between college grades and "real-life" outcomes, such as success on the job or in adult relationships. However, because colleges and many employers do place a high value on grades, they may relate to initial opportunities for employment or to college acceptance. So, the commonly held belief that students who receive better grades in school generally have more opportunities available to them and are more likely to succeed than those with poorer grades does have an element of truth to it. However, factors other than grades may be equally important. For instance, an employer may prefer an individual who had moderately high grades, participated in a variety of outside activities, and demonstrated a high level of motivation and good work skills over a student with top-notch grades who did not relate well to the interviewer when applying for a job and joined in no extracurricular activities in school.

Parents may ask whether their child's grades are likely to change much over time—will they improve or drop off as the child advances in school. Grades from year to year are moderately related to one another. elementary school grades tend to be predictive of high school grades. High school grades are typically the best single predictor of college performance. So, children who get average grades in the elementary school are typically average performers throughout school. The same is generally true for students whose grades are considerably above or below average.

This does not mean, however, that some students who begin school with a slow start and need remedial help may not get high grades later or that a student who does very well in first grade will do very well throughout school. As with life beyond school, a variety of factors impact on children so, for instance, a good remedial reading program may get a slow-starter on track or unfortunate circumstances may result in later difficulties for the first grade star. Additionally, a student who moves to a new school or gets a new teacher that has a very different style or very different grading standards may show a sudden shift in grades. However, students who are having serious academic problems in one school will usually still have trouble in another school because the causes of the problem still remain.

Another question is whether students who do well in one subject should be expected to do well in all others or whether grades will vary considerably from one subject to another. Although most students do a bit better or worse in one subject or another, there is often a pattern among grades and a student who earns A's in math does not typically earn D's in language arts. Again, however, a variety of factors are involved, and it is possible for a student to do very well in math but need help in reading.

Although it is unusual, it is not unknown for students to be in a gifted program in one area and need help in another. Also, most students are better at certain kinds of things than others. For instance, some children may do very well when asked to memorize answers but are at loss when required to devise creative solutions. If the kinds of things that a student is required to do in school in order to get a high grade shift away from the child's strengths, grades may fall. Similarly, children who have difficulty learning to work on their own may get lower grades as they progress through school and teachers begin to expect more independent work.

What can I do as a parent?

1. Don't place more importance on grades than they deserve. Instead, with the help of your child's teacher, identify your child's strengths and determine areas that need improvement. Rather than working with your child with the goal of getting good grades, try some of the following tips and improved grades should follow.

    a. Work with your child in developing good study habits.

    b. Help your child develop ways to work independently by helping establish schedules and teaching your child how to plan ahead.

    c. Teach your child a sense of responsibility for and pride in school work.

    d. Make sure to notice what your child does well and offer praise for this.

2. Be careful of monetary rewards for good grades. If children are already trying their best and getting intrinsic satisfaction from what they do in school, adding the extrinsic or outside reward of money may reduce the personal satisfaction of a job well done.

3. Establish realistic expectations for your child's grades. Learn what is realistic for your child and then praise your child for good effort and doing his/her best.

4. Attend carefully to any comments or notes that the teacher makes on the report card. These often tell you more than does the grade. If you have concerns or if you don't really understand what the grades mean, contact the teacher and discuss your child's progress. Plan your questions in advance and be sure to ask for specific tips on how to help your child.

5. Don't be alarmed if your child's grades change somewhat or if your child occasionally brings

home a grade which does not meet your expectations. Remember that children go through a variety of normal changes in growing up and that their performance may occasionally show the effects of this.

6. Do attend to a steady pattern of lower grades or a sudden large decline in grades. For example, if your child has always received A's and B's and then brings home several D's, talk to your child's teacher, the school psychologist or counselor, or the principal. Look at everything that is going on in your child's life and consider what might be responsible for this sudden change.

7. If your child is having a serious problem with grades, don't be too quick to move the child to another school in the hope that things will get better. It will likely be much more helpful to attempt to identify the causes of the low grades and to look for ways to help your child in the current environment.

8. Many parents have strong feelings about grades, and school policies on grading are often very much influenced by parents' preferences and opinions. If this is a topic that interests you, get involved. The local parent/school organization (PTA, PTO. . .) might be a good place to start. Find out what the school's policy is on grading, what has been tried in the past, and if any changes are anticipated. Talk to other parents and find out about the grading policies in neighboring schools. Use this information when the opportunity comes for shaping your school's grading policy.

NATIONAL
ASSOCIATION OF
SCHOOL
PSYCHOLOGISTS

Homework

Erika Manz
University of South Florida

Background—It is argued that both the quality and the quantity of homework affect student learning. Research indicates that the time students spend on homework has an important effect on their achievement and students assigned homework achieve at a higher level than those that are assigned none. Math homework in elementary school may improve arithmetic computation, problem-solving skills, and concept understanding. Homework that is graded or commented on has a stronger impact on achievement than homework that is not. Homework that is well planned and closely tied to the instruction in the classroom appears to be more effective than irrelevant assignments. Consequences for homework completion and noncompletion as well as parental checking of assignments may add to its effectiveness. Homework may have a compensatory effect, allowing less able students to compensate for their lower ability through increased study. Homework develops good work habits, gives an opportunity for practice and review, and offers an assessment of the student's understanding of classroom lessons.

Development—Homework should change at different ages and at different grade levels. The time spent working on homework should vary depending on age and grade level of the student. There is a wide variability within a classroom in regard to the time it may take for students to complete their assignments. The purposes and types of homework assignments should also vary by grade level and subject matter and can be classified as practice, preparation, extension, and creative homework.

An obvious factor that influences the effectiveness of homework is whether or not the child completes the homework assignments. There are several strategies parents and teachers can use to ensure that children complete their homework assignments.

1. Parents should be made aware by the teacher of the types and amount of homework their child will be expected to complete. Homework should be sent home with complete instructions so that parents are able to guide their child if necessary.

2. Parents can request that a daily assignment log be sent home with their child so that homework assignment completion can be monitored.

3. A consequence system can be developed by the parents, teacher, and child to motivate the child to complete his/her assignments. For instance, a system may be set up in which the child is able to earn points for each completed assignment. These points can be saved and put toward a reward.

4. Assignments focusing on novel subject matter that appear too difficult for the child should be modified or abbreviated so that the child can experience success while learning new material.

5. A peer tutor can be used to help students who have difficulty completing assignments by helping them stay focused on the assignments and guiding them through new material.

This paper was adapted from a chapter entitled, "Children and Homework" in Children's Needs: Psychological Perspectives by Timothy Z. Keith.

Increasing Academic Learning Time
Teacher Handout

Maribeth Gettinger
University of Wisconsin-Madison

Overview

The amount of time during which students are learning from group lessons or individual study is called productive, active, or, most commonly, academic learning time (ALT). Only a fraction of the total amount of time allocated for instruction, sometimes as little as 25%, is actually spent in learning. Recent effective-teaching research has shown that when students' ALT is increased, a concomitant increase in achievement will likely occur, especially for low-achieving students. Furthermore, ALT is considered to be a manipulable facet of classrooms, one resource that teachers can control through effective teaching and managerial practices.

To plan strategies for increasing ALT, it is necessary to first analyze how time is used. Teachers can keep logs of how time is allocated and used during a typical day or week. Such a time-profile assessment enables teachers to focus efforts directly on time components that need improvement. Learning time is composed of four components: (a) allocated time, which may be reduced by interruptions, transitions, and other non instructional activities; (b) instructional time, which may be only 50% to 90% of allocated time and is further reduced by students' inattentiveness and disruptiveness; (c) engaged time, typically 45% to 90% of instructional time and often reduced by inappropriate instruction; and (d) ALT, ranging from 40% to 90% of engaged time.

What can I do as a teacher?

Based on this disaggregation of learning time and an assessment of time use within each component, teachers can increase ALT in three general ways: (a) increase the proportion of allocated time that is actually used for instruction; (b) work to increase on-task or engaged time among students; and (c) enhance the productivity of learning time by matching instruction to individual needs and monitoring performance.

Increase instructional time

Teachers who are task-oriented and who plan and organize their teaching activities use more daily allocated time for actual instruction than teachers who do not plan as carefully. Effective time-management strategies for increasing instructional time include:

- **Establish contingencies for school attendance and punctuality.**
  - Reinforce attendance and punctuality consistently through praise, points, monthly certificates, or within-class competition.

- Structure classroom routines so that being present and on time are expected, e.g., give instruction for daily activities only once at the start of a class session.
- Adhere to a strict daily schedule; start and stop classes or lessons exactly on time.

- **Minimize interruptions.**
  - Schedule specific times for managerial, noninstructional activities, e.g., collecting money, cleaning up, making announcements.
  - Limit students' disruptiveness and the number of teacher reprimands for misbehavior; misbehavior can be minimized by establishing explicit rules for behavior and consistent consequences for compliance and noncompliance with rules.

- **Facilitate smooth transitions.**
  - Develop, teach, and practice step-by-step procedures for activity shifts.
  - Provide brief verbal cues, rather than lengthy instructions, for activities.
  - Prepare all materials for each activity before the day begins.
  - Reinforce smooth, quick transitions, e.g., time students during activity shifts and have them compete with one another or against a predetermined criterion.

- **Maintain a strong academic focus.**
  - Allocate group time for academic subjects and schedule short time blocks for individualized practice for students who require extra time.
  - Use peer tutors or parent volunteers to provide additional academic review time.
  - Schedule preferred activities immediately after less preferred ones; important activities should occur during students' peak levels of attending and functioning.

Increase Engaged Time

Teachers who exhibit structured, interactive, fast-paced, and directive teaching styles have students who are more highly engaged in learning. Teaching behaviors that maximize attention during whole-group instruction as well as independent seatwork include:

- **Clarify instructions and performance expectations.**
  - Have students write, repeat, or paraphrase task directions to ensure understanding; post classroom rules.
  - Keep task instructions worded simply and few in number; include precise statements of what students are expected to do.
  - Break tasks down into small segments and demonstrate steps for completing assignments.
  - During independent seatwork, move throughout the classroom monitoring children, praising students who follow directions, and administering consequences for those who do not comply.

- **Maintain an interactive teaching style.**
  - Include all students in discussions and provide frequent opportunities for student responding, e.g., choral responding, calling on students, asking students to comment on others' responses.
  - Use fast-paced, teacher-directed instruction and practice.
  - Maintain optimal difficulty level of instruction and questions to ensure that responding and feedback are primarily positive.

- **Adopt seating arrangements to encourage attending.**
  - Use seating that permits visual contact with all students.

- Move around the room continuously, going to students rather than having students come to the teacher.

Increase productive learning time

Although increasing instructional time and maintaining student engagement are important, the overall quality of teaching during instructional or engaged time and the appropriateness of instruction for individual students affect the amount of ALT that students receive. Students who attain high levels of productive learning time are likely to achieve more than students who accumulate less time. Guidelines for enhancing the quality of instruction include:

- **Use seatwork effectively.**
  - Monitor seatwork by moving around the room systematically; keep contacts with individual students brief.
  - Establish clear procedures about what students should do when work is completed; have alternative activities for fast students.
  - Develop a procedure for requesting and obtaining assistance that is not disruptive and allows students to continue working while they wait; e.g., an assistance report card attached to desks that students use to signal the teacher.

- **Provide immediate, corrective feedback.**
  - Feedback should indicate whether responses are correct and provide suggestions for reworking incorrect problems.
  - Strive for greater frequency, specificity, and academic relevance in corrective feedback.
  - To minimize time demands, correct students' work while circulating during seatwork periods, use self-correction, or have students correct each other's work.

- **Diagnose, prescribe, and monitor performance accurately.**
  - Assess students' current knowledge, skill level, and strengths and weaknesses to determine appropriate instructional goals, task difficulty, grouping, and scheduling.
  - Monitor students' performance during actual instruction, e.g., accuracy of responding when students are engaged in group or individual learning.

Resources

American Association of School Administrators. (1982) *Time on task: Using instructional time more effectively.* Arlington, VA: Author. Available from: American Association of School Administrators, 1801 N. Moore St., Arlington, VA 22209.

Gettinger M. (1986). Issues and trends in academic engaged time of students. *Special Services in the Schools,* 2(4), 1-17.

Paine, S. C., Radicchi, J., Rosellini, L. C., Deutchman, L., & Darch, C. B. (1983). *Structuring your classroom for academic success.* Champaign, IL: Research Press. Presents procedures for keeping students actively engaged in learning and making the most efficient use of class time. Highly practical approach with step-by-step description of techniques.

Steere, B. F. (1988). *Becoming an effective classroom manager: A resource for teachers.* Albany NY: SUNY Press. Reviews teachers' effectiveness research and presents practical suggestions for teachers.

NATIONAL ASSOCIATION OF SCHOOL PSYCHOLOGISTS

Children and Limited English Proficiency
Teacher Handout

Diane Kriger Wilen
Broward County, Florida Public Schools

Background—Cultural diversity is widespread within the United States and is mirrored within American schools. With this diversity come large numbers of children whose native language is not English and who may be described as Limited English Proficient (LEP). According to the U.S. General Accounting Office, there are varying estimates of the numbers of LEP children of school ages (5 to 17 years old) residing in the United States. Figures ranging from 1.2 to 2.6 million have been reported depending upon the indicators used. There are very large populations of LEP students in California, New York, Texas, Illinois, New Mexico, Arizona, New Jersey, and Florida. However LEP students are present to some degree in virtually every state. Many of these LEP students are immigrants and refugees, but some were born in the United States. School dropout rates are often high among LEP populations.

The availability of bilingual education programs for LEP students differs across states and school districts. A minimum number of LEP students per grade, school, and school district who are of the same language minority or of any language minority may be required prior to establishing a bilingual program. Thus, some students may not receive specialized services for their Limited English Proficiency. Even if LEP students receive bilingual education services, their teachers may neither speak their home language nor have direct experience with their culture.

Development—Previous life experiences, family issues, behavioral adjustment, and academic performance are all important for teachers to consider in evaluating the current status of LEP students.

Life Experiences—LEP children have often been exposed to stressful or traumatic life experiences at a very young age. They may have endured war political strife, separation from parents and siblings, frequent moves, poverty, hunger overpopulated refugee camps, dangerous exoduses from their countries, and general uprooting. Others who are in the United States illegally live in fear of the authorities.

Medically, many LEP children are in need of services which may not have been affordable or available to them in their countries. Vision, hearing, general physical and dental exams are often indicated.

Educationally, some LEP students have a history of inconsistent schooling. Many come from countries where education is not mandatory or even available to all children. Children may have attended overcrowded schools with limited resources. Some may have been forced to drop out of school to go to work while others, especially those with mental or physical handicaps, may have been denied education in their native countries. Lack of availability of special education programs for handicapped children may actually have been the impetus for coming to the United States.

Culturally, LEP children come to school with a set of experiences, customs and values which differ from those of most other students. They may celebrate different holidays and may not be familiar with American celebrations such as Halloween and Thanksgiving. Often, they eat different foods and have different meal times. Their clothing may be different. They may have different standards of etiquette. They may write their names in a different order (e.g., last, middle, first for Vietnamese) or may not write the date according to the United States custom of month, day, year (e.g., day, month, year for Hispanics). They may have different concepts of time and punctuality.

Family Issues—Because families of LEP children often lack English literacy, they can have difficulty participating in the educational process of their children. They may have trouble helping with homework and may feel inadequate to attend conferences or ask questions of educators. Often, they have different childrearing practices and values. What may be perceived by American teachers as over indulgence and lack of responsibility may be appropriate in a LEP family's culture.

Behavioral Adjustment—LEP children may manifest behaviors ranging from passivity to acting out upon entering the American school. They often experience temporary adjustment problems because of all of the stresses and changes they face in adapting to a new country, language, culture, school, and life situation. They need time to adjust to their new environment.

Academic Performance—LEP children come to school with varying degrees of literacy in their own language and in English. Their language may not have the same alphabet as English and may be written in a different fashion (e.g., Hebrew has different characters and is written from right to left). This may make learning English even harder. They may have experienced different teaching styles (e.g., more emphasis on rote as opposed to analytical methods). English oral communication skills are generally mastered more quickly than reading and writing language skills. Learning to read in English is often easier to those already literate in their native language. Current academic performance should be interpreted in light of educational background and life experiences. LEP students may have started school at a different age than is customary in the United States and may have come from schools where grade levels do not correspond with the K-12 system.

What can I do as a teacher?

- Learn as much about the cultural and language background of LEP students by reading, attending courses, and speaking with minority language groups.
- Ask LEP students by what name they would like to be addressed and pronounce it correctly.
- Pair a new LEP student with a veteran LEP student who can be a "buddy" and who preferably speaks the same language as the LEP student.
- Encourage homework hotlines staffed by bilingual teachers or aides to assist LEP students.
- Teach survival English first (e.g. bathroom, cafeteria, book, pencil) and label common objects in the classroom in English.
- Use a dictionary which contains translations from English to the child's native language and vice versa.
- Pair visual cues and nonverbal gestures with verbal communication in the classroom. Speak English slowly and give short, concise directions. Observe LEP children to see if they understand what they are to do. Repetition may be needed.
- Use mechanical aids such as language masters, tape recorders, overhead projectors, and computers and hands-on experiences to reinforce learning.
- Enhance self-image and cultural pride by
  - encouraging presentations about native foods, customs, costumes, dances and holidays.
  - encouraging learning about famous minority language individuals.
  - encouraging participation in extracurricular activities, and

- encourage development of talents and special abilities.
- Encourage parent participation by calling the family if they do not respond to notes sent home by using social workers to make home visits, and by communicating with parents in their native language whenever possible. The use of interpreters or bilingual school staff can often facilitate the latter.
- If students exhibit academic or behavior problems which appear unusual or extreme in comparison to other LEP students, seek help from other professionals such as school psychologists, social workers and counselors.

Resources

Feeley, Joan T. (1983). Help for the reading teacher. Dealing with the limited English proficient (LEP) child in the elementary classroom. *The Reading Teacher,* 36(7), 650-655. This article discusses techniques teachers can use to help LEP students with reading in the regular classroom.

Gollnick, Donna M., & Chinn, Philip C. (1986) *Multicultural Education in a Pluralistic Society.* Columbus, OH: Charles E. Merrill. This book discusses influences of cultural background and diversity on students and presents multicultural educational strategies.

The following are available from the National Clearinghouse for Bilingual Education, 1118 22nd Street, NW, Washington, DC 20037 telephone 800-321-NCBE and 202-467-0867.

- *Refugee Immigrant Education Materials Catalog.* This catalog includes listings of materials related to the education of Vietnamese, Cambodian, Laotian, Chinese, Spanish, Haitian, Ethiopian, Polish, Armenian, and other LEP populations.
- *Forum.* This free bimonthly newsletter contains timely articles and information on the education of LEP populations.
- *Products List.* This annotated listing provides easy access to materials on topics such as issues in bilingual education, curriculum and instruction, language and linguistics, ethnic and minority populations, parent and community involvement, and culture.

NATIONAL
ASSOCIATION OF
SCHOOL
PSYCHOLOGISTS

Children and Organizational Skills

Gail Epstein Mengel
Longmeadow, MA Public Schools

Background—The ability to organize and be organized is often taken for granted. As a result, when organizational skills are lacking, the failure that occurs is often mistakenly blamed on laziness, lack of motivation, irresponsibility, procrastination, confusion, or avoidance. Whether the task is organizing spaces, materials, information, or procedures, however, weak organizational skills can be a genuine obstacle to learning and performance. Not selective, it can affect young and old, rich and poor, gifted and slower learner. It can cause failure among bright children and fuel emotional distress in emotionally healthy children. When understood for the problem that it is, however, disorganization can be helped by the guidance and structure of parents and teachers.

Development—Because organizational skills have gotten only limited attention in research studies (mostly related to academic application-study skills), little is actually written about how they develop and grow. Parents may recognize certain telltale clues in their children or their past development that are common among disorganized children, however. These include having trouble with concepts of place and time (such as above, below, left and right; before, after, tomorrow, yesterday), learning sequences by rote (the "ABC song," the days of the week, months of the year), learning how to tell time and estimate its duration, and understanding the sequences of events. Handedness may have not been readily established. Language may have developed later than expected and finding the right word to express thought may be a weakness. Telling stories, jokes, or directions in order may reveal difficulty. Recalling a series of directions can be taxing.

Handwriting often contains reversals of letters, mixes capital letters with lower case letters, is hard to read and poorly spaced, is not written on the lines, and has "wandering columns." These children frequently lose their possessions, have messy workspaces, cannot maintain focused attention, manage their time poorly, have trouble remembering the daily or weekly schedule, and require structure, boundaries, and clear limit-setting. Histories of accident-proneness and clumsy coordination are not untypical.

To disorganized children, information they take in through their various senses seems to defy being sorted, classified, and categorized in meaningful or logical ways. They often fail to see the patterns and routines of simple procedures or everyday events. They become easily confused and sometimes disoriented. In a very real sense, they are frequently unsure of "which end is up."

What can I do as a parent?

Determine where the organization falters and create systems, strategies, routines and checklists to bridge these gaps. Make these systems apparent to the youngster (devise them cooperatively when working with adolescents and older children), and use them consistently. Point out how the system can be applied to similar tasks and procedures by highlighting the common patterns among the tasks that lend them this common management.

Make children conscious of how objects, ideas, and procedures are alike, the traits and characteristics they share, and how they might be grouped in various ways. Encouraging these sorting, categorization, and classification skills helps them to search for the underlying organization and patterns among and between things.

Show children how tasks are broken down into smaller steps so that they can see how the "whole" is built from the parts. This makes the large multi-stepped tasks less overwhelming and easier to approach. Awareness of time and time management is frequently a problem in the disorganized child. Make children aware of the passage of time and of time "markers" in the day, such as mealtimes, favorite TV show times. Time how long various tasks and chores take, have "races against time," and assign duties or consequences for specified amounts of time to increase time awareness.

When organizing, start small-in one place, step, or category at a time-and complete the organization within it before moving to another place, step, or category. This gives a more immediate sense of accomplishment and encourages continued involvement.

Devise checklists for long-term tasks or tasks with many steps. This helps to highlight the specific details of a job, and provides a sense of accomplishment as each completed step is crossed off the list.

For shorter term or simpler tasks, a checklist may be replaced by memory "triggers" that help to represent the steps to be taken. For example, going out the door to school each morning a student might, need to remember Books, Homework, Money and a Snack. A memory trigger "Bears Hate Milk Shakes conjures up an immediate image that can be easily remembered and triggers the memory for the items by the beginning letter of each word.

Organizing materials and possessions (as in cleaning up a desk or a room) and information (as in sorting through a mass of papers) is similar to sorting cards, somewhat like Solitaire. The objective is to sort according to similar groupings until all items and information are exhausted.

Organizing requires knowing how to make decisions-to include or exclude elements of a group— knowing where to "draw the lines" and make the boundaries. Teach and reinforce decision-making skills through modeling and discussion. Model how you make a decision by "talking it through" out loud, so the process can be observed and the important elements to the decision-making can be seen. "Talking it through" can also be used specifically to show how you are organizing materials and ideas.

Organizing requires "taking charge" and feeling in control of the situation. You can help increase the sense of control by allowing room for children's own decision-making. This can be done by presenting alternatives for them to choose from even though those alternatives may be selected by the parent.

Expect disorganization in adolescents' bedrooms or try not to be too disturbed about it unless it threatens the health and welfare of the youngster or the rest of the family.

Sometimes adolescents are disorganized because they have no goals or reason to become organized. Helping them to understand their strengths and abilities, interests, and aptitudes can provide some direction for future planning. This in turn can motivate them to set more immediate objectives for which to become more organized.

Stress and depression can fuel disorganization. Be alert to signs of unusual stress, agitation, decreased concentration, or increased social isolation, and changes in appearance, appetite, or sleep patterns. These may suggest that further assistance is needed to address emotional needs.

Resources

Smith, S.L. (1979). *No Easy Answers: Teaching the Learning Disabled Child.* Winthrop. This detailed description of the disorganized child is complete and untechnical. It helps parents who need and want to understand their learning disabled child thoroughly. It addresses parents' feelings and concerns, and suggests practical methods of dealing with these children and their organization problems at home.

Winston S. (1978). *Getting Organized.* Warner Books. This book provides practical, action-oriented, step-by-step methods for physically organizing all aspects of personal living, including time management, setting up and reorganizing a desk, establishing a filing system, organizing storage, and helping children's personal organization.

NATIONAL
ASSOCIATION OF
SCHOOL
PSYCHOLOGISTS

Using Peer-influenced Academic Interventions in the Classroom
Teacher Handout

David W. Peterson and Janice Miller

Overview of Peer-Influenced Interventions

Peer tutoring and cooperative learning methods facilitate interactions among students in order to increase academic achievement, enhance positive relationships among classmates, and improve attitudes toward school and self. By using these techniques, teachers can better address the individual learning needs of *all* the students in their classrooms.

The Regular Education Initiative (REI) focuses on the need to increase the effectiveness of instruction within the regular education classroom in order to avoid unnecessary labeling and segregation within special education. Peer-influenced interventions, with a strong research base in allocated learning time, assist in meeting the needs of high-risk learners in regular education.

Peer tutoring and cooperative learning methods can be used to reinforce and remediate basic skills, to promote critical thinking, and to enhance communication and interpersonal skills. Although there are differences between peer tutoring and cooperative learning techniques, both are important components of an effective classroom.

Cooperative Learning

Background

A wide variety of cooperative learning methods share an emphasis on setting a goal for a group of students and rewarding the group for their performance. This format actively encourages students to work together, to share information, and to support each other's learning.

Establishing a group goal motivates students to help one another. Research also suggests rewarding the group based on the combined performance of the individual members of the group. This helps ensure that no one member of the group does all the work. Teachers should base the group's reward or recognition on each student's learning within the group.

There is some controversy on the importance of social interaction in cooperative learning in order to promote achievement. However, students do achieve more if they give and receive help in response to other students' requests. The peer tutoring that can go on in groups may help students "think aloud," may lessen student anxiety in learning, or may be more easily understood than instruction provided by the teacher.

163

Implementing Cooperative Learning Programs

Selection of a Program

Start small. Teachers should try one method in one curriculum area. Next, teachers should consider what goal(s) they wish to achieve: increase achievement, improve self-esteem, improve student relationships? Different methods will achieve different goals. In addition, some methods are more appropriate for certain subject areas than others. Finally, those methods employing more explicit peer tutoring are easier to implement with less mature learners.

Setting Up Cooperative Groups

- Group Size: Younger students or those less experienced in group work should be placed into small groups initially. Limited material to be shared and limited time for group work also require smaller groups.
- Arrangement of Classroom: Arrange classrooms so that group members can see and hear each other. Also, students should be able to move from cooperative groups to individual work sites throughout the day.
- Assignment of Students: Generally, heterogeneity in groups (having students of varying ability, race, or sex) is important. whenever possible, teachers should assign students (i.e., rank order on achievement) to mixed groups.
- Measurement of Performance: The performance of the group may be measured by combining individual scores, assigning points for cooperative behavior in groups, randomly selecting and grading one student's paper from the group, or grading a group paper or presentation.
- Individual Accountability: In order to ensure that every student in the group participates, teachers can assign each student one part of the group task, can assign each student a role in the group (such as praiser, checker, recorder), or can use the results of individual tests to determine group rewards/recognition.
- Parent Communication: In order to respond to possible parent questions or concerns, teachers should develop a communication plan. A letter, newsletter, or meeting with parents before cooperative learning is implemented is recommended.
- Group Skills: Students may need to be taught how to work cooperatively in a group. Teachers can initially give students nonacademic tasks in a group, have students observe a group effectively working together, or establish contingencies for appropriate group behavior.

Peer Tutoring

Background

Peer tutoring contrasts with cooperative learning in that it usually involves students working in pairs, one as the tutor, and the other as the student. Peer tutoring increases student achievement by reinforcing ongoing classroom instruction, remediating skill deficits, and providing additional practice opportunities which are essential to effective learning.

Research clearly supports the effectiveness of peer tutoring, especially when programs are highly structured and sequentially organized. Peer tutoring is effective with students of all ages and abilities including "high-risk," learning disabled, behavior disordered, and mentally retarded students. Peer tutoring can be used in almost any content area, but is most frequently used in reading, math, and spelling.

Implementing Peer Tutoring Programs

Tutor Training

Thorough tutor training will often ensure a successful program. Training programs should specifically teach tutors how to: 1) organize and use instructional materials; 2) maintain the "student's" attention during the sessions using **positive** techniques, as well as use teaching behaviors which are positive and do not punish mistakes; 3) set clear expectations for the student's learning; 4) give clear directions regarding the ways in which students should respond (i.e., "when I point to the problem, you give the answer quietly"); 5) use proven error correction methods (e.g., model, lead, test), as well as cues and prompts; 6) praise correct responses; and 7) measure student progress and maintain records. **It is important that tutors, regardless of ability level, role play and practice these skills before beginning tutoring.**

Establishing Tutoring Pairs

While common sense should prevail in the selection and assignment of tutoring pairs, the following guidelines are suggested: 1) older students who are relatively proficient in the subject matter will probably be the best tutors; 2) nevertheless, do not rule out tutors with skill deficiencies. They can be paired with younger "students" (cross-age tutoring) to minimize their deficits and improve their skills as they teacher; 3) select tutors who are sensitive to others, responsible, and motivated to teach (seek the recommendations of other teachers); and 4) monitor compatibility during the program and do not hesitate to make changes if students are not doing well together.

Lesson Content

Lesson content should be closely related to the skills being taught in the classroom to promote generalization and the efficiency of classroom learning. Select key skills that are important to continuing success in the selected subject matter and ignore supplementary skills that are not essential. Develop lesson materials that: 1) are easy to use, 2) enable children to respond in a consistent fashion, and 3) provide tutors with structure. Drill and practice tasks are sometimes easier for younger children.

Supervising, Scheduling, and Maintaining the Program

It is important to closely supervise tutoring, especially in the early stages of the program. Observe and, if necessary, provide additional instruction in praising, effective teaching, etc. Students may also need assistance in record keeping.

Schedule tutoring sessions in collaboration with other teachers to minimize conflicts. If possible, tutoring should occur on a daily basis and sessions should be brief (20 to 30 minutes). In order to maintain a smoothly operating program, provide regular recognition for tutors and students. Hosting a luncheon, sending notes to parents, and sending articles to the school newspaper or board newsletter will all provide much deserved recognition to students and teachers for their hard work.

Evaluating Student Progress

Those using peer-influenced interventions should include a method for measuring students' gains. We strongly recommend the use of direct, daily measurements rather than norm-referenced tests. For example, measuring the number of words read correctly during a one-minute timing (cwpm) will provide a more accurate and sensitive measure of reading progress than any standardized test. Classroom test scores can also be evaluated to determine if carry-over is occurring. Teachers may also wish to ask students to evaluate the program and their own progress, and teacher-made attitude surveys can be used to assess affective gains.

Resources

Ehly, S. (1986). *Peer Tutoring A Guide for School Psychologists*. Washington, DC: National Association of School Psychologists. A step-by-step guide with useful tips on training tutors. An accompanying videotape is also available from NASP.

Jenkins, J. R., and Jenkins, L. M. (1981). *Cross Age and Peer Tutoring Help for Children with Learning and Behavior Problems*. Reston, VA: Council for Exceptional Children. An excellent summary that is a must for anyone starting a tutoring program.

Kagan, S. (1989). *Cooperative Learning: Resources for Teachers*. Laguna Niguel, CA: Resources for Teachers. An excellent compilation of practical cooperative learning techniques.

NATIONAL
ASSOCIATION OF
SCHOOL
PSYCHOLOGISTS

Reading

Bonnie Matthews
University of South Florida

Background—Reading is the process of deriving meaning from written information. It is probably one of the most commonly used skills in our society. The ability to read seems not only to be highly valued by our society but also expected. It is necessary for gaining independence and achieving success in most areas of our culture. Yet, many individuals are severely lacking in this ability. According to a report cited by Spadafore (1987), it has been estimated that 10-15% of school-age children will encounter reading difficulties. Consistent with this, the National Institute of Education reports that 13% of the 17-year-old students who graduate from high school are functionally illiterate (Anderson, Hiebert, Scott, & Wilkinson, 1985).

There is much agreement among professionals that reading, comprehending, thinking with language, and communicating with the written word are cultural phenomena. Although formal reading instruction is usually carried out by the school system, it is generally agreed that the development of these skills is affected by a child's home and family environment. In spite of the fact that there are many reasons that some children have difficulty in reading, there are a number of ways that parents can have a positive impact on the development of reading skills in their children.

Development—From very early on in a child's life, the foundation for success in reading is being laid. It is generally agreed that there are a number of stages in reading development. Spadafore (1987) outlined these stages as follows. Children aged 2-5 years are in the prereading stage. During this time children begin to acquire language development such as expressive (speaking) and receptive (understanding words) language. Sensory skills such as auditory and visual processing are also developing. Social maturation is occurring in the areas of increasing attention span and curiosity.

Children aged 6-7 are considered to be in the beginning reading stage. Typically, they are developing decoding skills such as letter sounds, sound symbol relationships, and sight word reading. They are better able to express (discuss) that they are understanding language. Also, they are developing interest areas and attitudes toward reading.

Children aged 6 or 7 through age 13 are usually considered to be in the basic reading stage. During the ages of about 8-11, children typically are able to learn higher level decoding skills such as word attack skills, silent reading, oral reading, improved speed and accuracy, word list reading, and paragraph reading. These children are also building comprehension skills such as knowing the literal meaning of words and being able to infer word meaning from context of words with which they are not yet familiar. Additionally, they are learning listening comprehension. Finally, beginning at about the age of 8 they are learning vocabulary skills such as root words, prefixes, and suffixes and word meanings. At about the age of 11 most children can read for fact finding. They often seem to be motivated to learn by reading. Finally, they show increasing vocabulary development. There is consensus that early identification of reading problems and early intervention is important to help a child develop good reading skills. If you see signs of a reading problem, the following questions should be considered:

—Is the level at which my child is reading appropriate for his/her age?

—Does the problem seem to be in a specific area of prereading or reading skills or does it seem to be in all areas of reading?

—Are there specific physical or mental limitations that my child has which may affect the child's reading or learning to read?

—Is the reading problem having a great effect on the child's school performance and functioning?

If the child's reading, for whatever reason, is hindering his school performance then it should be addressed as early on as possible. Assistance can be obtained in determining the nature and scope of the child's reading problem.

The Causes of Reading Problems—There are many possible reasons that a child may be experiencing difficulty in reading. The child may have problems in the area of vision, memory, processing (auditory and/or visual), lack of exposure (the child may not have seen many books, may not have been read to often, or because of lack of reading in the home may not think that reading is worthwhile), lack of motivation (the child may not see a reason to read), anxiety (parental expectations may be too high and the child is afraid to attempt reading for fear of making mistakes), etc. There may be more than one factor contributing to the child's reading problem.

What Can I Do As A Parent?—In determining if your child has a reading problem that should be addressed, parents should consider the following questions:

—Is my child reading at a level that is below age-appropriate expectations?

—Is the reading problem a result of circumstances that can be changed (i.e., getting glasses for a vision problem or increasing parental involvement at home that may have been lacking)?

—Is the reading problem only a sign of a more serious problem (i.e., language or neurological problem)?

In terms of ways to build a good foundation for reading or to deal with an already existing reading problem, the following guidelines as suggested by Frank Smith in his 1985 book, Reading Without Nonsense, may be helpful:

—Begin reading to the child while he/she is quite young.

—Read things that are interesting and useful to the child.

—Have the child read along with you, and always tell the child what the words are.

—Provide plenty of opportunities to compare objects and thoughts to written print.

—Ensure success for the child by keeping information meaningful and by refraining from expecting perfection

—Correct mistakes in a casual fashion, correcting those that seem most important for comprehension of the material.

Additional suggestions:

—Have everyone in the family obtain a library card and make regular trips to the library.

—Show your child that you think reading is important, by having a variety of reading material in the home.

—Emphasize in normal daily situations that reading is an interesting way to learn about the world we live in.

—Encourage any reading that your child does or seems to be interested in.

—Take time to talk with your child about anything he may be reading (whether it is a dictionary or a comic book).

Resources

If the above information is not sufficient to answer all of your questions or concerns, you can receive further information from educators such as teachers, school guidance counselors, reading specialists, and school psychologists.

Remember, if you think your child has a reading problem it is important to identify it early and provide the appropriate interventions.

References

Anderson, R., Hiebert, E. H., Scott, J. A., & Wilkinson, I. A. G. (1985). *Becoming a nation of readers*. Washington, DC: National Institute of Education.

Smith, F. (1985). *Reading without nonsense*. New York: Teachers College Press.

Spadafore, G. J. (1987). Children and reading. In A. Thomas & J. Grimes (Eds.), *Children's needs: Psychological perspectives* (pp. 471-476). Washington, DC: National Association of School Psychologists.

Children and Retention
Parent Handout

Andrea Canter and Karen Carey

Background

Every year, many children are held back in the same grade. Retention or nonpromotion has been used to help children who have not kept up academically with their classmates. Children might also be held back because they are small, "immature," or have later birthdays and seem to need a chance to grow. And, retention has been used to help children who have missed a lot of school due to illness or frequent moves, or who are just beginning to learn English.

What does the research say?

- Most children do not "catch up" when they are held back.
- Although some retained children do better at first, they often fall behind again in later grades.
- Children who are held back tend to get into trouble, dislike school, and feel bad about themselves more often than do children who go on to the next grade.
- "Transition kindergarten" is a type of retention and generally is no more helpful than promotion to first grade.
- Many students who drop out of school were held back one, two, or more grades.
- Retention might be less harmful for children who feel good about themselves, get along well with others, and have the skills to catch up easily.
- Retention might be helpful for a child who missed a lot of school due to illness or family moves, if he attendance problem is solved and the child will be only one year older than classmates.

What can parents do to help?

Neither retention nor promotion will help a child learn! But in order to succeed, your child might need something different, not the same things again that didn't work the first time. Parents and teachers can work together to help children succeed. By catching the problem early, there are more opportunities to help children before they have a sense of failure, and there are greater chances for success.

- Discuss concerns with your child's teacher. Find out what work your child is expected to do, and what work your child finds difficult. Ask a lot of questions—how does he or she get along with classmates? Does he or she remember to follow directions? Does he or she finish assignments on time? What changes has the teacher tried to help your child? Are there other ways to teach the same material? Are there other books and materials that might help your child learn? What are some activities that you can help with at home to help your child catch up? Ask the teacher far some ideas! And try to find a time to visit the classroom and watch your child at work.

171

• Help your child with schoolwork at home. Ask your child about homework each day. Help him or he to find a quiet time and place to study. Check to see if your child can explain the assignment to you or read the directions. Make sure your child understands that you think schoolwork is important.

• Make sure your child is ready for school each day! Be sure your child attends school on time every day, eats balanced meals, gets enough sleep, and receives good medical care. Children need to be alert and healthy to succeed in school!

Where can I get more help?

It can be frustrating to know your child is not succeeding at school. It can make a parent feel upset or angry. Before considering retention, parents can get help from other professionals at school. These people offer ideas for parents and teachers about how to change instruction. They also provide testing to find out if a child needs other services such as tutoring or special education and may have some different learning materials that will work with your child. They can help children who have low self-esteem or poor social skills so that they "fit in" and feel better about themselves. At your child's school, you might contact the:

- School psychologist
- School problem-solving or support team
- School social worker
- School nurse
- Guidance counselor
- Special education teachers
- Reading specialists
- Principal

For more information, contact your school psychologist or:
The National Association of School Psychologists, 8455 Colesville Rd., Silver Spring, MD 20910

Resources

"Should My Child Repeat a Grade?" (Brochure published by NASP see above address)
"Position Statement on Retention" (and supporting paper summarizing research); NASP (request from above address)
"A-Plus Junior Study Guide"

Children and Retention
Teacher Handout

Andrea Canter Karen Carey and Peg Dawson

Background—Every year over 2 million American school children are retained in the same grade. By ninth grade, approximately 50% of all students will have been held back at least once. While it is a common practice, a survey of the research literature shows that student retention, for the most part, is of questionable educational benefit an may have negative effects on achievement, self-concept, attitudes toward learning, and school drop-out rates. The practice of retention costs American taxpayers more than $9 billion dollars each year! Furthermore, retention appears to be a discriminatory practice as boys, Blacks and Hispanics are far more likely to be retained than are other students.

Research

Commonly held beliefs about the benefits of retention have been dispelled by decades of research.

- **Low achievers rarely "catch up."** Most children do not "catch up" when they are retained, and in fact are more likely to fall further behind. Some children show initial gains following retention but long-term studies show that these gains "wash out" within two or three years. Promoted peers with similar skills fare at least as well academically, and often do better.

- **Retention is generally unsuccessful even at kindergarten or first grade.** While retention appears to have more negative effects for older students, even retention of kindergarten children appears to be an ineffective intervention. Research indicates that students are more likely to be hurt by retention than helped, regardless of grade level. "Transition kindergarten is a type of retention and generally has not been proven to be effective."

- **"Immature" children do not benefit from an extra year to grow.** There simply is no evidence that children will mature faster or adjust better when retained. Students do not benefit emotionally from retention.

- **Retained students are more likely to drop out of school.** The drop-out rate among retained students is much greater than for similarly achieving students who have never been retained. The probability of dropping out increases with multiple retentions.

Does anyone benefit from retention?

Under some circumstances, retention is less likely to yield negative effects:

- Students who have positive self concepts, good peer relationships, and have adequate skills to catch up easily are less likely to have negative retention experiences.

- Students who missed a lot of school due to illness or family moves might be helped by retention.

173

However, this assumes that the attendance/health problems have been resolved and that the student is no more than one year older than classmates.

- There will always be individual students who appear to have positive experiences with retention. Unfortunately, educators are unable to consistently predict which students will be successful.

How can teacher help?

Since research fails to support retention, it is imperative that schools implement more effective strategies that enable at-risk students to succeed in the regular classroom.

- **Effective teaching strategies will enhance student success.** Mastery learning, direct instruction, adaptive education, team teaching, peer tutoring, cooperative clearing and curriculum-based assessment have all been shown to produce academic gains in students at all achievement levels. If the child works slowly, cut down the number or length of assignments. Look for ways to modify the curriculum. Reward students for their efforts! Teachers may need inservice training and consultation to help implement new methods in the classroom.

- **Catch the problem early.** If a child has difficulty keeping up with classmates, look for ways to help before the problem becomes serious. Observe the child while he/she works on assignments to determine the skills the child is missing. This can lead to a minimal amount of reteaching.

- **Establish activities that encourage parents to become involved in school.** Teachers can offer parents opportunities to observe instruction, to learn about class assignments, and expectations for success. Support staff can work with parents to increase their skills as "teachers" and as advocates for their children's learning. An atmosphere that welcomes parents as partners will promote better communication between home and school, and in turn will promote learning and appropriate behavior.

- **Seek assistance from the members of the school multi-disciplinary team.** Teachers can't be expected to solve all classroom difficulties alone! Members of the school team (psychologist, social worker, counselor, principal, nurse, Chapter I, etc.) have training and expertise to support efforts in the classroom and to help involve parents and appropriate community resources. It's important that students receive supportive services before they are entrenched in a cycle of failure.

For more information about retention, contact: The National Association of School Psychologists, Colesville Rd. #1000, Silver Spring, MD 20910.

Resources

Comer J. (1982). School Power.

Ehly, S. & Larson, S. (1980). *Peer tutoring for individual instruction.* Boston: Allyn & Bacon.

Graden J., Zins J., & Curtis, M. (1908). *Alternative educational delivery systems: Enhancing instructional options for all students.* Washington, DC: NASP.

McGinnis, E., Goldstein, A., Sprafkin, R. & Gershaw, N. (1984). *Skillstreaming the elementary school child: A guide for teaching prosocial skills.* Champaign, IL: Research Press.

Paine, S., & others, (1983). *Structuring your classroom for academic success.* Champaign, IL: Research Press.

NASP (1989). Supporting paper for Position Statement on Student Retention. (Available from NASP office)

Shepard, L. & Smith, M. (1989). *Flunking Grades: Research and policies on retention.* New York: Falmer Press.

Slavin, R. (1983) *Cooperative Learning.* White Plains, NY: Longman.

School Entry Decisions

Erika Manz
University of South Florida

Background—When are children ready to begin formal schooling? Readiness refers to the attainment of a developmental level at which one is capable of learning. But schools make multiple demands on children and children must be ready to do a number of things such as read, write, count, to follow directions, to sit quietly, to interact appropriately with other children, etc. Most educational researchers believe that children should attend school when they are "ready." However, the formal educational system has mandated chronological age as the criterion for school entry.

Development—Although there are agreed upon ages for appropriate abilities, behaviors, and developmental "stages," all children do develop differently and may not always develop their skills and behaviors in sequences or at typical ages. Therefore, it is difficult to predict school performance at 6 years of age from the behaviors and abilities a child possessed at 2 or 3 years of age. Considerable irregularities across skill areas are inherent in normal child development and therefore make it difficult to predict a child's school readiness or performance at a later time.

Factors—The following are key variables considered to relate to success in school:

—Chronological Age. Typically, children are placed in school if their birthdates fall between specified dates. It is possible that within one first grade classroom a child can be as much as 11 months, 30 days older or younger than a classmate. At this age, a year can make a great deal of difference both in terms of physiological maturity and opportunities for learning. Older kindergartners generally do better on achievement tests given at the end of the year than do younger kindergartners, particularly boys. Older children may also enter school with more knowledge.

—Sex. Girls tend to function better than boys of the same age on readiness and achievement tests.

—Intelligence. The most powerful single predictor of academic success is intelligence.

—Socioeconomic Status. Socioeconomic status (SES) is a more powerful predictor of success in first grade than chronological age.

—Race. Blacks generally tend to do less well than Whites of the same chronological age on readiness and achievement tests and are more frequently retained at each grade level.

—Preschool Experience. Children who have attended preschool tend to do better in the following years in both academic and social areas. This experience seems to have a greater benefit for low SES children.

What is being done to improve the decision-making process? What can be done? Researchers and educational professionals have several suggestions:

—Although raising the minimum age for school entry may help ease the teachers' burden slightly, several problems are left unresolved. First, lower SES children will be less likely than their peers to spend the extra year in preschool time in good learning situations. Second, handicapped children may not come to the attention of school personnel as quickly. Third, there will always be a younger group in every entering class and they will be substantially less ready.

—Some schools have attempted to resolve the problem by instituting a transitional first grade for children who have difficulty in kindergarten. Unfortunately, the class is composed mainly of lower functioning children who are inappropriate models for their classmates and the curriculum often simply repeats the previous year's curriculum.

—Some schools have adopted an early screening program for children as young as 3 years old. This approach appears to offer the best chance to head off later school failure with virtually none of the potentially aversive features of other approaches.

—An individualistic approach can also be considered. Determining whether there are serious concerns regarding a child's present level of functioning may determine if delaying entry should be considered.

This paper is a synopsis of a chapter by Ronald E. Reeve and Ilene J. Holt entitled, "Children and School Entry Decisions" in Children's Needs: Psychological Perspectives.

NATIONAL
ASSOCIATION OF
SCHOOL
PSYCHOLOGISTS

Children and Study Skills

Maribeth Gettinger
University of Wisconsin-Madison

Background—Being able to study effectively is important for a child's success in school. Many capable students at all grade levels may experience frustration and even failure in school **not** because they lack ability, but because they do not have adequate study skills. Good study skills benefit children beyond improving their academic performance. Children who have developed good study skills are also more likely to increase their feelings of competence and confidence as they learn. They tend to approach their school work with a positive attitude, rather than a negative and anxious one.

Development—Study skills may be viewed as basic learning tools; they enable students to acquire and retain information presented in textbooks and classrooms. More specifically, study skills include listening and reading, notetaking, outlining, managing time, and taking tests. Study skills may be organized into four general stages of learning that are common to all children. The first stage of studying involves taking in information from books, lectures, or presentations. Study behaviors that are associated with success at this stage include listening and reading. The second stage entails some organization of the information. Study behaviors that facilitate organization include underlining, notetaking, outlining, making lists, or asking oneself questions about the material. Stage three involves practicing or rehearsing the organized material and requires some type of review or discussion on the part of the learner. The final stage is the actual remembering or application of information. Skills in taking tests, writing, or preparing reports are used in this stage.

What can I do as a parent?

Parents need to remember that there is no simple formula for improving study skills for all children. More important than following any one particular method are building good habits, developing a system that works for them, and using the system effectively and consistently. Learning styles vary from student to student. Study hams that work for one person may not work well for another person-even for two children who come from the same family! Children need to discover how they learn and then work out a study system that fits in best with the way they learn things.

Here are some tips parents can pass on to their children for helping them develop good study skills. Without pressuring, parents may encourage children to:

1. **Establish a study routine.** Children should pick a place, find a time, and build a routine. Studying should be a part of the daily family routine. Students find that they learn more if they get into the habit of studying at the same time and in the same place each day. Of course, special family events or sudden demands will force them to break that routine from time to time, but they should try to stay in the routine as much as possible.

2. **Make sure study surroundings allow children to concentrate.** To concentrate on studies, some children may require total quiet; others may need a little background noise (such as music). Children should find the atmosphere that helps them focus on what they have to study without being

distracted by other activities or being so relaxed that they fall asleep. Children may need some cooperation from the family to do this (not disturbing them, taking phone messages, etc.).

3. **Keep assignments in one folder.** Students may have a separate notebook for each class, but they should keep all homework assignments in one folder. That way, they will be able to see all of the things they have to do and divide their study time accordingly.

4. **Work out a study system.** Rather than just reading straight through an assignment, most students find that they learn more if they work out a systematic method. This may involve skimming the material, underlining or taking notes, reviewing major ideas, and so on. Two key elements are to **read with a question in mind** and **take notes in their own words.** One popular system, known as the "SQ3R" method, involves these steps: (a) Survey: Quickly scan the reading assignment (look at headings, graphs, summaries, etc.); (b) Question: Make up a question to keep in mind as they read; (c) Read: Then, read to answer the questions they formulated; (d) Recite: Try to answer questions without looking at the reading assignment; and (e) Review: Immediately review the material to make certain notes are organized and major ideas are understood.

5. **Expand concentration time.** At first, children may only be able to concentrate for short time periods (10 minutes is typical, since it is the time between commercials on TV programs). Parents can help children work on building this up to longer stretches without breaks, so it will not take as long to get through assignments. Most children need to work up slowly and steadily, just like one does in weight training or aerobics.

6. **Develop time estimation skill.** One key to good studying is being able to estimate how long it will take to complete each assignment. Start by having children make an estimate on each assignment, then note how long it really takes to do the work, and note how well they do on the assignment (or how they do on the test for which they studied). Most students must keep adjusting and evaluating estimates until they become routinely accurate.

7. **Plan ahead.** Athletes cannot get in shape in one or two nights; they need to "work out" for several weeks. Studying works the same way. Children should start working on major assignments or reviewing for major tests well ahead and plan their strategy for finishing the assignment on time.

8. **Set goals.** Before beginning work on an assignment, help children decide how well they want to do on it and how much effort it will take to do that well. This will help them learn to divide study time effectively, so they do not spend too much time on relatively unimportant assignments.

9. **Reward achievements.** When children achieve one of their study goals, give them a little reward: make a snack, allow them to call a friend, or whatever. Often children will want someone (parent or friend) who can congratulate them on their achievements and with whom they can share what they have learned.

Resources

Cohn, M. (1979). *Helping your teenage student: What parents can do to improve reading and study skills.* New York: E. Dalton. Written especially for parents of middle and high school students, offering suggestions that parents can implement to foster effective study skills at home.

Duckett, J. C. (1983). *Helping children develop good study habits: A parent's guide.* Washington, D.C.: National Institute of Education. Brief, succinct guide for parents to improve children's study habits.

Hahn, J. (1985) *Have you done your homework? A parent's guide to helping teenagers succeed in school.* New York: John Wiley. Concise book that tells parents what it takes for students to be successful in school and provides tips on motivation and general study strategies.

Whitman, R. (1984). *Home team: Over 60 home learning tips from the American Federation of Teachers.* Washington, D.C.: American Federation of Teachers. Brochure that describes how parents can promote their children's learning, including suggestions relating to specific content areas.

Part V

Helping Out—
Emotional and Behavioral
Problems with Children and
Adolescents

Children and Anorexia and Bulima

Joseph P. Irilli, *Niles City Schools, Niles, Ohio*
Cathy J. Carty, *Youngstown City Schools, Youngstown, Ohio*

Background—Anorexia and Bulimia are serious, life threatening disorders with a wide range of physical and psychiatric components. Research suggests that the current diet and fitness phenomenon may be responsible for the increase in eating disorders. Evidence suggests that eating disorders may affect 18-20% of the students between the ages of eleven and nineteen. That means that the significance equals or exceeds all other low and high incidence handicapping conditions with which school personnel typically deal. The dieting phenomenon has increased well over 50% among normal weight adolescent girls as compared to the last decade. In a recent research study, 80% of the girls between the ages of ten and eleven were afraid of becoming fat and were dieting to lose weight. Since this is the time a young girl should be entering a period of rapid growth, excessive dieting may affect later development.

The literature suggests Anorexia Nervosa and Bulimia are disorders occuring predominantly among females. Both disorders occur in males, however, the current incidence rate is set at two percent of the population. The diagnostic criteria that is used for assessing eating disorders is that which are spelled out by the Diagnostic and Statistical Manual of Mental Disorders.

Anorexia Nervosa

—Intense fear of becoming obese, which does not diminish as weight loss continues.

—Disturbance of body image, e.g., claiming to "feel fat" even when emaciated.

—Weight loss of at least 25% of original body weight or if under 18 years of age, weight loss from original body weight plus projected weight gain expected from growth charts may be combined to make the 25%.

—Refusal to maintain body weight over a minimal normal weight for age and height.

—No known physical illness that would account for the weight loss.

Bulimia

—Recurrent episodes of binge eating (rapid consumption of a large amount of food in a discreet period of time, usually less than two hours).

—At least three of the following:

1. Consumption of high-caloric, easily ingested food during a binge.
2. Inconspicuous eating during a binge.
3. Termination of such eating episodes by abdominal pain, sleep, social interruption, or selfinduced vomiting.

4. Repeated attempts to lose weight by severely restrictive diets, self-induced vomiting, or use of cathartics or diuretics.

5. Frequent weight fluctuations greater than ten pounds due to alternating binges and fasts.

—Awareness that the eating pattern is abnormal and fear of not being able to stop eating voluntarily.

—Depressed mood and self-deprecating thoughts following binges.

—The Bulimic episodes are not due to Anorexia Nervosa or any known physical disorder.

Physical Symptoms	Emotional and Perceptual Characteristics	Behavioral Characteristics
Insomnia	Distorted Body Image	Unusual Eating Habits
Constipation	Inability to Think Clearly	Hyperactivity
Lanugo	Dichotomous Thinking	Frequent Weighing
Premature Aging	Overpersonalization	Laxatives
Hair Loss	Low Self-Worth	Diuretics
Dental Problems	Masked Anger	High Achievement
Amenorrhea	Perfection	Depression
Hypothermia		Shoplifting
Dehydration		Extreme Sensitivity

Development—Parents are often unable to recognize that their child suffers from a serious mental disorder. The early symptoms of eating disorders are similar to the values society places upon physical appearance, shape, weight, and achievement. Parents attribute other signs of the disorder such as negativism, weight loss, and body image self-consciousness, to typical adolescent behavior. Consequently, neither the youngster nor her parents recognize the behavior as symptomatic of a psychological disorder. Since the parents are not aware that their child has a mental illness, psychological intervention is likely to be sought too late. A major portion of a young person's day is spent in school, therefore, school personnel fulfill a vital role in the detection of an eating disorder. Their vigilance often assists in getting a child into an active treatment program before medical complications become irreversible.

Responsibility for an eating disorder must be at least partially placed upon society. We are now living in a society full of Anorexics, Bulimics and continual diets and yet our media continue to promote "you can never be too rich or too thin." This is a time when young people need to begin to question the values of our society. The media are continually portraying the thin, almost emaciated look as the goal to achieve. Given the impact that television, movies and magazines have on youth, the rate of Anorexia Nervosa and Bulimia are skyrocketing. They tend to glamourize a dreary, miserable illness with an element of mystery and exciting danger. It has become the obligation of parents, teachers, and other school personnel to help students overcome this illusion.

The prognosis for recovery becomes increasingly better if diagnosis is made early. Full recovery is defined by most researchers as being within ninety percent of an individual's normal body weight for age and height. The death rate is currently set between eight and fifteen percent of diagnosed Anorexics and Bulimics. Death is usually due to cardiovascular problems, electrolyte imbalances, and/or suicide. Approximately twenty to sixty percent of eating disordered individuals have a chronic eating disorder which redevelops whenever the individual is placed in a stressful situation. We feel that if parents work closely with school personnel a great contribution can be made in the prevention and treatment of eating disorders.

What can I do as a parent?

The successful prevention and treatment of Anorexia Nervosa and Bulimia may be enhanced by parents who are aware of some basic principles to use when dealing with their child.

—Educate yourself about all aspects of eating disorders especially diagnostic criteria, observable symptoms, physical problems, possible causes that have been identified and treatment options.

—Become aware of the strong impact that you have upon your child as his/her role model. If you're not confident in your own body image you may pass on your own insecurities to your children.

—Don't contribute to a possible disorder by focusing on calorie counting, eating habits, exercise and weight.

—Identify your own feelings toward your child, discuss facing reality and accepting feelings. Listen to your child and encourage her participation in family discussions.

—Help your child to combat societal pressures. The media continue to glamourize Anorexia Nervosa as the "Golden Girl" disease.

—Encourage your child to move toward individualism and autonomy while continuing to provide loving support and encouragment.

—Always maintain a balance between your child's need for your love and attention and a need for autonomy.

Resources

American Anorexia Nervosa Association, Inc., 139 Cedar Lane, Teaneck, NJ 07666.
Anorexia Nervosa and Associated Disorders, Inc., P. O. Box 271, Highland Park, IL 60035.
National Anorexic Aid Society, Inc., P. O. Box 29461, Columbus, OH 43229.

Books

Erichsen, A (1986). *Anorexia Nervosa: The Broken Circle.* London: Faber and Faber.
Garfinkel, P., and Garner D. (1982). *Anorexia Nervosa! A Multidimensional Perspective.* New York: Brunner/Mazel.
Garner D., & Garfinkel, P. (1985). *Handbook of Psychotherapy for Anorexia Nervosa and Bulimia.* New York: Guilford.
Kinoy, B.F. (1981). *When Will I Laugh Again?* New York: Columbia University Press.

Children and Anxiety

Thomas Huberty
Indiana University

Background—Anxiety is a familiar term and is a common experience for both children and adults at many times in their lives. For children, it is difficult to distinguish anxiety from fear, but generally anxiety is seen to be apprehension about future events that have not yet occurred. Fear, on the other hand, is a response to a situation, such as a child being afraid of an animal. The focus of this discussion is on anxiety, which is a feeling of apprehension without any apparent cause. Anxiety is a normal experience for all of us at one time or another, and becomes a concern when it becomes excessive and/or interferes with one's typical daily routine. Anxiety can be experienced by a person as a long-term feeling or it may occur in a specific setting, such as when taking a test.

Anxiety may occur in response to specific situations such as speaking in front of a group, or be shown in many situations. Children who are referred to as "high-strung may show some of the signs of anxiety. Some common characteristics of anxiety are oversensitivity to normal events, fear of future outcomes, concentration difficulties, distractibility, impulsiveness, inattention to schoolwork, excessive movement, sleeping problems, rapid breathing, nausea, headaches, stomachaches, unusual fatigue, and, in extreme cases, running away from a situation. Not all of these characteristics will be shown at one time, however, and all may be signs of other problems.

Development—Young children experience anxiety normally as a process of growing up. Infants tend to feel anxiety about falling, loud noises, and having physical needs met. Anxiety in infants is shown in generalized activity that becomes more specific with age. At about 7-9 months of age, babies start to show anxiety of new people. It is at this point that the child can distinguish typical caretakers from strangers and he/she is apprehensive (anxious) about the absence of familiar persons. This form of anxiety is shown by refusing to be held by strangers, clinging to parents, and crying when alone with unfamiliar people. This "stranger anxiety" usually ends by about 12-14 months. At about 18-24 months, children demonstrate a related type of anxiety called "separation anxiety." This anxiety is shown by crying, temper tantrums, and attempting to cling to parents or caretakers. While this form of anxiety appears to be similar to stranger anxiety, it is different from the child's perspective. The anxiety is not a response to what might happen to the child if held by a stranger, but to the possibility that the parents might not return and to what might be the consequences of their not returning. By the time children enter school, these forms of anxiety ordinarily have dissipated and the child is more secure about being with strangers and not concerned about being left by parents.

As children progress in school, they tend to become anxious about being accepted by peers, overall school performance, expectations set by parents, physical appearance, and feelings of competence. They also may hold increased anxiety about the stability of family relationships, death, and the future. Research has shown that girls tend to show more general anxiety than boys and more centered around social acceptance and popularity. The reasons for these findings are not clear, but may be related to the social roles that girls are expected to maintain in our society.

Recognizing the signs of anxiety and knowing when they indicate problems is not an easy task. If you see some signs of anxiety, the following questions should be considered:

—Is the anxiety typical for a child of that age?

—Is the anxiety seen across many situations or is it limited to a specific situation, such as speaking in front of the class?

—Is the anxiety of a long-term nature or has it occurred recently?

—Are there events going on in the child's life that are causing stress and pressure?

—Is the anxiety a sign of a larger problem, such as home and family difficulties?

—Is the anxiety having a great effect on the child's personal, social, and school functioning?

The last question is the most important, because if the child is having difficulty with everyday activities, the problems must be addressed regardless of their cause. By attending to the degree to which anxiety might be interfering with the child's functioning, answers to the other questions will become important in determining the nature, scope, and source of the child's anxiety. Once the entire situation is understood, then plans to work with the anxiety can be developed.

The Causes of Anxiety—The potential causes of anxiety are many, but the primary characteristic is that the child or adolescent is uncertain about something that has not yet happened. It matters little that the anxiety about a situation may not be realistic or justified. As long as someone feels uncertain whether something in the future might have a direct effect, he/she may become anxious. Anxiety is most likely to be shown when the person feels that something bad will happen and that they have no control over it. It is when people are apprehensive about the future and feel unable to do anything about it that anxiety is most likely to occur.

Nearly any event or circumstance can cause anxiety by creating a situation in which the person cannot predict an outcome and feels unable to make significant changes. Family problems (e.g., pending divorce, competition with siblings), excessive or unusual discipline practices, inconsistency in how children are handled or treated by adults, high expectations and standards set up by the child or others that are perceived to be unattainable, peer pressure to conform or "fit in," rejection (or, in some cases, acceptance as the child must now meet new expectations) by peers, high needs for achievement, concerns about success or failure, physical appearance, and ability level in a variety of areas are some of the factors that can contribute to the development of anxiety in children. It should be noted that anxiety often is shown in these situation, which is normal. Anxiety becomes problematic when it becomes so intense that the child's personal-social and/or school functioning begins to deteriorate.

Sometimes, there may be more than one factor contributing to the child's anxiety. The author once was asked to consult with school personnel about a 15-year old girl who complained of "test anxiety" in which she "froze" when taking a test. It was determined that she was indeed so afraid of getting a low grade that she could not perform. Moreover, she was concerned about disapproval from her mother if she got a low grade, and that she would have to compete even more with her new stepfather whom her mother had recently married.

What can I do as a parent?

In determining if anxiety is present and is a problem to be addressed, you as a parent should consider the following questions:

—Are there signs of anxiety that are not typical for my child's age?

—What are the signs of anxiety and how do they affect my child's personal, social and academic performance?

—Is the intensity of the anxiety much higher than the situation would indicate it should be?

—Are there unusual circumstances that might contribute to the anxiety that may change or be changed within the immediate future, such as family problems?

—Does my child feel that expectations and standards are too high to be met?

—Is the anxiety only a sign of a more serious problem that the child is experiencing?

—Is my child's behavior essentially normal, but people around him/her are having difficulty being tolerant of the behavior?

In terms some ways to deal with anxiety, the following guidelines might be helpful:

—Provide as much consistency as possible in handling and discipline.

—Set realistic goals and expectations for yourself and your child that are reasonable and attainable.

—Try to keep as consistent a schedule as possible in terms of homework, household chores, activities, etc.

—**Listen** to your child. Many times, a child will feel anxious about a specific situation and all he/she needs is to talk to someone who will listen and give advice only when asked.

—Do not assume that the child is just being difficult, as the anxiety may be a sign of a more significant problem.

—Do not assume that it will "go away," as you may end up not recognizing a potentially serious problem.

Resources

If the above questions and suggestions do not provide you with the help you need, it may be that the child's anxiety is a sign of a larger problem that must be addressed. In these cases, the school psychologist or counselor may be very helpful in providing you with information about your child as well as helping to obtain counseling or similar services. Your family physician, local mental health centers, ministers, or other professionals may be helpful in understanding the problem and providing you with help.

Bullying

George Batsche
University of South Florida

Benjamin Moore
Hommett School—The Baby Fold
Normal, Illinois

Definition of a "Bully"—A bully is a child who fairly often oppresses or harasses someone else; the target may be boys or girls, the harrassment physical or mental (Olweus, D.). Bullies are usually boys, although girl bullies do exist.

Definition of a "Victim"—A child who for a fairly long time has been and still is exposed to aggression from others; that is, boys or possibly girls from the child's own class or maybe from other classes often pick fights and are rough with them or tease and ridicule them. Two types of "victims" emerge:

- "Passive Victims"—Anxious, insecure, appear to do nothing to invite attacks and fail to defend themselves.
- "Provocative Victims"—Hot-tempered, restless, create tension by irritating and teasing others and attempt to fight back when attacked.

Some facts about the bully problem

- Approximately **one in seven** school children is either a bully or a victim.
- This affects approximately 5,000,000 elementary and junior high school students in the United States.
- Approximately 282,000 students are physically attacked in America's secondary schools each month.
- An estimated 525,000 attacks, shakedowns and robberies occur in an average month in public secondary schools.
- In a typical month about 125,000 secondary school teachers (12 percent) are threatened with physical harm and approximately 5200 actually are physically attacked.
- **Almost 8 percent of urban junior and senior high school students miss one day of school each month because they are afraid to attend.**

Why do some children and adolescents become bullies?

There is no "one reason why a child might become a bully. However, we do know what types of circumstances will likely help a child develop bully behavior. Bully behavior is developed mainly as a result of factors in the **environment**. This environment includes the home, the school and the peer group.

189

Bully behavior is learned. The good news is that because the bully behavior is learned, it can be unlearned, particularly if we do something about it when children are young.

What factors in the environment will likely contribute to a child becoming a bully?

- **Too little supervision of children and adolescents.** Without supervision, children do not get the message that aggressive behavior is the wrong behavior to have.

- **Bullying pays off.** Many children learn at a very young age that when they bully their brother sister or parents that they get what they want. Often we are too busy or too tired to "fight" with the child so we just give in. Each time we give in when the child is aggressive or just plain obnoxious, we are giving the child the message that **bullying pays off.**

- **Do as I say, not as I do.** Some children seem more likely to imitate adult aggressive, bullying behavior than other children. In some families, when children are punished for aggressive behavior (even if they see it in their home) they stop being aggressive. For most children, however, if they see aggressive behavior they will imitate it. When parents fight and one parent intimidates the other and "wins," the child gets the message that intimidation gets you what you want.

- **Harsh, physical punishment.** Although spanking a child will often put a stop to the child's behavior, spanking that is too harsh, too frequent or too physical teaches a child that it is OK to hit other people. In particular, this teaches a child that it is OK for bigger people (parents) to hit little people (children). **Bullies usually pick on younger, smaller, or weaker children.** They model, in their physical attacks, what happened to them **personally** in the home. **The worst thing that can be done is to physically punish a bully for bully behavior.**

- **Peer group that supports bully behavior.** Many parents do not know what their children are doing with the peer group. Their child may be running with other children who advocate bully behavior. In order for the child to "fit in," the child must bully like the peers.

- Getting more negative than positive messages. Children who develop bully behavior feel that the world around them (home, school, neighborhood) is more negative than positive. These children have more negative comments (get yelled at, told that they are wrong) than positive comments. They expect the world to be negative with them so they attack first. By picking on others, they feel more important and powerful. If they cannot feel important because parents and teachers make positive comments and "reinforce" them, then they will feel important in negative ways.

- **Poor self-concept.** Children who get more negative comments given to them than positive ones will develop a poor self-concept. These children then believe that the only way to be "accepted" is to pick on others.

- **Expecting hostility.** Because of the negative messages received and the poor self-concept, bullies expect their parents, teachers and peers to pick on them, blame them or otherwise humiliate them. Therefore, they attack before they are attacked, even when in reality they were not about to be attacked. They assume hostility when none exists. In many ways, the bully's philosophy is, **"The best defense is offense."**

School factors

- Larger schools report a greater percentage of violence.
- Schools with clear rules of conduct enforced by the principal report less violence.
- Schools with students that report fair discipline practices report less violence.
- Small class size relates to less violence.
- Schools where students mention that they are in control of their lives report less violence.

- A principal who appears to be ineffective or invisible to students reports more violence in that school.
- Schools with principals that provide opportunities for the teachers and students to be participatory members of decision-making report less violence.
- Cohesiveness among teaching staff and principal relate to less violence.

Why do some children and adolescents become victims?

Less is really known about "victims" but there is some information which will help us understand the victim situation to some extent.

- Most victims are anxious, sensitive, and quiet.
- Victims generally do not have many, if any, good friends at school.
- Victims seem to signal to others that they are insecure and worthless children who will not retaliate if they are attacked or insulted.
- Bullies often target children who complain, appear physically weak, seek attention from peers and adults and seem emotionally weak.
- These children may be overprotected by parents and school personnel and are therefore unable to develop coping skills on their own.

What can be done about the problem?

In General

- A strong commitment is needed in the home and school to change the behavior. Parents need support from school and mental health/community workers to enforce positive behavior patterns. **Parent training is essential.**
- Specific training is needed in the social skills that the child lacks to get along with other children. This can be dome in school through social skills training and in the home through increased supervision, more positive discipline and modeling.
- Increase, significantly, the amount of positive feedback that the child gets in the home and the school.
- The pattern of bullying begins at an early age; as early as age 2. Early intervention is essential. The older the child becomes, the more difficult change will be. After age 8-10, change is very difficult.
- Develop a strong value system in the home and in the school that gives a clear message that bully behavior is completely unacceptable.

Specifying things to do in the home

- If you have a serious bully or victim problem, contact the school psychologist in your child's school building and ask for help. In the meantime, the following steps will significantly help the problem.
- Be sure that you are being as positive as possible with your child. Shoot for 5 positive comments for every negative one that you direct to your child. You will have to work very hard and "catch them being good."
- Do not use physical punishment. Instead, use removal of privileges, time spent in their bedroom, work tasks around the house or helping younger children in the neighborhood or in the home as a consequence for bully behavior.

- When you see your (or another) child engaging in bully behavior, put a stop to the behavior immediately and have the child practice a more appropriate behavior instead. For instance, if you have a child who pushes his sister away from a toy in order to play with it, have the child practice (at least 3 times) asking for (and receiving) the toy the correct way.

- If the child is a victim, have the child practice telling the bully to, "stop bothering me" and then have the child walk away. The parent should be there to supervise the behavior of the bully and the victim.

- Parents must model, or show, the children in the home behavior between adults or between adults and children that is not bully behavior. If the children see parents yelling and bullying each other or if this is how the parent talks to the children, then the child will do that behavior as well. Remember to operate from the **"Do as I say AND as I do"** point of view.

- Supervision is of great importance. If you can, supervise the situations in which your child will have the opportunity to become either a bully or victim. If you cannot supervise the children under those circumstances, try to find someone who can. If you cannot supervise and cannot find someone, then do not allow the child to participate in that situation.

Specific things to do in the school setting

- Establish a school climate that clearly and emphatically disapproves of bullying. This can be accomplished through school-wide campaigns (including contests, posters, parties, dances, school events) that support behaviors which are the opposite of bullying. These behaviors can include "buddy systems," cooperative learning, peer tutoring, big brother-big sister programs and others.

- Establish a climate in which rules of conduct are enforced and are developed by the students and teachers cooperatively.

- Discipline practices should emphasize restitution and positive practice rather than expulsion, paddlings, and humiliation. That is, when students are caught bullying they should apologize, demonstrate the correct behavior, and then have to spend a specified period of time helping (public service) younger, less able children.

- Teachers and administrators should work to increase the number of positives directed toward children on a daily basis. The ratio, just as in the home, should be approximately **5** positives for each negative. Teachers must **"catch them being good."** This may be difficult but the teacher will have to give positives for behaviors they usually take for granted. The situation may occur where the teacher will have to "set up" a situation in order to give positives. This might include sending an older "bully" to a younger class in order to help a particular student with an academic exercise. The "bully" can then receive recognition for this behavior.

- In classrooms where there are a number of students with the "bully" problem, the use of social skills training sessions throughout the year may be necessary. If the teacher is unfamiliar with these skill training sessions, a call to the school psychologist can help with materials and technical assistance.

- On a building level, the establishment of a "discipline" committee is suggested. The purpose of the committee would be to identify the five top discipline problems in the school and to develop intervention plans that will be implemented regardless of where in the school the problem behavior occurred. The discipline measures should emphasize restitution and positive practice, not physical punishment, exclusion, or humiliation.

- Although it is very difficult to justify, bullies should not be removed from the school setting unless absolutely necessary. The teaching of social skills, the value campaign against bully behavior and the increased number of positives directed toward bullies for appropriate behavior are more productive, in the long run, than exclusion.

The above are only examples of where to begin thinking about and acting on the problem. Listed below are resources for both parents and teachers.

Resources for parents and teachers

Parents

Available from: The National School Safety Center Pepperdine University, Malibu, California 90265

- *School Crime and Violence: Victims' Rights*
- *Student and Staff Victimization*

Resources on changing children's behavior in the home and family: **The following are available from any bookstore and can be ordered if not in stock.**

Available from: Research Press, Box 3177, Department 5, Champaign, IL 61826, (217) 352-3273.

- *Living with Children: New Methods for Parents and Teachers by Gerald R. Patterson.*
- *Parents are Teachers: A Child Management Program by Wesley C. Becker.*

Teachers

The information below is available from Research Press (see above).

- *Skillstreaming the Elementary School Child and Skillstreaming the Adolscent by Dr. Arnold Goldstein and colleagues.*
- *Aggressive Replacement Training by Dr. Arnold Goldstein and Dr. Barry Glick.*
- *The Prepare Curriculum: Teaching Prosocial Competencies by Dr. Arnold Goldstein.*
- *Getting Along with Others by Nancy F. Jackson, Dr. Donald A. Jackson and Cathy Monroe.*

NATIONAL
ASSOCIATION OF
SCHOOL
PSYCHOLOGISTS

Delinquency

Kim Robinson
University of South Florida

Background—Statistics from the U.S. Department of Commerce (1983) indicate that 20% of all arrests in 1981 involved children under the age of 18. Furthermore, when the more serious crimes were considered, it was found that 33% of those arrested were juveniles. The percentage of children seen in the juvenile courts has increased from 2% in 1960 to 5% in 1979 (Statistical Abstracts, 1982-1983). Although juvenile crime has traditionally been considered a male problem, the percentage of females involved in juvenile delinquency is increasing at a higher rate than males. Between 1965 and 1981 delinquent offenses committed by females increased by 78%, nearly double the rate of increase for males (Knopf, 1984). When one considers the cost of the rising rate of delinquency in terms of monies involved in supporting the juvenile court system, treatment and rehabilitation of delinquents, as well as the personal costs that the victims of these crimes suffer, the seriousness of the juvenile delinquency problem is apparent.

Generally, the term delinquency refers to any illegal act committed by a juvenile (someone below the legal age of adulthood, which varies from state to state). A juvenile can be considered delinquent for breaking any federal, state, or local criminal laws. In addition, a juvenile can be considered delinquent for committing status offenses, which are behaviors that are not considered crimes for adults (truancy, running away, drinking alcohol, etc.).

It should be noted that many of the statistics relating to delinquency are based on arrest rates and involvement in the juvenile justice system. According to some research, this limits a large number of individuals who engage in delinquent behaviors but never become involved in the legal system. One study by Moore and Arthur (1983) suggests that as many as 80-90% of individuals may actually engage in illegal activities.

The term delinquent may conjure up the image of the stereotypical neighborhood thug. However, all delinquents are not alike. There has been considerable research to try to identify specific and reliable subgroups of delinquent youth. Quay (1964) has identified four meaningful dimensions of delinquent behavior that are widely used in the juvenile justice system. They are socialized-subcultural delinquency, unsocialized-psychopathic delinquency, disturbed-neurotic delinquency, and inadequate-immature delinquency.

Socialized-subcultural delinquents are relatively normal individuals whose delinquent behavior relates to association with an antisocial subgroup, like a gang. These individuals tend to be of lower socioeconomic status and do not tend to display other psychological problems.

In contrast, the *unsocialized-psychopathic delinquent* tends to be a loner. In addition, this type of delinquent displays limited remorse, anxiety, and guilt, and does not respond adequately to praise or punishment. This type of delinquent has been compared to the psychopathic adult.

The behavior of the *disturbed-neurotic delinquent* is often considered to stem from emotional problems relating to anxiety, depression, guilt, and inferiority. These individuals are less likely to engage in repeat offenses and aggressive behavior.

Finally, the *inadequate-immature delinquent* displays poor social awareness and poor social skills as well as a general inability to cope with the demands of home and school. Frustration and impulsivity appear to be the precursors of delinquent behavior in this type of delinquent, as opposed to peer pressure or anger.

It is probable that the reasons each of these groups display delinquent behavior are very different. It should also be considered that each of these groups may respond differently to various intervention programs.

Development—There are a variety of theories regarding the development of delinquent behaviors. However, it is a complex social behavior that most often cannot be attributed to any one causal factor.

There is no strong evidence that race, social, or economic factors are strongly related to delinquency. However, one model of delinquency identifies a juvenile's perceived or real inability to attain social or economic goals through legitimate means as the motivation for criminal behavior.

Aggression is a developmental variable that may be related to later delinquency. Disruptive/aggressive acts account for nearly 50% of social interactions among 12- to 18-month-olds. However, as language skills and social skills develop, the use of these strategies decreases (Holmberg, 1977). By the time a child reaches adolescence the occurrence of physical assault is rare. Rather, aggression is expressed through verbal taunts and cursing (Holmberg, 1977). It may be that violent adolescents are developmentally delayed in respect to the normal developmental sequence of aggression. Nondelinquent children outgrow aggressive behavior and develop more appropriate ways of expressing anger, solving problems, and getting what they want, but delinquent children may lag behind in the development of these alternative skills.

Another developmental factor lies in family characteristics of delinquent youth. Extreme punishment and inconsistent, neglectful discipline correlate with delinquency. Lack of parental support and nurturing are also linked to delinquency (Glueck & Glueck, 1968).

Another view of the development of delinquency considers it a learned behavior. Indeed, parental modeling of antisocial and criminal behavior has been associated with delinquency (Glueck & Glueck, 1968). This problem may be magnified due to a lack of exposure to role models who engage in the appropriate alternative behaviors noted above.

Farley and Sewell (1976) suggested that delinquent individuals are underaroused and thus seek stimulation through novel, exciting activities. Other researchers have suggested that there may be a subgroup of hyperactive children who can be characterized by lowered arousal levels. This would, in part, explain the overlap that has been demonstrated between hyperactivity and delinquency and aggression. However, there are many children who are hyperactive and do not display aggressive or otherwise delinquent behaviors.

There is also evidence that hard-core delinquents fail to respond effectively to punishment in the same way as normal people. This increased tolerance and quicker recovery from pain diminish their ability to learn from the negative consequences that may follow undesirable behavior.

What Can I Do as a Parent/Teacher?—In treating delinquency, professional support should be considered. However, in the case of delinquency, prevention is the most effective role of parents and teachers.

- A nurturing and supportive relationship, as well as a balanced and consistent system of discipline should be provided. Research suggests that parent training is often an effective intervention.

- Parents and teachers should proactively teach appropriate social, problem-solving, and coping skills. Research of various treatments of delinquency shows that programs that attempt to provide students with the skills to cope with the demands of the natural environment appear to hold the most promise.

- Schools and parents should work to insure that students educational and vocational needs are met so that the disparity between goals and reality can be reduced. Children need experiences with success.

References

Farley, F. A., & Sewell, T. (1976). Test of an arousal theory of delinquency: Stimulation seeking in delinquent and nondelinquent black adolescents. *Criminal Justice and Behavior, 3,* 315-320.

Glueck, S., & Glueck, E. (1968). *Delinquents and non-delinquents in perspective.* Cambridge: Harvard University Press.

Holmberg, M. C. (1977). *The development of social interchange patterns from 12 to 42 months: Cross-sectional and short term longitudinal analyses.* Unpublished doctoral dissertation, University of North Carolina at Chapel Hill.

Knopf, I. J. (1984). *Childhood Psychopathology.* Englewood Cliffs, NJ: Prentice-Hall.

Moore, D. R., & Arthur, J. L. (1983). Juvenile delinquency. In T. Ollendick & M. Hersen (Eds.), *Handbook of child psychopathology.* New York: Plenum.

Quay, H. C. (1964). Dimensions of personality in delinquent boys as inferred from factor analysis of case history data. *Child Development, 35,* 497-484.

U. S. Department of Commerce. (1983). *Statistical abstracts of the United States (1982-1983).* Washington, DC: Author.

NATIONAL ASSOCIATION OF SCHOOL PSYCHOLOGISTS

Children and Depression

H. L. Janzen, *University of Alberta*
D. H. Saklofske, *University of Saskatchewan*

Background—Depressed mood is a common and universal part of human experience that can occur at any age and has various causes. Over time, many children report or give the appearance of feeling unhappy, sad, dejected, irritable, "down" or "blue" but most of them quickly and spontaneously recover from these brief and normal moods or emotional states. However, for others, the depression can be severe and long lasting, and interfere with all aspects of daily life from school achievement to social relationships.

The incidence of more severe depression in children is probably less than 10% although exact figures are not known. Girls are more likely than boys to develop mood disorders. The associated risk of suicide increases significantly during adolescence.

Development—Recognizing and diagnosing childhood depression is not always an easy task. The onset of depression can be gradual or sudden, it may be a brief or long term episode, and may be associated with other disorders such as anxiety. The presence of one or two symptoms is not sufficient evidence of a depressive disorder. It is when a group of such symptoms occur together over time that a more serious mood disorder should be considered. The DSM-III-R manual published by the American Psychiatric Association classified depression according to severity, duration and type.

The definition of major depression requires the presence of five or more of the following symptoms for at least two weeks. One or both of the essential features of depressed or irritable mood, and loss of interest or pleasure in almost all activities must be observed. Other symptoms include appetite disturbance and significant weight loss or gain, sleep difficulties or too much sleep, slow or agitated and restless behavior (many depressed children become overly aggressive), decreased energy or fatigue, feeling of worthlessness or self-blame and guilt, concentration and thinking difficulties, and thoughts of death or suicide.

Less severe forms of depression include dysthymia (moderately depressed mood over one year) and adjustment disorder with depressed mood caused by some known stress and lasting less than 6 months. Depressive features will vary in relation to the age and developmental level of the child. For example, physical complaints, agitation, anxiety and fears are more often seen in younger children while adolescents are more likely to engage in antisocial behavior or become sulky, overly emotional, and withdrawn.

There are a number of suggested causes of childhood depression. Biological explanations of depression have examined the roles of hereditary, biochemical, hormonal, and brain factors. More recently, the amount of light associated with seasonal changes has been suspected to affect mood.

Psychological descriptions have linked depression to the loss of loved ones, disturbances in parent-child relationships, and threats to self-esteem. Attention has also been focused on the way children interpret and structure everyday experiences and the belief they have about their ability to control and shape their world. Any of a number of psychological stressors may be able to significantly affect the mood of some children.

Given the various kinds and causes of childhood depression, there are different treatments that may be required. The "treatment" for the disappointment that follows the loss of a ball game may be a visit to the local hamburger restaurant, or the feelings of failure and irritability caused by a poor school mark could signal the need to improve study habits and pay closer attention in school. When the signs of depression described above occur and persist, the professional assistance of a psychologist or psychiatrist should be obtained. Antidepressant (tricyclics and MAO inhibitors) and antianxiety medications are very beneficial in the treatment of severe depression. Several effective forms of psychological treatment include behavioral, cognitive-behavioral, and interpersonal (IPT) therapy. Combined medication and psychotherapy programs are frequently employed in the treatment of depression.

What can I do as a parent?

The list of suggestions follows the most frequently cited symptoms of childhood depression.

—Self-esteem and self-critical tendencies: give frequent and genuine praise; accentuate the positive; supportively challenge self-criticism; point out negative thinking.

—Family stability: maintain routine and minimize changes in family matters; discuss changes beforehand and reduce worry.

—Helplessness and hopelessness: have the child write or tell immediate feelings and any pleasant aspects 3 or 4 times a day to increase pleasant thoughts over 4-6 weeks.

—Mood elevation: arrange one interesting activity a day; plan for special events to come; discuss enjoyable topics.

—Appetite and weight problems: don't force eating; prepare favorite foods; make meal-time a pleasant occasion.

—Sleep difficulties: keep regular bed-time hours; do relaxing and calming activities one hour before bed-time such as reading or listening to soft music; end the day on a "positive note."

—Agitation and restlessness: change activities causing agitation; teach the child to relax; massage may help; encourage physical exercise and recreation activities.

—Excessive fears: minimize anxiety-causing situations and uncertainty; be supportive and reassuring; planning may reduce uncertainty; relaxation exercises might help.

—Aggression and anger: convey a kind but firm unacceptance of destructive behavior; encourage the child to his angry feelings; do not react with anger.

—Concentration and thinking difficulties: encourage increased participation in games, activities, discussions; work with the teachers and school psychologist to promote learning.

—Suicidal thoughts: be aware of the warning signs of suicide; immediately seek professional help.

—If depression persists: consult your family doctor for a complete medical exam; seek a referral to a psychologist or psychiatrist.

Resources

Depression and Its Treatment—by Drs. J. H. Greist and J. Jefferson, 1984. This is a very readable layman's guide to understanding and treating depression.

Stress, Sanity and Survival—by Drs. R. L. Woolfolk and F. C. Richardson, 1978. Numerous suggestions are given for dealing with worry, anger, anxiety, inadequacy and other signs of stress associated with depression.

Three Steps Forward: Two Steps Back—by C. R. Swindel, 1980. Written from a religious perspective, this book offers practical ways to face problems such as loss, anxiety, self-doubt, fear and anger.

Control Your Depression—by Dr. P. Lewinsohn, 1979. This leading expert offers meaningful and helpful suggestions based on his theory of depression.

Feeling Good: The New Mood Therapy—by David Burns, 1980. This book provides many useful ideas for changing depressed mood and feelings of sadness.

Danny's Descent Into Hell—by S. McCoy, Reader's Digest, January, 1988. This moving and insightful article describes a teenager's depression.

NATIONAL ASSOCIATION OF SCHOOL PSYCHOLOGISTS

Children and Drug Abuse

Mickey K. Randolph,
Susan G. Forman, Kathy L. Jackson
University of South Carolina
Columbia, South Carolina

Background—Each year a large number of teenagers begin using alcohol and/or drugs. A recent large scale national survey indicated that 92% of high school seniors had tried alcohol and 61% had tried marijuana. Forty-five percent of the boys and 28% of the girls reported regular heavy drinking. Daily alcohol use or daily marijuana use was reported by about 5% of these students.

Serious negative effects of even the most frequently used substances, tobacco, alcohol and marijuana, have been documented. Health, social, behavioral, psychological, and learning problems can result from substance abuse by children and youth.

Development—Substance use progresses through stages, with most teens initially experimenting with tobacco, beer, wine, and hard liquor. Marijuana use begins somewhat later. Some teens go on to experiment with depressants (ex. Quaaludes), stimulants (ex. amphetamines), psychedelics (ex. LSD), and opiates (ex. heroin). First use typically takes place in social situations with friends. A large percentage of teens experiment and do not repeat the experience. Some use substances occasionally without experiencing negative consequences. However, others begin to use compulsively and encounter a wide range of problems.

The average grade for first use of alcohol is grade 9, however 56% of high school seniors have reported initial use of alcohol before high school. Most marijuana use also seems to start during middle school and early high school. Surprisingly, almost 4% of high school seniors have reported that they tried an illegal drug before sixth grade.

A wide variety of social, developmental, behavioral, and psychological factors have been found to be associated with adolescent substance abuse. The most important of these are antisocial behavior during childhood, association with substance-using peers, poor school performance, parental substance use, and problems in family communication and family behavior management.

What can I do as a parent?

Parents and Children

1. Be a good role model, set a good example. Parents' habits and attitudes regarding alcohol and drug use influence their children's behavior. Children will notice why their parents drink, when they drink, how much they drink, and what they do while they're drinking. Drinking in front of children is not necessarily harmful, but drinking too much and in risk situations (ex. while driving) can be harmful because children learn behavior from watching their parents.

2. Help your children have a positive self-image. Children and youth who feel good about themselves are less likely to use alcohol and/or drugs to help them feel good. Parents can assist in their children's development of a positive self-image by:

—giving frequent praise;

—praising effort, not just achievement;

—helping them set realistic goals:

—when correcting, criticizing the behavior, not the child;

—not making constant comparisons with other children;

—giving them real responsibilities so that they see themselves as useful and important;

—showing them love through hugs, kisses, and words.

3. Learn to listen to your child. Real listening is more than not talking. Listening includes:

—watching your child's facial expressions and body language to uncover how they really feel:

—rephrasing your child's comments to show you understand what was said;

—using your own body language (make eye contact, nod your head, smile when appropriate) and tone of voice to give support and encouragement;

—using encouraging phrases to keep the conversation going ("Tell me more about it.")

4. Talk with your child about substance use. An appropriate time may be when a television program or news report deals with the issue. Find out how your child feels about the issue and clearly explain why they should not drink or use drugs.

5. Encourage healthy acitivies. When a child has positive interests he or she may be less likely to experiment with drugs or alcohol because of boredom. These activities can include school clubs, scouts, music, sports, or other hobbies. Family activities are also beneficial.

6. Set family rules regarding substance use. Children should know that substance use will not be allowed and what the consequences for breaking the rule will be. Parents should tell children what they expect them to do in situations where they may be pressured to use alcohol or drugs.

7. Teach your children to deal with peer pressure. Children can be taught that there are times that they must stand up for themselves and "say no." Parents can role-play these situations with their children to help them develop strategies to resist peer pressure.

8. Know the early warning signs of substance use. Despite parents' good efforts, some pre-teens and teens begin using alcohol and/or drugs. Some early warning signs include: poor school work, change in sleeping habits, change in peer group, withdrawal from the family, unpredictable temper tantrums, association with known substance users and appearance of intoxification. The school psychologist, school counselor, or professionals at the local drug and alcohol abuse council can be helpful in determining needed services for your child if alcohol or drug use is suspected.

Parents and the School—Support substance and abuse prevention and early intervention programs in your child's school. Prevention programs usually consist of a curriculum provided for an entire grade level. Early intervention programs target students most at risk for substance abuse. Effective programs focus on teaching students personal and social coping skills such as: how to resist peer pressure, how to make decisions, how to manage anxiety, how to control behavior, and how to communicate with others. These skills help kids cope with problems and difficult situations so they won't be tempted to turn to drugs or alcohol.

Parents and the Community—Parents can band together to fight substance abuse through parent groups. A parent group can be a support group (parents help each other in dealing with their children's substance use problems) or an action group that raises alcohol and drug issues with community organizations, churches, schools or local government agencies. Parents can help each other take positive, constructive action to prevent substance abuse among youth.

Resources

The Parent Handbook of Drug Abuse—by J. Baron. Drug Abuse Program of America. 1981. Provides a detailed discussion of the most commonly abused substances. Physical symptoms as well as social-emotional changes are discussed. Provides prevention techniques and treatment recommendations.

Getting Tough on Gateway Drugs—by R. L. Dupont. American Psychiatric Press, 1985. In addition to describing the most commonly used drugs, the author focuses on the role that families can have in preventing and/or stopping substance use.

The Parent Connection: How to Communicate With Your Children About Alcohol and Other Drugs—by R. Meyer. Franklin Watts. 1984. Focuses on how parents can tell if their child is using alcohol and/or drugs. There is a strong emphasis on communication skills and resolving attitudinal differences.

What, When and How to Talk to Children About Alcohol and Other Drugs: A guide for parents—by C.C. Milgram. Hazelden. 1983. Provides information on influences to use alcohol and drugs, ways to identify alcohol/drug abuse in your children and finally, ways to prevent substance use.

Encopresis

Kim Robinson
University of South Florida

Background—Encopresis is defined as repeated defecation in clothing or other inappropriate places, or the inability to control defecation, after the age when bowel control is usually achieved. There are two subtypes of encopresis: continuous and discontinuous. Continuous encopresis refers to cases where the child has never developed bowel control, and discontinuous encopresis refers to cases where the child had been completely toilet trained, but regressed to bowel incontinence (Levine, 1982). Another distinction of encopretic behavior is between retentive and nonretentive encopresis. Children with retentive encopresis withhold feces, often becoming impacted. Children with nonretentive encopresis pass normal bowel movements. The majority (80-95%) of all cases of encopresis are of the retentive type (Levine, 1975).

The severity of this encopresis varies according to age, physical and mental development, medical complications, and social-emotional factors. Treatment can vary from simple reinforcement programs implemented by parents and/or school personnel to complex medical and behavioral interventions.

Development—Normal development of bowel control is achieved around the age of 3 or 4 years by approximately 70% of children, although girls tend to be slightly ahead of boys in this area. The task of attaining bowel control is more complex than one might think. It requires the child to have developed the physical ability to control the sphincter muscles, the ability to postpone the urge to defecate, and the ability to give a signal to an adult or go to the bathroom independently. The amount of time needed to accomplish bowel control tends to be less the later that training is initiated (Schaefer, 1979).

Causes—Levine (1982) has identified factors that contribute to the potential risk of developing encopresis at different developmental levels. In the infancy and toddler years painful constipation, medical problems with the anorectal area, parental overreaction, and coercive medical interventions place a child at risk for developing encopresis. In the 2-5-year range factors that may place a child at risk include either extremely coercive or extremely permissive training, fear of toilets, and painful or difficult defecation. During the early school years, avoidance of public restrooms with limited privacy, failure to persist at the task, frenzied lifestyles, and psychosocial stresses are some possible contributing factors.

Another potential cause of soiling behavior may be in the reinforcing nature of the one-on-one time that the child experiences while the parent has to help the child clean up. This may be why some parents report that an older sibling may become encopretic after the birth of another child. Although it may be an unpleasant experience for the parent, to a young child it may seem like a good way to get some individual time. This may be countered by providing some time specifically for individual time for that child. A child may also use soiling as a punishing event for those in authority.

Because the majority of children with encopresis are of the retentive type, it is important to understand the development of this condition. Children who display this type of encopresis do not fail to retain their feces. In contrast they retain their feces too well. This condition is referred to as psychogenic megacolon. The child begins with simple constipation and voluntary retention. Eventually the child's rectum and colon become impacted with large amounts of fecal material. When this occurs the child adapts to the sensation of fullness and loses the ability to respond to bodily cues of the need to defecate.

As the fecal material is retained, water is absorbed making the stool harder over time. The painful defecation that results can often lead to further avoidance of defecation. When the pressure of the retained fecal matter causes the sphincter to dilate, seepage of new liquid fecal matter around the impaction and leakage out into underclothing can result. This type of soiling is often called overflow or paradoxical diarrhea (Schmitt, 1984).

It should also be noted that encopresis can result from various medical conditions such as defects in the spinal canal, inflammation of the spinal cord, Hirschprungs disease, as well as other injury, assault, or disease.

What Can I Do as a Parent?—If a child is developing normally in all other areas, but fails to achieve bowel control by an appropriate age (after 4 years), or the child abruptly loses continence (at least several instances in one month), a family physician should examine the child to determine whether any medical problems, including impaction, are present.

Treatment can range from a simple reinforcement program implemented by parents to intensive medical interventions including enemas and laxative treatment, as well as comprehensive treatment programs that use both positive and aversive behavior modification in combination with medical intervention. The more severe the problem, the more likely it will be resistive to treatment and will require consultation with professionals. A family doctor will usually be able to recommend appropriate services. In addition, the school psychologist and medical personnel may be able to assist in the development of an individualized treatment program.

In terms of dealing with encopresis the following guidelines might be helpful:

—The use of a positive reinforcement approach, rather than an aversive or punishment approach, will make corrective bowel training less stressful.

—Successful training programs reinforce appropriate defecation as well as nonsoiling and do not focus on retention of feces as this could possibly make matters worse (i.e., psychogenic megacolon).

—Treatment should include an educational component. Appropriate bathroom skills must be taught like any other skill: trained, practiced, and reinforced. In addition, training may be needed when the child goes to a different setting (i.e., preschool).

—A corrective bowel training program may require weeks or months of strict compliance with the program. This is especially true in the case of retentive encopresis.- The older the child the more imperative it is that an effective intervention be promptly identified so that the development of serious secondary emotional problems (extreme fear of peer ridicule, self-isolation, excessive dependency, etc.) can be prevented.

School personnel can help by making a private restroom available for use, allowing the student to use the toilet whenever they request, making extra clothing available, and excusing the student from gym class or showers to avoid public humiliation.

References

Levine, M. D. (1975). Children with encopresis: A descriptive analysis. *Pediatrics, 56,* 412-416.

Levine, M. D. (1982). Encopresis: Its potentiation, evaluation, and alleviation. *Pediatric Clinics of North America, 29,* 315-330.

Schaefer, C. E. (1979). *Childhood encopresis and enuresis.* New York: Van Nostrand Reinhold.

Schmitt, B. D. (1984). Encopresis. *Primary Care, 11,* 497-511.

Enuresis

Erika Manz
University of South Florida

Background—There are two types of enuresis, diurnal and nocturnal. Diurnal enuresis is characterized by a failure to learn daytime bladder control and nocturnal enuresis is a failure to achieve nighttime bladder control, or bedwetting. Both types can occur together. However, when diurnal enuresis is present it is important that the child be given a thorough medical evaluation to rule out possible medical problems. Simple bedwetting, or primary nocturnal enuresis, which accounts for 80% of all bedwetting, is bedwetting in which a child has never had at least a 2-month period of consecutive dry nights. The frequency of bedwetting may range from twice a month to twice a week. Most primary nocturnal enuretics wet the bed five to seven nights per week. Secondary nocturnal enuresis often results from more complex medical or emotional problems. Secondary nocturnal enuretics display a more sporadic pattern and a lower frequency of wetting. Enuresis can run in families and may be partly hereditary. Up to 75% of bedwetters are boys.

Development—Children with enuresis are not simply lazy or lacking willpower but are unable to control their bladder functioning while sleeping. It appears that roughly 75% of 4-year-olds will outgrow bedwetting on their own. Bedwetting will stop spontaneously after about 3 years, on the average.

Bedwetting may be caused by several factors. One may be physical factors such as infections and chronic disease or physical defects, specifically in the bladder and kidneys. Urinary tract infections are found in 5% of male bedwetters and 10% of female bedwetters. Most urinary tract infections are effectively treated with antibiotics. Forty percent of children treated for urinary tract infection will stop wetting the bed when the infection is cleared. Emotional factors have also been thought to cause bedwetting. Some researchers believe that emotional problems can result in enuresis, more so for girls than for boys. Serious emotional problems are common in secondary enuretics and children who are both day and night wetters. A generally accepted factor in bedwetting is learning. Simple bedwetting often occurs because the child has failed to learn to attend and respond to his or her need to urinate while asleep.

What Can I Do as a Parent?—After a medical examination, consult a specialist regarding the following treatments:

1. *Drug treatment.* Imipramine hydrochloride (trade name Tofranil) can be prescribed in doses of 25-75 mg and is given one hour before bedtime. This treatment is viewed as a temporary solution because only 50% of children treated with this drug become dry during treatment and almost all resume bedwetting by the following year. Therefore, the lasting effects of imipramine hydrochloride are equal to the effects of spontaneous remission. Side effects of this treatment are increased heart rate, muscle tremor, profuse sweating, increased blood pressure, loss of appetite, and retention of urine.

2. *Behavioral treatments.* Four types of behavioral treatment of enuresis involve using a direct method of training at home by the parents. The effectiveness of these treatments depends on the willingness and ability of parents and children to follow the procedures correctly.

The **bell and pad training** relies on a urine alarm device that consists of a pad and a battery-operated alarm. They are commercially available from Sears and other suppliers. The alarm sounds when the child wets the bed and the parent must wake the child. Seventy-five percent of children experience initial arrest and about one third experience relapse following the treatment. Unsuccessful results may be due to inappropriate or incorrect use of the treatment. When **overlearning** is used, the chance of relapse is cut in half and the lasting cure rate for the two methods combined is 60%.

Retention control training teaches the child to increase bladder capacity by having the child drink large quantities of fluid on a predetermined schedule and rewarding the child for holding for longer and longer periods of time. Although this method is a useful adjunct to the bell and pad training, it is less effective when used by itself. The retention control method had a lasting cure with 30% of the children.

Another behavioral method is **dry-bed training**, which consists of waking the child at scheduled times to train dryness, positive practice, bell and pad, and cleanliness training. Relapse after dry-bed training (39%) is similar to that following the bell and pad training alone (41%). Furthermore, dry-bed training is more complicated and difficult to carry out than the bell and pad method alone.

Full-spectrum home training involves the strongest possible combination of behavioral procedures and is outlined in a self help book for parents by A. C. Houts and R. M. Liebert entitled, *Bedwetting: A Guide for Parents and Children.* This treatment includes bell and pad, cleanliness training, retention control, overlearning, and additional steps to ensure effectiveness. Eighty-one percent of children achieve initial arrest of bedwetting, 24% relapse after one year, and 61% demonstrate permanent results.

This paper is a synopsis of a chapter entitled, "Enuresis" from *Childrens' Needs: Psychological Perspectives* by Arthur C. Houts.

Fears and Phobias

Bonnie Matthews
University of South Florida

Background—Fear has often been described by professionals and educators as a reaction to a threatening situation. For example, an individual may experience fear when being chased by a growling dog or by a bully approaching with clenched fists. Phobias have been described as "fears which are severe, persistent behavioral patterns of avoidance" (Kendall et al., 1991). According to the *Diagnostic and Statistical Manual of Mental Disorders, 3rd Edition, Revised* (DSM-III-R; 1987), the most common phobias involve animals, particularly dogs, snakes, insects, and mice. Other common phobias include witnessing blood or tissue injury, closed spaces, and heights. When an individual is presented, in any way, with the phobic stimulus, he/she exhibits signs of anxiety. The phobic response may be elicited by nothing more, in some individuals, than the thought of the stimulus (i.e., imagining being near a dog or being in a high place).

Fears and phobias have been documented in individuals of all ages. Regarding children, Kratochwill, Sanders, and Wiemer (1991) report that the number of fears and phobias appears to vary with the age of the child. From their review of recent research results, they report that the number of fears tends to fluctuate from four to more than seven and that severe fears tend to be experienced by a fairly large proportion of children and adolescents. As a result of much research conducted on fears and phobias, effective treatments have become available. The review by Kratochwill and his colleagues (1987) indicates the following about fears associated with different aged children. Children aged 2 through 6 tend to have fears that are less reality based than those of other children of ages. For example, they tend to be afraid of things like ghosts and monsters. Children aged 7 through 12 tend to have fears that reflect threatening situations that seem more realistic. For example, they tend to be afraid of things like bodily injury and natural disasters. Children aged 13 through 18 tend to exhibit political fears as well as fears about personal-social relationships and fears of physical injury.

The Causes of Fears and Phobias—There are many theories about the potential causes of fears and phobias but the major characteristic of fears and phobias in children is that the child feels threatened by some situation. Phobic responses go one step further in that the fear about the situation is so severe that it interferes with their lives and the lives of those around them. Additionally, the fear may be to an unrealistic degree. Fears become problematic when they become so intense that the child's personal-social and/or school functioning begins to be negatively affected.

What Can I Do As A Parent?—In determining if fears are present and if the problem warrants further attention, you as a parent can consider the following questions.

—Are the behaviors associated with the fears typical for my child's age?

—What are the symptoms of the fear and how do they affect my child's personal, social, and academic functioning

—Does the fear seem more severe than the situation would seem to warrant?

—Is the fear only a sign of a more serious problem that my child is experiencing?

—Is my child's behavior essentially normal, but people around him/her are finding it difficult to tolerate the behavior?

Suggestions for parents:

—Do not discount the emotional response of your child. His/her feelings may be very real to him/her.

—Listen to your child. Often times the fear may be decreased by providing the child with correct or specific information about the feared situation.

—Allow the child to discuss the fear with you. The child needs to know he/she has your understanding and support.

—Seek professional help if the fear seems to be interfering with your child's daily functioning or if it persists for a longer period of time than seems appropriate.

Resources

If further information is desired, you may find it helpful to consult with the school guidance counselor or school psychologist. Additionally, your local mental health centers, pediatricians, and clergy may be of assistance in providing you with information more specific to your child's needs.

References

American Psychiatric Association. (1987). *Diagnostic and statistical manual of mental disorders* (3rd ed., rev.). Washington, DC: American Psychiatric Press.

Kendall, P. C., Chansky, T. E., Freidman, R. K., Kortlander, E., Sessa, F. M., & Siqueland, L. (1991). Treating anxiety disorders in children and adolescents. In P. Kendall (Ed.), *Child and adolescent therapy: Cognitive-behavioral procedures.* New York: Guilford Press.

Kratochwill, T. R., Sanders, C., & Wiemer, S. (1987). Children and fears and phobias. In A. Thomas & J. Grimes (Eds.), *Children's needs: Psychological perspectives* (pp. 214-221). Washington, DC: National Association of School Psychologists.

Firesetting

Kim Robinson
University of South Florida

Background—Children are responsible for 40-70% of documented intentional fires (Baizerman & Emshoff, 1984) and the incidence rates of firesetting appear to be growing rapidly. Although curiosity about fire occurs as a normal part of development, the consequences of "playing with fire" can be tragic. A dangerous combination lies in the decreasing level of parent supervision and the unlimited access to matches and lighters in American society.

Although any instance of firesetting is of concern, the firesetter could be engaging in anything from curious fire-play to recidivist arson. Wooden and Berky (1984) identify four types of firesetters: (a) young children (under age 10) who start fires accidentally; (b) delinquent firesetters acting out against society; (c) older children who have other problems and set fires as a cry for help (the largest group); and (d) severely emotionally disturbed firesetters (the least prevalent type of firesetter).

Development—Fascination with, and attraction to fire is a typical phenomenon in the development of young children. Curiosity about fire is most common in 2- to 7-year-olds. Interest in fire usually dissipates around the age of 9 or 10. At this age a child is no longer considered a curiosity firesetter and the possible existence of other problems must be investigated (Fineman, 1980). However, there have been cases of pathological firesetters at earlier ages.

Like many other behavior problems, firesetting occurs more frequently in the male population. Young children who set fires tend to do so in or near their own homes. Older children are more likely to set fires in a social context, away from the home environment (Sensor, 1985). Research by Patterson (1982) indicates that firesetters exhibited less serious behavioral problems in their early behavioral history. The early behavior pattern of the firesetter appears to escalate from high-frequency, low-intensity behaviors like non-compliance to the low-frequency, high-intensity behavior of firesetting.

A social learning theory of the development of pathological firesetting was proposed by Fineman (1980). In some cases, natural curiosity may be reinforced by social factors such as negative attention and the sensation of power surrounding the child's first experience with fire. The child may then develop the symptom of firesetting as a pathological coping mechanism.

Although all instances of firesetting or suggestions of future plans to set fires should be considered serious, assessing the level of seriousness of a child's involvement in a fire-related incident is a very difficult task. Some of the issues that should be addressed include the following:

—The age of the child. Is the behavior typical for a child of a given age?

—Frequency and duration. Has the behavior occurred before? Across different settings? For how long? Does the child plan to do it again?

—Does the child display other behavior problems?

—What were the circumstances preceding the behavior?

—Motivation. Was the incident motivated by curiosity, excitement, accident proneness of the child playing with matches, anger expression, etc.?

—Did the firesetting incident have major or minor ramifications (burn marks on the carpet or incineration of the family household)

—Is the behavior a sign of other family, school, or interpersonal problems?

Parents and teachers should consult other professionals to assist in determining the level of severity of the behavior and the most appropriate intervention. As with most behavior problems, proper early intervention can result in prevention.

What Parents and Teachers Can Do—The most desirable intervention for firesetting is prevention. Families and schools should utilize educative strategies to teach children the dangers as well as the practical and appropriate uses of fire. In addition, the child's environment should be "fire-safe." Children should not have access to matches or lighters and should be supervised so that the opportunity for fire-play is reduced.

In responding to the "curiosity" firesetter, the parents and/or school should act quickly. The school psychologist can assist the school and the family in addressing the firesetting behavior. One option is to have a respected individual from the community or school speak to the child about the seriousness of the behavior. The school can then support the child's appropriate behavior through the implementation of a fire safety curriculum.

The Juvenile Firesetter Handbook (Federal Emergency and Management Agency, 1984) suggests several behavioral management strategies including: (a) putting the child in charge of fire safety education for younger students or siblings, (b) developing a contract with an adult to earn rewards for appropriate behavior, (c) restitution strategies where the child must help repair or earn money to repair damages, and (d) educational strategies as well as several other behavior management strategies. Another option is referring the curiosity firesetter to the local chapter of the National Firehawk Foundation. This program pairs trained fire fighters with firesetters in an educational and therapeutic relationship.

The serious or pathological firesetter should be referred to the agency where the assessment and intervention needs of the child and family can be quickly and appropriately met.

The key to helping the pathological juvenile firesetter is to reduce stress, teach alternative problem-solving and attention-getting skills, encourage the child to develop appropriate ways to express anger and monitor and verbalize aggression, and most importantly, provide stronger rewards elsewhere. In addition, the child must learn to reduce impulsivity. Fear and anxiety in relation to setting a fire must be raised to reduce the firesetting impulse and stop the behavior. This paper is a synopsis of a chapter by Melissa Gordon (1987).

Resources

Firesetting. In A. Thomas & J. Grimes (Eds.), *Children's needs: Psychological perspectives.* (pp. 221-228). Washington, DC: National Association of School Psychologists.
National Firehawk Foundation. P.O. Box 27488, San Francisco, CA 94127. (415) 922-3242.

References

Baizerman, M., & Emshoff, B. (1984). Juvenile firesetting: Building a community based prevention program. *Children Today, 3,* 8-12.
Federal Emergency and Management Agency, U.S. Fire Administration. (1984). *Interviewing and counseling juvenile firesetters.* Washington, DC: Author.
Fineman, K. (1980). Firesetters in childhood and adolescence. *Psychiatric Clinics of North America, 3,* 483-500.
Patterson, G. (1982). *Coercive family process.* Egene, OR: Castalia.
Sensor, C. (1985). Firesetting. In J. Grimes & A. Thomas, (Eds.), *Psychological approaches to problems of children and adolescents (pp. 3-19).* Des Moines, IA: Iowa Department of Public Institutions.
Wooden, W., & Berkey, M. (1984). *Children and arson: America's middle class nightmare.* New York: Plenum.

Children and Head Injury

Robert Diamond
University of Virginia Health Sciences Center

Background—As many as 4 out of 100 individuals may have a significant head injury each year. Head injury is more common in children than adults, and more common in boys than girls. Mild, or minor, head injuries, which do not involve prolonged loss of consciousness or medical complications, are fortunately much more common than the severe injuries. Typical causes of head injury include auto accidents, athletic injuries, falls, and interpersonal violence. Even a common childhood activity such as bicycle riding can cause thousands of head injuries each year. The most common result of head injury is a disruption of intellectual abilities, however, other consequences may include personality changes, impulse control problems, headaches, and seizures. An encouraging fact about the intellectual and behavioral after effects of head injury is that in nearly all cases change is expected in the direction of improvement.

Development—Following head injury, there is a period of a gradually decreasing rate of recovery. In the first few months following head injury there is a rapid recovery of a substantial portion of preinjury abilities. More moderate gains may continue for up to two years. Verbal language abilities and well learned material recover rapidly, while the recovery of reasoning and new learning abilities may take much longer. The early recovery of language abilities may leave head injured persons in the difficult position of seeming more capable and recovered than they actually are.

Physical, psychological, and environmental factors are involved in the recovery from head injury. For more severe head injuries, there are numerous specialized head injury rehabilitation programs. Particularly for minor head injuries, psychological and environmental factors can be vital. One point of concern is that head injured individuals may be negatively affected by expecting to return too soon to preinjury levels. The consequences of minor head injury are often subtle and not easily detected without specialized testing. It is also often difficult for families and for those who work with children to connect learning problems to a minor head injury which occurred some months previously. In this situation, a child may be perceived as unmotivated, lazy, negative, disturbed, or lacking in ability. The mistaken perceptions will only compound difficulties and interfere with recovery.

What can I do as a parent?

An ounce of prevention is worth a pound of cure. It is better to prevent a head injury than to deal with the consequences of one. Use seat belts and child safety seats in automobiles. If your children are engaging in high risk activities (bicycle riding, horseback riding, using all terrain vehicles, playing football, etc.) require them to wear protective headgear.

Better safe than sorry. Seek medical attention if your child has had even a momentary loss of consciousness or period of unresponsiveness. Other indicators of a need for a medical check include confusion, grogginess, visual problems, difficulty remembering what happened immediately before or after the injury, a severe headache which develops a few hours after the injury, vomiting, uneven pupil size, and limb weakness on one side. If you aren sure whether or not you should see a physician, see a physician.

Don't compare apples and oranges. Recognize that medical professionals are primarily concerned with physical health. Following a minor head injury, your child may clearly not be at medical risk. Your physician's reassurance that there has been a complete recovery is medically accurate. However, in many cases subtle cognitive difficulties may continue for an extended period. Medical professionals with their different criteria, may lead you to expect that everything will be just as it was before the injury. A comprehensive psychological evaluation of your child may be necessary to identify deficits and direct any intervention. Your school psychologist may either perform this evaluation, or be able to refer you to a clinical neuropsychologist.

Don't keep the schools in the dark. If your child has had a severe head injury, be sure that the individuals involved in the rehabilitation program coordinate efforts with the school. The types of intellectual deficits which are seen following mild head injury in children are often first noticed in the school setting. If teachers and other school personnel are not aware that your child has had a head injury, their expectations may not be consistent with your child's capabilities. This discrepancy may lead to the stress and negative conditions which can prolong difficulties.

Let nature take its course. The most important function of the family, the school, and others in the head injured child's environment is to allow the natural process of recovery to occur. Everyone involved with your child should understand that there may be some decline in in tellectual efficiency, but that improvement is expected. The degree of improvement is difficult to predict, and may range from a complete recovery of preinjury abilities to a persistent loss of certain abilities. It will be best to maintain an attitude of realistic optimism. Evaluation by the school psychologist or a clinical neuropsychologist can identify those children in need of more intensive rehabilitation.

Resources

For medical questions or concerns about physical symptoms:

- The emergency room or trauma center at your local hospital
- Your child's physician
- Hospital nursing and medical staff

For questions about recovery and possible effects of head injury on your child's learning abilities:

- Hospital neuropsychology, education, physical therapy, speech therapy, and occupational therapy staffs (if involved)
- Instructional and support staff at your child's school, particularly the school psychologist and special education resource teacher
- National Head Injury Foundation: 18A Vernon Street, Framingham, MA 01701; (617) 879-7473

Obsessive Compulsive Disorder in Children

Joyce Krumbein Slater, Ph.D.
Milford School System, Milford, Connecticut

Definition

According to the Diagnostic and Statistical Manual of Mental Disorders, 3rd Edition, Revised (DSM-III-R), Obsessive Compulsive Disorder (OCD) involves having "recurrent obsession or compulsions sufficiently severe to cause marked distress, be time consuming, or significantly interfere with the person's normal routine, occupational functioning, or usual social activities or relationships with others."

Obsessions are unwanted, persistent thoughts, ideas or worries that repeatedly besiege a person's mind. These ruminations are typically experienced as intrusive, unpleasant and senseless. The obsessions are recognized as the product of one's mind, but the person seems to have little or no control over them. Common obsessions include repetitive thoughts of violence (e.g., hurting a loved one), contamination (e.g., becoming infected by touching something), and doubt (e.g., unsure if something has been done correctly or questioning the basic nature of things such as "Is the sky really blue?").

Compulsions are repetitive and intentional behaviors performed usually in response to obsessions in order to reduce anxiety. Typically, the behavior is not related to the obsession, but it seems to reduce initial anxiety. The most common rituals include excessive hand washing, checking, counting, hoarding, touching, having to do certain things (not all) perfectly and seeking constant reassurance.

Background

Severity of OCD varies—many cases are so mild that treatment is not necessary, some are so severe that compulsive rituals ruin the individual's life, taking up most of their waking hours. Since effective treatment is now becoming available, more OCD sufferers are beginning to seek help. Recent studies conducted by the National Institute of Mental Health found that 2.5% (1 in 40) of the population has suffered from OCD at some point in their lives.

Causes of OCD

There is a growing body of research suggesting that OCD has its roots in the biological sphere. New research indicates that OCD involves abnormal metabolism in specific areas of the brain. Specifically, the neurotransmitter (brain messenger) serotonin has been called into question. To date, serotonin has been related to depression, anger, impulsivity and OCD.

Imaging techniques have revealed that the frontal lobe region and a portion of the basal ganglia

217

behave differently in OCD patients. In addition, there appears to be a relationship between Tourettes syndrome (uncontrollable motor and vocal tics) and an increased incidence of OCD.

Treatment

Treatment may include family interventions, behavior therapy and/or drug treatment. Drug treatment is seldom used alone. Traditional psychoanalytic or psychotherapeutic techniques have not proved to be effective in the treatment of OCD.

Family Intervention involves counseling the family to be neither antagonistic nor accommodating. Principles of behavior therapy are discussed with the family in addition to helping the family negotiate with the patient. Most importantly, the family learns to disengage from the patient's rituals, i.e., to become involved in the patient's rituals as little as possible.

Behavior Therapy has proven to be very valuable, especially in treatment of children. The patient is taught to focus on specific behaviors and to systematically lessen anxiety. Techniques used include exposure (facing the things they fear) and response prevention (refraining from carrying out compulsive rituals). Children very often need external motivation which may include contingency contracting and/or a menu of rewards. Patients usually have homework (practicing behavior techniques at home) and treatment is most often short term.

Drug Treatment at present primary involves Clomipramine (Anafranil) or Fluoxamine (Faverin), which enhance serotonin neurotransmission. Fluoxetine (Prozac), a serotonin uptake inhibitor, has also shown promise in reducing obsessions and rituals. Pharmacological treatment is a last resort, especially for children. When necessary, drug treatment is employed but only in conjunction with behavioral and family intervention.

What can I do as a parent?

- Deciding when to seek treatment is a matter of personal choice, although family members and the child's pediatrician may be helpful in making the decision.
- If parents suspect that their child has OCD, it is important to get a professional assessment. Because of embarrassment, most OCD sufferers go to great length to conceal their disorder. OCD, therefore, can be confused with many other childhood illness such as depression, anxiety disorders, learning disabilities, and school avoidance.
- Instituting behavior therapy also requires guidance and support and should not be initially attempted without the aid of a professional.
- Parents should be neither antagonistic nor accommodating. They should seek to become involved in their child's rituals as little as possible.
- Finding an experienced behavior therapist can often be difficult. Departments of psychiatry affiliated with medical schools may be a good source. Other excellent resources are listed at the end of this handout.

What can I do as a teacher?

- Remember, children with OCD may outwardly function as normal individuals. Because of fear of being stigmatized, OCD sufferers often go to extreme lengths to hide or camouflage their OCD. Teachers need to be psychologically sensitive to children with OCD, taking great care not to embarrass or ridicule them.
- It is important for teachers to be neither antagonistic nor accommodating, careful not to feed or reinforce a child's rituals.

- If a teacher suspects OCD, it is important to consult the school psychologist or other mental health professional in the school. Diagnosis and assessment should be made by a trained professional.
- Once a child is diagnosed, teachers should work with the child's therapist or school psychologist in order to help set up proper guidelines for school performance. For example, a child who continually erases might be rewarded for papers which come in without erasure marks.
- Remember, one of the goals of behavior treatment is to shape normal behavior for the OCD sufferer. It is perfectly reasonable for teachers to require normal classroom behavior of children with OCD. Reward rather than punishment should be used.
- A menu of reinforcement (list of reward activities) has proven most effective with school age children. Remember, what adults may think is a reinforcer may not be thought so by a child.

Resources

Obsessive Compulsive Foundation, P.O. Box 9573, New Haven, Connecticut 06525, (203) 772-0565
Anxiety Disorders Association of America, 6000 Executive Boulevard—Suite 200, Rockville, Maryland 20852-4004, (301) 231-9350

References

American Psychiatric Association. *Diagnostic and Statistical Manual of Mental Disorders*—3rd edition—*Revised*, Washington, D.C.: American Psychiatric Press, 1987.
Greist, J. H. (1989). *Obsessive Compulsive Disorder: A Guide.* Madison, WI. Obsessive Compulsive Information Center, University of Wisconsin.
Livingston, B. (1989). *Learning to Live with Obsessive Compulsive Disorder: A Guide.* Madison, WI. Obsessive Compulsive Information Center, University of Wisconsin.
Livingston, B. (1989). *Learning to Live with Obsessive Compulsive Disorders.* New Haven, CT., Obsessive Compulsive Foundation.
Rapoport, J. L. (1989). *The Boy Who Couldn't Stop Washing.* New York, New York: E.P. Dutton.

NATIONAL
ASSOCIATION OF
SCHOOL
PSYCHOLOGISTS

Physical Abuse

Nancy Conti
University of South Florida

Background—Currently in this country, 30.6 children per every 1,000 are reported abused (Gargiulo, 1990). Each year an estimated 200,000 children are abused and 2,000 of them die from the abuse (Meier, 1985). Five to 10% will suffer lasting impairment (Justice & Justice, 1990). It is suspected that the above statistics do not reflect the actual number of children in the United States who are physically abused. This is due to differences in how physical abuse is defined and the inability to detect those children who are never taken for medical treatment or identified as abused.

Definitions range from those that are very specific and include the types of instruments used and the resulting injuries (Gargiulo, 1990), to definitions that simply refer to abuse as physical injury (Meier, 1985; Stern, 1987). This is further complicated by changes in definition across time and cultures (Vizard, 1987).

An accurate assessment of the number of abused children is also affected by the inability to detect all who are abused. Many children do not receive medical treatment and some are simply not identified (Gargiulo, 1990; Justice & Justice, 1990). This may be due to where the abuse is located on the body and the family changing residence when abuse is suspected by the physician, teacher, neighbor, etc.

Development—Abuse most often occurs in the home by a parent who was likely to have been abused as a child also (Stern, 1987; Vizard, 1987). Most often the mother is the abuser (Justice & Justice, 1990; Meier, 1985), followed by "fathers, boyfriends, relatives, neighbors, babysitters, and others" (Meier, 1985).

Although the younger the child the more at risk the child is for injury, school-age children are the most frequently identified group of abused youngsters. Abuse will vary across gender also, with boys between the ages of 5 and 9, and girls ages 14 and up having the highest rate of abuse (Creighton, 1987; Justice & Justice, 1990; Moore, 1985).

Causes of Physical Abuse—To assess why abuse occurs within a family, three factors must be considered. These include: (a) what the parent(s) bring to the situation; (b) what the child brings; and (c) the situation factors.

Parent factors that have been found to contribute and/or be associated to the initiation and maintenance of abusive behavior towards a child include, but are not limited to:

—Marital problems

—Minor criminal offenses and/or history of violence

—Becoming a parent at an early age

—Lack of a support system

—Parents who were typically victims of abuse as children

—Parents who believe in harsh punishment

—Parents who use and/or abuse drugs and alcohol

—Parents with mental illness, anxiety, and/or high stress (Gargiulo, 1990; Justice & Justice, 1990; Newberger & Newberger, 1981; Vizard, 1987).

Child factors typically found in abusive families include, but are not limited to:

—Prematurity and/or neonatal problems (i.e., colic)

—Physical handicaps

—Illness

—Unwanted pregnancy

—Hyperactivity

—Difficulty with bladder or bowel control

—Twins

—Temperament of the child (i.e., difficult personality)

—Difficult to control (Justice & Justice, 1990; Meier, 1985; Newberger & Newberger, 1981; Vizard, 1990).

Situational factors associated with the initiation and maintenance of child abuse include, but are not limited to:

—Relationship of parents

—Relationship between parent(s) and child

—Stress on the family due to environmental situations (i.e., housing problems and unemployment)

—Single parent homes (either divorced or never married)

—Large number of family members

—Isolation (lack of support) from family and friends (Browne & Saqi, 1987; Justice & Justice, 1990; Meier, 1985; Newberger & Newberger, 1981).

Precipitating the abusive interaction, various factors that may be parent, child, or situational can be triggers that initiate the abuse. These factors include: child misbehavior; parent-to-parent or parent-to-child argument; scapegoating of the child for problems in the family; child crying; parent fatigue; and parent frustration with parent, child, or situational factors (Meier, 1985).

What Can I Do as a Parent?—Parents who abuse their children or are aware of physical abuse by another adult either within the family or a family friend are frequently ashamed of the situation and may fear the legal repercussions (Vizard, 1990). The facade of ignorance often leads to maintenance of the abuse and perpetuates dysfunctional family relations, in addition to the potential for severe physical and/or emotional injury to the abused child. Often abusive families do not perceive the situation as problematic, because most abusive adults were themselves abused as children and view such behavior as acceptable (Justice & Justice, 1990).

Parents faced with an abusive situation must understand that the primary goal of the legal system and mental health agencies is to prevent further abuse of the child and to maintain the family unit. Although in some cases it is necessary to remove the child for a period of time, the ultimate goal is reunification of the family (Gallinger, Meier, & Carney, 1985; Gray, 1981).

Treatment for abuse typically focuses on the parent, the child, and the family unit. Parent issues that need to be addressed include, but are not limited to:

—Helping the family develop support systems

—Developing better communication within the family

—Techniques for dealing with anger

—Child management and parenting skills

—Education in child development

—Assisting the parent in gaining employment (Justice & Justice, 1990)

Treating the abused child is often more complex than treating the parent. Children must deal not only with their own feelings, but must also be taught to understand why the abusing person behaved the way they did. Treatment for children typically includes:

—Helping the child to trust others

—Teaching them to play

—Allowing the child to release their anger

—Teaching the difference between touching that is good and touching that is not good

—Teaching social skills

—Building the child's self-esteem and dealing with self-blame

—Helping the child to understand that the parent/adult was reacting to problems in his/her life and that the parent/adult really loves the child (Dalen, 1989; Gray, 1981; Justice & Justice, 1990).

What Can I Do as a Teacher?—The educational system can be a key component in the prevention of child abuse. Schools are the ideal place to prepare future parents by incorporating parenting courses into the high school curriculum and to provide child management classes to parents in the community (Gray, 1981; Whitfield, 1987).

Teachers have the benefit of seeing children on a regular basis and can therefore initiate legal/human services intervention in the identification of child abuse. They are trained in child development and to identify signs of abnormal behavior and/or development. Legally, teachers are bound to report suspected child abuse and must be aware of local procedures (Maher, 1987). Indicators of child abuse may be manifested either physically and/or behaviorally. Teachers should be alert to the following signs:

—Bruises and burns: be aware of sharp outlines or geometric patterns; repeated bruises or burns; in unusual locations.

—Lacerations and abrasions

—Missing or loose teeth

—Families who move frequently (Gargiulo, 1990; Stern, 1987)

Areas where children are injured by their own doing include the "shins and knees, outer arms, forehead and around the ears." Abrasions are also not uncommon. If additional information is desired, teachers should contact their local pediatrician (Stern, 1987, p. 49).

Behavioral indicators to which teachers need to be alert include, but are not limited to:

—Pulling from or becoming fearful of physical contact

—Desiring attention (no matter how it is attained)

—Occasional temper tantrums

—Expressing fear when faced with the abusing adult

—Behavioral extremes, exhibiting either extreme aggressive behavior

—Sleepy in class

—Excessive tardiness or absence

—They do not initiate interaction, but will respond

—Try to hide injuries (Gargiulo, 1990; Maher, 1987; Moore, 1985).

Resources

Community resources such as family crisis centers, community centers, and self-help groups are available through schools, churches, and local agencies. To access this support, contact your local school, church, or pediatrician.

References

Browne, K., & Saqi, S. (1987). Parent-child interaction in abusing families: Its possible causes and consequences. In P. Maher (Ed.), *Child abuse: The education perspective* (pp. 77-103). Oxford, England: Basil Blackwell Limited.

Creighton, S. J. (1987). Quantitative assessment of child abuse. In P. Maher (Ed.), *Child abuse: The education perspective* (pp. 23-34). Oxford, England: Basil Blackwell Limited.

Dalen, A. V. (1989). The emotional consequences of physical child abuse. *Clinical Social Work Journal, 17,* 383-394.

Gallinger, D.,Meier, J. H., & Carney, J. (1985). Sociolegal approaches for helping assaulted children and their families. In J. H. Meier (Ed.), *Assault against children: Why it happens, how to stop it* (pp. 117-140). Boston: Little, Brown and Company.

Gargiulo, R. M. (1990). Child abuse and neglect: An overview. In R. L. Goldman & R. M. Gargiulo (Eds.), *Children at risk* (pp. 1-36). Austin, TX: PRO-ED.

Gray, J. D. (1981). Prevention of child abuse and neglect. In N. S. Ellerstein (Ed.), *Child abuse and neglect: A medical reference* (pp. 51-72). New York: John Wiley & Sons.

Justice, B., & Justice, R. (1990). *The abusing family.* New York: Plenum Press.

Maher, P. (1987). School responses to child abuse cases: The reactive role. In P. Maher (Ed.), *Child abuse: The educational perspective* (pp. 190-209). Oxford, England: Basil Blackwell Unlimited.

Meier, J. H. (1985). Definition, dynamics and prevalence of assault against children: A multifactorial model. In J. H. Meier (Ed.), *Assault against children: Why it happens, how to stop it* (pp. 1-46). Boston: Little, Brown and Company.

Moore, J. G. (1985). *The ABC of child abuse work.* Brookfield, VT: Gower Publishing Company Limited.

Newberger, C. M., & Newberger, E. H. (1981). The etiology of child abuse. In N. S. Ellerstein (Ed.), *Child abuse and neglect: A medical reference* (pp. 11-20). New York: John Wiley & Sons.

Stern, C. (1987). The recognition of child abuse. In P. Maher (Ed.), *Child abuse: The educational perspective* (pp. 35-58). Oxford, England: Basil Blackwell Unlimited.

Vizard, E. (1987). The historical and cultural context of child abuse. In P. Maher (Ed.), *Child abuse: The educational perspective* (pp. 7-22). Oxford, England: Basil Blackwell Unlimited.

Whitfield, R. (1987). Strategies for prevention: Education for good child care practice. In P. Maher (Ed.), Child abuse: *The educational perspective* (pp. 169-189). Oxford, England: Basil Blackwell Unlimited.

Children and Running Away

James R. Deni
Appalachian State University
Boone, North Carolina

Background—Children running away from home is not a new problem, but today children are running in increasing numbers. Each year in the United States approximately 1.5 million children run away from home. Most children who run away are between the ages of 10 and 18 years old. It is estimated that one child in eight will run away from home overnight before his or her 18th birthday. Runaways are equally divided between males and females. The most common destination is a relative's or friend's house. However, some travel 100 to 200 miles away from home, especially those having transportation and money. Most runaways return home within one day, while the average stay is three days. Many are forced to live on the streets engaging in theft, violence, selling drugs, forgery, and prostitution to make a living.

Development—Current studies on runaway behavior do not establish a single reason for children running away. However, the most frequently cited cause is parent-child relationships. Adolescents themselves cite communication problems as a major source of conflict in their homes.

Rates of runaway behavior are much higher in single-parent families and families in conflict. The majority of runaways are trying to escape situations they perceive as problems they cannot or will

not deal with. They run because they are unhappy with the existing environment, sometimes to avoid abusive and insensitive parents. Many of them feel "pushed out" or "thrown away." Many of the throwaways result from the inability of parents to cope with adolescent behaviors such as drugs, sexual activity, defiance of authority, and poor academic performances. Parental behaviors such as incest, child abuse, and inadequate response to economic pressure may also lead to runaway behavior in children.

Although factors leading to runaway behavior cannot be found in a single source or given age, they will be cumulative and there will be prior indications and warning signs. Early warning signs are angry rejection by a child, verbal threats of running away, constant battles over autonomy, drug abuse, alcoholism, school failure, parent-child conflict, truancy, juvenile delinquency, child abuse, communication problems, sharp changes in behavior or personality, inadequate or poor peer relationships, low self-esteem, and poor social skills. Certainly these warning signs are not unique to runaway behavior; however, one or more of these signs may increase the chances of a youth running away. A simple measure of conflict and perceived helplessness is the number of times a youth has run away.

What can I do as a parent?

Prevention is the best treatment for runaway behavior in youths. Remember that children run away as a result of years of perceived or real problems they cannot or will not deal with.

- Make time to listen to your children. Many children run away looking for someone who has time to listen, even about a hope or a dream.

- Remember that children have feelings and thoughts also but may lack the language and vocabulary to express their feelings.
- Treat them as you would another adult, with respect. Respect from children today is not automatic; it must be earned.
- Maintain open lines of communication with your children. Communication can be constructive or destructive to a relationship. Parents should try avoiding responses that children perceive as preaching, moralizing, criticizing and blaming. These and similar responses many times inhibit growth in relationships.
- Maintain open lines of communication with school personnel. Be an involved parent and know how your children are doing in school. Ask how you as a parent may help at home.
- Be an informed parent. Know your children's friends and where your children are at night. Being a parent means accepting responsibility for their behavior.
- Establish some basic rules at home. Contrary to popular belief, most children want and need basic rules governing their behavior. Limit the rules to a few and enforce them consistently and make them cooperatively.
- Seek professional help when needed. Do not be afraid to ask for professional (e.g. School Psychologists, Mental Health, etc.) help when problems between you and your children persist. Individual and/or family counseling may be needed.

Resources

National Center for Missing and Exploited Children. Phone (202) 634-9821. Provides assistance to parents and law enforcement agencies in locating missing children and preventing child exploitation.

National Runaway Switchboard. Toll free 1-800-621-4000 or 1-800-HIT-HOME. Provides counseling and referral services 24 hours a day; free and confidential.

Runaway Hotline. Toll free 1-800-231-6946 (in Texas 1-800-392-3352). Provides confidential relay messages from youths to parents without revealing locations.

Children and Sexual Abuse

Linda C. Caterino
Adjunct Professor, Arizona State University
Tempe, Arizona

Background—Child sexual abuse is usually described as the sexual exploitation of a child by an adult or significantly older peer (usually 5 or more years). It is a broad term and includes genital exposure, kissing, fondling, oral-genital contact, digital penetration, and vaginal or anal intercourse as well as child pornography and child prostitution. The abuse may be a single act by a stranger or incest with a family member carried on for many years.

It is estimated that there are 10.7 cases of child abuse a year per 1,000 children. However due to a lack of reporting, the figures may be even higher. The American Humane Society estimates that there are between 200,000 and 300,000 cases per year with 5,000 cases being incest. Girls are reported to be abused four times more frequently than boys. The majority of the offenders are male (99%), with only 11% being strangers; 60% of the offenders were known to the victim with 29% being relatives.

Development—Two basic patterns for sexual abuse have been described. They are categorized as sex pressure and sex force offenses. In sex pressure offenses, the offender usually an authority figure known to and possibly related to the child, entices the child into going along with the sexual activity through material or emotional bribery. The goal is to gain control of the child by developing a willing sexual relationship.

Sex force offenders use intimidation or physical aggression. No attempt is made to form an emotional relationship with the child and the child is only seen as an object for sexual gratification of the offender.

Many cases of intrafamilial sexual abuse are committed by the father or stepfather against their children. He usually seeks to engage the child through private interactions. The relationship may progress from exposure to masturbation, fondling, kissing, and then oral, anal, or vaginal intercourse. The children are then cautioned not to tell so that the offender may be able to maintain the relationship for years. Typically, incestuous relationships last for 3-5 years. The child usually keeps silent because he or she is afraid of the offender or out of fear of destroying the family. At times an adolescent may tell through concern for a younger sibling or due to an unrelated argument. Accidental disclosure may also occur. Even after a child has told, he or she may be pressured by family members to withdraw the complaints.

Long term effects of sexual abuse as measured by retrospective responses of adults who were childhood victims include depression, suicidal behavior anxiety, feelings of isolation and stigma, poor self-esteem, and a tendency toward revictimization and substance abuse. Other researchers have identified obesity, character disorders, prostitution, psychosis, and schizophrenia as effects of sexual abuse.

What can I do as a parent?

Parents should be aware of the symptoms of child sexual abuse, including:

I. Physical Symptoms—
   a. changes in eating habits.
   b. changes in sleeping habits, including nightmares and insomnia
   c. difficulties in sitting or walking
   d. pain, swelling, or itching in the genital area
   e. frequent urinary tract infections
   f. painful urination
   g. vaginal or penile discharge
   h. bleeding in the genital or anal area
   i. torn, stained or bloody underwear
   j. bruises
   k. venereal disease, particularly in children under 13 years
   l. pregnancy
   m. excessive masturbation

II. Emotional Reactions
   a. excessive fearfulness about particular people or places.
   b. clinging behavior
   c. withdrawal
   d. regressive behavior
   e. a change in attitude toward school (refusal to attend, excessive absences, drop in grades, unwillingness to change for or participate in P.E., arriving early or leaving late for school).

III. Cognitive Reactions
   a. knowledge of sexual behavior too far advanced for his or her age and education
   b. changes in fantasy play

IV. Social Reactions
   a. poor peer relations
   b. indiscrimating hugging, kissing, or seductive behavior with other children and adults
   c. excessive aggression

Suspected child abuse should be reported immediately. Most states usually require only an oral report which can be made on the phone. The national hotline is 1-800-4-A-CHILD and some states also provide a 24-hour toll free number.

Resources

Victims of child abuse can be helped through psychological therapy including art therapy, music therapy, play therapy, etc. Relaxation and behavioral techniques are also useful. Several successful family programs have also been developed to deal with incest behavior. Parents United, and Daughters and Sons United have established programs in many major U.S. cities.

There are also numerous prevention programs using media and/or books which can be helpful in educating children and adults about sexual abuse.

For parents

Adams, C. & Fay J. (1981). No More Secrets: Protecting your child from sexual assault. San Louis Obispo, CA: Impact Publications. A practical guide for parents to help them discuss sexual assault with their children.

Newman, S. (1985). Never Say Yes to a Stranger: What Your Child Must Know To Stay Safe. New York: Putnam. Meant to be read by parents and children together this book illustrates different situations in which children can be approached by strangers and ways to deal with the encounter.

Sanford, L. (1980). The Silent Children: A Parent's Guide to the Prevention of Child Sexual Abuse. Garden City, New York: Doubleday. This book presents specific techniques parents can use to prevent child sexual abuse as well as methods of discussing sexual abuse with children. It also provides information for parents with specific needs such as parents of developmentally disabled children.

For children and adolescents

Hyde, M.O. (1984). *Sexual Abuse: Let's Talk About It.* Philadelphia, PA: Westminster. This book meant for adolescents defines sexual abuse and gives examples of what to do in abuse situations.

Sweet, P. (1981). *Something Happened to Me.* Recine, WI. Mother Courage. A sensitive, beautifully illustrated book meant for younger children.

Terkel, S. & Rench, J. (1984). *Feeling Safe, Feeling Strong: How to Avoid Sexual Abuse and What to Do if it Happens to You.* Minneapolis, MN: Lerner. Presents short vignettes concerning sexual abuse situations ranging from unwanted touch to obscene phone calls and rape.

Stealing

Lynn Ellen Thompson and Diane Van Dusen
University of South Florida

Background—Less is known about children who steal than about children with other difficulties, due to practical and ethical considerations associated with the detection and treatment of stealing. However, research does suggest that children and adolescents who steal are at a greater risk for adjustment and legal difficulties later in life.

According to the literature family characteristics that may be associated with stealing are: inconsistent parental discipline, parents who do not reward prosocial behavior, poor monitoring of child's behavior, tension or other family stressors (for example, divorce or unemployment may be present), and finally, parents may not view stealing as a problem.

Research has shown that there are two different types of stealing: confrontative, in which the child confronts the victim and may use force, and nonconfrontative, in which the child does not confront the victim and force is not a factor.

Development and Causes—Researchers have suggested several possible factors associated with childhood stealing. Stealing is often rewarded simply by possessing the stolen item. Moreover, feelings of power or control may be associated with successful stealing. If parents and teachers do not detect that stealing has occurred and the child receives no negative consequences for his or her actions the temptation to steal is increased.

Peer pressure may contribute to a child's stealing because she or he may be easily influenced by the group or find independent thinking difficult. In addition, many adolescents may have feelings of insecurity or confusion and may steal in order to maintain membership in a peer group.

Children experiencing home, school, or financial problems may be more likely to become involved in delinquent activities, which may include stealing. In addition, being labeled a troublemaker by parents, teachers, or oneself may promote the development of a deviant self-concept and increase the likelihood of stealing.

Three parental disciplinary styles have been identified. In the first, assertion of power, a parent threatens a child who may fear punishment. Withdrawal of love, or the second style, is associated with a threatened loss of affection for misbehavior. Induction, or explaining why a child should or should not engage in different behaviors, with an emphasis on possible consequences to self or others, is the third discipline style. Research has shown that a relationship exists between induction and the ability to resist temptation in adolescent boys.

Finally, it has been shown that children with parents who steal often imitate their parents' behavior.

What Can I Do as a Parent?—In terms of dealing with stealing the following suggestions may be helpful:

—Respond to the situation, do not try to deny or cover up your child's stealing.

—Respond in a calm, matter-of-fact style.

—Use an inductive discipline style, emphasize why the child should not steal and what the possible consequences of stealing are for the child and society.

—Do not reward non-stealing, as undetected stealing may also be rewarded.

—Define stealing consistently as "the child's taking or being in possession of anything that does not clearly belong to him/her" (Reid, 1975, p. 137).

—Do not be influenced by doubts about proof of ownership or reduce your concern because the item is of minimal value.

—Consider individual and/or family counseling if problems persist.

What Can I Do as a Teacher?—The following guidelines may be helpful in providing you with ways to handle stealing in your classroom:

—Respond to the situation in a calm fashion.

—Avoid labeling one student as a thief, use classwide intervention procedures.

—Assess the level of stealing, what is being stolen, and how often stealing occurs.

—Have the student's parents mark all of the child's belongings. Check students belongings every 15 minutes. If all items are marked, the student is praised for having only his/her items. Any item in the student's possession that is not marked is considered stolen and the student should be reprimanded and fined.

—Make tokens available to the entire class for work completion. These tokens can be exchanged for prizes or free time. Free time is lost for any incidents of stealing.

—Companionship of a staff member, whom the student really likes, can be made dependent upon no stealing incidents for the day, or the week, according to the severity of the problem.

Postscript

If classwide interventions are not successful, or problems at home persist, contact your school psychologist for more individual intervention strategies.

Resources

Miller, G. E., & Klungness, L. (1986). Treatment of nonconfrontative stealing in school-age children. *School Psychology Review, 15,* 24-35.

Miller, G. E., & Klungness, L. (1989). Childhood theft: A comprehensive review of assessment and treatment. *School Psychology Review, 18,* 82-97.

Rosen, H. S., & Rosen, L. A. (1983). Eliminating stealing: Use of stimulus control with an elementary student. *Behavior Modification, 7,* 56-63.

Schwartz, S., & Johnson, J. H. (1988). *Psychopathology of childhood: A clinical-experimental approach* (pp. 307-340). New York: Pergamon Press.

Switzer, E. B., Deal, J. E. & Bailey, J. S. (1977). The reduction of stealing in second graders using a group contingency. *Journal of Applied Behavior Analysis, 10,* 267-272.

Weger, R. M. (1987). Children and stealing. In A. Thomas & J. Grimes (Eds.), *Children's needs: Psychological perspectives* (pp. 571-578). Washington, DC: The National Association of School Psychologists.

Wetzel, R. (1966). Use of behavioral techniques in a case of compulsive stealing. *Journal of Consulting and Clinical Psychology, 30,* 367-374.

Williams, R. L. M. (1985). Children's stealing: A review of theft control procedures for parents and teachers. *Remedial and Special Education, 6,* 17-23.

References

Reid, J. B. (1975). The child who steals. In G. R. Patterson, J. B. Reid, R. Jones, & R. E. Conger (Eds.), *A social learning approach to a family intervention: Vol I. The socially aggressive child* (pp. 135-138). Eugene, OR: Castalia.

NATIONAL
ASSOCIATION OF
SCHOOL
PSYCHOLOGISTS

Children and Suicide

William O. Hahn
Behavior Management Consultants
New Kensington, PA

Background—It is estimated that a child or adolescent will commit suicide every 90 minutes. Suicide among the young has become the third leading cause of death. An estimated 25 percent of all high school students contemplate suicide at some time during the school year. Experts disagree whether this suicide rate is increasing or has plateaued. It is known, however that this death rate has more than doubled over the past 20 years. Add to these statistics those children who attempt suicide or consider it as the only alternative and we have a problem of almost epidemic proportions.

Development—While suicide is considered to be a uniquely individual act, there are some common trends and identifiable traits. Children as young as 2 or 3 may attempt suicide, but they do not usually utilize a lethal method. Even children between the ages of 6 and 10 tend not to use lethal methods. This seems due to the fact that younger children are almost "protected" from self-destruction by virtue of their immaturity. A common factor present in suicidal young children, which tends to prevail even into adolescence, is a strong sense of abandonment or rejection by a significant other. As children become older stress factors may intensify and add to the problem. Significant stressors such as addition of a third party to the family, sibling birth, parental divorce, and as was mentioned, a sense of abandonment all play an important part. Losses such as these often result in a decrease in self-esteem and an increase in anger or rage. Thus suicide for the child becomes either an attempt to alter an intolerable situation, a cry for help, or a means of gaining attention, love, and affection from significant others.

In adolescence, the usual clues to suicidal behavior include the following:

1. Loss of significant other
2. Recent suicide of a peer or family member
3. Legal difficulties
4. Unwanted pregnancy
5. Family stress
6. Recent and/or frequent changes in school
7. Difficulties in relationships
8. Depression and withdrawal
9. Disorientation and isolation

As with younger children, these teenagers often find themselves in what they consider to be an intolerable situation. Unfortunately, they become rigid in their thinking, unable to see any alternatives other than suicide. Often there are prevailing feelings of hopelessness, (that is, the feeling that there is no hope, and that the future looks bleak). With these types of views, and an inability to see alternatives, the child's only solution becomes a suicide. Five danger signs of suicide are as follows:

1. A suicide threat or statement indicating a desire to die,
2. A previous attempt,
3. Severe depression,
4. Marked changes in personality or behavior,
5. Making a will or giving prized possessions away.

What can I do as a parent?

It is important for the parents to be aware of his/her child's moods, feelings, and attitudes. Sudden mood swings or marked changes in behavior decreasing grades and/or withdrawal from friends often signify the onset of depression. The parent must realize that this is often not just a "phase" that the child is going through, but indications of a problem. Of primary importance in helping these distressed children is letting the child know that no matter what, you are there as a parent to help them, that you care for them, and love them. While you might not be able to heal their pain, resolve their problems, or even understand what they are going through, you must let them know that you are willing to listen and help them in whatever way possible.

As a parent, if you begin to notice signs of depression, or more importantly, signs of suicidal behavior you should begin by talking with your child. Let them know that you will listen, and that you are not going to judge them. Encourage them to express their feelings and really listen. Try not to criticize or downplay their feelings. At some point, it will become necessary to ask them if they have thought about suicide. (You are not putting an idea into their heads—the majority of children and adolescents know what suicide is, so you are not giving them any suggestions.) If they have seriously thought about suicide, then it is time to seek professional help, either through the school, local mental health agency, private agency, suicide hotlines, or your family physician. If in addition to the suicidal thought, the child has a plan of suicide, then serious consideration should be given to hospitalization of the child for his own protection. Any time that you fear that your child might be suicidal, it is imperative that you seek the help of qualified professionals. It is also advisable that you remove any guns from the house, as this is the most lethal of all methods, and also one that is prone to be used impulsively.

After the suicidal crisis is over you must continue to support, listen, and care for your child. You don't want them to think that they must threaten suicide in order to get your attention. It is also important to follow-up with a mental health agency, in order to resolve the difficulties that stimulated the suicidal behavior. Remember, youth suicide is a family problem.

Resources

Baucom, J. Q. (1986). *Fatal Choice.* Chicago: Moody. Provides an excellent, easy-to-read overview of the problem of adolescent suicide, and offers methods that parents can institute to prevent suicide.

Bolton, I. M. (1983). *My Son, My Son.* Atlanta: Bolton. This book represents the reactions of a mother (who is a counselor) to her son's suicide. This book provides excellent suggestions for dealing with the aftermath of suicide.

Hewett, J. H. (1980). *After Suicide.* Philadelphia: Westminster. Offers suggestions for both professionals and nonprofessionals in dealing with the aftermath of suicide.

Johnston, Jerry (1987). *Why Suicide.* Nashville: Oliver Nelson Books. This book explores the many reasons for adolescent suicides, provides methods to preventing suicides, and also offers clues to determining if a child is suicidal.

Suicide Intervention in the Schools
Administration and Teacher Handout

Scott Poland
Cypress-Fairbanks ISD, Houston, Texas

Incidence

The problem of youth suicide has dramatically increased in recent years:

- 300% since 1950
- 200% since 1970
- Adolescents are especially at risk. Recent surveys of eighth through twelfth grade students found that 30 – 50% of the students have seriously thought about suicide and 8 to 14% have attempted suicide.
- Suicide is the 2nd leading cause of death for adolescents with approximately 2,000 to 2,500 deaths annually. It is estimated that there are 100 to 120 attempts for every death.

The suicide of elementary age students is rare with less than 200 suicides occuring annually. Young children have less thought out plans and may engage in reckless behavior. Children pass through developmental stages in their understanding of death and educators need to be familiar with these stages.

Role of the school

- To detect suicidal students
- To assess the severity level of the suicidal student
- To notify the parents of the suicidal student
- To work with the parents to secure the needed supervision and services for the student.
- To monitor the student and provide on-going assistance

Warning Signs

Everyone should know the following warning signs of suicide and the referral procedures to follow to assist the student.

- Suicidal threats
- An attempt at suicide
- Prolonged depression
- Dramatic change of behavior or personality
- Making final arrangements

Confidentiality

NO ONE SHOULD KEEP A SECRET ABOUT SUICIDAL BEHAVIOR. The parents of the suicidal student must be notified. School districts and their employees have been sued for failing to notify parents, inadequately supervising and failing to get psychological help for suicidal students. The liability issues are forseeability and negligence.

Empowerment

All school employees play a role in preventing youth suicide. Listen and hear what the student is saying. Trust your judgment and inquire directly, openly and honestly about the student's suicidal thoughts. Take definite action to get help for the student.

Key myths debunked

Suicide is not inherited. It is not someone's destiny. There are many people alive today who were suicidal at one time. Young people are often ambivalent about suicide and go back and forth between wanting to live and wanting to die. The young person who talks or writes about suicide may be at risk and cannot be ignored.

Factors and forces in youth suicide

Researchers have identified as many as 28 different causes. There is no one type of young person that is more at risk. The following factors are involved in many youth suicides.

- Depression
- Drug and alcohol usage
- Angry and rebellious behavior
- Gun availability
- Impulsive and reckless behavior

Assessment

School employees such as counselors and psychologists should have special training to determine the severity risk level for a suicidal student. "No suicide contracts" should be utilized to gain a promise from the student not to follow through on his or her suicidal plans. Alternatives to suicide should be emphasized.

Getting assistance for suicidal students

Community services such as crisis hotline centers, hospitals, and private practitioners are available to assist. Parents need to be encouraged to reach out to their child through increased supervision and communication. Parents need to take suicidal threats seriously and professional help must be sought whether or not the child's behavior is manipulative. It may be necessary to document in writing that parents were notified and encouraged to get assistance in the community. School personnel should continue to monitor and assist the student.

Curriculum

There is a debate about the advisability of classroom presentations on suicide prevention. A presentation that is well integrated with a mental health unit is recommended. The information presented must also emphasize friend intervention and prevention. All information presented should be carefully selected.

Postvention

Few events are more scary than the suicide of a student. Care should be taken not to glorify the student. Memorials should be downplayed. The suicide of the student must be acknowledged and students must be allowed the opportunity to express emotions and ask questions. This discussion should be done in either small groups or a classroom format but not in an assembly. Networking counseling efforts should assist the friends of the deceased to manage their grief and should assist other students previously known to be suicidal.

Media

Coverage should be downplayed. Back page coverage if any at all is preferred. Suicide should not be portrayed as mystic, romantic, simplistic or unexplainable. Details of the method should be avoided. Emphasis should be placed on where suicidal students can get help.

Resources

Organization: American Association of Suicidology, 2459 S. Ash, Denver CO 80222 (303) 692-0285
Books: *Suicide Intervention in the Schools*, Scott Poland, Guilford Press, New York, (1989) 800-365-7006
Suicide Prevention for the California Public Schools, (1987), California Department of Education, PO Box 271, Sacramento, CA 95802-0271

Children and Tourette Syndrome
Teacher Handout

Randi Walls
Youngstown Public Schools

Background—Tourette Syndrome (TS) is a tic disorder which developes in childhood or adolescence and can last a lifetime. It is characterized by involuntary, repetitive muscle movements (motor tics) and the uttering of uncontrollable sounds and words (vocal or phonic tics). Although no cause has been definitely identified for TS, one theory is that it is caused by a chemical imbalance in the brain.

TS is more complex and extreme than other tic disorders. In order for a diagnosis of TS to be made, the individual must exhibit, at some time, both multiple motor and one or more phonic tics. The location, number frequency, complexity, and severity of the tics change over time. They can completely disappear and reappear later. Therefore, an actual case of TS is difficult to diagnose; its symptoms can be easily confused with mild, temporary tic conditions (such as nervous eyeblinking often seen in young children), other tic disorders, and physical disorders. Further, TS can be accompanied by learning disabilities, attention-concentration difficulties, hyperactivity, or emotional problems. It can increase or subside during adolescence but generally tends to diminish in adulthood. TS occurs more often in males, is thought to be hereditary, and appears across races, ethnic groups, and socioeconomic levels.

TS is not life threatening nor degenerative. It is diagnosed primarily via the symptoms and a study of the person's history. There is no known cure; it is treated medically and behaviorally. The Tourette Syndrome Association estimates that there are approximately 100,000 persons in the U.S. with TS, which may extend to as much as 3.5 million when including persons who have chronic, multiple motor tics as well as those who have TS.

Development—Tics usually develop in a progression over time from the simple to the complex, with motor tics developing sooner than phonic tics, although all may emerge simultaneously. Examples of tics are as follows:

- **Simple motor:** Eye blinking, facial twitching, tooth clicking, grimacing, shoulder shrugs, kicks.
- **Complex motor:** Sustained "looks," face/hand gestures, bending, throwing, licking of shoulder. Complex motor tics are more ritualistic and of longer duration that simple motor tics.
- **Simple phonic:** (Also called vocal tics). Barking, sniffing, throat clearing, spitting, grunting.
- **Complex phonic:** (Also called vocal or verbal tics). Syllables, words, phrases ("how about it," "stop that"), repeating one's own or someone else's words, unusual tone, accent, rhythm of speech, aggressive utterances, obscenities. Obsenities, although often identified with TS, actually are exhibited by a minority of individuals with TS.

Tics can be preceded by "sensations" or "urges," and although the tics can be suppressed for a brief period, they must eventually be released by an individual. Tics can increase with stress or subside when the person is absorbed in an activity. This should not mean that they are easily or predictably controlled, however. Unfortunately, extreme TS symptoms are too often viewed by others as malicious or oppositional behavior.

Each person with TS is different and the difficulties that are encountered vary from person to person. Often, these difficulties continue to influence daily functioning even when the tics are mild, disappear or are controlled through the use of medication. Some other conditions or problems which may occur with TS include:

- difficulties with writing and similar motor activities.
- difficulties with speech and language such as stuttering or halting speech, difficulty expressing ideas or finding words, difficulty understanding others, problems with following directions.
- weaknesses in visual-spatial perception.
- difficulties with attention and concentration.
- hyperactivity.
- obsessive-compulsive behaviors such as intrusive thought about fears or compulsions to touch things or perform complicated movements.
- problems with social and emotional functioning, including poor self-concept and peer relation difficulties, irritability and tantrums, anxiety, or depression.

Interventions—Medication, which may or may not be needed, and behavior therapy are the treatments of choice for the control of tics and associated behaviors. Support for the family is also very important. In the school setting, TS students often attend regular education classes or may receive assistance from programs for students with learning disabilities, speech and language handicaps, behavior disorders, or health related special education programs. A team approach should be used when working with a TS student and should typically include school officials, the family, and a physician. Assessments should include those of cognitive ability, academic achievement, speech and language functions, social and emotional status, neuromotor functioning, and family history. Caution should be used in interpreting test results which may be underestimated as a result of the TS. A treatment plan should take into account the student's history and environment, not just symptoms or test scores. It is important to remember that TS can be overdiagnosed as well as underdiagnosed.

What can I do as a parent?

As is indicated above, each child with TS is an individual. As a result, intervention plans depend on the individual profile of the child. Staying in contact with the family will allow for modification of your intervention strategies as the student's needs change. The following are some suggestions which may be tried for a child with TS:

Interventions designed to deal specifically with TS:

- In the classroom, try to reduce stress and distractions.
- Consider the seating arrangement which is most appropriate for your student.
- Allow for good and bad days which result from the changing nature of the disorder. Try to allow for concentration difficulties which might result when the student is trying to suppress the tics.
- Allow for physical movement such as running errands, performing a daily class chore, or visiting or helping another teacher.
- Learn about the medication your student is taking and be alert for side effects. Report any changes to the student's parents.
- Make staff aware of the student's difficulties and needs.

Interventions designed to deal with associated learning problems:

- For difficulties with written language, shorten assignments, modify writing activities to allow more time, and teach the student how to outline and take notes.
- Allow the use of a tape recorder for recording lectures and to assist the student with self-expression. The student can practice by speaking into the recorder.
- For reading difficulties, recorded books can be helpful. Help the student deal with losing his/her place or getting stuck when reading a sentence or passage.
- Provide a calculator for math calculations, if written computation is difficult. To reduce distractions, divide written problems visually, e.g. fold paper to expose only one or a few problems at a time.
- Teach the student to underline key words and phrases.
- Allow oral test taking. Provide multiple choice answers, if possible, and allow additional time.
- Use visual aides in lessons to help with focus and spatial difficulties (e.g., color highlights, arrows, shapes, and window box or ruler to follow line across page).
- Consider the use of computers or typewriters which may be helpful to some students, but not to others.

Interventions designed to deal with associated social and emotional difficulties:

- Let the TS child know that you accept him/her and that you understand his/her difficulties.
- Foster a sense of accomplishment. Let him/her know that his/her contributions are valuable.
- Do not be afraid to reasonably challenge him/him and reinforce his/her efforts.
- Look for special talents/interests to develop and to recognize in the classroom or school setting, including helping others with assignments or projects.
- Provide positive and immediate feedback, stressing the student's successes, e.g. how many words were spelled correctly.
- Be sensitive and sincere in your comments and efforts to work with the child.
- Be AWARE. An informed teacher can share knowledge about TS with the class and serve as a positive model for other students (people fear the unknown).

Resources

Associations:

The Tourette Syndrome Association can provide a comprehensive list of articles, books, handouts, videos/films, and similar materials for parents and professionals such as teachers, school psychologists, and school nurses. Contact: Tourette Syndrome Association, Inc., 42-40 Bell Blvd., Bayside, NY 11361/(718) 224-2999
Many local or state organizations also can be contacted.

Texts:

Cohen, D.J., Bruun, R. D., & Leckman, J. F. (1988). (Eds.), *Tourette's Syndrome and tic disorders, clinical understanding and treatment.* John Wiley and Sons.
Friedhoff, A. J. & Chase, T. N. (1982). (Eds.), *Gilles de la Tourette Syndrome.* New York: Raven Press.

Videos:

- Tourette Syndrome: The sudden intruder   • Stop it. I can't!

These are available for sale from the National Tourette Syndrome Association office, but may be available for borrowing from state or local associations.

Note: The author would like to thank Marilyn DeSalvo, for her contribution to this handout.

Part VI

Working It Out—
Adapting to Life Crises and
Changes

NATIONAL
ASSOCIATION OF
SCHOOL
PSYCHOLOGISTS

Adolescent HIV/AIDS
Parent Handout

Margaret K. Greer, Barbara L. Armstrong, & Dianna L. Dean
Medical University of South Carolina, Charleston, SC

Introduction

Everyday in the United States, 90 new cases of AIDS are identified and 60 people die from this fatal disease! **AIDS** has become the **seventh leading cause of death for teens and young adults** between the ages of 15 and 24 year. AIDS is now the number one cause of death between the ages of 24 and 34 years. In one year (between July 1988 and July 1989), the number of infected teenagers increased by 43%, and most of these teenagers became infected via heterosexual contact.

Every 13 seconds, a teenager contracts a sexually transmitted disease. More than 50% of adolescents have engaged in sexual intercourse prior to their 18th birthday. Eighty percent of males and 70% of females engage in sexual intercourse by age 20. Half of these teenagers practice unprotected sex during their first encounter, and many have multiple sex partners. These statistics are astounding, and they illustrate that sexual activity is on the rise not the decline. Sexual activity does not reflect poor parenting skills, rather the need to help adolescents act responsibly.

As parents it is difficult to acknowledge **teenagers as sexual beings.** It is equally hard to address their **experimental behavior** with drugs and alcohol. However, we must not assume these issues are foreign in our household, and we must take a proactive stand and **educate our children.** AIDS is in its second decade. If we, as parents, are to fight this epidemic **changes in attitude and behavior toward the disease and those it infects/affects are essential.** Open the lines of communication and bring HIV/AIDS out of the closet.

What is HIV/AIDS?

Definition

- HIV is the Human Immunodeficiency Virus. This virus attacks the immune system, which is the body's defense against infection. Over time, HIV breaks down the immune system. When the immune system is weakened, the individual becomes very ill with life threatening infections or cancer.
- AIDS is the Acquired Immune Deficiency Syndrome. This syndrome occurs in a person whose immune system has been damaged by infection with HIV.

Medical Symptoms Include Chronic Episodes of:

- Fever.
- Night sweats.

- Diarrhea.
- Weight loss.
- Fatigue.
- Swollen lymph nodes.
- Persistent cough.
- Skin rashes.
- Neurological impairments such as dementia, memory loss, partial paralysis, and loss of coordination.

Classification

Group   I   Acute infection
Group   II   Asymptomatic infection
Group   III Persistent generalized lymphadenopathy
Group   IV   Other disease
                 Subgroup   A   Constitutional disease
                               B   Neurologic disease
                               C   Secondary infectious diseases
                               D   Secondary cancers
                               E   Other conditions

Progression and Treatment

Although the progression varies with each individual, the appearance of indicator diseases seems to be similar in adolescents and adults. The incubation period (time from exposure to development of *actual* symptoms) is approximately 7 to 9 years, so it is often difficult to trace back to the time, place, and circumstances of exposure. On the other hand, if exposure to the virus is suspected, he/she should promptly seek testing because positive HIV antibody test results can be detected 6 months after exposure in over 90% of individuals.

To date, there is no cure for AIDS. Retrovir (AZT) therapy has been approved for treatment of HIV infection in children, adolescents, and adults. This therapy may help to slow disease progression and help to improve quality of life. Experimental medications are also being investigated, and to locate the nearest drug trial site, call 1-800-874-2572.

How Does an Adolescent Become Infected with HIV?

1. Sexual activity (vaginal, anal, or oral) with a person who is infected with HIV.
2. Recipient of infected blood or blood products.
3. Sexual abuse by HIV infected individual.
4. Injection with HIV infected needle.
5. Vertical (in utero) transmission. With the advent of new therapies, more children who were born to HIV infected mothers will live into adolescence.
- Individuals do **not** become infected with HIV by casual contact!

Social/Emotional Considerations

As you would expect the social/emotional issues surrounding HIV/AIDS are complex. There is a tendency toward isolation, depression, disorganization, and grief. Once a family learns of their loved ones' diagnosis, it is common to experience feelings of shock, fear, disbelief, anger, and sadness. During a time when **acceptance, love and support are vital,** many adolescents are forced to face their illness alone for fear of abandonment. As parents it is important to *face the diagnosis,* deal with your teenagers' feelings (low self esteem, poor self image), and **take steps to get help** (education, counseling, medical treatment, financial assistance, legal advice).

Adolescence is a time of experimentation often with sex, drugs, and alcohol. Teenagers don't think in terms of their own vulnerability; they often "live for the moment." This behavior can have costly results. Teenagers find it difficult to talk to parents about "touchy" issues, and often will not confide if they are curious, scared or hiding something. Peer pressure and social stigma play important roles in a teenagers' behavior.

We must join forces and **fight AIDS, not the people who have AIDS.** Teenagers and their families need support. We want to educate our youth in an effort to prevent the spread of HIV/AIDS. However, we must realize that for those already infected we can not turn our backs. As parents, we must:

- Respect privacy and confidentiality.
- Listen to teenagers and acknowledge their feelings.
- Open lines of communication.
- Educate children about HIV/AIDS, sexual activity, and substance abuse.
- Get involved with support groups for yourself and your teenager.
- Pursue substance abuse treatment if needed.
- Learn about HIV/AIDS and its treatment.
- Advocate for needed professional support and services.

What Can I Do as a Parent?

Set the Example & Provide Information About HIV/AIDS

- Discuss sexual and alcohol/drug issues with your teenager. Lack of knowledge only encourages careless experimentation which puts your teenager at risk for HIV infection.
- Now is the time to prepare your adolescent for the future. If safe behaviors are learned now, then these safe practices are more likely to be continued into adulthood. Provide specific and practical information regarding risk of HIV infection and how to engage in safe behaviors. Discuss which behaviors do and do not put them at risk.
- Age of initial sexual activity dramatically influences safe sexual practice, so encourage your teen to delay sexual activity. Discuss relationships and safe, viable options to sexual intercourse.
- Even when teens know safe behaviors and plan to use them, they are less likely to practice these safe behaviors while under the influence of alcohol or drugs, so alcohol and drug use needs to be openly discussed in both the home and school settings.
- If you as a parent are involved in unsafe practices, whether in sexual encounters or drugs, you are not only putting yourself at risk. Your child may very well follow this example, so please consider this risk and seek help immediately.

Support School and Community Involvement

- Remember that sex education programs do **not** promote sexual intercourse.
- Despite media coverage of HIV/AIDS, surveys of adolescents' knowledge indicate that they are generally unaware of their risk, and even if aware, continue to participate in risky behaviors.

- Promote positive attitudes and understanding/compassion for individuals who are infected. Help to support school/community efforts to provide appropriate care and intervention for infected adolescents.
- Learn information about where a teen can be tested, what testing involves and implies, and when it is appropriate. If your son/daughter wants to be tested for the HIV antibody, pre & post-test counseling should be provided by a qualified health official. Don't become distressed by this request for testing, they need your support and guidance.

Resources

National AIDS Hotline: 1-800-342-AIDS.
National AIDS Information Clearinghouse: P.O. Box 6003, Rockville, MD, 20850, 1-800-458-5231.
Gardner, W., Millstein, S., & Wilcox, B. (Eds.). (1990). *Adolescents in the AIDS epidemic.* San Francisco: Jossey-Bass.

Adolescent HIV/AIDS
Teacher Handout

Margaret K. Greer, Barbara L. Armstrong, & Dianna L. Dean
Medical University of South Carolina, Charleston, SC

Introduction

Everyday in the United States, 90 new cases of AIDS are identified and 60 people die from this fatal disease! **AIDS** has become the **seventh leading cause of death for teens and young adults** between the ages of 15 and 24 years. AIDS is now the number one cause of death between the ages of 24 and 34 years. In only one year (between July 1988 and July 1989), the number of infected teenagers increased by 43%, and most of these teenagers became infected via heterosexual contact.

Every 13 seconds, a teenager contracts a sexually transmitted disease. Moe than 50% of adolescents have engaged in sexual intercourse prior to their 18th birthday. Eighty percent of males and 70% of females engage in sexual intercourse by age 20. Half of these teenagers practice unprotected sex during their first encounter, and many have multiple sex partners.

AIDS is in its second decade. If we are to be successful in fighting this epidemic, we must **change our attitudes and behavior toward the disease and those it infects/affects.** Preventing the spread of HIV requires education, counseling, and behavioral changes.

What is HIV/AIDS?

Definition

- HIV is the Human Immunodeficiency Virus. This virus attacks the immune system, which is the body's defense against infection. Over time, HIV breaks down the immune system. When the immune system is weakened, the individual becomes very ill with life threatening infections or cancer.
- AIDS is the Acquired Immune Deficiency Syndrome. This syndrome occurs in a person whose immune system has been damaged by infection with HIV.

Medical Symptoms Include Chronic Episodes of:

- Fever.
- Night sweats.
- Diarrhea.
- Weight loss.
- Fatigue.
- Swollen lymph nodes.
- Persistent cough.
- Skin rashes.
- Neurological impairments such as dementia, memory loss, partial paralysis, and loss of coordination.

Classification

Group I   Acute infection
Group II   Asymptomatic infection
Group III   Persistent generalized lymphadenopathy
Group IV   Other disease

           Subgroup   A   Constitutional disease
                            B   Neurologic disease
                            C   Secondary infectious diseases
                            D   Secondary cancers
                            E   Other conditions

Progression and Treatment

Although the progression varies with each individual, the appearance of indicator diseases seems to be similar in adolescents and adults. The incubation period (time from exposure to development of *actual* symptoms) is approximately 7 to 9 years, so it is often difficult to trace back to the time, place, and circumstances of exposure. On the other hand, if exposure to the virus is suspected, he/she should promptly seek testing because positive HIV antibody test results can be detected 6 months after exposure in over 90% of individuals.

To date, there is no cure for AIDS. Retrovir (AZT) therapy has been approved for treatment of HIV infection in children, adolescents, and adults. This therapy may help to slow disease progression and help to improve quality of life. Experimental medications are also being investigated, and to locate the nearest drug trial site, call 1-800-874-2572.

How Does an Adolescent Become Infected with HIV?

1. Sexual activity (vaginal, anal, or oral) with a person who is infected with HIV.
2. Recipient of infected blood or blood products.
3. Sexual abuse by HIV infected individual.
4. Injection with HIV infected needle.
5. Vertical (in utero) transmission. With the advent of new therapies, more children who were born to HIV infected mothers will live into adolescence.

- Individuals do *not* become infected with HIV by casual contact!

Social/Emotion Considerations

Adolescence is a time of experimentation often with sex, alcohol, and drugs, and this "live for the moment" behavior can yield costly results. With youth comes a false sense of security laced with misconceptions. Statistics frequently seem distant and unrelated personally, as adolescents deny vulnerability. Yet, statistics on HIV/AIDS demand attention to this national crisis.

The psychosocial impact of AIDS in the adolescent population is complicated by social stigma and low self-esteem associated with the disease. Some teens are able to rely on family strength for emotional as well as financial support, yet many teens are faced with a family in crisis or they are homeless and relying on the dangerous resources of street life. HIV infected adolescents may be forced to deal with the disease and its ramifications alone due to fear of rejection or abandonment by the family.

Professionals, paraprofessionals, volunteers, etc. become an integral part of the HIV infected adolescent's support system providing information, resources, counseling, and emotional/financial assistance. Adolescents respond to the HIV diagnosis as adults do. They experience shock, fear, guilt, denial, anger, and depression.

Teenagers are heavily influenced by peer pressure, and their lives may be in a state of disorganization by virtue of their sexual practices or substance abuse behavior. Intervention should:

- Respect and protect confidentiality.
- Consider cultural and ethnic issues.
- Impart hope and provide support.
- Acknowledge feelings.
- Reinforce strengths, facilitate independence, foster self esteem.
- Encourage participation in peer support group.
- Identify goals and strategies to accomplish same.
- Keep lines of communication open.
- Prepare for the future.
- Boost morale and share positive information when possible.

What Can I Do as a Teacher

Set The Example by Acknowledging the Problem

- Recognize that sexual and drug experimentation is common in this age group and thus puts them at risk for HIV infection.
- Many sexual and drug use behaviors learned in adolescence put them at continued risk into adult years.
- Despite media coverage of HIV/AIDS, surveys of adolescents' knowledge indicate that they are generally unaware of their risk, and even if aware, continue to participate in risky behaviors.
- The earlier schools/teachers start an educational program, the safer the youth of today will be.
- Age of initial sexual activity dramatically influences safe sexual practice; therefore, the longer youths delay sexual activity the more likely they are to engage in safe behaviors.
- Even when teens know safe behaviors and plan to use them, they are less likely to practice these safe behaviors while under the influence of alcohol or drugs.

Provide Education About HIV/AIDS

- Remember that sex education programs do *not* promote sexual intercourse.
- Conduct an anonymous survey/questionnaire, so you will be able to utilize educational materials and classroom discussion geared toward students' needs.
- Provide specific and practical information regarding risk of HIV infection and how to engage in safe behaviors. Discuss behavioral changes (abstinence, alternative sexual expression, "safer sex" practices, informing sexual partners).
- Address the issue of what behaviors do and do not put them at risk. Recognize that this is often a difficult subject to discuss and a team teaching approach (classroom teacher along with school psychologist/nurse/other teacher/or guidance counselor, etc.) may be more comfortable and efficient.
- Effective education should address/increase adolescents' sense of personal susceptibility.
- Promote positive attitudes and understanding/compassion for individuals who are infected.

- Address issues to initiate and **maintain** healthy behaviors.
- Provide information on where a teen can be tested, what testing involves and implies, and when it is appropriate.
- If a teen wants to be tested for the HIV antibody, pre & post-test counseling should be provided.
- Design an evaluation package to measure knowledge gained and to review program strengths and weaknesses.

Infection Control/Risk Management

- Policies and procedures should be developed to handle any and all blood spills.
- Provide access to gloves and disinfectant (bleach at a dilution of 1:10 which was mixed within the last 24 hours).
- Urgent care of a bleeding individual should never be delayed due to lack of available gloves.
- Use of gloves and disinfectant is recommended when dealing with: blood blood-contaminated fluids
- Hand washing is recommended when dealing with:

| urine | stool | vomitus |
| tears | nasal secretions | oral secretions |

Resources

National AIDS Hotline: 1-800-342-AIDS.

National AIDS Information Clearinghouse: P.O. Box 6003, Rockville, MD, 20850, 1-800-458-5231.

Gardner, W., Millstein, S., & Wilcox, B. (Eds.). (1990). *Adolescents in the AIDS epidemic.* San Francisco: Jossey-Bass.

Adopted Children
Parent Handout

Linda M. Neiheiser

Overview

"If you've found and welcomed home your child, your adoption experience hasn't ended . . . It's just begun." This accurate statement, used as an advertisement for the education and support organization, Adoptive Families of America, reflects the true situation of adoptive families. Adoption is not a one-time event, but rather one method of forming a family that impacts on the adoption triad members—the birthparents, the adoptee, and the adoptive parents—as well as extended family members and future offspring as a lifelong, intergenerational process. Just as the child grows and develops, so do adoption issues over time. Adoptive parents need to be aware of these issues to assist their children in healthy development.

Seven Core Issues

Adoption experts Sharon Kaplan and Deborah Silverstein have mapped out seven basic issues in adoption affecting all members of the triad. Working through these issues can be an enriching and rewarding experience:

- Loss. Adoption is a way of forming a family in which all triad members experience loss in the process. Birthparents lose their biologic child, adoptees lose their birthparents and extended family, and adoptive parents lose the biologic child they planned to have and perhaps the adopted child they imagined they would have adopted. This experience of loss remains throughout the lifespan, with adoptees in particular looking for familiar biologic faces in the crowd, considering a search, or perhaps conducting one. Losses in adoption lead to other issues for all triad members. The following elaborations pertain to the adoptee:

- Rejection. Adoptees sometimes feel they suffered loss because they were not worthy to have what they lost, leading to feelings of rejection by not only the birthparents, but the entire country of origin as well, with transracial adoptees experiencing the same feelings of rejection from their race. This rejection may manifest itself in impaired self-esteem. Adoptees may attempt to be perfect to avoid rejection again, or they may force situations of rejection, due to anticipating that it would occur eventually.

- Shame. Related to feelings of defect in oneself, shame may manifest itself in adoptees as they believe they will never be the perfect child they need to be to avoid "rejection" by the adoptive parents, as well as shame for feeling rejected by the birthparents.

- Grief. The rituals used in our society to grieve for a loss are missing in adoption losses, making the grieving process difficult for some adoptees. The stages of grief consist of denial of the loss, anger, bargaining to reclaim the loss, depression, and acceptance or partial acceptance of the loss. Adoptees do not begin the grieving process until middle childhood, and do not fully understand it until late adolescence. Failure to grieve on the child's part may result in either acting out or depression.

- Identity. Adoptees experience genealogical discontinuity and feel sometimes as if they are borrowing their identity their adoptive family. By not feeling as if they belong, to either birth or adoptive families, adoptees may behave as "people pleasers" to be accepted, or may seek out groups or cults for a feeling of acceptance.

- Intimacy. Adoptees may experience difficulties in close relationships, due to possible previous bonding and attachment problems. Some adoptees may refrain from becoming involved in intimate relationships, fearing they may unknowingly be involved with a biologic relative.

- Control. Adopted children usually have no control over their adoption placements, making them feel as if they joined the family in a haphazard way. This may lead some adoptees to experience difficulty in understanding cause and effect, which may be seen in an inability to take responsibility for their actions.

These core issues impact upon the adoptee differently with each stage of development.

What can I do as a Parent?

- Adoptive parents need to realize that they, too, experience these same core issues, and it is imperative they address the issues to adequately assist their children in doing the same. Considerations for assisting adopted children include:

  —Recognize your own feelings pertaining to these issues.

  —Be aware of the vulnerabilities of both you, your spouse and your child, as well as other children in the family.

  —Initiate dialogue in a natural way, related to the child's developmental level.

  —Discuss specific questions and concerns.

  —Address your child's fears and fantasies.

  —Accept and support your child's decision to search for the missing pieces in his background, when it is appropriate, if he chooses to do so. Do not take away the child's control once more by searching for her. Instead, allow for emotional and monetary support, and assist the child in social system areas of which she may have no knowledge.

  —Seek the aid of an adoption specialist if your child is in need of assistance for behavioral problems which may have an adoption connection.

  —Join adoption organizations and read the current literature and monthly publications, to be better prepared to answer your child's questions, as well as to understand how adoption affects both the birthparents and adoptive family.

- Adoptive parents must also realize that, although adoption appears to be a socially-accepted method of forming a family, it is often considered inferior or "second-best" by those not personally touched by adoption. This pejorative belief is evidenced in the negative way adoption is portrayed on television, in movies, and in journalistic writings. This view of adoption as problematic gives a false image of adoption that is detrimental to the adoptee.

  Most adoptive families enjoy healthy relationships and form lifelong attachments. However, it is the few disruptive adoptions that receive public attention, leading some to believe that all adoptions are headed for the same fate. Adoptive parents need to confront these various stereotypes, myths and misconceptions about adoption to allow for their children to grow up in a more accepting society, with respect to differences.

—Talk with friends and family about adoption as one of many methods of family formations in contemporary society, comparing it with single-parent, 2-parent, step-parent, and blended families among others.

—Speak about adoption at your child's school, or give presentations at group functions in your community. Encourage professionals, such as medical and academic personnel to become more knowledgeable of adoption. Use positive adoption language when speaking to each of these.

—Write letters to the editor of your newspaper, or to magazine publishers, television general managers, cinema presidents, etc. when adoption is treated negatively.

—Donate adoption books or provide subscriptions to adoption publications to your school library. Video and audiotapes are also available for purchase, to be given to your child's school.

Adoption language

Positive, or constructive, adoption language should be familiar lexicon to all adoptive families. Not only does it assign dignity, respect, objectivity and responsibility to the birthparents for making an adoption decision, it also does the same for adoptive parents and adoptees involved in the adoption process.

It is important to clarify that your child *was* adopted, rather than *is* adopted, to avoid the pitfalls of labeling. Be aware of prejudicial attitudes when the adoption is referred to by individuals, with no clarification of how the adoption is related to the subject at hand, such as "This is Mr. and Mrs. Johnson and their adopted son, Joe, our neighbors." Question why the adoption was referred to, if it has no bearing on the general context.

Avoid terminology such as "real parent," "natural parent," or "one of your own." Preferred terms are "birthparent" for the child's biologic connection, and "parent" to indicate yourself. "Adoptive" should be used as an adjective to describe the parent only when it is relevant to the topic of adoption.

Children are not "put up for adoption" or "given up." rather, the birthparents "arranged an adoption," or "made an adoption plan." Similarly, birthparents don't "keep their babies," but instead "continue to parent" the child themselves.

"Foreign" adoptions are best described as "transnational/international," "transcultural," or "transracial" adoptions, with each specifying a particular type of adoption.

Adopted Children
Teacher and Administrator Handout

Linda M. Neiheiser

Overview

Adoption is a social service that provides a child with a new, permanent set of parents when the biologic parents cannot fulfill a parenting role. The practice of adoption has been in existence since recorded history, with the Code of Hammurabi (2800 B.C.) evidencing the oldest set of written adoption law. However, contemporary society's perception of adoption—that of a solution for meeting the needs of the child—is vastly different from the centuries-old practice of adoption as a system providing childless adults with heirs for political, religious, or even labor purposes.

Adoption has long been viewed as a single event for the members of the adoption triad—birthparents, adoptee, and adoptive parents—requiring minimal intervention by social service personnel. Yet the changing methods, current complexities, and greater enlightened view of adoption as a lifelong, intergenerational process uniting the triad members forever demand an interdisciplinary approach in working with adoptees. School personnel and medical clinicians, among others need to be more aware of adoption issues to adequately service adopted children.

Overrepresentation

Although adopted children comprise approximately 2–3% of the general population, their percentages are higher in psychological treatment facilities. This overrepresentation may be due to a number of factors, including adoptive parents' greater receptivity to the mental health professions than non-adoptive parents as one explanation for adoptee overrepresentation; identity consolidation concerns, especially during the adolescent state, which would explain adolescent adoptees' large numbers in such mental health programs; and actual problem behavior.

Research studies also bear out the large numbers of adoptees in health settings. Yet it should be noted that most of these studies look solely at adoptees engaged in treatment programs, rather than at adoptees as a whole in society, in comparison to non-adoptees. The figures may, therefore, be inflated. Still, adopted children do have issues to face throughout their lives that non-adoptees do not, such as loss.

Loss

Adoptive families form bonds and lifelong attachments, much like biologic families. However, the adoptive family is different in that it is formed through loss. All the triad members lose something in the process. Birthparents lose their birthchildren. Adoptees lose their biologic parents and extended family members, and may lose the opportunity to ever meet their birthparents, especially if the adoptee is from another country. The adoptive parents suffer loss, too—loss of confidence in their right to be a parent—which may affect the way they interact with their adopted child.

Developmental Issues

Prior to kindergarten, children are not aware of adoption issues, even if they have heard their own adoption story. But upon entering school, they begin to realize that most of the other children they meet are not adopted, and they begin to question their adoption story and other explanations their parents have given them.

The middle childhood years—ages seven through eleven—are an increasingly troublesome time for some adoptees, who begin to understand the significance of their loss. This new realization often leads adoptees to grieve for their loss, in ways that parents and teachers sometimes have difficulty understanding. A child who reacts with intense grief over a trivial loss may be expressing his unresolved feelings about the previous, deeper loss. This is normal and necessary, and does not indicate the child is unhappy in his present family.

Adopted children this age may also blame themselves harshly for anything that does not go right. They may be attempting to take control, to compensate for their loss of control in the adoption process. They may also be expressing a need to be perfect—to avoid being "rejected" once more, as adoptees sometimes feel they have been in the adoption placement. Loss, grief, inferiority, insecurity, feelings of abandonment, separation anxiety, and loss of trust are issues adoptees face during the middle childhood years.

During adolescence, adoptees begin the struggle to establish their identity, much like non-adopted adolescents. The adoptee has the additional challenge of forming this identity with an absence of biological markers, and may seek to uncover information concerning the birthparents. Again, this curiosity is normal and does not indicate the adoptee is unhappy in the adoptive family. Yet some adolescent adoptees need assistance in working through their concerns of a lack of genetic information, medical history, ethnic origins, or knowledge of their birth family's skills, talents, and abilities.

What can I do as an educator?

- Teachers, counselors, and administrative staff can begin to educate themselves on the various aspects of adoption to adequately assist adopted children or adolescent adoptees who may be experiencing difficulties. Attending area-sponsored adoption conferences or having an adoption expert speak at an in-service day are ways to familiarize school staff with the adoptees' issues of loss and grief, current adoption practices, and appropriate adoption language, as well as to dispel myths and misconceptions concerning adoption. This new knowledge can also be applied to working with adolescent birthparents.

    Ask adoptive parents to volunteer making brief presentations to classrooms, focusing on children's developmental levels of understanding, using the following guides:

    —At the preschool level, discuss the various ways families are formed. A unit on families, highlighting the uniquenesses of and similarities between two-parent families, single-parent families, blended families, extended family situation, adoptive families and step-parenting unions would be appropriate.

    —Kindergarten children could be led in a similar discussion, with information included on how babies are born, if this is permitted in your school. It is an area of interest to children this age, and could be discussed using pets as examples.

    —Elementary school-age children clearly note differences. An emphasis at this stage should be that of adoption as a "not better or worse situation"—just a different one. Include the family formation discussion, and allow for questions—both for the children and from them.

    —Secondary level students should be given the opportunity to discuss their perceptions of adoption. Present students with scenarios, to allow true feelings to emerge. This will provide the opportunity to dispel misconceptions and present factual information on current adoption practice. Some of these students may be prospective birthparents or may have already made adoption plans, in addition to the adolescent adoptees that may be present in the class. This added dimension should be considered.

- Review curriculum in your school. Is it sensitive to the feelings of adopted children? Do teachers ask children to write autobiographies, beginning with their birth? Are infant photos requested from every child for projects? Which teachers have students create family trees? Are genealogical studies or comparisons of inherited traits conducted? These lessons need modification, but they should be modified for the entire class, not just for the adoptee. Altering a lesson solely for an adopted child singles them out as different, and this can be hurtful to the child. Teachers should realize that many of these still-common lessons appear archaic when one considers the various family formations prevalent today. Genograms provide greater scope than family trees for multi-family situations.

- Transnational adoptees may know very little about the countries of their birth, and may not be interested in presenting information to the class on those particular countries. They should be permitted choice of projects as other children, rather than assigned their countries of origin. Some transnational adoptees may be of older age at placement, and may need assistance with the English language, as well as American customs. Preparing the class with cultural differences and incorporating the aid of a classroom "buddy" may assist the new adoptee.

- Adolescent adoptees may feel the need to discuss adoption-related concerns with someone other than a parent. If educators are familiar with adoption issues, they may consider forming a support group within the school, or discussing these concerns one-on-one with the adoptee. Additional assistance may be provided by area adoption support organizations. In addition to the issues, educators should also be knowledgeable of adoption language.

- Positive, or constructive, adoption language should become part of the vocabulary of every educator who works with adoptees, to assign respect and objectivity to the triad members involved in an adoption decision:

  —The phrase, "Put up for adoption," dates back to the 1890s, when 90,000 city orphans were brought to small, midwestern towns and exhibited or "put up" high on train platforms, in churches and town halls, for farm families to view them and select the ones to be taken home as extra laborers. More fitting terminology includes "chose adoption," "arranged an adoption," or "made an adoption plan," with "give up for adoption" seen as negative, implying ownership.

  —Birthparents don't "keep their babies;" rather, they continue to "parent the child." Keeping babies, as in giving them up, implies ownership.

  —Preferred terms for family relationships include "birthparent," "birthmother," or "birthfather" to describe the biologic couple who conceived the child, and "parents," "mother," or "father" to describe the adoptive parents. Neither parents nor child should ever be labelled "adoptive parents" or "adopted child," except in discussions of adoption. Terms to avoid include "real parent," "natural parent," or "one of your own."

  —Adopted children grow up and become adolescent or adult adoptees. They do not remain "adopted children."

  —"Foreign" adoption has negative connotation, leading to the preferred terms of "transnational/ international," "transcultural," and "transracial" adoption, with each term specifying a particular type of adoption.

Adoption Resources for Parents and Educators

The National Adoption Information Clearinghouse (NAIC) was established by Congress to provide professionals and the general public with easily accessible information on all aspects of adoption, including infant and intercountry adoption and the adoption of children with special needs. NAIC maintains an automated bibliographic data base of documents on adoption, a data base of adoption experts, listings of adoption agencies, crisis pregnancy centers, and other adoption-related services, excerpts of state and federal laws on adoption, and information on ongoing research projects concerning adoption. To receive a catalog and publication order form, call or write: National Adoption Information Clearinghouse, Suite 1275, 1400 Eye Street NW, Washington, DC 20005. 202/842-1919.

Search information may be obtained from any of the following

American Adoption Congress (AAC), 1000 Connecticut Avenue NW, Suite 9, Washington, DC 20036. Hotline number 1-800-274-OPEN.

Adoptee Liberty Movenet Association (ALMA). P.O. Box 154, Washington Bridge Station, New York, NY 10033.

Independent Search Consultants (ISC), P.O. Box 10192, Costa Mesa, CA 92627.

International Soundex Reunion Registry (ISRR), P.O. Box 2312, Carson City, NV 89702-2312.

Adoptive parent groups

Adoptive Families of America, 3333 Highway 100 North, Minneapolis, MN 55422. 612/535-4829. A national, nonprofit membership organization of more than 15,000 families and individuals and more than 250 support groups. Monthly publications and national conferences.

North American Council on Adoptable Children, 1821 University Ave., Suite N-498, St. Paul, MN 55104. 612/644-3036. An international, nonprofit organization with representatives in each state to assist adoptive parents and support groups. Monthly publications and national conferences.

National Committee for Adoption, 1930 Seventeenth St. NW, Washington, DC 20009. 202/328-8072. A nonprofit, private organization made up of member groups whose goal is to promote adoption. A hotline provides information to couples interested in adoption and referrals for counseling.

Resolve, Inc. P.O. Box 474, Belmont, MA 02178. 617/643-2424. A national, nonprofit charitable organization which offers information, advocacy and support to people with problems of infertility and to adoptive families, and education to associated professionals. Monthly publications, both national and local.

Other resources

An annotated listing of books and other materials available can be obtained by contacting any of the following:

Our Child Press, 800 N. Maple Glen Lane, Wayne, PA 19087. 215/964-0606. A resource for books on adoption, written for adoptive parents, adoptees, birthparents, and others interested in adoption.

Parenting Resources, 250 El Camino Real, Suite 111, Tustin, CA 82680. 714/669-8100. Education, counseling and mediation services provided to triad members. Multi-media materials available.

Perspective Press, P.O. Box 90318, Indianapolis, IN 46290-0318. 317/872-3055. A resource for books on adoption, as well as national speakers.

Your school's library or media service should be examined to see if adoption-related materials are available and current for those children wishing to learn more about adoption. Guidance counselors may also want to consider subscribing to the various monthly publications for their department.

Children and Asthma
Teacher Handout

Steven E. Curtis
Utah State University

Overview

There are over 8 million children with asthma in the United States, including over 2 million children under the age of 15. Childhood asthma is the leading cause of school absences due to a chronic physical disorder and is associated with heavy medication usage, many emergency room visits, frequent hospitalizations, and occasionally, death. These negative experiences of the asthmatic child may result in poor grades, low self-esteem, and possibly a desire to drop out of school in the later grades. Asthma can be controlled if prescribed medical procedures are followed and if the child learns asthma management skills. Teachers can play an important role in helping the asthmatic child be successful and happy in school.

Characteristics of Asthma: Asthma is a respiratory disorder, often manifested by wheezing and labored breathing, which has three significant characteristics: intermittence, variability, and reversibility. Asthma is intermittent in that attacks are not always experienced on a regular basis. For example, some children may experience attacks all year long; while others may experience attacks only in one particular season. Asthma is variable, in that attacks vary in severity from mild episodes, manifested by chest tightness or a mild wheeze, to "status asthmaticus," which denotes steadily worsening asthma. Asthma is also reversible, which distinguishes it from other types of respiratory disorders, such as emphysema. Asthma-related airway obstruction may reverse spontaneously or with treatment, and symptoms may be present at one moment and then subside a short while later.

Causes of Asthma: The cause of asthma has often been thought to be emotional, but emotions do not cause asthma. Asthma is actually caused by a physiologic hyperresponsivity of the airways that seems to be genetically determined. Asthma attacks occur when these hyperresponsive airways are exposed to certain stimuli called "triggers." Some emotions can act as triggers of attacks for certain children.

Mechanisms of an Asthma Attack: Asthma attacks occur when there is a blockage in the airways. This blockage occurs when one or more triggers cause tight constriction of the muscles surrounding the airways (called bronchoconstriction), resulting in smaller airways and restricted airflow. The airway linings then swell and the membranes lining the airways secrete extra mucus. This causes further restriction of the airways, resulting in breathing difficulties and possible wheezing. Wheezing is the sound of air being forced through the mucus in the restricted airways and is often audible from a distance.

Common "Triggers" of an Asthma Attack: Common triggers include allergens (e.g., pollens, foods, dust, mold, feathers, or animal dander); irritants (e.g., smoke, air pollution, and cold air); exercise; respiratory infections; aspirin and related substances; and emotional responses (e.g., hard laughing or crying). Triggers vary from child to child and are usually identified by physicians who conduct allergy histories and perform skin tests.

Symptoms of an Asthma Attack: Symptoms of an asthma attack may include wheezing, tightness in the chest, shortness of breath, pains in the chest, coughing, face perspiration, hunched shoulders, and/or an uncomfortable look on the face. During an attack, several or all of these symptoms may be present.

Medical Treatment of Asthma: Traditional medical treatment has focused on managing asthma versus curing the disorders since a medical cure is not known at this time. Medications used in the management of asthma include adrenergic agents, theophylline, and cromolyn. Corticosteroids are used with acute exacerbation of asthma. These medications all increase the flow of air through the airways in order to relieve and prevent trouble breathing.

Attack Prevention: Attack prevention includes: identifying and avoiding know triggers; recognizing early signs of an asthma attack; and acting on early signs to prevent more serious attacks from occurring. Once triggers are identified they should be avoided as much as possible. When early signs of an attack occur, the child should take action to manage the attack, in order to prevent a more severe attack from developing.

Attack Management: Attack management involves these steps: relaxation, drinking warm liquids, and using medications as prescribed. When early signs of an attack are noted, the child should stop any activity, sit down, and rest for at least 10 minutes. During this time it is helpful for the child to engage in "belly breathing" and some type of relaxation technique. Relaxation techniques are best taught by trained professionals, such as school psychologists. The child should also slowly drink warm liquids in order to help the airways relax. During this time, medication should be taken as prescribed. These procedures should be followed during the early signs of an attack as well as during a full blown attack. When these management steps bring little or no relief, the child's parents should be contacted to discuss the possibility of physician referral.

What can I do as a teacher?

Teachers can help in the following ways:

1. Many children have undiagnosed asthma which could be treated if diagnosed by a physician. Teachers observing children with symptoms of asthma who are previously undiagnosed should contact the parents to suggest a medical referral.

2. With asthmatic children who have been previously diagnosed, contact between parents and teachers should take place to discuss the following: the physician's recommendations; the type and frequency of medications; possible side effects from medication; behavior to expect from the particular asthmatic child during an asthma attack; specific strategies to be used to prevent and manage attacks once they occur; and ways to keep the channels of communication open between school and home.

3. Teachers should pay close attention to the prescribed times for taking medication in case students need to be reminded to take them.

4. Teachers should pay close attention to potential side effects of asthma medication. Possible side effects include tremors, drowsiness, fatigue, headaches, or stomachaches. If these side effects are noted, the parents should be contacted so they can contact the physician.

5. Teachers should be aware of the triggers causing the child's asthma attacks in order to help the child avoid these triggers and prevents attacks.

6. If the child has exercise-induced asthma, the teacher should help the child follow medical procedures recommended prior to exercise. Exercise induced asthma does not mean the child cannot exercise. The asthmatic child should exercise on a regular basis and take medications as prescribed to ward off attacks.

7. If an attack occurs the teacher should follow the above attack management procedures and the procedures discussed by parents. When a child's condition has improved after an attack, the child should return to class.

When to call the parents or doctor: If you have any doubts about the severity of an attack, call the parents immediately to discuss a possible visit to the physician. Parents should always be called if the child's fingernails or lips are turning blue or if the child seems to be breathing shallowly and focusing all attention on breathing.

Resources

American Lung Association (1982). *Superstuff: A pediatric asthma self-management program.* New York: American Lung Association. *Superstuff* is a small book with information designed to help children learn asthma self-management skills.

National Heart, Lung, and Blood Institute. (1984). *Living with asthma: Manual for teaching families the self-management of childhood asthma.* (NIH Publication No. 85-2364). Bethesda, MD: National Institutes of Health. *Living with Asthma* is a packaged self-management program for childhood asthma. The program may be used by a variety of professionals and may be obtained in most university libraries. Within the materials is information about asthma, visuals, and handouts to give to parents.

The National Heart, Lung, and Blood Institute (NHLBI) has a Reading and Resource List of information sources for asthma, which include handouts, books, videos, and information about asthma programs. Free copies may be obtained by writing to NHLBI, Asthma Project, Building 31, Room 4A21, Bethesda, MD 20205.

Local chapters of the American Lung Association are good sources for free asthma information pamphlets.

Cancer

Nancy Conti
University of South Florida

Background—Cancer is defined by Van Eys as "the uncontrolled and uninhibited growth of a certain cell . . . it is a frequent and normal consequence of cellular behavior" (Van Eys, 1981). Types of cancer and the effect on the body differ primarily in the location of the cell undergoing abnormal growth (i.e., blood, bone, central nervous system). Although environmental factors are considered to be variables in the development and/or promotion of cancer, psychological factors are not (Katz, 1980; Van Eys, 1981). Gender differences were also noted in development of cancer with boys diagnosed more often than girls at a ratio of 1.2:1 (Hanson & Mulvihill, 1982).

Although cancer is the second leading cause of death (after accidents) in children under 15 years of age, advances in medical technology have led to a shift in treatment focus from prolonging and dealing with death to concentrating on the quality of the child's life (Cincotta, 1989; Hanson & Mulvihill, 1982; Katz, 1980; Kung, 1981). Cancer is no longer a completely incurable disease. The type of cancers most often found in children include: leukemia, Hodgkin's (cancer of the lymph gland), Wilm's tumor (cancer of the kidney), bone tumors, soft tissue sarcomas, Retinoblastoma (cancer of the eye), and brain tumors, with the most frequent childhood cancer being a form of leukemia (Siegel, 1980). The onset of leukemia, Wilm's tumor, brain tumors, and Retinoblastoma most frequently peak at approximately age 4, whereas Hodgkin's and bone cancer are rarely seen before age 5 and adolescence respectively (Hanson & Mulvihill, 1982; Miller, 1989). There are three medical interventions for the treatment of childhood cancer. These include chemotherapy, radiation therapy, and surgery. Some of the typical side effects of chemotherapy are "mouth and lip ulcers, nausea and vomiting, hair loss, weight gain, fluid retention, pain and weakness in arms and legs, fevers, burns on the skin, susceptibility to disease, possible cognitive and affective impairment, reduced fertility, secondary malignancies" (Katz, 1980). Side effects of radiation include "nausea and vomiting, hair loss, skin burns, headaches, impaired physical growth, and reduced fertility" (Katz, 1980; Levine, Blumberg, & Hersh, 1982). The side effects of surgery are "disfigurement, reduced functioning," and possibly the use of prosthetic devices (Katz, 1980; Levine, Blumberg, & Hersh, 1982).

Development—The most frequently observed responses by children to their illness and treatment are anxiety, fear, sadness, guilt, and loneliness (Katz, 1980; Levine, Blumberg, & Hersh, 1982; Spinetta, 1981a,b; Van Eys, 1981). Additional responses may vary according to the age of the child. For example, children below age 4 or 5 may experience feelings of abandonment by their parents; children ages 5 through 6 are aware they have a serious illness, but may not be able to verbalize their feelings; and those age 7 through 8 are aware and able to speak to other children about what they are feeling. Children above age 8 are even more aware of their condition and have a greater ability to relay their feelings (Levine, Blumberg, & Hersh, 1982; Spinetta, 1981a,b). Further difficulties observed in children include the impact to the child's self-esteem. The children must adjust to the fact that their illness is serious enough to threaten their lives and that the treatment may be lengthy and uncomfortable. Children may also be concerned about whether and when they will return to school and how their peers will react to the changes they have undergone. The necessary adjustments combined with the child's

267

need to be accepted by his/her peers and engage in normal childhood activities may result in a negative impact on the child's self-esteem and the child having difficulty sufficiently adjusting to the situation (Katz, 1980).

The child's reaction to the side effects of treatment may vary according to the child's age. For preschool-age children there are typically few or no problems resulting from the physical effects of treatment (such as baldness), but cognitively the child may interpret the treatment as punishment for bad behavior or the withdrawal of their parent(s)' love. School-age children are more aware of their physical appearance and therefore more sensitive to the effects of treatment. They may also blame their parents for not protecting them and allowing this to happen. For adolescents, the physical effects of treatment will be highly anxiety producing (Katz, 1980).

The reactions of the siblings may include such feelings and behaviors as: guilt for being healthy, fear, separation anxiety, school problems, depression, jealousy, feelings of responsibility for the condition of the sick child, rejection or resentment towards the parents for not being available for the well child and not protecting the ill child from becoming sick, shame at having an ill sibling, and physical problems that include stomach pains, enuresis, and headaches. The physical symptoms displayed by the sibling(s) may be equivalent to those of the sick child (Bendor, 1990; Levine, Blumberg, & Hersh, 1982; Sourkes, 1980; Spinetta, 1981c). Gender and age of siblings will also affect how they react to the situation. Girls are more likely to become withdrawn, and boys are more likely to become aggressive. Infant siblings are most likely to be adversely affected due to parental preoccupation with the sick child. Older siblings will be better able to understand the situation and engage in caretaking activities (Spinetta, 1981c).

According to Katz (1980), parents may also manifest behavioral and psychological reactions to the situation which may include:

1. Denial.
2. Guilt over not adequately protecting their child or identifying the problem earlier.
3. Overprotection.
4. Overidentification—parents may assume that they know how the child is feeling and impose this on the child.
5. Separation anxiety.

A possible reaction by the father may be for him to throw himself into his work in order to escape a problem he does not know how to deal with. Lack of money for the medical bills is often the given reason. The mother is often left alone to deal with the emotional needs of herself and her family (Kung, 1981).

What Can I Do as a Parent?—First and most important, parents must respect the rights of the child. The child has a right to know what is happening to his/her body due to the illness and treatment. The child also has a right to their feelings about the situation and should be given the opportunity to express those feelings. Finally, any devices (prosthetic devices, wigs, hats, etc.) the child needs to most fully regain normal functioning should be provided (Aronson, 1980; McCue, 1980).

To most adequately provide for the needs of the sick child, parents must should attempt to do the following:

1. Come to terms with and accept the illness and treatment requirements.
2. Be aware of the potential outcomes of the illness.
3. Be aware that the child, due to age, may have limited understanding of what is happening. Parents should be as open and honest with the sick child and the siblings as possible.
4. Be supportive of each other.
5. Engage in coping strategies.

6. Allow the siblings to discuss their feelings with the parents.

7. Allow the sick child to express their anger toward their siblings.

8. Maintain discipline and work toward maintaining normality (Kaplan, 1980; Levine, Blumberg, & Hersh, 1982; Sourkes, 1980; Spinetta, 1981a,c).

What Can the Schools Do?

1. Be aware of the medical situation and maintain contact with the parents.

2. Ensure the most normal environmental conditions possible for the child.

3. Make appropriate curricular changes based on the needs of the child.

4. Educate those teachers who will have contact with the child to the physical and psychological side effects.

5. Assist the child in how to talk to his/her peers about what has happened. (Deasy-Spinetta, 1981; Fryer, Saylor, Finch, & Smith, 1989).

Resources

If additional information is desired, please contact your physician, school psychologist, or guidance counselor

References

Aronson, J. (1980). I may be bald, but I still have rights. In J. Kellerman (Ed.), *Psychological aspects of childhood cancer* (pp. 184-191). Springfield, IL: Charles C. Thomas.

Bendor, S. J. (1990). Anxiety and isolation in siblings of pediatric cancer patients: The need for prevention. *Social Work in Health Care, 14,* 17-34.

Cincotta, N. (1989). Quality of life: A family decision. In Van Eys (Ed.), *Cancer in the very young* (pp. 63-73). Springfield, IL: Charles C. Thomas.

Deasy-Spinetta, P. (1981). The school and the child with cancer. In J. J. Spinetta & P. Deasy-Spinetta (Eds.), *Living with childhood cancer* (pp. 153-168). St. Louis, MO: C.V. Mosby.

Fryer, L. L., Saylor, C. F., Finch, A. J., & Smith, K. E. (1989). Helping the child with cancer: What school personnel want to know. *Psychological Reports, 65,* 563-566.

Hanson, M. R., & Mulvihill, J. J. (1982). Epidemiology of cancer in the young. In A.S. Levine (Ed.), *Cancer in the young* (pp. 3-11). New York: Masson Publishing USA, Inc.

Kaplan, D. M. (1981). Interventions for acute stress experiences. In J. J. Spinetta & P. Deasy-Spinetta (Eds.), *Living with childhood cancer* (pp. 41-49). St. Louis, MO: C.V. Mosby.

Katz, E. R. (1980). Illness impact and social reintegration. In J. Kellerman, (Ed.), *Psychological aspects of cancer* (pp. 14-46). Springfield, IL: Charles C. Thomas.

Kung, F. H. (1981). From diagnosis to survival. In J. J. Spinetta & P. Deasy-Spinetta (Eds.), *Living with childhood cancer* (pp. 81-85). St. Louis, MO: C.V. Mosby.

Levine, A. S., Blumberg, B. D., & Hersh, S. P. (1982). The psychosocial concomitants of cancer in young patients. In A. S. Levine (Ed.), *Cancer in the young* (pp. 367-390). New York: Masson Publishing USA, Inc.

McCue, K. (1980). Preparing children for medical procedures. In J. Kellerman (Ed.), *Psychological aspects of cancer* (pp. 238-256). Springfield, IL: Charles C. Thomas.

Miller, R. W. (1989). The frequency of cancer in the very young. In J. Van Eys (Ed.), *Cancer in the very young* (pp. 19-31). Springfield, IL: Charles C. Thomas.

Siegel, S.E. (1980). The current outlook of childhood cancer—The medical background. In J. Kellerman (Ed.), *Psychological aspects of cancer* (pp. 5-13). Springfield, IL: Charles C. Thomas.

Sourkes, B. M. (1980). Siblings of the pediatric cancer patient. In J. Kellerman (Ed.), *Psychological aspects of cancer* (pp. 47-69). Springfield, IL: Charles C. Thomas.

Spinetta, J. J. (1981a). Adjustment and adaptation in children with cancer: A 3-year study. In J. J. Spinetta & P. Deasy-Spinetta (Eds.), *Living with childhood cancer* (pp. 5-26). St. Louis, MO: C.V. Mosby.

Spinetta, J. J. (1981b). Living with childhood cancer. In J. J. Spinetta & P. Deasy-Spinetta (Eds.), *Living with childhood cancer (pp. 3-4). St. Louis, MO: C.V. Mosby.*

Spinetta, J. J. (1981c). The sibling of the child with cancer. In J. J. Spinetta & P. Deasy-Spinetta (Eds.), *Living with childhood cancer* (pp. 133-142). St. Louis, MO: C.V. Mosby.

Van Eys, J. (1981). The truly cured child: The realistic and necessary goal in pediatric oncology. In J. J. Spinetta & P. Deasy-Spinetta (Eds.), *Living with childhood cancer* (pp. 30-40). St. Louis, MO: C.V. Mosby.

NATIONAL ASSOCIATION OF SCHOOL PSYCHOLOGISTS

Children and Chronic Illness

Margaret L. Potter
Moorhead State University, Moorhead, Minnesota

Background—Most childhood illnesses last for only a few days or at most, several weeks. However 10 to 20 percent of all children have chronic illness where the treatment may continue for years. For two percent of these children, the illness is severe and regularly interferes with daily activities. There is a wide variety of chronic illnesses, of problems associated with such illnesses, and of reactions to the illness on the part of the child, parents, teachers and friends. Because each situation is unique, it is important to be able to be creative and flexible when dealing with problems that do come up.

Development—Depending on the specific illness, the severity and effects of a chronic illness may change as the child grows older and as the body goes through normal maturational changes. Especially during adolescence, previously routine treatments may need to be changed both because of the adolescent's changing body and because of the teen's increasing need for independence, responsibility and privacy.

Also changing as the child grows older is the child's understanding of illness:

Birth to 18 months—Infants do not realize that illness is not a part of normal life. Very young children do not understand that objects and people still exist even when they cannot see them, thus separations from family may be especially painful.

18-36 months—Toddlers understand their illness only as something that interferes with their own world. They have a magical view of causes and effects leading them to believe that if they want something to happen it will happen; or they may believe it was something they thought or did that made them sick. Toddlers also need to feel that they have some control over their world.

3-7 years—Preschoolers are beginning to think more logically, but still tend to believe that bad things, like being sick, result from wrong doing, outside forces, or events that happened close together in time or location. They define illness by what they can actually see or feel and may develop conflicting theories about their illness.

7-12 years—Elementary school-aged children still understand best that which they can feel or see. By about age nine or ten, they start to understand some of the unobservable active processes of their bodies, but they tend to believe firmly that it is germs that cause illness. At about age 11 or 12 they start to understand the body's own healing process.

Adolescents—Adolescents are increasingly capable of understanding the complexities of how their body operates. Some teens may take an intellectual view of their illness and try to learn as much as possible about it. They may develop their own personal ideas about illness combining emotion, fact, fantasy and even, still a measure of self-blame. Adolescents may also assert their independence by refusing or sabatoging treatment routines.

What Can I Do as a Parent?

- Experts agree that it is best to treat chronically ill, even terminally ill, children as normally as possible. Be matter-of-fact about the illness. As much as possible, maintain normal age appropriate expectations for your child including completion of assigned household and school responsibilities. Do not let the illness overshadow the person, or overtake your family.

- Whenever possible, let your child/adolescent assume responsibility for their own care and have a say in that care. This helps them feel as if they have some control over their lives. Even toddlers can be given choices about which cup to drink their medicine from or whether to take it before or after putting on their pajamas. Adolescents should be treated as active partners in treatment and educational decisions.

- Help your other children to develop their own identities and to understand the similarities and differences between themselves and their ill sibling. Tell them about the illness at a level they can understand and keep them informed about what is happening.

- Find a contact person in the school whom you can keep posted about any changes in your child's condition or treatment. Since teachers change, a more logical contact person might be the school nurse, counselor or assistant principal.

- Keep communication channels open. Work closely with all of the people involved in your child's care. Do not be afraid to ask questions or to ask to have information repeated.

- Get to know other families that are also dealing with a chronic illness. If there are no organized groups near you, ask your school or doctor to suggest someone with whom you and your child can share problems and experiences.

- If your child's progress in school is hampered by the illness, he or she may be eligible for special services under federal and state laws. Check with your school—services available may include hospital/homebound tutoring, physical and occupational therapy, classroom assistance, counseling, etc.

- Work with the school to develop a written plan of how to deal with make-up work, schedule modifications, emergency situations and so on.

- Recognize that it is normal for you and your child to periodically feel frustrated, angry, sad, anxious, guilty, or even to deny the seriousness of the illness. Just try not to let these feelings interfere with your child's treatment plan.

Resources

- *The Exceptional Parent*—A monthly magazine providing practical information and articles for parents of children with special needs. Your local library should have a copy.

- *The Chronically Ill Child: A Guide for Parents and Professionals.* A. McCollum, Yale University Press. 1981. An excellent book that discusses many of the practical issues with which families must deal from birth to young adulthood.

- *Encyclopedia of Organizations*, Gale Research. The most recent edition of this reference book available at public libraries is the best source for addresses of organizations serving people with chronic illnesses or low-incidence handicaps.

- *Closer Look*, National Information Center for the Handicapped, Box 1492, Washington, D.C. 20013.

- *Notes from a Different Drummer* (1977) and *More Notes from a Different Drummer* (1984). B. Baskin and K. Harris, Bowker Publisher. These reference books provide descriptions of children's books that portray the handicapped.

NATIONAL
ASSOCIATION OF
SCHOOL
PSYCHOLOGISTS

Children and Responses to Disaster
Formulating a Disaster Plan

Debby Waddell
Alex Thomas

Background—Disasters can take many forms. They may be

- weather-related, as in tornadoes, hurricanes, or floods;
- accident-related, as in bus or automobile deaths or drowning;
- illness-related as in AIDS, cancer or other deaths due to illness, or
- bizarre and unusual, as in the case of snipers or a murder.

For some of these disasters, pre-planning can be done, i.e., when death from cancer is anticipated or when weather forecasts warn of hurricanes. Others may be sudden and allow no time for pre-planning. Yet another variable is whether the disaster occurs at school (i.e., a suicide in the school or a tornado during school hours) or outside of school hours (i.e., weekend hurricane or automobile accident). All of these factors will undoubtedly affect the specific response to the disasters, but some common elements can be found in all of these situations.

Formulating a Disaster Plan: When disaster strikes, teachers and school staff members need to be immediately ready to cope with their reactions and the reactions of their students. The need to deal with student reactions comes at a time when staff members are still dealing with their own reaction and may be least prepared to think quickly and cope with others' reactions. Nonetheless, this must be done. With some advance planning, this process can be much smoother than if disaster takes you by surprise and no preformulated plan is in effect. Once a plan is in effect, adjustments can quickly be made to deal with the specific nature of the current crisis.

If formulating a disaster plan, the following ideas may be helpful.

- Determine if your district is small enough to have a single crisis team or if separate building teams are needed with an umbrella district team for times of widespread disaster.
- Team members should be selected on the basis of each member's expertise.
- Designate a team leader.
- Designate the disaster team or teams. This will likely include administrators, school psychologists, counselors, and other staff members without responsibility for individual classrooms.
- Designate an individual who will deal with the media. This is very important.
- Plan ways of using community resources and network with these agencies or individuals in advance. Potential resources include mental health agency personnel and clergy with special training in counseling.
- Prepare for weekend or after-hours meetings of disaster teams and coordinators, perhaps setting

up a phone-tree for quick notification. Be sure to check contract language prior to requiring after hours involvement, where necessary.

- Determine how PTO/PTA leaders might bring meals for staff members working late into the evening or arrange child care for staff members' children to free them for disaster team efforts.

All staff members should be aware of the disaster plan. Not only teachers, but clerical staff, aides, bus drivers, and maintenance staff need to be apprised of the plan. Including staff members in planning and sharing the plan at a district inservice day or teacher meetings allows time for discussion when stress and pressure are minimal.

Another task that can be done in advance of disaster is preparing information on typical reactions to disasters and planning ways for distribution of such information. The teacher and parent handouts accompanying this information are designed for just such purposes. Pairing these handouts with one detailing events and resources in your community is suggested. A possible format for such a handout is:

- Specific, factual information about the event.
- Details about how the district is handling the crisis.
- Information about contact people within the district including phone numbers.
- Information about community resources including phone numbers.
- Titles of books pertinent to disasters as well as books dealing with feelings. Ask librarians to use the bookfinder to prepare a list of such books available in your library (school and public) for a variety of topics (death, tornadoes, children and serious illness, etc.). This will facilitate quick access if the list is needed. Preparing such a list may suggest topic areas in which your libraries are weak and allow time for ordering additional materials.

Disaster plans can include steps to be taken immediately upon learning of a disaster as well as longer-term plans. The following items might be included:

Immediate Reaction to Disaster

- Determine how staff members and students will learn of the disaster.
  - Provide accurate information to all concerned at approximately the same time to help control the spread of rumors. The PA system or messages to teachers might be used. depending on the nature of the disaster. A death or other intimate disaster may require a more personal manner of imparting information.
  - Notify staff members in advance if time allows. Word of a death occurring over a weekend can be spread by phone or at an early-morning staff meeting.
  - Target certain parents for special notification. For instance, if a member of an athletic team is killed, phoning parents of other team members might be indicated.
- Decide about scheduling changes.
  - Decide whether to maintain normal schedules or set aside regular scheduling in an all-out effort to deal with the crisis. Obviously this decision will depend on the extent of the crisis and might even vary from grade to grade and from class to class. For instance, if a sophomore commits suicide, that class will probably need more assistance than the senior class.
  - A most important step in any disaster is reopening the school and returning to a normal routine as soon as possible.

274

- Formulate plans for school dismissal.
  - Typically keeping children in school for the regular school day is best when dealing with disaster. However, if early dismissal is required, parent notification becomes an item of priority.
  - There may be occasions when an extended school day is necessary. For instance, if a shooting has occurred and the gunman/women is at large and most of the students walk home from school, dismissing students would be hazardous.
  - Plans may need to be made for shielding children and staff from the media. Cordoning children as they are loaded into school buses may prove to be very effective for this purpose.

Intermediate Steps for Crisis Control

- Provide support and counseling for students.
  - Regular instruction will probably need to be suspended while the disaster is discussed.
  - Individuals trained in counseling might target classrooms for their most immediate services where children are most severely affected.
  - Teachers need to know how to get assistance from another professional quickly should the need arise.
- Disseminate factual information about the crisis to parents.
  - The most effective method of providing factual information to parents may be to prepare a letter to be sent home.
  - Some parents may need to be contacted by phone, especially if their child's reaction to the disaster seems extreme.
- Decide how to deal with funerals or memorial services if death(s) are involved in the disaster.
  - When possible, have parents take their own children to the services.
  - If parents are unable to go, staff members may volunteer to do this. Permission slips may be needed.
  - Successful suicides should not be treated as honored heroes in school assemblies and funeral attendance should, in most cases, be only with parents accompanying the children.
  - At times, school buses may be used. Permission slips may be needed.
  - Plans for make-up work or forgiveness for assignments not completed due to attending the services should be made and discussed with staff members so that a consistent plan is used.

Long-term and on-going disaster intervention

- Provide for on-going opportunities to deal with the crisis. This might include:
  - Continue to have additional support staff and outside professionals available to students.
  - Make additional resources available to teachers who will be dealing with student reactions daily.
- Think ahead to effects which might be delayed. For example:
  - A similar incident in another location may trigger renewed feelings.
  - The one year anniversary of a disaster may provide an opportunity for planning a special remembrance, thereby diverting renewed reactions if the anniversary date is ignored.

Children and Responses to Disaster
Parent Handout

Debby Waddell, *Handouts Editor*
Alex Thomas, *Communique Editor*

Background—Disasters can take many forms. They may be

- weather-related, as in tornadoes, hurricanes, or floods:
- accident-related, as in bus or automobile deaths or drowning;
- illness-related as in AIDS, cancer or other deaths due to illness; or
- bizarre and unusual, as in the case of snipers or a murder.

The emotional effects of a disaster on you and your child can be tremendous. One of the difficulties experienced by parents during disasters is that they have not had adequate time to deal with their own reactions when they are called upon to deal with the impact of the disaster on their child. This handout is designed to help you and your child during a disaster.

Emotional Reactions to Disaster

Emotional reactions vary in nature and severity from child to child. Children's reactions to a disaster are determined by their previous experiences, their temperament and personality, and the immediacy of the disaster to their own lives. Nonetheless, some commonalities exist in how children (and adults) feel when their lives are disrupted by a disaster.

Loss of Control. By their very nature, disasters are something over which we have no control-if we did, we would stop them from happening. The feeling of loss of control can be overwhelming.

Loss of Stability. Disasters also interrupt the natural order of things. Stability is gone and this is very threatening; it can destroy trust and upset equilibrium for extended periods. After all, if this disaster could happen, then most anything else might happen too.

Self-centered Reactions. Children's immediate reaction to disaster often includes a fear for their own safety. They may be intensely worried about what will happen to them, to an extent that you think is unreasonable. However young children have difficulty putting the needs of others before their own. Children need repeated reassurance regarding their own safety and the outcome of the disaster as it relates to them.

Stages of Reactions to Loss. Some reactions to disasters are similar to reactions to other losses or grief. These include denial, anger, depression, bargaining and acceptance. Not every person experiences all of these feelings, and they do not always occur in just this order. A person may feel angry, then depressed, then angry again. How feelings are expressed will vary with the age of the child. A very young child may express denial by refusing to talk about the situation or clowning when others are talking about the disaster. Older children may go to their rooms or insist on going to the mall. Anger in a young child may involve a tantrum and in older child may be manifested as yelling at a parent.

What To Say To A Child During Or After A Disaster

- Knowing what to say is often difficult. When no other words come to mind, a hug and saying, "This is really hard for us," will always work.

- Try to recognize the feeling underlying your child's actions and put it into words. Saying something like "It makes us mad to think about all the people and homes that were hurt by this hurricane," or "I can see you are feeling really sad about this," can help.

- Sometimes children may have an overwhelming fear that they are unable to put into words, and you may need to voice for them. For instance, if a friend loses his mother during a flood, you might want to say to your child, "You may be scared that something will happen to me and Daddy (or Mommy) too. We are safe, and the flood waters are leaving, so we aren't going to die from this flood."

- Be honest with your child about what has happened and what is happening.

- Don't deny the seriousness of the situation. Saying to a child "Don't cry, everything will be okay" does not reflect how the child feels and the child knows that, at least in the immediate future, this is not true.

- Help your child know what words to use with others. For instance, if the disaster has resulted in death, the child may feel overwhelmed about what to say to friends at the funeral home. You may need to help by suggesting some simple appropriate words.

- Plan a practical concrete activity to help student deal with feelings.

    - Involve students in decisions about what to do to help restore their sense of having control in their lives. Possible activates include:

        - Collecting money for disaster victims.

        - Planting a tree as a memorial for a death.

        - Designing cards and writing notes to someone involved in the disaster.

        - Drawing pictures and putting up a bulletin board.

        - Writing poems or stories for a class book about the disaster.

- Inform parents about how their children are reacting and what is being done in the classroom to deal with the disaster. A handwritten, dittoed note will suffice in this situation.

- Decide how to handle attending funeral or memorial services if the disaster involves deaths.

    - Whenever possible, have parents take their own children to services.

    - If necessary, arrange transportation for a student to a memorial service. If you will be teaching during the service, a parent or another staff member may take the student. (Permission slips may be needed). The person chosen should be prepared to deal with the student's emotional reaction to the service.

    - Provide information about the funeral and its structure to prepare the students for the experience. Students who aren't going may still want to know what will happen. For young children, this may be their first experience with death, and information may be especially important for them.

- Allow for the fatigue which children may experience due to stress and changed sleep patterns.

    - Plan for less intense instructional activities for a few days.

    - Introduce snack time for a few days to provide extra nourishment which tired children may need. Room parents or the PTA/PTO may be willing to provide snacks.

- Delay tests which will allow fair evaluation of student performance after stress levels are reduced.

Long-term and on-going disaster intervention

- Provide on-going opportunities to deal with the crisis.
  - Let students know there continue to be people available who are willing to listen. Tell them who is available and when and where to find these people.
  - Discuss feelings with the entire class or individual children who feel most affected.
  - Discuss the disaster in the context of other subjects, e.g. discuss suicide prevention in a junior high health class, discuss weather-related disasters in elementary social studies class.
  - Provide facts to help allay fears. For instance, if a classmate dies of cancer, facts about prevalence and cures may help students who are fearful when they feel unwell.
- Think ahead to effects which might be delayed. For instance:
  - Be aware that similar incidents in another location may trigger renewed feelings.
  - Plan a special remembrance for the one-year anniversary of the disaster, thereby diverting renewed reaction if the anniversary date is ignored.
- Listen and watch for long-term reactions.
  - Prepare for long-term reactions which are normal, such as the continued need to discuss a hurricane or shooting.
  - Watch for pathological long-term reactions. Pathological long-term reactions are more severe than those experienced by most children and might include (1) persistent reexperiencing of the traumatic event through intense recollections, dreams, flashbacks or hallucinations, (2) persistent avoidance of stimuli associated with the trauma or numbing of responsiveness, e.g., restricted affect, diminished interest in usual activities or (3) signs of increased arousal, e.g. sleep difficulties, irritability, hypervigilance, disturbances in concentration, exaggerated startle response.
- Find ways to emphasize a return to stability.
  - When the disaster abates, return to previous schedules and maintain these for a time, even if some change in routine was planned, in order to provide a sense of security and comfort.

NATIONAL
ASSOCIATION OF
SCHOOL
PSYCHOLOGISTS

Children and Responses to Disaster
Teacher Handout

Debby Waddell, *Handouts Editor*

Alex Thomas, *Communique Editor*

Background—Disasters can take many forms. They may be

- weather-related, as in tornadoes, hurricanes, or floods:
- accident-related, as in bus or automobile deaths or drowning;
- illness-related as in AIDS, cancer, or other deaths due to illness; or
- bizarre and unusual, as in the case of snipers or a murder.

Pre-planning can be done for some of these disasters i.e., when a death from cancer is anticipated or when weather forecasts warn of hurricanes. Others may be sudden and allow no time for pre-planning. Yet another variable is whether the disaster occurs at school, i.e. a suicide in the school or tornado during school hours or outside of school hours, i.e. a hurricane or automobile accident. All of these factors will undoubtedly affect the specific response to the disasters, but some common elements can be found in responses to all of these situations.

Teachers have two essential jobs in the aftermath of disasters. First, to make plans for the practical aspects of how the disaster will be handled in their own classroom and second, to understand and cope with student reactions. The first of these responsibilities will likely be shared with other building personnel, but each teacher will have to structure the response within his/her own classroom. The second responsibility, coping with student reactions, again will be shared-this time with the parents and individuals such as school psychologist, school counselor, or an outside mental health professional. The on-going need to deal with student reactions during the school day, however will fall on individual teachers. This handout is designed to provide assistance in the first of these two areas. The accompanying parent handout deals with emotional reactions to disaster and the possible responses.

Determining appropriate steps to be taken immediately upon experiencing a disaster and deciding what to do in the days and weeks that follow is crucial. The following ideas are suggested:

Immediate Reaction to Disaster

- Inform students of the disaster.
    - Typically some school-wide decision is made regarding notification of staff and students. Often the PA system or a message to all teachers is used so the same information is given to everyone at the same time and the spread of rumors is controlled. A death or other intimate event may require a more personal method of imparting information.
    - Your responsibilities are:
        - Ensuring that the information your students receive is appropriate to their

developmental level and is stated in vocabulary they can understand. You may need to restate information in several ways so that every student understands.

- Controlling panic among your students. Your calm demeanor and take-charge attitude can do much to control panic. It is okay for students to know that you are upset, for instance by shedding tears over a death. While it will be natural for you to experience emotion, it is important to students that you maintain composure and control of the situation.

- Decide about scheduling changes.

  - Decisions about scheduling changes may be made by administrators. However you will have to make decisions about what is to happen in your classroom. Generally, returning to a normal routine is appropriate.

  - If students seem very unsettled, returning to a normal routine may not be the best choice. Possible immediate responses to disaster include discussing what has happened, clarifying information and facts, and listening carefully.

Intermediate Steps for Crisis Control

- Arrange support and counseling for students.

  - Building administrators will probably have made arrangements for support services. Your job is to know how, where, and when to access these services and to channel students in need of these services to the appropriate individuals.

  - Children particularly affected by the disaster should be carefully observed. They may require extra support and assistance.

  - Continue to have group discussion time at the beginning of the day. This may be useful in clearing the air of rumors and helping the students get ready for school work.

  - Plan a practical concrete activity to help student deal with feelings.

- Involve students in decisions about what to do to help restore their sense of having control in their lives. Possible activities include:

  - Collective money for disaster victims.
  - Planting a tree as a memorial for a death.
  - Designing cards and writing notes to someone involved in the disaster.
  - Drawing pictures and putting up a bulletin board.
  - Writing poems or stories for a class book about the disaster.

- Inform parents about how their children are reacting and what is being done in the classroom to deal with the disaster. A handwritten, dittoed note will suffice in this situation.

- Decide how to handle attending funeral or memorial services if the disaster involves deaths.

  - Whenever possible, have parents take their own children to services.

  - If necessary, arrange transportation for a student to a memorial service. If you will be teaching during the service, a parent or another staff member may take the student. (Permission slips may be needed.) The person chosen should be prepared to deal with the student's emotional reaction to the service.

  - Provide information about the funeral and its structure to prepare the students for the experience. Students who aren't going may still want to know what will happen. For young children, this may be their first experience with death, and information may be especially important for them.

- Allow for the fatigue which children may experience due to stress and changed sleep patterns.
  - Plan for less intense instructional activities for a few days.
  - Introduce snack time for a few days to provide extra nourishment which tired children may need. Room parents or the PTA/PTO may be willing to provide snacks.
  - Delay tests which will allow fair evaluation of student performance after stress levels are reduced.

Long-term and On-going Disaster Intervention

- Provide on-going opportunities to deal with the crisis.
  - Let students know there continue to be people available who are willing to listen. Tell them who is available and when and where to find these people.
  - Discuss feelings with the entire class or individual children who feel most affected.
  - Discuss the disaster in the context of other subjects, e.g. discuss suicide prevention in a junior high health class, discuss weather-related disasters in elementary social studies class.
  - Provide facts to help allay fears. For instance, if a classmate dies of cancer, facts about prevalence and cures may help students who are fearful when they feel unwell.
- Think ahead to effects which might be delayed. For instance:
  - Be aware that similar incidents in another location may trigger renewed feelings.
  - Plan a special remembrance for the one-year anniversary of the disaster, thereby diverting renewed reaction if the anniversary date is ignored.
- Listen and watch for long-term reactions.
  - Prepare for long-term reactions which are normal, such as the continued need to discuss a hurricane or shooting.
  - Watch for pathological long-term reactions. Pathological long-term reactions are more severe than those experienced by most children and might include (1) persistent reexperiencing of the traumatic event through intense recollections, dreams, flashbacks or hallucinations, (2) persistent avoidance of stimuli associated with the trauma or numbing of responsiveness, e.g., restricted affect, diminished interest in usual activities or (3) signs of increased arousal, e.g. sleep difficulties, irritability, hypervigilance, disturbances in concentration, exaggerated startle response.
- Find ways to emphasize a return to stability.
  - When the disaster abates, return to previous schedules and maintain these for a time, even if some change in routine was planned, in order to provide a sense of security and comfort.

Children and Divorce

Sharon W. Royal and Howard M. Knoff
University of South Florida, Tampa

Background—The number of children affected by divorce is staggering. The divorce rate has more than tripled since 1960, doubling between 1970 and 1981. It is now estimated that approximately 40 percent of all marriages will end in divorce and that 40 to 50 percent of all children born in the past decade will spend some time living in a single-parent family. These divorce experiences do have long-term impact on children's-especially boys-development and adjustment, an impact evident in the home environment and in the school setting.

Development—The repercussions of the divorce process depend on several factors:

1. *The age of the children at the time of the divorce*

   a. *Infants'* reactions to divorce can closely be related to their primary caregivers' emotional status and adjustment. The child's emotional development is often dependent on the parent-child bonding, nurturing, and identification processes that begin very early in life.

   b. *School-aged children* are at greater social and academic risk than their peers in families unaffected by divorce. They commonly react with depression, withdrawal, grieving, fear fantasies of responsibility for the break-up and of possible reconciliation, anger shame, decreased school performance, a sense of loss or rejection, and conflicts over which parent to express loyalty to.

   c. *Adolescents'* reactions can be similar to those of younger children, and, in addition, they may feel anxious about the future and their own potential marriages. In some cases, however, adolescents may more easily adjust to their parents' divorce. An increasing maturity gives a growing understanding of the circumstances surrounding the divorce experience. Also, by the middle teens, academic and athletic activities, and most social relationships become paramount in their lives, blunting somewhat the impact of a parental marital crisis.

2. *Gender*—Divorce more seriously affects boys than girls, and older boys show more significant emotional and academic problems than younger boys. Over time, girls appear able to make a satisfactory adjustment, but boys' difficulties may persist. Within the home, girls respond more favorably to permissive child-rearing styles, while boys do better with an authoritative approach which directs the child using reason, problem-solving, yet firm structure. The authoritarian attitude stressing punishment, force, and rejection to control a child's behavior has been unproductive with either sex.

3. *Length of time since the divorce*—In general, it does appear that most children can adjust to divorce over a period of years. Older children whose parents have been divorced a long time may come to function quite well despite experiencing lingering emotional traces of sorrow and anger.

4. *Parents' own emotional stability* is clearly important to their children's divorce adjustment. Many divorced parents may need up to two years to overcome the emotional effects of divorce. During the first year these parents may be less able to accomplish their parenting tasks, more likely to make unrealistic maturity demands on their children, be more inconsistent with discipline approaches, and less

affectionate and involved with them. By the end of the second post-divorce year these difficulties begin to be resolved.

What Can I Do as a Parent?—Certain pre-divorce preparations can help reduce children's social-emotional reactions to the significant stresses surrounding an impending separation or divorce.

1. Children need to be informed, hopefully by both parents in a joint discussion, about an upcoming separation or divorce.

2. They need to be continually reassured that:

- their parents still love them,
- they are not responsible for the divorce,
- their needs will be taken care of,
- their parents will be available as much as possible to talk with them about their concerns or fears,
- everyone will try to work together to make the situation as comfortable as possible, but they are still expected to perform their responsibilities with respect to home and school, and that
- it's all right to feel bad about the situation, but there are people who care and can help them through these bad feelings.

3. Ongoing emotional support can be provided by the school psychologist or in private counseling sessions.

Also, parents can arrange post divorce circumstances in a way which will greatly enhance children's long-term adjustment. Such considerations include:

- limited financial loss to the custodial parent
- a minimum of conflict and hostility between parents
- consistency between parents with respect to child-rearing and disciplinary practices
- a loving, positive relationship between the child and both parents
- an authoritative approach to discipline by the custodial parent
- frequent and reliable visitation with the non-custodial parent and that parent's family
- an emotional climate that permits child and family discussions of divorce-related issues and concerns
- specific school characteristics such as smaller school populations, environments emphasizing structure and orderliness, traditional rather than open classroom structures, and nearness of school to home
- family support factors such as the availability of helpful relatives (especially relatives of the noncustodial parent), friends, child-care assistance (nursery schools, for instance), and involvement of the custodial parent in social/recreational groups and experiences.

By being sensitive to these kinds of issues, concerned parents can help their children make the best possible adjustment to this distressing life event.

Resources

Frande, L. B. (1983). *Growing Up Divorced*. Fawcett Crest.
Gardner R. (1977). *The Parents' Book About Divorce*. Doubleday.
Glass, S. M. (1980). *A Divorce Dictionary: A Book for You and Your Children*. Little, Brown.
Salk, L. (1978). *What Every Child Would Like Parents to Know about Divorce*. Harper and Row.
Stein, S. B. (1979). *On Divorce: An Open Family Book for Parents and Children Together*. Walker.

NATIONAL
ASSOCIATION OF
SCHOOL
PSYCHOLOGISTS

Children and Divorce: Access/Visitation Arrangements

Steven I. Pfeiffer
Child Development Center
Oshner Clinic & Alton Medical Foundation

Background—Divorce in the United States is almost as popular as marriage itself. The divorce rate has doubled in the past ten years, and it is expected that in the very near future almost half of all children will spend some time living in a single-parent family.

Approximately 90 percent of the children of divorce remain in their mother's custody. Although joint custody or co-parenting has grown in popularity in both the media and with divorcing parents, most courts still assume that the stability of a single home is preferable to children shuttling back and forth between feuding parents. Particularly with younger children, sole custody provides the greater likelihood of ensuring a secure attachment, parent-child bonding, and identification with one adult caretaker.

Four general rules are commonly followed by the court in deciding custody disputes:

1. A young child should be placed in the custody of his mother.
2. A girl should be placed in her mother's custody, while a boy should be placed in his father's custody if he no longer requires his mother's constant care.
3. If the child is old enough to form an intelligent judgment, her choice of custodian will be given consideration.
4. It is typical practice to grant the rights of visitation to the parent not awarded custody. Visitation would be restricted or refused only if it may result in serious emotional or physical harm to the child.

Types of Custody Arrangements—In most situations, four custody plans are the usual options available to divorcing families. They are governed, however, by state law, and an attorney would be in the best position to advise of the alternative arrangements.

Sole Custody: Sole custody is an arrangement in which one parent has custody of the child(ren) and the other parent has visitation privileges. This is the most traditional and common arrangement, and the custodial parent is expected to make the majority of the child's daily life decisions. However, both parents can participate in many of the decisions regarding their child's education, religion, medical and dental care, summer experiences, etc. Commonly, a specific schedule of visitation is included in the separation agreement and divorce decree such as, "Father will pick up the children on alternate weekends on Friday 6:00 p.m. and return them Sunday at 6:00 p.m." This plan is particularly useful when parents are unable to cooperate sufficiently, and thus benefit from the structure which ensures parents' equitable rights.

Divided/Shared Custody: This is a less common and unusual plan. The child spends half of the time with one parent and half with the other (such as 6 months with each parent, or alternating years). Each parent enjoys reciprocal visitation privileges. This particular plan is most workable when both parents live in the same school district, share similar values and child rearing styles, and enjoy minimal conflict and hostility in dealing with one another.

Split Custody: This plan divides the children between both parents. One or more child(ren) live permanently with one parent and one or more live with the other parent. One advantage of this arrangement is that each parent has full access to at least one child-typically a child of the same sex as the custodial parent. On the other hand, a risk with this plan is that siblings are split up, contributing to their feelings of loss, rejections, self-blame, confusion, guilt and shame.

Types of Access/Visitation—One important aspect of custody is access to the child by the noncustodial parent (if joint custody is not initiated). Five types of access exist:

Free Access: Unrestricted contact between the child and the noncustodial parent, where access typically occurs as a response to the needs of the child.

Flexible Regular Access: The child visits with the noncustodial parent on a regular basis, such as on weekends and one midweek evening. Both parents understand that the regular arrangement can be modified and renegotiated if neccessary.

Rigid Regular Access: Similar to the regular arrangement, except that considerably less flexibility is allowed for change.

Irregular or Occasional Access: There is no set pattern or schedule, with visitation occuring on a sporadic or occasional basis, usually at the convenience of the noncustodial parent. Generally, access is not more regular because one or both parties are reluctant to maintain closer contact, because the custodial parent is not enthusiastic about visitation, or because either parent has relocated to a distant geographical location.

No Access: There is no longer contact between the noncustodial parent and the child(ren).

Development—Regardless of the custody/visitation plan, children face a difficult set of adjustments as a result of separation and divorce. It is not unusual for children to continue to experience a range of adjustment problems as long as two-to-three years following parental divorce.

Most children find the option of free access most desirable. Children themselves report that one source of frustration and unhappiness is restricted access to a parent. Children who spend little time with their noncustodial parent during the first year after the marital breakup seem particularly vulnerable to develop psychological problems. More frequent and regular contact seems to be important, particularly for preschool and schoolaged children. For various reasons, infants and adolescents don't seem to be as adversely affected by less frequent access.

It is generally agreed upon that an ongoing relationship between the child and the noncustodial parent is extremely important. It is also widely recognized that children are dissatisfied with infrequent visitation arrangements.

What Can I Do As A Parent?—Three principles can help guide parents through the often painful and stressful process of divorce when children are involved.

1. Child custody decisions should be made **expediently**, with the philosophy of the **child's needs foremost** during the legal proceedings. "The least detrimental alternative" is a reasonable perspective that helps parents decide upon the "best" type of custody and access/visitation arrangement.

2. Divorcing parents need to be **flexible** and **tolerant** when approaching the visitation plan. Visitation schedules should be viewed as structured guidelines that assure parents' equitable rights, and childrens' access to their noncustodial parent on a consistent and regular basis.

However, **modifications** will need to be made on occasion, and as the child gets older and circumstances change, **periodic revisions** may be warranted.

3. Children **benefit from ongoing relationships with both of their parents** following divorce. Infrequent and irregular visitation arrangement prove less satisfactory for both the noncustodial parent and for the children, and seem to contribute to the adjustment difficulties often seen following a marital breakup.

The custodial parent's attitude toward visits is a crucial factor in the relative success or failure of the visitation arrangement. Children have an uncanny ability to pick up even subtle parental cues that reflect negative feelings and attitudes toward their ex-spouse. The custodial parent must learn to "compartmentalize" any animosity she feels toward her ex-spouse, so that she can encourage and support her children's continued relationship with their other parent. This is not an easy task, and may require the professional help of a mediator or psychotherapist.

Resources

Gardner, R.A. (1970). *The boys and girls book about divorce.* New York: Bantam Books. Gardner normalizes the many confusing and painful feelings that children experience when their parents divorce, and offers practical suggestions on how to set up a reasonable access/visitation plan.

Goldstein, S. & Solnit, A. J. (1984). *Divorce and your child.* New Haven: Yale University Press. This paperback book is a manual for parents with many helpful guidelines on child custody, medication, and access/visitation.

Majid, K. & Schreibman, W. (1980). *Divorce is . . . a kid's coloring book.* Gretna, La.: Pelican. A delightful coloring book for preschool and early school age children that uses drawings as a means of touching upon 25 issues about divorce.

Wallerstein, J. & Kelly, J. (1980). *Surviving the break up: How children and parents cope with divorce.* New York: Basic Books. Written by two experts on the effects of divorce and access/visitation, this paperback book offers much information of what parents and children typically go through during a marital breakup. The two authors do a nice job of explaining why visits with the noncustodial parent are so hard, what "games parents play" that tend to discourage visiting, and how to ensure a more positive access relationship.

Dysfunctional Families

Martha E. Scherer
University of South Florida

Background—Dysfunctional or troubled families may be experiencing difficulties ranging from inadequate parenting skills and maladaptive patterns of interaction to psychological problems in one or more members of the family. The level of dysfunction may vary depending on the severity of stressors, such as job loss or illness, affecting the family. A number of school-related problems have been associated with maladaptive family functioning, including conduct problems, aggression, delinquency, eating disorders, drug abuse, depression and suicidal gestures, school phobia, hyperactivity, and child abuse (Graden & Christenson, 1987).

Different types of problems within the home appear to be related to different types of school-related problems (Christenson, 1990). For example, children with antisocial behavioral patterns often come from homes where: (a) discipline methods of the parents are inconsistent and harsh; (b) monitoring of children's whereabouts, activities, and peer associations is infrequent and inconsistent; (c) positive family management including encouragement, social interest, and use of social reinforcers is lacking; (d) parental problem-solving skills are not well developed; and (e) parents are not involved actively in their children's daily lives (Ramsey, Walker, Shinn, O'Neill, & Stieber, 1989).

The relationship of maladaptive family functioning to school-related problems should not be interpreted as a causal relationship. The assignment of blame is neither warranted by the existing research nor useful in helping children to overcome school-related problems. In fact, most parents want their children to be successful in school but, for various reasons, do not know how to help their children with school work or how to create a positive attitude toward learning (Christenson, 1990).

What Can I Do as a Teacher?—Probably the first issues that teachers need to deal with are questions of blame and of the possibility of improvement in the child's behaviors. These two issues are closely related. If we place the blame for maladaptive child behavior on the family, we are likely to believe that there is nothing we can do to bring about change. In this case, we have defined the problem as outside our range of influence. That is not true. We need to avoid blaming and focus on helping children develop the skills they need to function successfully in the school environment.

For some children, the school environment may be the only safe and stable place in their lives. Children can learn appropriate behavior for school that they may or may not be able to use in their home environments. Behaviors that are appropriate and desirable for school may be behaviors that the child simply has not learned at home or that are not effective at home. It may be necessary to teach social skills directly to children who have not learned them. It may be necessary to demonstrate, through a rich schedule of reinforcement, that the new skills are effective in producing results that the child values.

One important thing we know is that children who develop competently despite being at risk because of maladaptive family functioning possess two important attributes. They seem to be "protected" by having positive social skills and a positive orientation toward the future (Graden & Christenson, 1987).

Collaboration with parents is the best and preferred plan for interventions to improve any child behavior. When families are dysfunctional, collaboration with parents is even more important. Again, the blame issue must be resolved prior to parent contact so that it will not create, or add to, parental defensiveness and thus block the effectiveness of the parent-teacher partnership. When working with these parents, teachers will probably be most successful if they focus on specific, definable behavior, outline precisely what is to be done, focus on positive rather than punitive interventions, and are persistent in their efforts to effect improvements.

When the home situation appears to be severe enough to warrant family counseling or therapy, referrals can and should be addressed through the school administration. Whenever abuse is suspected, it **must** always be reported.

What Can I Do as a Parent?—Parents who recognize that their own family interaction patterns are dysfunctional may wish to seek family counseling to begin to address the problems. Parent training classes are often available through various schools and social agencies at no cost or for a minimal fee. These classes often help parents to establish more effective relationships with their children. Parental support (e.g., encouraging schoolwork, listening to children read, participating in learning activities at home, providing rewards for improvements on daily in-class assignments, providing opportunity and supplies for learning at home) has been shown positively to affect children's academic success (Christenson, 1990). Implementing these practices in the home can go a long way toward improving your child's school performance.

Collaboration with your child's teachers is an important part of helping to improve behavior and academic achievement. Children do better when expectations and values are consistent both at home and at school. If consistency between these two environments can be achieved, children have a much better chance of achieving their potential.

References

Christenson, S. L. (1990). Differences in student's home environments: The need to work with families. *School Psychology Review, 19,* 505-517.

Graden. J. L., & Christenson, S. L. (1987). Children and troubled families. In A. Thomas & J. Grimes (Eds.), *Children's needs: Psychological perspectives* (pp. 651-658). Washington, DC: National Association of School Psychologists.

Ramsey, E., Walker, H. M., Shinn, M., O'Neill, R. E., & Stieber, S. (1989). Parent management practices and school adjustment. *School Psychology Review, 18,* 513-525.

Children and Foster Homes

Nancy A. McKellar
Wichita State University

Background—Children live in foster homes when their biological parents cannot care for them. This form of substitute care is often selected for younger children and those with less serious behavior problems. Common reasons for foster care placement center on multiple problems presented by one or both parents, rather than the child. The longer the child is in foster care, the more likely that child is to stay there.

Development—Foster children are first and foremost children with all the problems typical of others their age. Additionally, they have specific difficulties associated with their status as foster children.

1. **Adjustment to separation from the biological family**—Separation from the biological family generally causes short-term emotional trauma and pain for the child, leading to confusion, uncertainty, problems of identity, conflicts of loyalty, and anxiety about the future. Regardless of the age of the child or the circumstances of placement, the child reacts to the trauma of being separated from the biological family in much the same manner as persons who have lost loved ones in other ways. These common reactions include the stages of shock, protest, despair and detachment. Foster children experiencing shock may appear to be adjusting adequately to the separation from their biological family, but their emotional involvement with their new situation is minimal. Sleep difficulties, teeth grinding, and upper respiratory infections may be observed. During the protest stage, foster children may experience anger anxiety, and helplessness. They may appeal for help in negative, inappropriate ways, yet reject such help when it is given. Foster children in the stage of despair react apathetically to the demands of their world, appearing to be disorganized and helpless and to lack motivation. In the detachment stage, a period of adjustment, foster children feel accomplishment in having adjusted and seek out new relationships in which they invest themselves emotionally. They may still hope to return to their biological family but these ideas are more reality-based than previously.

2. **Effects of traumatic events that have prompted foster care placement**—her children sometimes reason that if they were removed from their biological families, with whom they identify, because the family was unworthy, then they must also be unworthy. They may suffer the long-term effects of abuse and/or neglect.

3. **Difficulties associated with being in the foster care system**—Foster children are identified to their peers as being different because they always have a different name from the family with whom they live; may not have the information about their past that would be necessary to participate in some class activities; and may not have money for "extra" school items, such as field trips and yearbooks. Placement in foster care will mean that a child moves into a new home and usually into a new school and community. The moves required of foster children entail the trauma of separation from their biological families and may also include being moved from one foster home to another. Often these moves are sudden, at least from the child's viewpoint, making them particularly difficult to handle emotionally. Moving results in practical problems that include inaccurate or outdated health records, unidentified or untreated handicapping conditions, and exclusion from some sports and other extracurricular activities.

4. **Problematic behaviors exhibited at home and/or school**—Children who do not feel secure in their foster home may regress to immature behaviors, such as temper tantrums, whining, or clinging. A foster child may behave inappropriately in an attempt to disrupt the foster home placement and/or to cope with the grief of separation from the biological family. Foster children may try to protect themselves from the possibility of additional rejection by constantly criticizing a foster parent or the teacher; withholding whatever the child thinks the adult wants, such as completed homework or compliance with rules; and skipping school or running way.

What can I Do As A Parent?—Foster children have two sets of parents, the biological and the foster parents. The following suggestions are for foster parents:

1. Discuss with your foster child, in a caring, empathic, and knowledgeable manner the reason for the child's placement in foster care and what decisions are being made regarding the child's future.

2. Help your foster child build self-esteem and identity by encouraging the child to develop a relationship with at least one other person who really cares about the child, can affirm the child's worth, and can be a good listener for the child's concerns and conflicts. This person might be yourself, a relative, teacher counselor or teacher aide.

3. Avoid using punishment, particularly corporal punishment, to discipline your foster child. These techniques can be humiliating or degrading and will work against your efforts to improve the child's self-respect. Instead, try to use discipline techniques like natural and logical consequences plus positive reinforcement of appropriate behavior.

4. Take an active part as a parent in the educational process of your foster child.

5. When you are told that your foster child will be receiving some special school services, such as speech therapy or psychological testing, ask when to expect the services to begin. If your child has not received the services within a reasonable time, ask the principal or teacher the reason for the delay.

6. Protect your foster child's right to family privacy by not discussing information unrelated to your child's educational needs with the school. However be sure to inform the teacher of any special needs, problems, and interests your child has.

7. If your foster child appears upset after visiting the biological parents, try to remember that emotionally upsetting visits are less harmful to the child than the devastating feelings of abandonment resulting from no visits at all. Inform the teacher when such visits occur so that the teacher can more easily recognize the cause of the child's periodic difficulties.

Resources

Foster Parent Education Program, Institute for the Study of Children and Families, Eastern Michigan University, Ypsilanti, Michigan 48197. This program is a valuable source of practical information related to foster children.

Helping Children Cope with Separation and Loss, by C. L. Jewett. Harvard Common Press, Publisher. 1982. These specific techniques and guidelines for helping children cope with grief over loss (of the biological family and/or previous foster families) will be helpful to anyone working with foster children.

The Practical Guide to Foster Family Care, by B. L. Kaplan and M. Seitz. Charles C. Thomas, Publisher. 1980. Impacts of fostering on the child and the foster family are discussed in this sourcebook for foster parents, along with practical information on such topics as relating to the biological family, disciplining the foster child, dealing with the school and community, financing, and separating when the child leaves.

NATIONAL
ASSOCIATION OF
SCHOOL
PSYCHOLOGISTS

Children and Holidays Helping Children Cope with Loss During Holidays
Parent Handout

Deborah D. Waddell
Psychologist, Columbus, Ohio

Background Information—Family gatherings and traditions make holidays special. The joy that these traditions bring into our lives is upset when a family member has died. At times of loss, facing holidays can be difficult for adults and children alike.

Development—Ritual and tradition are a very important part of holidays for children. Safety and security are experienced in the rituals which occur year after year. Through traditions, children can trust that life will go on and they will be okay. Altering family tradition significantly after a death may only compound the sadness which the family feels about the loss of a loved one. Despite this, not every tradition may be possible with the changed family structure so some different ways of celebrating holidays may need to be developed. Carefully balancing tradition and change is important in helping children deal with loss on holidays.

Holidays may be filled with conflicting emotions for children. Especially if the loss is recent and sadness has been the predominating emotion in recent days and weeks. Children may feel torn by their desire to enjoy the holiday and their feelings of grief. They may experience guilt about enjoyment of the holiday and confusion about how to act.

How children experience and deal with loss at holiday time is impacted by several factors:

- Children at different ages deal with grief differently. A young child may be unaware that Mother's Day is any different from any other day and can easily be so wrapped up in Christmas celebrations that grieving is put aside. On the other hand, an older child may feel much like you do, being acutely aware of how the loss will change holidays and struggling with the conflicting emotions of remembered joys from holidays past and grief about the loss.

- The amount of time since the loss also affects how it is experienced on holidays. If the loss was early in the year, grief may resurface at Thanksgiving, Hanukkah, or Christmas, but it is likely to be less intense than if the loss occurred recently.

- The role that the deceased person played in the children's holidays in past years will affect how apparent the loss is. If grandpa lived far away, the loss may seem less a part of the holiday to children than if he lived nearby so his traditional place at the table is empty.

- The loss will be felt differently on different holidays and some will be harder than others. The first holiday after the loss, the birthday of the deceased, or Mother's and Father's Day may be harder than other days. Christmas or Hanukkah, when there are presents or toys, may not be as difficult as Thanksgiving which centers on family and thankfulness.

What Can I Do As A Parent?

- Let children be the guide. Don't force thoughts of the loss on them when they are thinking of something else, but be sensitive to their moods. If they seem particularly sad or mention the loved one, be available to talk. Often, it's helpful to reflect feelings with statements like "You're really missing dad right now. So am I. It's hard to think of Thanksgiving without him." On the other hand, your children may need to hear from you that it is okay to be excited about a holiday and that sadness does not go on forever.

- Talk with your children about what is important to them in celebrating the holiday and how traditions can be continued with the new family structure. Children may be willing to take on extra responsibility to keep traditions alive. A delicate balance needs to be maintained between letting children assume some tasks which help maintain family customs and expecting them to take over roles and responsibilities which really belong to adults. For instance, a teenager may be quite capable of baking with younger siblings but should not be expected to take on all the holiday responsibilities of a deceased parent.

- Instead of celebrating differently, add a new custom to your traditional ones. Select this new custom together so everyone is comfortable with the choice. Some ideas you might suggest to your children include:

    - Giving a memorial gift or service to a charity which has special meaning related to the deceased person may be helpful. For instance, if the person died of a heart attack, a donation to the Heart Association may be appropriate. If a doctor hospital, or agency was particularly helpful during your loss, a plate of cookies for Christmas or flowers on Mother's Day can be a special remembrance.

    - Living memorials like plants or trees are often appropriate. Perhaps your family would like to have a Christmas tree which can be planted after the holidays in memory of the deceased person. Planting dad's favorite flowers in the yard or by his grave on Father's Day is also meaningful.

    - Allowing time for a special prayer or poem before a family meal may feel right. Thanksgiving might be particularly hard if your family tradition includes special prayers of thanksgiving for the good things that have happened in the past year. You can't be thankful for a loss of a loved one, but you can be thankful for the special times you had and the ways in which the deceased person enriched your lives.

    - Visiting the cemetery on special days is important to some families. Children might make a wreath or select flowers to leave at the grave.

- Plan some extra time for your child during the holidays. This time might be spent reading holiday stories, taking a walk, or preparing holiday food together. These times provide opportunities to share feelings about the holiday.

- Don't overcompensate with many extra or special gifts. No material item can replace the loss of a loved one. Extra gifts may actually lead to more disappointment if children think the message is that the gifts are meant to compensate for the loss but discover that grief is still real.

- Try not to interfere with the joy children experience on holidays even though joy may seem the least possible emotion for you. If you are having a particularly hard time dealing with the merriment of a holiday, perhaps a friend can substitute for you in some activities with your children. Save a special event for you to share with the children. Perhaps a visit to Santa is extra special and this could be your opportunity to participate in your children's holiday excitement. Ask a friend to accompany you if you think you can't manage alone.

- Talk to your child's teacher if a holiday may be particularly stressful for your child. Plan how

Mother's Day cards or Christmas gifts made in class will be handled. Your child might select some other special person to remember at this time.

- Take some time for yourself and allow for the sense of loss you will have to cope with during the holiday season. Holidays are painful after a loss and the anticipation of the pain can be overwhelming. However, avoiding the holidays by trying to ignore old customs or skip all holiday celebrations won't fix the pain and can make the holiday more difficult for your children. Supportive friends and other family members can give you a much needed break or offer a listening ear when things are particularly difficult.

Resources

Many cities have groups for children dealing with loss. Your school psychologist may know of such groups or you may wish to contact local hospitals, mental health centers, or Hospice organizations to inquire about such groups.

Seasons of grief: Helping children grow through loss is a book by Donna Gaffney which offers ideas for helping children at the time of a death and throughout the following year. This 1988 book is published by New American Library.

Holiday help: Coping for the newly bereaved is a booklet available for $3.00 from ACCORD, 1930 Bishop Lane, Louisville, KY 40218. Phone 1-800-346-3087. This booklet contains ideas for adults, but many can be adapted for children also.

NATIONAL
ASSOCIATION OF
SCHOOL
PSYCHOLOGISTS

Children and Hospitalization

Don Brunnquell
Minneapolis Children's Medical Center

Background—About one-third of children will have been hospitalized at least once before they reach adulthood. Long or repeated hospitalization may create long-term problems, especially if the child has had other stresses such as family problems or significant loss. Short-term effects such as difficulty sleeping, fear of medical treatment, increased limit testing and changes in activity level are common, but generally disappear within a month after hospitalization. All of these problems can be minimized and often eliminated by good preparation, communication during the hospital stay, and open discussion afterwards.

Development—Since children are different at each age, hospitalization affects each age and each child differently. The chart below suggests the child's needs and possible responses at each age:

Age	Needs	What You can Do
Infancy (0–12 mo.)	Attachment, security	Stay with your child, including overnight "rooming-in" whenever possible insist on as few other caregivers as possible Help with your child's care whenever possible
	Routine	Maintain "home schedule" as much as possible
Toddler (12–30 mo.)	Security, routine	Stay with your child including overnight "rooming-in" whenever possible Maintain routines Minimize number of caregivers
	Independence	Involve child in care if possible Avoid over protection
	Impulse control	Encourage age-appropriate activities
Preschooler (30 mo.–5 yrs.)	Security, routine Understanding	Stay with your child, including "rooming-in" whenever possible Give accurate, honest information repeatedly in simple ways. Hospital tours
	Self-worth	Reassure child this is not punishment Avoid over protection
School Age (6–12 yrs.)	Maintain self-esteem and competence	Age appropriate activities Involvement in care
	Maintain positive body image	Preparation and hospital tours. Honest communication and information
	Maintain social self-esteem	Visits by family and friends Cards and letters
Adolescence (12-18 yrs.)	Maintain Trust	Honest, complete communication
	Maintain independence	Age-appropriate activities
	Maintain social self-esteem	Visits and phone calls
	Maintain positive body image	Realistic discussion of body lifestyle changes

What can I do as a parent?—In addition to consulting the chart about the needs of children at different ages and what you can do, here are some general ideas for all ages. Most important is that your child feel you want to talk with him or her about the experience before, during and afterward. While a visit to the hospital may be difficult for your child, preparation and working through feelings can help your child to avoid being overwhelmed. These tips can help your child to see hospitalization as a time to learn and grow.

—Bring your family to a preadmission tour if they are provided.

—This is an ongoing process. Talk to your child before, during and after hospitalization.

—Find out first what your child thinks and feels. Use play, drawings, books, and brief informal chats to explore your child's thoughts and feelings. Then give your child information. Encourage your child to ask questions.

—Younger children think and play in specific ways. Play with them and be as clear as possible. Use play material and role playing as well as words.

—Young children often are especially worried about separation from parents or feel guilty about doing something wrong. Reassure your child that he or she did not cause the illness. Also tell your child that you will come along to the hospital, will take your child home, and that you still love your child. Bring a stuffed animal, doll, toy or blanket from home.

—Give accurate information in words and ways that children understand. Honesty is important to build trust. It's okay to think about realistic concerns, but help your child to eliminate misunderstandings.

—Help your child to know that scary and hurt are not the same, that you want to talk about what is happening, and that talking helps.

—Encourage normal activities during the hospital stay as much as possible. Games from home, school work, and visits from friends can all help.

—Include brothers and sisters. They have worries, too, and they can influence the attitude of the child who will be hospitalized.

—Plan some special celebration or activity for when your child is home again. It helps your child to know that he or she will be coming home.

—Make sure you have the information you need. Talk to your doctor so you feel informed and comfortable. Children know when their parents are nervous, which in turn can make children nervous.

Resources

For medical questions:

—Your child's physicians and their office staff
—Nursing staff at the hospital.

For questions about your child's needs and reactions:

—Hospital child life, psychology, and social work staff
—Hospital nursing staff
—Your child's physicians
—School nurse, psychologist, teacher
—Your own family and friends, who have had experiences with hospitalization and can be a support to you
—Association for the Care of Children's Health, 3615 Wisconsin Avenue, N.W. Washington, D.C. 20016.

Books

Going to the Hospital, by A. Greenwalk and B. Heed. Family Communications, Publisher. 1977. A Mr. Rogers' book for preschoolers and young children. Informs readers generally about hospitalization and encourages further exploration and discussion.

Curious George Goes to the Hospital, by H. Rey and M. Rey. Houghton-Mifflin, Publisher. 1966. In this book for preschool and early school-age children the familiar monkey character Curious George models positive reactions to various aspects of hospitalization.

The Hospital Story, by 5. Stein. Walker Publisher. 1974. This book for preschool and young school-age children follows the experience of a girl having a tonsillectomy and also contains a text for parents. It deals with the emotional as well as medical aspects of the experience.

Why am I Going to the Hospital, by C. Cotta and C. Livingston. Lyle Stuart, Publisher. 1981. A book for preschool and school-age children dealing with the causes and experiences of hospitalization, including the emotional aspects.

The Teenage Hospital Experience: You Can Handle It!, by E. Richter. Cowad, McCenn, and Geoghan, Publishers. 1982. A book for adolescents, based on interviews with teenagers and caregivers, that address the issues of independence and social support vital to teenagers.

National Association of School Psychologists

Children and Moving

Elaine Clark and Douglas Goldsmith
University of Utah

Background—For many children in the United States moving has virtually become a way of life. In fact, it is estimated that there are approximately eight million school-age children who move to new schools in new communities each year. In order to facilitate a smooth transition, it is important for parents to be aware of, and anticipate, potential adjustment problems when their children's lives are disrupted by a move. Parents and school psychologists can work together both prior to, and following, a move in order to effectively assist' children during the adjustment period.

Development—While some children experience only minimal distress in response to the challenge of moving; others experience a number of adjustment problems. The responses of children toward moving may range from depression to anger and even threats to run away. Perhaps the best predictor of a child's response to moving is the child's status at the time of the transition. Because moving tends to exaggerate a child's existing strengths and weaknesses, it is generally most advantageous to well-adjusted, adaptable children who have made consistent progress in school. In contrast, moving tends to be detrimental to those who have experienced difficulties prior to moving. In some cases, children with previous problems may enroll in a more suitable school or begin to associate with a healthier peer group and actually benefit from the move.

In order to anticipate problems which might arise, it is necessary to consider the age of the child. Children in earlier grades are preoccupied with the task of separating from their parents and transferring their allegiance from home to school. For these children moving may result in a temporary regression since some will cope with the transition by becoming more dependent upon their parents. Adolescents are also very vulnerable at the time of a move. Faced with overwhelming personal and social demands, secondary school students often experience a great deal of stress with the prospect of leaving their friends and forming new ones. Since the peer group is essential for adolescents as they form their own identity and increase their independence, the loss of a peer group may result in depressed and anxious feelings. An adolescent may also feel confused about ways to develop new friendships when peer groups appear unapproachable.

There is no clear relationship between factors such as the number of moves, the distance between moves, or even the reason for moving and a child's adjustment. In fact, some children who have moved frequently develop excellent social skills which allow them to make new friends quite easily. While a number of families move because of being transferred to a new job, a growing number of children experience their first move because of a divorce. If following the divorce the move is due to an inability to sustain the previous lifestyle, the children tend to respond with anxiety and depression. However, those who move because of the remarriage of the custodial parent are often enthusiastic, especially if the move leads to an improved financial status. Parental attitudes also impact the child's adjustment, especially when, in their attempt to cope with their own feelings, they are less available to their children for emotional support. Thus, children whose parents are angry, frustrated, and depressed about an impending move are likely to have a more difficult adjustment than those whose parents view the change as a positive transition. It is important, however, to keep in mind that for some children, the least complicated move, such as from elementary to junior high school, is a formidable task. But in general, while moving may have serious consequences for some children, there is little evidence to conclude that the difficulties are long lasting; on the contrary, whatever the effects, they appear short lived.

What Can I Do as a Parent?—If you are like the majority of people moving, you will be moving because of a job change. In this case, you may not be able to select the exact location. However, since most communities require children to attend schools in their residential district, try to carefully select the community where you will live. Visiting schools in potential communities will provide you with an opportunity to talk with principals and teachers about your concerns, including questions pertaining to the curriculum. Although it may not be possible, moving during the school year has certain advantages for school-age children. Not only does this increase a parent's opportunity to communicate with the new school beforehand to insure a smoother transition, it provides children with a greater opportunity to make new friends. Some children, however, may be so overwhelmed by the challenges of the new curriculum that they may not be able to fully enjoy the social benefits. Hopefully today's emphasis on individualized instruction will help to alleviate some of the difficulty adjusting to a new curriculum, particularly when entering school at a time other than the beginning of the school year.

Discuss the move as soon as possible with the children. Give them plenty of information about the move and encourage them to discuss their feelings about it. This may be in the context of discussing your feelings or through the use of storybooks that have been written about children who have moved to a new home. Depending upon the circumstances of the move and maturity of the children in the family, you may wish to discuss the reasons for moving. But by all means, inform them about the date and location of moving. It may be helpful to mark the date on a calendar and circle the location on a map. If the entire family is unable to visit the new location before the actual move, familiarize everyone by showing them pictures of the new house, neighborhood, school, and other places of interest. Try to include them in as many decisions as you feel comfortable with, such as the color of their bedroom.

Inform the school where your child is currently attending about the move. Your child's teacher and principal may have some excellent suggestions about preparing your child for the move and smoothing the transition. They can assist you in making contact with the new school. Make the transfer arrangements as soon as possible. Be sure to send your child's educational record in plenty of time to assure proper class placement. You may also wish to inquire about extracurricular activities, dress codes, and any other tips to help your child adjust. A number of communities have school-based programs which are designed to assist families make a smoother transition. Since children in the lower elementary grades seem particularly upset by change in routine and adjustment to new surroundings, support groups in the school can be especially important. Also, for the young adolescent who suffers the loss of a peer group, the support group can help to reduce the tendency to become overly dependent on you as the parent by encouraging the adolescent to gain support from new peers. It can also provide them a quick indoctrination about the lifestyles and expectations of the new peer group.

As the moving day approaches, encourage the children to help in the actual preparations. Allowing them to pack their own belongings helps them to maintain some control over the move. Try not to throw away too many of their old toys and belongings since these items assure continuity for children and provide a sense of security during the transition. Furthermore, help the children say goodbye to their friends. Collecting addresses and exchanging photos help children maintain positive feelings about their old friends, and enable them to be more open to meeting new ones. Since some libraries have programs to help children in such a transition, locate the nearest library. Furthermore, seek advice from neighbors and friends who have made similar moves, and don't hesitate to contact school personnel for help. Once you have moved in, spend time together as a family, showing everyone around and participating in community activities. Encourage the children to join clubs and invite new friends home for visits. Lastly, try to be tolerant of any adjustment problems you observe. Each child adjusts in a different way, and some will require greater attention. If your child does not seem to adjust within a reasonable amount of time, however, you may wish to seek the help of a school psychologist.

Resources

The following is a list of recommended books. A public library is likely to have these and other books which pertain to moving.

Green, P. (1980). *Gloomy Louie.* Whitman. Despite Louie's distress about moving, a series of events help him gain a more positive viewpoint and gain self-confidence.

Hurwitz, J. (1979). *Aldo Applesauce.* Morrow Press. A humorous and sensitive book about the fears of moving to a new school.

Nida, P. C. and Heller, W. M. (1985). *The teenager's survival guide to moving.* This book explains how to survive and adapt to the stresses of moving.

Zolotow, C. (1973). *Janey.* Harper and Row. The story shows how two children who no longer live near each other can still be friends.

Children and Reactions to Death

Charles P. Heath
Deer Valley Unified School District, Phoenix, Arizona

Background—Children must deal with the loss of significant others more often than most adults realize. Each loss results in the child going through the same process of grief resolution, though the length and intensity may vary. Loss is viewed as a cumulative process, in which, without complete resolution of a minor loss, subsequent less significant losses are likely to provoke similar stress. While exact figures are not known, it is estimated that five percent of the children in the United States (1.5 million) lose one or both parents by age 15.

Development—The child's level of cognitive development plays a primary role in the extent to which a child will understand the loss of a parent. Specific reactions as well as their duration are different for adults and children.

A child's need to ask the same questions about the death over and over is more of a need for reassurance that the story has not changed rather than a need for factual accuracy. Children also seek adult reactions so they can gauge their own reactions. Emotions may be expressed as angry outbursts or misbehaviors that are often not recognized as grief-related.

Developmental Phases in Understanding Death—These age references are not rigid but should be used as rough guides. Also, children may regress to an earlier stage when emotionally upset.

Infants & Toddlers: Prior to age 3 children are not able to achieve complete mourning. However, they do seem to explore the state of nonbeing by games such as peek-a-boo.

Three to Five: Children deny death as a formal event; death is seen as reversible. The dead are simply "less alive". The child seems to regard death mainly as a separation, a departure.

Four to Six: Children are prone to misinterpret superficial events as being intrinsically involved in death. For example, knowing someone who died in a hospital may make the child want to stay away from hospitals to avoid death. Prior to age seven, children use "magical thinking" where personal wishes, thoughts, and actions are believed to be the causes for what happens.

Five to Nine: This is the age when children begin to understand the finality of death. Death is seen as an accident rather than inevitable. One dies under certain circumstances and if those circumstances do not occur then one cannot die. Death is also seen as something that will happen to others, not to ourselves. Finally, for this age there is a tendency to view death as a person. The death-man is usually regarded as a creature of the night.

Ten to Twelve: Children have the mental development and emotional security to express an understanding of death as a final and inevitable event associated with cessation of bodily functions.

Adolescence: As the adolescent begins to gain more independence and starts looking toward the future, there is the realization that all future plans require time and death may come at any time to prevent these plans from reaching fruition. They realize that one grows up only to die.

Developmental Phases of Grief Resolution—These phases are the same for children and adults; they are not discrete phases and some overlap may occur; and the length and intensity of each phase is dictated by the seriousness of the loss.

Phase One: Characterized by shock and numbing followed by a reaction of alarm. The alarm is centered around questions of who is going to care for the child. Denial and disbelief may also be exhibited during this initial stage.

Phase Two: This time of acute grief is characterized by yearning, searching, disorganization, despair, and ultimately reorganization. This phase is also characterized by strong feelings of sadness, anger, guilt, and shame. Once the stage of intense feelings starts, it can take 6-12 weeks for the worst pain to subside and as much as two years before the grief process is completed.

Phase Three: This phase involves the integration of loss and grief where the child begins to reorganize daily activities. Less frequent and less intense crying is seen. The child is also able to verbalize an awareness of the loss.

What Can I Do as a Parent?—As a surviving parent there are several things which can be done to support the grieving child.

1. Explain the death in a clear and direct manner. If the remaining parent cannot do this, then the child should be informed by another adult who is close to the child.

2. The child should be told the dead person will never return and that the body will be buried in the ground or burned to ashes.

3. The remaining parent should not deny the child an opportunity to share in the expression of pain.

4. Adults should avoid using their children as confidants for their own comfort and understanding.

5. The single most important message to relay to the child is, "You are not alone; I am with you.

6. Touching and holding a child can do more than any words to relay a parent's message.

7. Children should be allowed to attend the funeral, if it is their wish.

8. Prior to the funeral someone should explain to children what is likely to take place, who will be there, and how people are likely to react.

9. The choice of whether to view or touch the deceased should be left up to the child.

10. It is important to establish continuity in the daily routines of children.

11. Changing to a new school or moving to a new neighborhood should be postponed.

12. If it is determined that a child is experiencing pathological grief, rather than normal grief reactions, counseling may be necessary in order to help facilitate the grieving process.

Resources

Grollman, E. (Ed.) (1967). *Explaining death to children.* Boston: Beacon. Information on both death and dying is presented by several professionals. Each discusses death based upon his or her background perspective.

Grollman, E. (1976). *Talking about death: A dialogue between parent and child.* Boston: Beacon. The narrator explains death to a child whose grandfather has died. This explanation is accompanied by a Parent's Guide which also lists agencies that may be of assistance.

Kopp, R. (1983). *Where has Grandpa gone?* Grand Rapids, MI: Zonderman. Discusses different aspects of death and grief including the function of funerals. Includes a special "read along" section for adults to read to children to help explain the meaning of death and ways to cope with the loss.

LaTour, K. (1983). *For those who live: Helping children cope with the death of a brother or sister.* Dallas, TX: Kathy LaTour. Designed to help with the readjustment by the family after the death of a child or sibling. Examines how surviving children react to the death of a sibling. Discusses problems that both parents and children are likely to encounter during the grieving process.

Manning, D. (1984). *Don't take my grief away: What to do when you lose a loved one.* New York: Harper & Row. Written more from the perspective of the bereavement of a spouse when losing a husband or wife. Assists in understanding what happens when someone dies, dealing in a realistic yet healing way with the necessity of accepting the loss and facing the feelings of loss, separation, and even guilt that we experience.

Seizures

Lorene Heuvelman
University of South Florida

Background—When the term "seizure" is used many parents and teachers become fearful of the prognosis and future development of the child. The most common seizure diagnosis is **Epilepsy**, which by definition means recurrent seizures. Although a seizure disorder is a serious pathology, there is a great deal of variability in the way the disorder manifests itself within each individual. The strength and duration of seizures are dependent on the affected area in the brain, the extent of the damage to that area, and the connections between the damaged area to other healthy areas in the rest of the brain (Noyes & Kolb, 1968). Seizures can take many forms; all involve some loss of consciousness but only some include motoric involvement.

There are three most common types of seizures and they are defined by the way the seizure manifests itself in the brain. First, if the seizure stays contained within a small, localized area it is classified as a **Partial seizure**. Partial seizures do not begin with a loss of consciousness, rather the child will experience motor activity that is involuntary. A second type is a **Generalized tonic-clonic or Grand mal seizure**, which includes much of the cortex and may even disrupt the brain stem. The generalized seizure can consist of four stages. The first stage is the "aura" stage. However, not everyone experiences this preseizure sensory symptom (Sands & Minters, 1977). The second stage disrupts consciousness, may be followed by body rigidity (tonic phase) and the muscles begin to contract violently (clonic phase). These jerks and twitches, which most people are aware of when they think of seizures, occur during this clonic phase. Once the person has completed stage three, they will lapse into a temporary coma stage. This final stage can last about an hour and the individual can wake up sore, fatigued, tired, confused, and with complete amnesia of stages two through four. Finally, a seizure that does not include major motor activity but does disturb consciousness for a short time is called an **Absence or Petit mal seizure**. These seizures do not usually involve major motor activity. Rather, the child will lose consciousness to a certain degree. These seizures have often been mistaken by teachers and parents as daydreaming or inattention. The seizure may last only a few seconds and include some minor twitching (e.g., eye blinking, staring). Absence attacks are often seen in children, but are rarely found in individuals over the age of 15.

Development—The cause of seizures in children aged two to 15 often can be traced to a genetic predisposition. That is, there is a family history of seizure disorders. Other causes may include treatable infections or metabolic disorders, brain injury, or unknown causes. Seizures from infections or metabolic disorders can be symptomatic to the disease and once the disease or infection is cured the seizures may remit. A brain injury during birth or later in life may be the culprit and then the prognosis is not as predictable. Medication may control the seizures but it is not clear whether the disorder will cease as the child matures. Over 50% of the seizure disorders in children are idiopathic in nature, which means there is no known cause (Boll, 1978).

Most parents and teachers want information about possible effects on intellectual and social/emotional growth as well as effective treatments. All of these are important concerns, but unfortunately, only a few have some good empirical answers. The intellectual development of children with seizure disorders does appear to be somewhat affected. The more severe the seizures, the more generalized the affected area, the longer the duration, and the earlier the onset together may increase the likelihood that **some** intellectual impairment may occur (Dodrill, 1981). Some studies have found that children with seizure disorders have a higher probability of learning disabilities than "normal" children. Therefore, it seems important to reduce the possible negative effects on cognitive development by consistent medical treatment, follow-up, and supervision from parents and teachers.

The social/emotional growth is a major concern to many parents and teachers. Researchers have noted that children in psychotherapy have a tendency to perceive themselves as different, outcasts, and disabled (Christ, 1978). The child's parents may be instrumental in helping him/her understand the impairment and the teachers should educate the other students on the disorder.

Treatment—There are only a few treatments for seizures, but medication seems to be the most respected treatment to date. Over 75% of children with seizure disorders are treated with medication and a great majority of their seizures are controlled (Sands & Minters, 1977). There are also some seizure disorders that have been helped with surgery. Finally, some attempts have been made to control seizures by use of biofeedback and psychotherapy (Lubar & Shouse, 1977). However, biofeedback and psychotherapy have been more helpful in providing coping strategies for individuals to deal with the other aspects of having a seizure disorder (e.g., anxiety over having seizures and where they may occur, social stigma, and isolation) rather than the control of the actual seizure itself.

What Can I Do as a Parent?—As a parent there are many things you can do if your child is diagnosed with a seizure disorder. The most important is good medical care and follow-up to deal with the physical effects of the disorder. However, the parents need to take the primary role in dealing with the child's social/emotional growth. You as parents will need to consider the following questions:

—Does my child make statements about being different or weird in comparison to his/her playmates?

—Does my child withdraw or isolate himself/herself from other children?

—Is my child more anxious than other children when participating in group activities?

—Is this anxiety only a sign of a more serious worry that he/she may have a seizure?

—Do other people and children respond differently to my child once they are aware that my child has a seizure disorder? Is my child aware of that?

In terms of dealing with your child's social/emotional growth, the following guidelines might be helpful:

—Talk openly about the disorder with the child and explain that he or she is not an epileptic child but instead has a disorder called epilepsy.

—Be honest about the prognosis; tell the child you are uncertain if he or she will "grow out of it" but that it is a possibility (depending on the etiology).

—Try to normalize the disorder by letting the child know that everyone has something about them that they don't like or wish they could change.

—Encourage the child to talk to you about his/her feelings and how others may have treated him/her badly due to ignorance of the disorder. Listen to what the child has to say.

—Talk to your child's teacher and ask him/her to include a discussion on seizure disorders. If the teacher does not feel they can lead a discussion of this type, call your local epilepsy organization (Shaw, 1983) for information on speakers. Or you might lead the discussion if you feel you have the education.

—Encourage the child to ask questions of his/her doctor about the disorder and its prognosis. Give the child some control.

—Go to the library together and research information about epilepsy with the whole family. Let the child know that you are all in this together; he or she is not alone.

Resources

Your best resource at the start will be your physician. They can inform you about the many facets of the disorder that could not be described in detail above. They should also have current reading materials or resources that you can get from the library that they feel provide accurate and up-to-date information about development, treatment, and prognosis. Your school psychologist may also be able to refer you to some reading materials and quality resources. Use their expertise, but do some research yourself.

References

Boll, T. J. (1978). Diagnosing brain impairment. In B. Wolman (Ed.), *Clinical diagnosis of mental disorders.* New York: Plenum Press.

Christ, A. E. (1978). Therapy of the child with true brain damage. *American Journal of Orthopsychiatry, 48,* 505-515.

Dodrill, C. B. (1981) Neuropsychology of epilepsy. In S. B. Filskow & T. Boll (Eds.), *Handbook of clinical neuropsychology.* New York: Wiley.

Lubar, J. F., & Shouse, M. N. (1977). Use of biofeedback in the treatment of seizure disorders and hyperactivity. In B. Lahey & A. Kazdin (Eds.), *Advances in clinical child psychology* (Vol. 1). New York: Plenum Press.

Noyes, A. P., & Kolb, L. C. (1968). *Modern clinical psychiatry.* Philadelphia: Saunders.

Sands, H., & Minters, F. C. (1977). *The epilepsy fact book.* Philadelphia: F. A. Davids.

Shaw, E. B. (1983). Resources available to the patient with epilepsy. In T. R. Browne & R. G. Feldman (Eds.), *Epilepsy: Diagnosis and management* (pp. 139-143). Boston: Little, Brown.

NATIONAL
ASSOCIATION OF
SCHOOL
PSYCHOLOGISTS

Children and Siblings of the Handicapped

Sally Linton Burton
University of Idaho

Background—The diagnosis of a handicapping condition brings about a variety of changes for all family members. Recent studies show that siblings are significantly affected by the presence of a family member with a handicap. Currently, approximately 12% of all students in public schools are receiving special education services. Most of these special education students have siblings, although statistics on the number of siblings are currently unavailable. More importantly, parents and professionals are often unaware of the special needs and unique concerns of these nonhandicapped siblings.

Typical problems confronting siblings include: embarrassment, guilt, isolation, resentment, excessive caregiving responsibilities, and greater pressure to achieve.

Embarrassment—Children with handicaps may embarrass their siblings by having seizures, or calling attention to themselves through some unusual behavior which may cause peers, neighbors, or strangers to stare.

Guilt—Siblings may occasionally get angry at their brother or sister with a handicap and may suffer feelings of guilt because they realize their anger has been directed towards behavior that their sibling could not control.

Isolation—Siblings may feel a sense of isolation about sharing news about their brother or sister with their friends because of the negative reaction they might get. It may be difficult or embarrassing to explain to their friends why their brother or sister is in special education classes and needs special attention. Siblings may also have to restrain their enthusiasm about an accomplishment of their sibling with a handicap because their friends may consider this a trivial achievement and laugh at their brother or sister.

Resentment—Siblings may sometimes resent the reduced amount of their parents' time and energy they receive because of the special needs of the child with a handicap. Often the siblings may misinterpret their parents' priorities and engage in inappropriate behavior in an attempt to get their fair share of their parents' attention. These attention-getting techniques may later be generalized to other situations so siblings act out against teachers and other authority figures.

Excessive Caregiving Responsibilities—Siblings are normally the best equipped and most convenient babysitters for their brother or sister with a handicap, but such responsibilities may directly conflict with the sibling's own needs. If excessive child care responsibilities deprive siblings of the opportunity to have time to themselves or pursue their own interests, they may resent both their parents and their brother or sister with a handicap.

Future Concerns—Siblings are very concerned about the future of their handicapped brother or sister. They want to know about living and financial arrangements for the handicapped individual and their own chances of having a handicapped child.

Pressure to Achieve—Often parents may transfer unrealized expectations that they develop for the child with the handicap to the nonhandicapped sibling. These increased expectations can create stress if parents and/or the sibling let these expectations become unrealistic.

What Can I Do As A Parent?—Household chores should be evenly distributed among all family members and not become the sole responsibility of nonhandicapped siblings. Nonhandicapped children can become resentful if individuals with handicaps do not have to participate in family or household chores. Children with handicaps may team up with another family member to take some minimal part in household chores.

Open communication is essential in a family who has a handicapped child. The full impact of the handicap should be talked about honestly with all family members including the nonhandicapped siblings. Your nonhandicapped child has a right to factual and age-appropriate information regarding the handicap. If this information is withheld, they may invent answers to their questions such as what caused the handicap and may even blame themselves for the condition.

Future concerns of the handicapped individual should be dealt with as a family. Siblings may want to know if they will have children with disabilities and who will take care of and become responsible for the handicapped child when the parents become unable to do so. A visit with one of your local advocacy groups such as The Association for Retarded Citizens or a discussion with the family lawyer can help the family and the nonhandicapped siblings prepare for the future.

Encourage and reinforce your children to express their true emotions about their handicapped sibling with you. If the child is mad at their handicapped sibling for embarrassing them at school, share with them how you would feel if it were you that was embarassed. Acknowledge their feelings and allow them the right to be mad. Nothing diffuses the anger of a child more than parental respect of their feelings. Share with them stories of your own childhood and how you felt when your brothers or sisters made you angry. After all, you should expect kids to act like kids.

If there is a sibling support group in your area, check it out for yourself. If it meets your approval, encourage your child to participate in the group. Your willingness to acknowlege sibling concerns will foster an atmosphere of cooperation between you and your child.

Spend special time alone with your nonhandicapped children. Make plans to spend time alone with them and talk just about their activities, dreams and accomplishments.

Being a sibling of an individual with a disability offers several benefits. Some of these benefits include the ability to develop a sense of humor about dealing with awkward or unusual situations, tolerance and patience of others with lesser advantages and/or abilities and flexibility. When you see these qualities in your nonhandicapped child, take the time to praise him/her.

Resources

Meyer D. J., Vadasy, P. F., & Fewell, R. R. (1985). *Living With A Brother or Sister with Special Needs*. Seattle, WA: University of Washington Press. *Living With a Brother or Sister With Special Needs* is a book written for young readers. The book offers factual information and emotional support to brothers and sisters with handicaps. This book provides useful and clear explanations about specific handicapping conditions. The book constitutes an excellent resource book for parents and siblings.

Powell, T. H., & Ogle, P. A. (1985). *Brothers and Sisters-A Special Part of Exceptional Families*. Baltimore, MD: Paul H. Brookes. The authors are special educators who have combined a review of research on siblings of children with handicaps together with their own experiences and recommendations to produce a book which will be of considerable value to parents. The chapters include discussions about the unique needs of siblings with specific strategies to help them maximize their psychological and emotional growth.

Seliman, M. (Ed,) (1983). *The Family With a Handicapped Child*. New York: Grune and Stratton, Inc. This volume focuses on a range of topics including legal issues, community service providers, working with families, counseling, and therapeutic interventions. Most importantly, there is a chapter entitled "Siblings of Handicapped Persons" by the author which includes an overview of research findings and discusses psychological prospects for siblings.

NATIONAL ASSOCIATION OF SCHOOL PSYCHOLOGISTS

Children and Single Parent Homes

Cindy Carlson
University of Texas at Austin, Austin, Texas

Background—A single parent family is one in which someone raises his or her children alone without the household presence of a second parent or a parent substitute. It is estimated that a majority of U.S. children will at some point in their lives live in a single-parent family. Currently, one of five white children and one of every two black children under the age of 18 years live with a single parent. Over 90% of children in single-parent families live in households headed by their mothers. Alarmingly, more than 50% of these female-headed one-parent families fall below the poverty line in the United States.

The single parent, primarily mother-headed, family has typically been viewed as a "broken" or "deficient" family structure with expected adverse consequences for the development and socialization of children. It is important to note that many of the adverse effects on children associated with being reared in a single-parent home are not found in research studies when the effects of social class and low income are controlled. Thus, it is inappropriate to view the single-parent family as deficient; however this family type is vulnerable to task overload and to stress as the same number of roles, with comparable level of quality to an intact family, must be accomplished by one adult, typically on a single income. Thus a primary task of single parents is being able to create and utilize existing social support effectively such that the development of their children can be maximized with minimal stress.

Development—There are no consistent age-related behavioral indicators associated with being reared in a single-parent family. Both the circumstances surrounding and the resources available to single parent families vary widely and are more likely to influence the development of children than status as a single parent. Furthermore, deficits in development may not appear in preschool or early school-aged children, unless they are overly stressed, but may increase over time. The following is a summary of child behaviors and problems associated with single-parent homes, as well as factors likely to increase risk of developmental difficulties. In general, these behaviors are applicable to children preschool through adolescence, unless otherwise indicated, and are likely to worsen with time if the family circumstances underlying the development of child problems is not changed.

Boys:

- Externalizing behavior problems at home and/or at school, e.g., impulsivity, inattention, inability to delay gratification, acting out.
- Lowered achievement motivation and academic performance (deteriorates over time).
- Lowered performance on mathematics-related tasks (deteriorates over time).
- Less secure masculine identity (most acute when father loss occurs prior to age five).
- Peer difficulties (related to difficulties in other areas).
- Lower self-esteem, locus of control, and ego-strength (deteriorates over time).
- Gains in independence, maturity and empathy.

Girls

- Lowered performance on mathematics-related topics.
- Lower self-esteem, lower sense of personal control, higher anxiety.
- Gains in independence, maturity, and empathy.

Risk Factors

- Mother-headed homes
- Caused by divorce
- Children are male
- Children are younger (below 5 years of age)
- Greater numbers of children in the family
- Inadequate financial and social support
- Lack of father or male surrogate involvement
- Nonauthoritative parenting style
- Low maternal education
- White or Hispanic versus Black

What Can I Do as a Parent?—It has been argued that when one parent is absent, the remaining parent will have a more intense effect upon the child. Single-parents should, therefore, recognize that the quality of their parenting is critical to their child(ren). However attempting to accomplish the work of two-parents is seldom feasible. Rather, single-parents would do best to view themselves as parent and family managers or coordinators who engage in quality parenting but who also locate and maintain resources to assist in the effective rearing of their children.

Authoritative Parenting—Parenting behaviors that have been found to have a positive effect on both boys and girls include clear setting of rules and adequate control and supervision balanced with extensive verbal interaction, nurturance, and warmth. The ability to establish clear authority is particularly important for single parent mothers with sons. If you have difficulty controlling your children, it is very important that you acquire these skills. Attend parent education classes, read child-rearing books, or consult a mental health professional for assistance.

Encourage Math & Sciences—Single-parent, mother-headed homes are consistently associated with children's lowered quantative performance in school. To offset this effect, take particular interest in your child's school performance and curiousity in these subjects. In addition, make available, when possible, resources that will assist your child in developing interest and competence in these areas. Resources might include, for example, the public library, computer software, weekend recreational events, vacations, magnet schools or summer programs specializing in science and math. If math and science are not your interests, discuss your concern with your child's math and science teacher to gain their assistance in encouraging your child in these areas.

Sex-Role Orientation—Sex-role orientation is primarily a concern of single-parent mothers with sons. You can facilitate the male sex-role identification of your son by creating opportunities for your child to establish close relationships with one or more male adults. This, of course, is particularly important if your son has infrequent or no contact with his biological father. Male role models might include relatives such as a grandfather or uncle, coaches, neighbors, friends, or use of community groups such as Boy Scouts or Big Brothers. In addition, involvement in sports appears to be particularly important for males in female-headed homes, as athletic competence is centrally related to self-esteem and popularity in the male peer culture of school aged children and adolescents.

Clear and Appropriate Roles—In single-parent homes, the many tasks of managing a household fall on the shoulders of one adult. Such tasks include housecleaning, care of younger children, fixing meals, and laundry. To avoid strain, it is generally necessary to get assistance with household tasks, either from children in the family or from resources outside the family. An important consideration in the use of children to fulfill family roles and responsibilities is the developmental competence and capacity of the child. Elementary school-aged children, for example, seldom have the maturity to accomplish the above noted household tasks without assistance and supervision. However they can assist the single-parent with subcomponents of these tasks, e.g., picking up toys and clothes, setting the table. While the risk for elementary school-aged children is demanding behavior that the child is unable to accomplish, the concern with adolescent children may fall to the other extreme, with adolescents appearing capable of fulfilling adult roles, but actually risking their own social and emotional development. Adolescents may easily slip into the emotional and practical vacuum created by the absent adult in a single parent home, particularly if the parents absence is recent and the adolescent is the same sex as the absent parent. Although adolescents present a picture of maturity to parents, they are seldom emotionally capable of handling the adult responsibilities of financial or emotional support to their parent. Thus, single parents with adolescents must balance appropriate sharing of household tasks against the sometimes unconscious desire, when distressed, to replace an absent adult figure. If you are uncertain about what are appropriate expectations for your child, regardless of age, check either with other parents or with school personnel.

Single-Parent Mental Health—Single-parent mothers and fathers, regardless of financial status, report stress, anxiety, a lack of energy, and often loneliness as a result of juggling the demands of work, parenting, and socializing. Your capacity to parent is not only a function of your knowledge and skills, but also a function of your emotional well-being. Often child behavior problems reflect anxiety created in the child by a parent's depression, apathy, or expressed helplessness. It is, therefore, critical that you find ways to nurture, support, and sustain your mental health. Regular exercise may be helpful. Single-parent support groups and organizations are generally available through communities and churches, and can provide information, social, and recreational support. Consider seeking professional assistance if child or family problems remain unresolved or reoccur.

Resources

Going It Alone: The Family Life and Social Situation of the Single Parent, by R. Weiss, Basic Books, New York, 1979. This book presents sensitive and comprehensive coverage of single parent family issues. Available in paperback.

The Boys and Girls Book About One-Parent Families, by R. Gardner Bantam Books, New York, 1978. This book is written to help children cope with some of the common problems that arise in their single-parent family. The book is written at the third to fourth grade level. Discussion between parent and child while reading is advised. Paperback.

Raising Sons: Practical Strategies for Single Mothers, by J.E. Rodgers & M. F. Cataldo, Signet Books, New York. 1984. This book presents a positive view of single-mother/son childrearing with numerous useful child management suggestions. Paperback, high school reading level.

Parents Without Partners, Inc. 7910 Eoodmont Avenue, Suite 1000, Bethesda, MD 20814, (800) 638-8078. A nationwide organiztion for single parents that provides an informative monthly newsletter as well as local chapter in many communities that organize educational and recreational events.

Children in Stepfamilies

Susan Kupisch
Austin Peay State University, Clarksville, Tennessee

Background—Many children experience the divorce and remarriage of their parents. Single parent and remarriage families comprise nearly forty-five percent of all families with children. It is estimated that almost half the children under age eighteen will spend some time in a single parent home and that one in five children will live in a stepfamily.

Although parents may view the second marriage as a positive step, their children may not. Living within a stepfamily creates new expectations and demands; therefore, unanticipated problems usually arise. A stepfamily is defined as a family in which at least one adult has a child or children prior to the new marriage. The children may live with the couple or visit periodically. Some children find home to be with both mom and dad, as in the cases of joint custody. Stepchildren have to establish new bonds while maintaining old ones. Many feel they have lost members of their original family because one parent lives away, brothers or sisters are separated, and/or grandparents no longer visit.

Because the "real" family is viewed as the first marriage family, communities have not fully accepted the stepfamily. Some religions only sanction first marriages and most do not fully accept alternatives. Legally, absent parents and stepparents have no protected parental rights. Socially, stepchildren and stepparents often feel out of place in family events and school functions. The stepfamily has been called a family with no history and no roots.

Development—Families that make it a success generally do not expect a storybook family life. The home contracts and expands as children move in and out to meet schedules and household needs. Space is used for many purposes. A bedroom for the weekend becomes a den during the weekdays and playroom for the summer. In the stepfamily children may relate to the same adult in different ways. Mary might be viewed as mother for one child and as a friend by another.

Stepfamilies also find that the patterns of living are not as simple as before. It takes four to five years to become stable. From the beginning, there are many individuals trying to adjust to one another. Instead of marriage starting a new phase of life for the couple, it may interrupt an ongoing phase of development for the adults, as well as the children. The remarriage of parents may come when a teenage daughter is struggling with her own problems or when the new wife is mothering young children but also having to manage teenagers who are only a few years younger in age. These complications compound marital problems and strain personal relationships within the family.

Many families feel that vacations and traditional family gatherings help build family unity. But when children cross household lines, family traditions are broken. For the stepfamily, the holiday dinner, the vacation at the beach, and the weekend break easily become points for argument. Building a new unit further signals the loss of previous family experiences.

Perhaps feeling guilty about past mistakes, such as wanting a divorce or putting children through difficult times, many stepparents perceive their image to be tainted. They suspect that others view them negatively. It is not uncommon for the custodial mother to insist that the children use the stepfather's surname to save embarrassment. This tells the children that they have something to hide.

Remarriage requires the members to blend personal habits, disappointments, and expectancies.

They may find others in the family unsupportive or even resentful because of religious beliefs, loyalty to the ex-spouse, or other personal reasons. For the stepfamily, lifestyles, values, and attitudes must be meshed quickly in order for the new family to form. Blending is complex due to the number of people involved, their needs, and their family histories.

Feelings of sadness and anger due to the loss of contact with the absent parent, and conflicts about parent loyalty plague many stepchildren. Many have fears of rejection and abandonment. For many, adjustment to the stepfamily means the readjustment to yet another family structure in a brief period of time. Also being expected to love the new stepparent can create confusion for a youth whose identity remains with the other parent.

Guidelines for Parents—A critical time for discussing stepfamily issues is prior to the event itself. Several early problems in the second marriage relates to unresolved issues in the first marriage family. Being aware of typical trouble signs helps us recognize the stress when it appears.

- Grieve and let go: Close the chapter on the first marriage. Allow the spouse to continue to be a parent but don't be in the middle of the relationship.

- Court the new family: Marriage is a lifestyle arrangement and in a stepfamily several people are involved. Children need to be included in activities related to getting to know each other.

- Clarify expectations: Discussing interests, likes, and expectancies helps each member feel more secure with the unit and how to fit in.

- Find space to live: Each member needs personal space which is respected. Privacy, sharing, and who rules must be worked out from the beginning.

Guidelines for Stepparents:

- Accept being a stepparent: A stepparent cannot replace the natural parent and attempting to do so creates more confusion and resentment. Take an appropriate role by assuming a caring, noncompetitive place in the family.

- Accept the mate's ex-spouse: Each mate brings into the marriage a history of past relationships which cannot be erased. With children, communication with ex-spouses is important in arranging schedules, discussing resources, and making parental decisions.

- Allow children time with the absent parent: The child's desire to be with and love the separated parent need not be threatening. Being pressured to choose between parent and stepparent creates loyalty conflicts.

- Develop patient discipline: The stepparent is probably more critical of the child's behavior than is the parent. If a foundation of caring is not established, discipline will be viewed as punitive and unfair.

- Arrange family meetings: Open communication is needed within the family experiencing new demands and adjustments. The periodic family meeting to hash over feelings serves as an appropriate way for problem solving.

Guidelines for Stepchildren:

- Express feelings and thoughts honestly: Feelings of fear, anger, and sadness are not uncommon during times of family change and uncertainty. Although it may be difficult for children to recognize and acknowledge feelings about the family, support people can communicate the willingness to listen and reassure.

- Ask parents about expectations: Anxieties and frustrations can be significantly reduced by preparing for events. As expectancies change they need to be communicated to children. Having

320

experienced several significant life changes, children in remarried units may have a special need for reassurance.

- Realize that marriage and divorce are adult decisions: Many children blame themselves for their parent's divorce. Helping children understand the adult nature of such decisions can diminish inappropriate fantasies.
- Love takes time: Children need to be permitted the time to develop the respect and love for new family members. Given opportunities to spend time together and know one another emotional relationships will usually flourish.

Resources

Books for Stepparents

Jensen, L. & Jensen, J. (1981). *Stepping Into Stepparenting: A Practical Guide.* Palo Alto, CA: R & E Research Association.

Lewis, H. C. (1980). *All About Families the Second Time Around.* Palo Alto, CA: A gentle, yet direct exploration of feelings, fears, dilemmas, and roles in families of remarriage..

Visher E., & Visher J. (1982) *How to Win as a Stepfamily.* Palo Alto, CA: Stepfamily Association of America. Highly practical "how-to-succeed" guide for stepfamilies.

Books for Children

Berman, C. (1982). *What Am I Doing in a Stepfamily?* Palo Alto, CA: Stepfamily Association of America. This illustrated book touches the issues relevant to the young stepchild.

Gardner R. (1982) *The Boys and Girls Book about Stepfamilies.* Palo Alto, CA: Stepfamily Association of America. A warm and honest book that provides reassurance and answers to many of the important questions children ask about stepfamilies.

Getzoff, A., & McClenahan, C. (1983). *Stepkids: A Survival Guide for Teenagers in Stepfamilies.* Palo Alto, CA: Stepfamily Association of America. Packed with solid, realistic advice and awareness of the teenager's point of view.

NATIONAL
ASSOCIATION OF
SCHOOL
PSYCHOLOGISTS

Transition Planning for Handicapped Students
Parent Handout

Edward M. Levinson and Lynne M. McKee
Indiana University of Pennsylvania

Overview—Transition services refer to the services handicapped children require in order to make a successful adjustment to work and community living. In the past, efforts at successfully integrating young handicapped adults into the community have frequently been unsuccessful. Unfortunately, research indicates that following high-school, many handicapped students have high rates of unemployment and underemployment, and have a difficult time adjusting to independent community living.

The successful transition of handicapped students from the school environment to work/community living is a process involving special educators, vocational educators, mental health and mental retardation specialists, and prospective employers/community agency representatives. However the most important members of the team are the handicapped student and his/her parents. The degree to which parents of handicapped students are involved in their child's transition is directly related to the success of that transition.

What Can I Do As A Parent?—Although transition planning should begin no later than age 13, there are many things which the parents of younger children can do to increase the likelihood of a successful transition:

- Actively participate in your child's Individual Education Plans (I.E.P.) from the time he/she begins school. Take an active role in seeing that the education plan includes:

  - Daily living and independent living skills including personal hygiene (e.g. care of body/hair, appropriate clothing for various occasions and weather conditions, etc.), basic housekeeping, money handling, transportation, and use of leisure time.

  - Social skills including appropriate eye contact and conversation, turn-taking, sharing, giving and accepting compliments and criticism.

  - Academic skills including reading, mathematic, oral and written communication skills.

  - Occupational and vocational skills including an awareness of realistic career options, an awareness of one's own strengths and weaknesses, and an understanding of personal preferences (e.g., I like and am good at working with young children; I don't like working with mechanical devices). As the child grows older I.E.P.s should increasingly emphasize career and vocational exploration and the development of work habits and behaviors, marketable vocational skills, and job seeking skills.

- Read stories to/with your child which involve various careers. (see Resources.) Biographies which tell of handicapped individuals achieving success in various careers can be especially useful in showing the child that many handicapped persons can live fulfilling and productive lives. Use these stories to identify and discuss the skills (listed above) which are required for successful work and community adjustment.

- Use daily opportunities to talk about various jobs and the skills necessary to be successful in these jobs. Stops at the grocery store, for example, can be used to discuss occupations such as check out clerk, stock person, bag person and the skills necessary to perform these tasks.
- Model appropriate work behavior. Dress appropriately for your job, be prompt in going to work and discuss with your child why these behaviors are necessary in getting and keeping a job.
- Discuss your reaction to criticism, what you do when you are sick, and not going to work, etc.
- Discuss with your child the steps which you took in choosing your career. For example, "I really liked working with people and I found that I enjoyed driving, so I decided to become a delivery person."
- Be aware of training/employment opportunities as they relate to your geographical area and to your child's abilities. Vocational/technical schools and vocational rehabilitation programs can be helpful in providing training and job placement services to a variety of handicapped persons.
- Some mildly handicapped students may be eligible to receive assistance in attending community colleges or universities.
- Allow your child to explore various occupations by having him/her serve as a volunteer in various job sites. Hospitals, libraries, animal shelters, nursing homes, etc. are frequently in search of volunteers. By volunteering in such programs, your child can experience the satisfaction of working in a real job site and can further explore his/her interests and abilities as they relate to various careers.
- Begin considering the type of living arrangements that will be appropriate for your child after he/she leaves school (e.g. independent, supervised apartment, group homes, living at home with you, etc.). Discuss these possibilities with your child.
- Give your child frequent opportunities to develop daily living skills. Allow him/her to participate grocery shopping, cooking, housekeeping, and home maintenance activities.
- Openly and freely discuss the transition process with your child. Remember that it is your son or daughter not you, who is going to be "living" the life prepared through the transition process. Although it is important that you guide him/her toward realistic goals, it is equally important that you take his/her interests and feelings into account when considering the transition to adult living.

Resources

Teachers, vocational counselors, and local librarians can be excellent sources of additional information on transition services and career awareness. Some books which deal with the successful adjustment of handicapped individuals to adult life include:

Aaseng, N. (1980). *Winners never quit.* Lerner Publications Co., Minneapolis, Minnesota.
Gelfand, R. & Patterson, L. (1962). *They wouldn't quit: Stories of handicapped people.* Lerner Publications Co., Minneapolis, Minnesota.
Keller H. (1980). Helen Keller: *The story of my life.* Watermill Press, Mahwah, New Jersey.

NATIONAL
ASSOCIATION OF
SCHOOL
PSYCHOLOGISTS

Transition Planning for Handicapped Students
Teacher Handout

Edward M. Levinson and Lynne M.McKee
Indiana University of Pennsylvania

Overview—Transition services refer to the services handicapped children require in order to make a successful adjustment to work and community living. In the past, efforts at successfully integrating young handicapped adults into the community have frequently been unsuccessful. Unfortunately, research indicates that following high-school, many handicapped students experience high rates of unemployment and underemployment, and have a difficult time adjusting to independent community living.

The successful transition of handicapped students from the school environment to work/community living is a process involving special educators, vocational educators, mental health and mental retardation specialists, prospective employers/community agency representatives, parents, and students. Transition planning should begin no later than age 13 and the Individual Transition Plan should be an integral part of the student's Individual Education Plan from this point onward.

What Can I Do As A Teacher?—As the teacher of handicapped students, you assume a critical role in enhancing the likelihood that students will make a successful transition from school to adult life. Because of your daily contact with students, you have considerable opportunity to observe academic and behavioral strengths and weaknesses and to direct the student toward appropriate career goals. Furthermore, as the individual most responsible for designing and implementing the Individual Education Plan, you have the opportunity to assure that those skills necessary to a successful transition are included in the curriculum. Successful transition to work/community life is generally thought to involve competencies in the areas of daily living skills, personal-social skills, and occupational/ vocational skills. The degree to which academic instruction incorporates these skill areas is related to the likelihood that a student will make a successful transition to adult life. Depending upon the individual needs of the student, consider incorporating instruction in such daily living skills as:

- Caring for personal needs
- Managing finances
- Basic cooking and housekeeping skills
- Appropriate telephone skills
- Telling time
- Being mobile within the community
- Engaging in appropriate recreational and leisure activities
- Teaching social skills should be an integral and ongoing part of any curriculum. Skills to be emphasized include:

- Maintaining good hygiene and appearance
- Making appropriate eye contact during conversations
- Exhibiting appropriate behavior across various situations
- Exhibiting adequate problem solving skills
- Accepting and giving compliments
- Accepting and giving criticism
- Making and keeping friends—trustworthiness, kindness, etc.

The development of occupational/vocational skills includes developing appropriate work habits and behaviors, possessing marketable vocational skills, and exhibiting appropriate job seeking skills. Understanding and exploring occupational and vocational alternatives is also important. Consider the following:

- When instructing reading/language arts, emphasize how these skills will be useful in adult life, and incorporate such applications in your instruction. For example, reading skills are necessary for driving a car (students may read the Drivers Education Manual, read signs along the roadway, etc.), grocery shopping (students may read the labels on boxes and cans), eating out in restaurants (students may read menus), etc.

- When instructing mathematics, emphasize how these skills are necessary in daily life and teach them within such a context. The importance of knowing how to tell time can be related to getting to work on time, knowing when a favorite television program is coming on, etc. Measurement skills can be taught within the context of food preparation. Computational skills can be taught within the context of making purchases.

- Consider setting up a simulated work environment in your classroom. Students can be "paid" (tokens, stars) based on "work" (academic) performance, maintaining proper hygiene, and displaying appropriate social skills. Token reinforcers can be exchanged for material reinforcers (available at the class "store") on a preestablished schedule. Specific suggestions on the implementation of these programs can be found in: Levinson, E.M. (1984). A vocationally oriented secondary school program for the emotionally disturbed. **The Vocational Guidance Quarterly**, 33(1), 76-81, and Levinson, E.M. (1985). Vocational and career-oriented secondary school programs for the emotionally disturbed. **The School Counselor** 33(2), 100-106.

- Incorporate discussions of careers into the curricula on a regular basis. For example, when studying health, discuss health related careers (e.g. nurses aide, laboratory worker, medical secretary), when studying science, discuss science related careers.

- Invite individuals into the class to speak about various careers and the skills required to be successful in these careers. Consider the ability level and interests of the students when deciding who to invite as speakers.

- Field trips should be used to expose students to various occupations.

- Provide students with an opportunity to role play job interview situations and provide students with feedback about their performance. Consider videotaping interviews and using the videotape in instruction.

- Provide students with an opportunity to practice filling out job application forms and reading the "want-ads."

- As a teacher, you play an important role in guiding students toward realistic career goals. Many students underestimate their abilities in terms of future careers (e.g. "I'll never be able to do anything,") or overestimate their abilities (e.g., "I want to be a brain surgeon."). Other students gravitate toward glamorous, but unrealistic occupations (e.g. actress, professional athlete, etc.). In fact, most handicapped individuals do possess the skills required to be successful at some job. You can both encourage those who underestimate their job potential while, at the same time, steering those with unrealistic expectations toward more practical career considerations.

Resources

A wide variety of resource materials on both functional curricula and career awareness/vocational planning are available through Regional Resource Centers or the Special Education or Vocational Education Offices of your district. Some which may be of special interest include:

Rettig, J.L. (1986). *Careers: Exploration and decision.* David Lake Publishers, Belmont, California.

Wircenski, J.L. (1982). *Employability skills for the special needs learner: An integrated program of reading, math, and daily living skills.* Aspin Publishers, Rockville, Maryland.

NATIONAL ASSOCIATION OF SCHOOL PSYCHOLOGISTS

Children and War-Responding to Operation Desert Storm**
Parent Handout

Debby Waddell, *Columbus, Ohio*

Alex Thomas, Miami University, *Oxford, Ohio*

Background—With the crisis in the Middle East, your child is experiencing something totally new and potentially quite frightening. American children today have never experienced war as a reality. Our children need support in dealing with this crisis.

Also unique is the impact of the media on our children's thinking. They have been exposed to violence-both real and fictional-in unprecedented amounts since they were born. Violence is replayed on television almost as soon as it occurs, and wars play on the nightly news.

Today's children also live in the world of Star Wars and Super Heroes. Adults may realize Luke Skywalker is fiction, but for children this is not so easy. Youngsters have difficulty separating reality and fantasy. Children who believe in Santa Claus can as easily believe in Darth Vader and Freddie Kruger. Separating the realities of Desert Storm from media fantasy may require adult help. As parents, it is our responsibility to help our children distinguish between fantasy and reality.

Emotional Responses—Emotional responses vary in nature and severity from child to child. Nonetheless, there are some common ways in how children (and adults) feel when their lives are impacted by war.

- **Fear:** Fear may be the predominant reaction-fear for the safety of those in the military as well as fear for their own safety. Children's picture of war may include a bomb dropped on their home. Their worries may seem unreasonable, but to them, they are quite possible. Children will hear rumors at school and may let their imaginations run wild. They may think the worst, however unrealistic it may be. The threat of terrorism may also add to their fear.

- **Loss of control:** Military actions are something over which children-and most adults-have no control. Lack of control can be overwhelming and confusing. Children may grasp at any control which they can have.

- **Anger:** Anger is not an unusual reaction. Unfortunately, anger is often expressed to those with whom children are most secure. Children may be angry at parents who are in the military to the extent that they do not even want to write letters. Knowing that those who are involved in the military are volunteers only helps to justify anger. Patriotism and duty are abstract concepts, for children, especially younger children, who are experiencing the reality of separation from a loved one.

** Although Operation Desert Storm concluded in 1991, this handout can serve as a model for similar events.

- **Loss of stability:** War interrupts the natural order of things. It is very unsettling. Stability is gone, and this is very threatening. It can destroy trust and upset equilibrium.
- **Isolation:** Children who have a family member involved in Desert Storm but don't live near a military base may feel isolated. Children of reserve members called to active duty may not know others in the same situation. Such children may feel jealous of friends' undisturbed families and may strike out at signs of normalcy around them.

Another group of children who may feel isolated are dependents of military families who have accompanied a remaining parent back to a hometown or who are staying with relatives while both parents are gone. Not only do these children experience separation from parents, but they also experience the loss of familiar faces and surroundings.

What Can I Do As A Parent?

- Acknowledge your children's feelings.
  - Knowing what to say is often difficult. When no other words come to mind, a hug and saying "This is really hard for you/us" will always work.
  - Try to recognize the feelings underlying your children's actions and put them into words. Say something like, "I can see you are feeling really scared about this," or "It makes us mad to think that our dad had to go to Saudi Arabia" can be helpful.
  - Sometimes children may have an overwhelming fear that they are unable to put into words which you may need to voice for them. For instance, if a parent is away, children may wonder what will become of them if the parent does not return. Try saying, "You never have to worry because we/you will be well taken care of. You won't be alone. Let me tell you our plan."
  - At times when your children are most upset, don't deny the seriousness of the situation. Saying to children, "Don't cry, everything will be okay," does not reflect how the child feels and does not make them feel better. Nevertheless, don't forget to express hope and faith that things will be alright.
  - Older children, in particular, may need help identifying what they individually believe about war and the role the United States has chosen in this conflict. Questions such as "Could my parent shoot someone?" and "How can anyone kill an Iraqi soldier who is only 12-13-no older than I?" are issues which may need discussion.
- Help your children put their fears in perspective.
  - Acknowledge the sanctity of each human life while letting children know that the chance of any one individual returning from the Middle East is very high. Death rates in U.S. conflicts have steadily dropped from the time of the Revolutionary War to a low of 0.5% in the Vietnam War. With increases in technology and medical advances, military statisticians suggest a potential loss ratio of 0.3% from battle and 0.1% from other causes in the Middle East.
- Help children to feel personally safe.
  - Discuss what is realistic modern technology versus science fiction. Help children to understand that the longest range missile that Iraq has can barely reach Israel. Discuss how far Iraqi war planes can fly without refueling (about 1000 miles) and the impossibility of refueling anywhere between Iraq and the United States. Let children share their fears, most of which are unrealistic and a result of rumor and anxiety, and put them in perspective as to what is realistic.

- Help children understand that precautions are being taken to prevent terrorism (e.g. bomb sniffing dogs, passport checks, heightened airport security) which might actually make them safer now than they usually are.
- Deal with fears such as Desert Storm may be the beginning of the end of the world, or that bombs will reach the local community.

- Try to maintain normal routines to provide a sense of stability and security.
- Help children to feel a sense of control by taking some action.
  - Send letters, cookies or magazines to those in the military.
  - Help your older child find a family who has a parent in the Middle East and arrange some volunteer babysitting times for that family.
  - If a family member is away, make plans for some special activities:
    - Gatherings with other families who are also missing a loved one help provide support for you as well as for your children.
    - Special parent and child times can provide an extra sense of security which might be badly needed. Let your child know that you will set aside a particular half hour each day to play. Make the time as pleasant and child centered as possible. Return phone calls later and make your child the real focus of that special time.
- Involve children in planning how to cope. Control and ownership are fostered when children help to plan strategies for dealing with a situation.
- Prepare for difficulties with children at night.
  - Maintain regular bedtime routines such as storytime to provide a sense of security. Special stuffed animals or blankets may be especially important right now.
  - Sit near your child until he/she falls asleep for a few nights. Gradually withdraw this support by checking back in two minutes and continuing to lengthen this time until your child feels secure again.
  - A light may be needed in or near your child's room.
  - Siblings may want to sleep in the same room until they feel more secure again.
  - Don't let your children focus too much of their time and energy on Desert Storm. If children are choosing to watch CNN News for hours each evening, find other activities for them. You may also need to watch the news less intensely and spend more time in alternative family activities.
  - Use outside support services if your child has a severe reaction. Your school psychologist or counselor can assist or provide names of other professionals trained to deal with children.
  - Try not to let financial strains be a major concern of children. Although economic impact of Desert Storm may result in job cutbacks or going from a civilian job to active duty in the military may cut family income, children are not capable of dealing with this issue on an on-going basis. Telling children that you need to be more careful with spending is appropriate, but be cautious about placing major burdens on children.
  - Take time for yourself and try to deal with your own reactions to the situation as fully as possible. This, too, will help your children.
  - Always be honest with your child and do not be afraid to talk to others about your fears and concerns.

Children and War-Responding to Operation Desert Storm**
Teacher Handout

Debby Waddell, *Columbus, Ohio*

Alex Thomas, *Oxford, Ohio*

Background—Students in the U.S. today have never experienced war as a reality. Although the United States has engaged in some brief military actions, never have our students experienced anything like the events that began with Iraq's invasion of Kuwait and the initiation of Operation Desert Storm.

Also unique to the experience of students of the nineties is the impact of the media on their thinking and feeling. They have been exposed to violence-both real and fictional-in unprecedented amounts. Real violence is replayed on television almost as soon as it occurs. Sesame Street can be interrupted by a report of a sniper in an elementary school and news shows bring conflicts between other countries into American homes.

Today's students also live in the world of Star Wars and Super Heroes. Luke Skywalker may be quickly relegated to the realm of fiction by adults, but for students this is not so easy. Youngsters have difficulty separating reality and fantasy. Students who believe in Santa Claus can as easily believe in Darth Vader and Freddie Kruger. These same students may have difficulty separating the realities of Desert Storm from fantasy of the media.

Almost every American student is likely to have some personal contact with Desert Storm. If a family member is not involved, a friend or a classmate's father or sister may be. All students need the support of caring adults to help them deal with this crisis.

Emotional Responses—Emotional responses vary in nature and severity from student to student. Students' reactions are determined by their previous experiences, their temperament and personality, and the immediacy of the crisis to their own lives. Nonetheless, some communalities exist in how students (and adults) feel when their lives are impacted by war.

- **Fear:** Fear may be the predominant reaction of many students-fear for the safety of relatives and friends in the military or fear for their own safety. Students' picture of war may include a bomb dropped on their home or school. Their worries may seem unreasonable, but to them, they are quite real. Students may hear many rumors at school and let their imaginations run wild. They may think the worst however unrealistic it may be.

The threat of terrorism may be a reason for students to fear for their personal safety, although statistically the chance of any one student being a victim of terrorism is very remote. Nonetheless, terrorism is one more item students may add to their list of worries.

- **Loss of control:** Military actions are something over which students, and most adults, have no

** Although Operation Desert Storm concluded in 1991, this handout can serve as a model for similar events.

control. Feelings of loss of control can be overwhelming. Students may grasp at any control which they can have.

- **Anger:** Anger is not an unusual reaction. Unfortunately, anger is often expressed to those with whom students are most secure. Students may be angry at parents who are in the military to the extent that they do not want to write letters. Knowing that those who are involved in the military are volunteers only helps to justify anger. Patriotism and duty are abstract concepts, especially for younger students who are experiencing the reality of separation from a loved one.

- **Loss of stability:** War interrupts the natural order of things. Stability is gone, and this is very threatening. It can destroy trust and upset equilibrium. After all, if this war can happen, then most anything else might also happen.

- **Isolation:** Students who have a family member involved in Desert Storm but do not live on or near a military installation may experience feelings of isolation. If a student's parents are reserve members called to active duty, he or she may be the only one in the school or class who is directly impacted by the crisis. That student may feel jealous of other students and their undisturbed families and may strike out at signs of normalcy around them.

Another group of students who may feel isolated are dependents of military families who have accompanied a remaining parent back to a hometown or who are staying with relatives while both parents are gone. Not only do these students experience separation from parents, but they also experience the loss of friends, teachers, and surroundings with which they were familiar.

What Can I Do As A Teacher?

- When in doubt about what to do, always be honest with students. There is never an absolute right thing to say or do. When in doubt, be honest.

- Help students put their fears in perspective.

- Acknowledge the sanctity of each human life while letting students know that the chance of any one individual returning from the Middle East is very high. Death rates in U.S. conflicts have steadily dropped from the time of the Revolutionary War to a low of 0.5% in the Vietnam War. With increases in technology and medical advances, military statisticians suggest a potential loss ratio of 0.3% from battle and 0.1% from other causes in the Middle East.

- Help students to feel personally safe. One of these techniques may help:

  - Using proportions from a map, make a human map. Have some students stand where Iraq, Saudi Arabia, and other Middle East countries are, let others represent European countries, and have some represent the United States.

  - Discuss the distances and how long they take to travel. Even high school students may profit from an activity such as this.

  - Discuss what is realistic modern technology versus science fiction. Help students to understand that the longest range missile that Iraq has can barely reach Israel. Discuss how far Iraqi war planes can fly without refueling (about 1000 miles) and the impossibility of refueling anywhere between Iraq and the United States. Let students share their fears, such as Iraq's converting a plane to carry enough fuel to get to the United States, and put them in perspective as to what is realistic.

  - Help students understand that precautions are being taken to prevent terrorism (e.g. bomb sniffing dogs, passport checks, increased airport security) which might actually make them safer now than they usually are.

  - Deal with fears such as Desert Storm may be the beginning of the end of the world as some have predicted based on Revelations or other religious teachings, or that bombs will reach the local community, which may originate from playground rumors.

- Allow students to express feelings. For a class that has numerous students directly involved, a special time might be set aside regularly to discuss feelings and issues. For a class with less direct involvement, specific students might need extra time to talk with you or with the school psychologist or guidance counselor. You might also put families within your school who are directly involved in contact with each other.

- Consider initiating some values clarification activities. Students may need help identifying what they individually believe about war and the role the United States has chosen in this conflict. Questions such as "Could my parent shoot someone and how do I feel about that?" and "How can anyone shoot an Iraqi soldier who is only 12-13-no older than I?" are the types of issues which may need discussion.

- Help students to feel a sense of control by taking some action.

  - Send letters or cookies to those in the military.
  - Initiate a flag flying project where students develop community participation in flying flags until the crisis is resolved.
  - Put together a volunteer babysitting network through which older students sit for families where parents are away.
  - Ask students to think about the men and women in the Middle East prior to the Pledge of Allegiance or involve them in an additional patriotic activity.

- Involve students in planning how to cope. Control and ownership are fostered when students help to plan strategies for dealing with a situation. Students often have practical and creative ideas for coping.

- Be careful not to stereotype or demean the Iraqi people. Children can easily generalize negative statements and develop prejudice.

- Pay special attention to students who may feel isolated. If only one student in a class has a parent who is involved, others can make that student feel special for awhile by attending to their feelings and needs. If a student has relocated because of separation from parent(s), set up a network of others to get the new student involved.

- Identify support services for students and families needing assistance beyond what can be provided in school. Try contacting mental health agencies or local churches and synagogues.

- Be sensitive to financial strains which war might exacerbate. If a civilian parent is placed on active duty, his/her salary may drop. If many military personnel are deployed from an area, support jobs such as waitresses or cashiers may be at risk due to decreased business.

Part VII

Fact Sheets

Fact Sheet

Adopted Children at School*

Introduction

Adoption as a way of building families is a positive and effective response to needs and issues for all the participants: for the birth parent or agency seeking a plan for the raising of a child in a permanent home, for the child in need of a family, and for potential parents for whom parenting through adoption can contribute to fulfillment of hopes for their family. In the majority of cases adoptions lead to positive outcomes. Nearly 80% will do well and make successful adaptations without special interventions. It is, however, clear from data on a number of factors in adoptive family life, child development, educational, behavioral and emotional adaptation, and utilization of health and human services that growing up adopted is a process that has major impact on personal and family experience. Adoptive family life is by its very nature complicated and different in ways that may require special support and attention at multiple points to reduce developmental risks and to enhance the likelihood of the most positive outcomes. It is important to recognize that children who have been adopted have unique experiences that can contribute to risks and vulnerabilities.

Adoptive families' needs for competent services often are not met by traditional child and family serving systems, programs, and services. Surprisingly, the training of human service professionals does not routinely include experiences that provide knowledge and skills relevant to the particular needs and issues of adoptive families. Social work training often includes preparation for work regarding adoptive placement and legalization procedures, but seldom extends to clinical training for recognizing or dealing with the extended adjustment to adoption-related issues that continue throughout the lifespan. Psychologists have seldom been exposed to adoption issues in their training.

Well developed sensitivity to the special issue of adoptive families and children and specialized psychological, social, educational, developmental, behavioral and mental health services, which are not readily identifiable or accessible for many families, will be needed if we are to meet the needs of this growing population. Adoption is extraordinarily common and is a pattern being extended to provide for children with increasingly diverse and intense needs, from varied backgrounds and with a broadening range of potential or current handicapping conditions. School personnel can be very helpful in increasing sensitivity to adoption issues and reducing stress for children. This article surveys some of the major issues for adoptive families and offers some guidelines for school responses to the needs of adopted children.

Target population and Indicators of adoption as a risk factor

It is estimated that 2% of the U.S. population are adopted people. In comparison with their representation in the general population, adopted children and families are heavier than average

* Authored by Susan E. Erbaugh, Ph.D., Chief of Psychology and Clinical Director, Minneapolis Children's Medical Center, MN.

consumers of mental health and related services. Recent surveys indicate that 8% to 10% of outpatient child and adolescent mental health visits and up to 20% of inpatient bed utilization in inpatient child and adolescent psychiatric units and residential treatment centers involve young people who have been adopted. In general population surveys, 10% to 15% of children and teens have symptoms indicating mental health service needs; among adopted youth these figures rise to a range of from 20% to 25%. There are some suggestions that adoptive families may have the resources and inclination to utilize mental health services more frequently and both adoption and the use of such services are correlated with socioeconomic status. However, other data sources also support the impression that there are increased risks for psychological and developmental problems among adopted children, as compared to peers living with birth families under otherwise similar circumstances.

Research on the symptoms of adopted children referred to mental health services suggests a variety of patterns of emotional, behavioral, and learning disturbances (Brodzinsky & Schechter, 1990). Studies of adopted children receiving clinical service have indicated increased rates of Attention Deficit-Hyperactivity Disorder (Dalby et al., 1982; Deutsch et al.), academic achievement problems (Brodzinsky, et al., 1984), personality, "character", conduct, and behavior problems (Austad et al., 1978; Brodzinsky et al, 1984; Dalby et al., 1982), and increased vulnerability to depressive mood disorders, suicide risk, severe acting-out behavior, and relationship problems (runaway, school drop-out, alienation from adopted families) in adolescence. Studies with adopted children and adolescents who have never been seen for clinical services also suggest higher levels of behavioral maladjustment, lower levels of academic achievement, and lower levels of social competence than for the general population (Brodzinsky et al., 1987) suggesting greater vulnerability for adopted as compared to non-adopted children.

The vulnerability which may be related to early life experiences is not revealed in symptoms of disturbed adjustment until the school age, but from childhood on, a variety of symptoms occur with higher frequency among adopted children. While there have been a number of descriptions of a postulated "adopted child syndrome" and a good deal of recent attention to the problems of allegedly "unattached children," empirically-based studies (McRoy, Grotevant and Zurcher, 1988) do not confirm the development of a consistent pattern of disturbance among adopted children in general. It appears that some of the inconsistency in findings may be related to failures to differentiate or to control for the effects of age at adoption, life circumstances prior to adoption or qualities of family life following adoption. When the adopted person is an older child, a person from a traumatic or stressful early life, or a child with identified or unrecognized handicaps, the risk for a variety of problems in development is increased. The risk in these situations is, however, not simply related to the fact of adoption.

On a more positive note, some studies of non-clinical samples have not shown greater incidence of adjustment problems among selected groups of adopted children. Studies comparing adjustment of children born into disadvantaged circumstances and adopted into more advantaged homes have shown that these children fare better than their peers who remain in less advantaged circumstances.

In extreme cases, the permanence of an adoption may be disrupted as a result of unresolved mental health issues or interactional problems for children, youth, or family members. The rate of adoption disruptions has increased dramatically in recent years, as more and more "difficult to place" or "special needs" children have been adopted. In 1970, only about 2% of adoptions were disrupted. More recent studies indicate the figure had climbed to about 10% by 1986 (Brodzinsky & Schechter, 1990). While this remains a minority outcome, it testifies to the increasing level of stress upon adoptive families and their children, and to the need for competent and effective intervention to improve the outlook for these children at risk (Barth et al.; Festinger, 1986; Illinois Department of Child and Family Services, 1988; Winkler et al., 1988).

340

Adoption scenarios

There is an increasing range in patterns of adoptive family building, carrying differing levels and types of issues or potential risks. There may be cumulative and interacting risk factors as we deal with adoptions stressed by more complex patterns of genetic, prenatal, early life or psychosocial risk factors preceding an adoption. Early placement into fully informed, well prepared, and supported families minimizes risk and enhances positive outcomes, but the unique experience of adoption plays out in increased rates of developmental and/or behavioral problems in even these relatively advantaged situations. The list below suggests the range of variations, some of which carry attendant risks for successful child and family development:

- Adoption among biological relatives
- Non-relative adoption of healthy same-race newborns
- Adoption of "older children" (after the first 6 months of life)
- Adoption after neglect, deprivation, trauma, physical or sexual abuse
- Adoption with known or unknown genetic risks for medical, developmental, or behavioral/emotional disorders
- Adoption of "special needs" children who have already demonstrated symptoms of handicapping conditions or disorders
- Subsidized adoptions of difficult to place children
- Transracial, international and cross-cultural adoptions
- Open, cooperative, independent, or designated adoptions with varying patterns of access to information and contact with birth parents
- Changing profiles of adoptive parents regarding age, marital status, etc.
- Adoption into non-traditional families, such as very large families, mixed foster, adoptive and birth-child families, international or multicultural families

Potential sources of risk

Several clusters of factors, which work in interaction, need to be taken into account in understanding complications and risks to positive outcomes that may differentiate the developmental course for families with children who are adopted. Current research suggests that multiple factors, in different combinations may be associated with increased risk. Risk factors may arise from:

- Genetic history
- Prenatal environment
- Preplacement history
- Infant/child temperament and individual differences
- Early adaptation of the adoptive family
- Communication about adoption
- Stressful family events after adoption
- Extrafamilial context and social support systems
- Developmental life cycle adaptations of the adoptive family and child

Of course, each of these factors implies positive potential as well as possible risk, and the quality of adoptive family life and developmental outcomes can be enhanced by appropriate efforts to balance recognized risks with experiences that can improve the resilience and coping capacity of children and families. McRoy, Grotevant and Zurcher (1988) describe three clusters contributing to seriously disturbed adjustment: 1) difficult child factors in benign families; 2) marital and parenting problems; and 3) difficult adopted children in troubled or abusive environments. They further note that for some cases, ineffective and conflicting mental health services appeared to have made problems worse rather than better.

Theoretical perspectives on adoption adjustment

Research and service planning in the area of adoption has been guided by a multitude of theoretical contributions which have been reviewed elsewhere (McRoy, Grotevant, & Zurcher, 1988; Winkler et al. 1988). An extensive review of these theoretical perspectives is beyond the scope of this paper, but it is worth noting that a comprehensive understanding of adoption adjustment needs to take into account a broad set of influences of interest to 1) behavioral genetics; 2) attachment and bonding theories; 3) relationship and "goodness of fit" theories; 4) developmental life cycle theories; 5) psychodynamic theories; 6) cognitive and attribution theories; and 7) sociological "adoptive kinship theory" (Kirk, 1984, 1985, 1988).

Developmental issues

Adoption is a life experience that becomes a permanent and recurrent issue in the matrix of life and influences the process and outcome of major psychosocial developmental tasks through the child and family life cycles. Psychosocial vulnerabilities may make themselves particularly evident at times when cognitive and psychosocial development puts the spotlight on certain aspects. Brodzinsky, Singer and Braff (1984) have described the following series of stages of development of adoptees' concepts of the meaning of adoption:

Stage		Concept
0	—	No information, understanding or concern
1	—	Birth and adoption concepts fused (Preschool age)
2	—	Differentiate life/death, birth/adoption (5–7 year olds)
3	—	Concern with *permanence* of adoption (8–9 year olds)
4	—	Interest in *legal* foundation for permanence (10–11 year olds)
5	—	Permanence understand, accepted (12–13 year olds)
6	—	Full comprehension of transfer of parental rights (adolescence)

It is interesting to note that in early elementary school years, the concepts of adoption undergo dramatic and rapid change. This suggests that "telling" about adoption may need to be repeated at successive stages, to allow children to apply their increasingly sophisticated cognitive tools to mastery of the meaning of their life stories. It has been suggested that preoccupation with the dawning awareness of adoption issues may interfere with early school adaptation and achievement and may be a contributor to learning inhibition or achievement problems for some children.

Adolescent identity formation and individuation experiences bring adoption issues to the forefront in some families. Questions or problems may emerge at this time, after a period of apparently positive development. Their appearance does not necessarily mean major trouble is ahead, but may highlight the particular challenges associated with growing up adopted.

Psychosocial issues for adopted children

In the course of child and family development, the stresses associated with adoptive family life may make themselves felt as complications, threats or deviations from the successful accomplishment of normative developmental tasks. While there is no uniform pattern underlying problems in adoption adjustment, the following issues have been described as sensitive (Brodzinsky, 1990; Bourguignon & Watson, 1988; Brinich & Brinich, 1982; Coleman et al., 1988; Grobe, 1986; Kral & Schaffer, 1988; Smith & Miroff, 1981; Sorosky, 1979; Winkler et al., 1988):

- Unresolved grief shared by birth parents, infertile adoptive parents and adopted persons
- Traumatic loss experiences and subsequent vulnerability to later losses or separations
- Concerns about trust, security and attachment
- Lowered feelings of self-esteem and self-worth
- Feelings of guilt, shame or inadequacy shared by parents and children
- Disturbances of self-image, identity
- Sense of isolation, alienation, differentness
- Genealogical bewilderment, rootlessness
- Anger, or resentment toward birth and/or adoptive families and society
- Loss of a sense of power, control over own life
- Sense of rejection and fear of further rejection
- Good parent/bad parent splits and shifting identifications
- Children's changing concept or understanding of adoption and its significance
- Inhibition of curiosity and discomfort with inquiry
- Need to search for birth relatives or origins

Adoptive parent and family issues

Adoptive parents and families as developing systems may also be stressed by factors that can complicate the adjustment and functioning of the parents and their reaction to the challenges of child-rearing. Adoptive parent and family issues may include questions, doubts or conflicts about:

- Secrecy, denial or revelation of history; timing and manner of "telling"
- Rejection, acknowledgment or accentuation of difference related to adoptive family status
- Marital tensions regarding unresolved issues including infertility or adopted decisions
- Attachment, bonding and "claiming" of the child
- Over-protectiveness
- Inhibited parenting capacity
- Parental accountability, aspirations and perfectionism
- Entitlement, ownership issues
- Empathy, "goodness of fit" perceived compatibility
- Sense of belonging, family identity
- Reactions to adolescent sexuality, fertility
- Fears of rejection, abandonment (heightened by searching)
- Family boundary and membership issues
- De-identification among siblings
- Social supports for adoptive family life in the extended family and/or community
- Attributions of conflict or problems to adoption

Sensitivity to adoption issues among school personnel

The comfort level and successful adaptation of adoptive parents and children in the school environment can be enhanced by heightened sensitivity to their issues and feelings. Special consideration of the following may be warranted:

Terminology and the meanings of words. Adoptive families are very "real" and for many adopted children it is the birth parent who is a fantasy figure. Adoptive parents feel very "natural" in their role and these are their "own" children. Children and parents will often prefer to be identified first as children, mothers, fathers, or sisters, without the routine use of prefixes referring to adoptive status. Careful attention to the meanings of the words we choose can go a long way toward welcoming and supporting families built through adoption.

Dealing with cultural and ethnic diversity in inclusive and respectful ways. Adoptive families become, in a sense, minority families, through their choice of this way of family building. Incorporating the differences in individuals and families into classroom and school contexts may require some special preparation and thoughtfulness.

School forms and procedures. Lack of access to some records, prior history, background or health information, changes or differences in names and time lags between placement and final legalization of adoption can create some awkward moments that need to be handled with tact and diplomacy.

Assignments and activities: Some flexibility and consideration of the circumstances with which adopted (as well as foster) families live is needed when approaching "family tree," "roots," autobiography, heredity or ethnic heritage activities, when asking for baby pictures or when probing areas of ancestry or personal history. Adopted children can benefit and participate meaningfully in activities related to their sense of personal historical continuity if their special life circumstances can be acknowledged and accommodated and positive support provided to counter feelings of inadequacy or embarrassment.

Labeling, scapegoating, peer teasing, and negative expectations: Caution is warranted to protect children who have been adopted from prejudicial attitudes and attributions with potentially negative impact on self-esteem.

Adoptive parents as experts, advocates and resources: In the process of preparation for adoptive family life many parents have accumulated an impressive store of information that can be a rich resource to others who care for children. Consider ways to capitalize on their experiences.

Responses to school structures and routines: Some children who have been adopted, and especially those adopted at older ages, may go through periods of unusual sensitivity to issues of constancy and predictability in relationships and routines. Some may react intensely to the absence of a teacher or the presence of a substitute or new staff. Others may have difficulty with transitions and changes or seem to be slow to warm up or to establish close and trusting relationships with adults. All will benefit from attention to esteem and relationship building and to limits and structure that are gentle, firm, fair and consistent.

Roles for the school psychologist

Quality of life and successful adaptation to the school environment for children who have been adopted can be enhanced by the involvement of school psychologists in the familiar and important roles of diagnostician, observer, interpreter, facilitator, family liaison, and referrer. Their resources can be of vital importance in preparing the child, the family and the school for a smooth entry, in anticipating and preventing some rough spots and facilitating collaborative problem-solving. Referral to outside clinical services for these children and their potential as well as current adoptive families may be needed at multiple stages in the process, including, for example, to work with: 1) children in the process of removal or placement away from their birth parents or legal termination of parent rights; 2) children in foster care or other temporary placements who are waiting for placement in permanent families; 3) children or teens at risk who are newly placed with adoptive families in need of support; 4) children, adolescents or families who develop adjustment problems months or years after placement; 5) adolescents struggling with identity confusion or bewilderment about their genetic past; and 6) individuals contemplating or engaged in the process of searching for birth parents or birth children.

In selecting psychotherapists or mental health service resources for adoptive families, it will be important to identify professionals or agencies that are informed and experienced regarding work with adoptive families. Professionals who both know about child development and mental health and appreciate the special features of the adoption experience and the commitments adoptive families have taken on will be the most helpful.

Conclusion

Adoptive family building occupies an important place in the kaleidoscope of patterns of family life, providing for the care and nurturance of children in permanent homes. Awareness of and responsiveness to the particular needs of adopted children and their families must keep pace with the evolving and changing patterns of family building and with the continuing relevance of adoption issues throughout the life cycle. School psychologists are in a pivotal position for recognizing, communicating and responding to the needs of this growing segment of the population of children and youth.

A packet of handout materials of interest to parents, school personnel and others concerned with the special needs of adoptive families and children may be obtained by sending a request and a self-addressed stamped business size envelope to:

> Susan E. Erbaugh, Ph.D.
> School Years Clinic
> Minneapolis Children's Medical Center
> 2525 Chicago Avenue South
> Minneapolis, MN 55404

References

Austad, C. C. and Simmons, T. L.—"Symptoms of adopted children presenting to a large mental health clinic", *Child Psychiatry and Human Development, 9:* 20–27, 1978.

Barth, R. P., Berry, Yoshikami, Goodfield and Carson—"Predicting adoption disruption", *Social Work, 33:* 227–233, 1988.

Blum, L. H.—"When adoptive families ask for help", *Primary Care, 3:* 241–249, 1976.

Bourguignon, Jean-Pierre and Watson, Kenneth W.—*After Adoption: A Manual for Professionals Working with Adoptive Families,* Illinois Department of Children and Family Services, 1988.

Brinich, P. and Brinich, E.—"Adoption and Adaptation", *Journal of Nervous and Mental Diseases, 170*: 489–493, 1982.

Brodzinsky, David M.—"Adjustment to Adoption: A Psychosocial Perspective", *Clinical Psychology Review, 7*: 25–47, 1987.

Brodzinsky, D. M., Radice, C., Huffman, L. and Merkler, K.—"Prevalence of Clinically Significant Symptomotology in a Nonclinical Sample of Adopted and Nonadopted Children", *Journal of Clinical Child Psychology, 16*: 350–356, 1987.

Brodzinsky, D. M., Schechter, D. E., Braff, A. M., and Singer, L. M.—"Psychological and Academic Adjustment in Adopted Children", *Journal of Consulting and Clinical Psychology, 52*: 582–590, 1984.

Brodzinsky, David and Schechter, Marshall D.—*The Psychology of Adoption*, Oxford University Press, New York, 1990.

Coleman, Loren, Tilborn, Karen, Hornby, Helaine and Boggis (Eds), *Working with Older Adoptees*, University of Southern Maine, 1988.

Dalby, J. T., Fox, S. L. and Halsam, R. H.—"Adoption and Foster Care Rates in Pediatric Disorder", *Journal of Developmental and Behavioral Pediatrics, 3*: 61–64, 1982.

Deutsch, C. K., Swanson, J. M., Bruell, J. H., Cantwell, D. P., Weinberg, F. and Baren, M. — "Over-representation of Adoptees in Children with Attention Deficit Disorder", *Behavior Genetics, 12*: 231–238.

Feigelman, William and Silverman, Arnold S. — *Chosen Children: New Patterns of Adoptive Relationships*, New York, Praeger Publishers, 1983.

Festinger, T. — *Necessary Risk: A study of adoptions and disrupted adoptive placements*, Washington, D.C.: Child Welfare League of America, 1986.

Gilman, Lois — *The Adoption Resource Book,* Harper and Row, New York, 1984.

Grobe, Pamela V. (editor) *Adoption Resources for Mental Health Professionals*, Mental Health Adoption Therapy Project, Children's Aid Society, Mercer, PA, 1986.

Illinois Department of Children and Family Services, *Toward Successful Adoption: A study of predictions in special needs placements*, 1989.

Jenista, Jerri Ann and Chapman, Daniel — "Medical Problems of Foreign-Born Adopted Children", *American Journal of Diseases of Children, 14*: 298–302, 1987.

Jewett, Claudia L. — *Adopting the Older Child*, Harvard Common Press, Boston, 1978.

Jewett, Claudia L. — *Helping Children Cope with Separation and Loss*, Harvard Common Press, Boston, 1982.

Kentucky Department of Social Services and Department for Mental Health and Mental Retardation Services, *Meeting the Mental Health Needs of Adoptive Families*, 1988.

Kirk, H. David — *Shared Fate: A Theory and Method of Adoptive Relationship* (revised edition), Ben-Simon Publications, Port Angeles, Washington, 1984.

Kirk, H. David — *Adoptive Kinship: A Modern Institution in Need of Reform* (revised edition), Ben-Simon Publications, Port Angeles, Washington, 1985.

Kirk, H. David — *Exploring Adoptive Family Life: The Collected Adoption Papers of H. David Kirk* (edited by B. J. Tansey, Ben-Simon Publication, Port Angeles, Washington, 1988.

Kral, R. and Schaffer, J. — Treating the adoptive family. In C. Chilman, F. Cos and E. Nunnally (Eds.) *Families in trouble related to alternative life styles*. Milwaukee, Sage Press, 1988.

Kraft, Adrienne D., Palombo, J., Mitchell, M. A., Dean C., Meyers, S., and Schmidt, A. W. — "The Psychological Dimensions of Infertility", *American Journal of Orthopsychiatry, 50:* 618–628, 1980.

McRoy, R. G., Grotevant, H. D. & Zurcher, L. A. — *Emotional disturbance in adopted adolescents:* Origins and development. Praeger, New York, 1988. Adopted Children (Cont.)

Melina, Carl M. and Melina, Lois — "The Family Physician and Adoption", *American Family Physician, 31*: 109–118, 1985.

Smith, Jerome and Miroff, Franklin I. — *You're Our Child: A Social/Psychological Approach to Adoption*, Washington, D.C., University Press of America, 1981.

Sorosky, A. D., Baran, A. and Panno, R. — *The Adoption Triangle*, Garden City, NY, Anchor, 1979.

Spencer, Marietta — "The Terminology of Adoption", *Child Welfare, 58*: 451–459, 1979.

Winkler, Robin C., Brown, Dirck W., VanKeppel, Margaret and Blanchard, Amy — *Clinical Practice in Adoption*, Pergamon Press, New York, 1988.

Fact Sheet

Attention Deficit Hyperactivity Disorder ADHD

1. *What are the diagnostic criteria of attention deficit hyperactivity disorder (ADHD)?*

The following diagnostic criteria were taken from the *Diagnostic and Statistical Manual* (3rd Edition, Revised) of the American Psychiatric Association:

A. A disturbance of at least six months during which at least eight of the following are present:

1. Often fidgets with hands or feet or squirms in seat (in adolescents, may be limited to subjective feelings of restlessness)
2. Has difficulty remaining seated when required to do so
3. Is easily distracted by extraneous stimuli
4. Has difficulty awaiting turn in games or group situations
5. Often blurts out answers to questions before they have been completed
6. Has difficulty following through on instructions from others
7. Has difficulty sustaining attention in tasks or play activities
8. Often shifts from one uncompleted activity to another
9. Has difficulty playing quietly
10. Often talks excessively
11. Often interrupts or intrudes on others
12. Often does not seem to listen to what is being said to him or her
13. Often loses things necessary for tasks or activities at school or at home
14. Often engages in physically dangerous activities without considering possible consequences

B. Onset before age of seven

Diagnosis usually follows from behavior rating scales completed by teachers and parents as well as a professional (such as a school psychologist) conducting formal classroom or home observations. Medical personnel rely on behavior rating scales (such as the one developed by Conners) as well as the input from school personnel. The problem with the definition of ADHD being tied to attentional deficits is that many of the behaviors required for diagnosis are ones that the ADHD child does not always demonstrate. For instance, these children can often sustain attention to high stimulation tasks such as Nintendo and often do well with attention in a one-to-one setting.

2. When are these children identifiable?

50–60% of the children are identifiable by age 2; 90% by age 5. It is rare for the diagnosis to be given, for the first time, after age 6 or 7.

3. Are most of these children identified and do they receive services?

According to Russell Barclay, Ph.D. (University of Mass-Amherst), only 15% of ADHD children actually receive services—85% do not.

4. How do we measure the severity of the problem?

This really varies with the situation. In situations where there is a lot of activity and movement (such as during play or free time), ADHD children are less noticeable and their behavior has less impact on others. The greatest difficulty arises when ADHD children are expected to engage in structured tasks which require self-control and little flexibility in how the task is to be carried out.

Severity is also a function of how much the ADHD interferes with the child meeting the expectancy of others and in how many situations the ADHD interferes (for instance, home, school, church).

5. How do ADHD children differ from non-ADHD children on behavior rating scales?

ADHD children score higher than non-ADHD children on scales measuring impulsivity, aggression, hyperactivity, and ability for self-control.

6. What is the peak age for excessive gross motor activity for ADHD children?

2–3 years of age.

7. What are the early signs of ADHD?

During Infancy: Difficult to care for, difficult temperament, may have sleeping and eating problems, noncompliant.

In Nursery School: Noncompliant and overactive, does not follow rules, verbally and physically aggressive.

In School: Noncompliant, out-of-seat behavior, disruptive, immature, underachieving, has trouble finishing work.

At Home: Noncompliant, cannot be trusted, a conduct problem in the neighborhood.

8. What predicts a poor prognosis for ADHD children in adolescence?

Aggression during childhood, resistance to improving on medication, resistance to psychological and educational interventions, absence of father in active parenting.

9. What are the proposed causes of ADHD?

This is still hotly debated. The causes range from biological variation, hereditary-genetic predisposition to environmental causes.

10. What do we know about the discipline style of families with ADHD who have not received specific training?

Due to the behavior profile of the ADHD child (excessive behavior, demands, etc.) families of ADHD children often demonstrate the following:

- More directive, commanding, more negative, less responsive, and less reinforcing parenting.

These parents are not inadequate individuals. Rather, parenting an ADHD child requires specialized skills which most parents do not have without participating in parent training.

11. What is the most frequent medical treatment for ADHD?

The use of Ritalin (methylphenidate). The effects of the medication are in the following areas:

—Increased attention span and concentration
—Decreased impulsivity
—Decreased task-irrelevant activity
—Decreased aggressiveness
—Increased compliance
—Improved handwriting
—Improved peer relations

Ritalin will not automatically increase achievement in school nor will it increase a child's IQ.

What are the side-effects of Ritalin?

—Decreased appetite
—Some insomnia
—Irritability—particularly in the afternoon
—Prone to crying
—Increased restlessness—particularly in the late evening
—Motor Tics—in less than 5% of the cases

3% of ADHD children fail to tolerate any dosage of stimulant medication

Other stimulant medications used include Cylert and D-amphetamine

12. Do ADHD children have other handicapping conditions in addition to ADHD?

- Approximately 30% of ADHD children are also identified as learning disabled
- There is a 70% overlap between ADHD children and a diagnosis of conduct problems. Approximately 2/3 of ADHD children have conduct problems at home and approximately 1/2 have identified conduct problems at school.

13. What treatment components are always necessary in treating ADHD?

AT HOME:

- Parent Training
- Home-Based Reinforcement Methods

- Training in self-control and impulsivity reduction
- Training positive social behaviors

STRUCTURING THE CLASSROOM FOR SUCCESS:

- Increase the frequency of consequences
- Increase the immediacy of consequences
- Make classroom rules more apparent
- Utilize the "Think Aloud-Think Ahead" technique
- Involve home-based consequences where possible
- Coordinate parent training programs with in-class methods

ADHD Children are about 35% behind developmentally in their ability to handle the pace and format of school work (this does not mean the level of work). Therefore:

- 4th grade material should be presented at about the 2nd grade level in terms of the amount of work given at one time, the amount of prompts needed (e.g., using a self-instruction card on the child's desk, using non-verbal gestures, displaying a list of rewarding activities, etc.).
- *Direct Instruction* should be provided by the teacher at least 30-45 minutes per day.
- Incomplete school work should not be sent home. Homework, however, is OK.
- ADHD children should be allowed to move about, to stand by their desks (etc.) if this is necessary to facilitate the completion of school work.
- Instruction that uses alot of participation should be used.
- Time limits (e.g., using a wall clock, a timer, etc.) should be verbalized and used

In the 1st and 2nd grade, the average attention span is 2 1/2 to 3 minutes. This increases with age, but ADHD children will always lag by about 30% when compared to agemates.

High School ADHD students need a "case manager" that the student can meet with at the beginning of the day, once during the day, and at the end of the day for organization and follow-up.

14. *Additional Information*

The Supreme Court of California recently ruled that ADHD is a disability under Section 504 of the Vocational Rehabilitation Act, the civil rights act for the handicapped.

Model School Programs

June Swanson-Department of Pediatrics
    University of California-Irvine
    School for ADHD

Houston Public Schools
    contact: Ben Williams

A great deal of the information in this fact sheet was taken from the work of Russell Barclay—either through workshops or his text: *Hyperactive Children.* Information was also taken from the work of Alan Kazdin.

Fact Sheet

Bullying

1. *What is the definition of a "bully?"*

A bully is a child who often oppresses or harasses somebody else. His or her target may be boys or girls, and the harassment may be physical or mental. Bullies are usually boys, although girl bullies do exist.

2. *Who do bullies oppress or harass?*

Bullies oppress or harass individuals whom we can call "victims." A victim is a child who for a fairly long time has been and still is exposed to aggression from others; that is, boys or possibly girls from the child's own class or maybe from other classes often pick fights and are rough with them or tease and ridicule them. Two types of "victims" emerge:

- *"Passive Victims"* are anxious, insecure, and appear to do nothing to invite attacks and fail to defend themselves.
- *"Provocative Victims"* are hot-tempered, restless, and create tension by irritating and teasing others and attempt to fight back when attacked.

3. *What are some basic facts about the bully problem?*

- —Approximately one in seven school children is either a bully or a victim.
- —This affects approximately 5,000,000 elementary and junior high school students in the United States.
- —Approximately 282,000 students are physically attacked in America's secondary schools each month.
- —An estimated 525,000 attacks, shakedowns, and robberies occur in an average month in public secondary schools.
- —In a typical month about 125,000 secondary school teachers (12 percent) are threatened with physical harm and approximately 5200 actually are physically attacked.
- —**Almost 8 percent of urban junior and senior high school students miss at least one day of school each month because they are afraid to attend.**

4. *Why do some children and adolescents become bullies?*

There is no "one" reason why a child might become a bully. However, we do know what types of circumstances will likely help a child develop bully behavior. Bully behavior is developed mainly as a result of factors in the environment. This environment includes the home, the school and the peer group. *Bully behavior is learned*. The good news is that because the bully behavior is learned, it can be unlearned, particularly if we do something about it when children are young.

5. *What factors in the environment will likely contribute to a child becoming a bully?*

—**Too little supervision of children and adolescents.** Without supervision, children do not get the message that aggressive behavior is the wrong behavior to have.

—**Bullying pays off.** Many children learn at a very young age that when they bully their brother, sister or parents that they get what they want. Often we are too busy or too tired to "fight" with the child so we just give in. Each time we give in when the child is aggressive or just plain obnoxious, we are giving the child the message that **bullying pays off.**

—**Do as I say, not as I do.** Some children seem more likely to imitate adult aggressive, bullying behavior than other children. In some families, when children are punished for aggressive behavior (even if they see it in their home), they stop being aggressive. For most children, however, if they see aggressive behavior they will imitate it. When parents fight and one parent intimidates the other and "wins," then the child gets the message that intimidation gets you what you want.

—**Harsh, physical punishment.** Although spanking a child will often put a stop to the child's behavior, spanking that is too harsh, too frequent, or too physical teaches a child that it is OK to hit other people. In particular, this teaches a child that it is OK for bigger people (parents) to hit little people (children). Bullies usually pick on younger, smaller, or weaker children. They model, in their physical attacks, what happened to them personally in the home. The worst thing that can be done is to physically punish a bully for bully behavior.

—**Peer groups that supports bully behavior.** Many parents do not know what their children are doing with the peer group. Their child may be running with other children who advocate bully behavior. In order for the child to "fit in," the child must bully like the peers.

—**Getting more negative than positive messages.** Children who develop bully behavior feel that the world around them (home, school, neighborhood) is more negative than positive. These children have more negative comments (get yelled at, they are told that they are wrong) given to them than positive comments. They expect the world to be negative with them so they attack first. By picking on others, they feel more important and powerful. If they cannot feel important because parents and teachers make positive comments and "reinforce" them, then they will feel important in negative ways.

—**Poor self-concept.** Children who get more negative comments given to them than positive ones will develop a poor self-concept. These children then believe that the only way to be "accepted" is to pick on others.

—**Expecting hostility.** Because of the negative messages received and the poor self-concept, bullies **expect** their parents, teachers and peers to pick on them, blame them or otherwise humiliate them. Therefore, they attack before they are attacked, even when in reality they are not about to be attacked. They assume hostility when none exists. In many ways, the bully's philosophy is, **"The best defense is offense."**

6. *Are there specific school factors that relate to bullying behavior?*

Yes. Among the specific school factors currently known are the following:

—Larger schools report a greater percentage of violence.

- Schools with clear rules of conduct enforced by the principal report less violence.
- Schools with students that report fair discipline practices report less violence.
- Small class size relates to less violence.
- Schools where students indicate the relevance of school to their lives report less violence.
- Schools where students mention that they are in control of their lives report less violence.
- A principal who appears to be ineffective or invisible to students reports more violence in that school.
- Schools with principals that provide opportunities for the teachers and students to be participatory members of decision-making report less violence.
- Cohesiveness among teaching staff and principal relate to less violence.

7. *Why do some children and adolescents become victims?*

Less is really known about "victims" but there is some information which will help us understand the victim situation to some extent:

- Most victims are anxious, sensitive, and quiet.
- Victims generally do not have many, if any, good friends at school.
- Victims seem to signal to others that they are insecure and worthless children who will not retaliate if they are attacked or insulted.
- Bullies often target children who complain, appear physically weak, seek attention from peers and adults, and seem emotionally weak.
- These children may be overprotected by parents and school personnel and are therefore unable to develop coping skills on their own.

8. What can be done about the problem?

IN GENERAL:

1. A strong commitment is needed in the home and school to change the behavior. Parents need support from school and mentalhealth/community workers to enforce positive behavior patterns. *Parent training is essential.*

2. Specific training is needed in the social skills that the child lacks to get along with other children. This can be done in school through social skills training and in the home through increased supervision, more positive discipline, and modeling.

3. Increase, significantly, the amount of positive feedback that the child gets in the home and the school.

4. The pattern of bullying begins at an early age—as early as age 2. Early intervention is essential. The older the child becomes, the more difficult change will be. After age 8-10, change is very difficult.

5. Develop a strong value system in the home and in the school that gives a clear message that bully behavior is completely unacceptable.

SPECIFIC THINGS TO DO IN THE HOME

1. If you have a serious bully or victim problem, contact the school psychologist in your child's school building and ask for help. In the meantime, the steps immediately below will significantly help the problem.

2. Be sure that you are being as positive as possible with your child. Shoot for 5 positive comments for every negative one that you direct to your child. You will have to work very hard and **"Catch them being good."**

3. Do not use physical punishment. Instead, use removal of privileges, time spent in their bedroom, work tasks around the house, or helping younger children in the neighborhood or in the home as a consequence for bully behavior.

4. When you see your (or another) child engaging in bully behavior, put a stop to the behavior immediately and have the child practice a more appropriate behavior instead. For instance, if you have a child who pushes his sister away from a toy in order to play with it, have the child practice (at least 3 times) asking for (and receiving) the toy the correct way.

5. If the child is a victim, have the child practice telling the bully to "Stop bothering me" and then have the child walk away. The parent should be there to supervise the behavior of the bully and the victim.

6. Parents must model, or show, the children in the home behavior between adults or between adults and children that is not bully behavior. If the children see parents yelling and bullying each other or if this is how the parent talks to the children, then the children will do that behavior as well. Remember to operate from the, "Do as I say and as I do" point of view.

7. Supervision is of great importance. If you can, supervise the situations in which your child will have the opportunity to become either a bully or victim. If you cannot supervise the children under those circumstances, try to find someone who can. If you cannot supervise and cannot find someone, then do not allow the child to participate in that situation.

SPECIFIC THINGS TO DO IN THE SCHOOL SETTING

1. Establish a school climate that clearly and emphatically disapproves of bullying. This can be accomplished through school-wide campaigns (including contests, posters, parties, dances, school events) that support behaviors which are the opposite of bullying. These behaviors can include "buddy systems," cooperative learning, peer tutoring, big brother-big sister programs, and others.

2. Establish a climate in which rules of conduct are enforced and are developed by the students and teachers cooperatively.

3. Discipline practices should emphasize restitution and positive practice rather than expulsion, paddlings, and humiliation. That is, when students are caught bullying they should apologize, demonstrate the correct behavior, and then have to spend a specified period of time helping (public service) younger, less able children.

4. Teachers and administrators should work on increasing the number of positives directed toward children on a daily basis. The ratio, just as in the home, should be approximately 5 positives for each negative. Teachers must "Catch them being good." This may be difficult but the teacher will have to give positives for behaviors they usually take for granted. The situation may occur where the teacher will have to "set up" a situation in order to give positives. This might include sending an older "bully" to a younger class in order to help a particular student with an academic exercise. The "bully" can then receive recognition for this behavior.

5. In classrooms where there are a number of students with the "bully" problem, the use of social skills training sessions throughout the year may be necessary. If the teacher is unfamiliar with these skill training sessions, a call to the school psychologist can help with materials and technical assistance.

6. On a building level, the establishment of a "discipline" committee is suggested. The purpose of the committee would be to identify the five top discipline problems in the school and to develop intervention plans that will be implemented regardless of where in the school the problem behavior occurred. The discipline measures should emphasize restitution and positive practice, not physical punishment, exclusion or humiliation.

7. Although it is very difficult to justify, "bullies" should not be removed from the school setting unless absolutely necessary. The teaching of social skills, the value campaign against bully behavior, and the increased number of positives directed toward bullies for appropriate behavior are more productive, in the long run, than exclusion.

The above are only examples of where to begin thinking about and acting on the problem. Listed below are resources for both parents and teachers.

9. *Resources for Parents and Teachers*

PARENTS

- Available from: The National School Safety Center, Pepperdine University, Malibu, California 90265

    1. *School Crime and Violence: Victims' Rights*
    2. *Student and Staff Victimization*

- Available from: Research Press, Box 3177, Department S, Champaign, IL 61826, (217) 352-3273

    1. *Living with Children: New Methods for Parents and Teachers* by Gerald R. Patterson.
    2. *Parents are Teachers: A Child Management Program* by Wesley C. Becker

TEACHERS

The information below also is available from Research Press (see above):

1. *Skillstreaming the Elementary School Child* and *Skillstreaming the Adolescent* by Dr. Arnold Goldstein and colleagues.
2. *Aggression Replacement Training* by Dr. Arnold Goldstein and Dr. Barry Glick.
3. *The Prepare Curriculum: Teaching Prosocial Competencies* by Dr. Arnold Goldstein
4. *Getting Along With Others* by Nancy F. Jackson, Dr. Donald A. Jackson, and Cathy Monroe

NATIONAL
ASSOCIATION OF
SCHOOL
PSYCHOLOGISTS

Fact Sheet

Divorce and Our Children

1. *Prevalence*

—The divorce rate in the U.S. has tripled since 1960, although it declined somewhat in the 1980's.

—In 1989, 1,186,000 divorces were documented in the U.S.

—Almost half of the children born in the last decade will experience the divorce of their parents.

—Because 75-80% of divorced parents remarry, and the divorce rate for remarriages is higher than for first marriages, many children will experience divorce more than once.

2. *What do we know about the effects of divorce on children?*

—A small number of comprehensive studies completed so far show that divorce has potential long-term impact on children's development and adjustment (especially for boys) in all settings.

—Divorce has been related to:

increased anxiety
aggressiveness, noncompliance, and acting-out
poorer social skills
reduced academic achievement
a higher likelihood of grade retention
a higher likelihood of referral for psychological services
difficulties in peer and other interpersonal relationships

3. *What factors affect children's reaction to divorce?*

A. *Age of the child*

—*Infants'* reactions to divorce are closely tied to the emotional status and adjustment of their primary caregiver (usually the mother). Care must be taken to assure that the emotional and physical environment of an infant remains reasonably intact during and after the divorce.

—*Preschoolers*, with intellectual and language skills still emerging, may show stronger emotional reactions than younger or older children (for example, anxiety, nightmares, eating disturbances, bedwetting) because they misinterpret the reasons for their parents' separation (self-blame) or cannot express their feelings.

—*School-age* children may show signs of:

depression
withdrawal

fear

fantasies that they were responsible for the divorce

hopes for reconciliation

anger

shame

a strong need for explanations

conflicts over their loyalties to parents

decreased academic and social performance

There is some debate regarding whether more negative outcomes are seen with younger or older school-age children.

—*Adolescents* may react with:

more problems in interpersonal relationships

concerns about their *own* potential for successful marriage

shame and embarrassment

problems with independence issues

—Some experts believe adolescents can be more severely affected than younger children because they are exposed to more parent conflict.

B. *Sex of child*

—Boys experience far more problems than girls in the areas of social-emotional and academic development following divorce. These problems are most prevalent from 1st through 7th-grade.

C. *Length of time since divorce*

—Many factors other than the mere passage of time affect children's adjustment to divorce, but, in general, children may reach a good level of adjustment in 2 to 4 years assuming that other major life changes don't occur (e.g., remarriage of a parent).

4. *What factors facilitate children's adjustment to divorce?*

At home:

—minimal financial loss and changes in the standard of living for the custodial parent and children

—availability of family and community support systems

—lower levels of conflict and hostility between divorced parents

—agreement on and consistency of child-rearing and discipline practices between divorced parents (especially if a warm, but firm and predictable authoritative style is used)

—frequent, consistent, quality contact between children and noncustodial parent—arranged before the divorce

—openness in the family emotional climate for discussion of divorce and related issues in language appropriate for the child's age

At school:

—a safe and orderly classroom environment

—continued high expectations for performance

—maintaining students' time on task

—frequent monitoring of student progress and rewards for progress

—counseling support as needed or desired

—good home-school communication

5. *How can school psychologists and other mental health professionals help to facilitate children's adjustment following divorce*

—Despite the general research, not all children experience major adjustment problems during and after divorce. Professionals can help parents distinquish between normal, developmentally-related behaviors and problems associated with the stress and emotional upheaval of divorce that may require intervention.

—If divorce is imminent, school and community mental health professionals can help parents be aware of, and maximize, conditions that help children cope (for example, agreeing on consistent child-rearing and discipline methods, providing frequent and consistent visitation with the noncustodial parent, learning how to talk to a child about divorce).

—School psychologists can help to coordinate efforts between the home and school so behavioral problems are handled in a clear and consistent manner. They also can inform teachers and other school personnel about the possible effects of divorce on children at different age levels. Teachers can learn to identify signs and symptoms in students so mental health resources can be made available.

—Community mental health services offer an array of programs for crisis intervention; social skills training; parent training; brief counseling for children and adults involved in divorce; child, parent, and family support groups; community education programs dealing with divorce; and interagency coordinating services.

For more information and resources:

Gardner, R. A. (1970). *The boys and girls book about divorce.* New York: Bantam Books.

Gardner, R. (1977). *The parents book about divorce.* New York: Doubleday.

Glass, S. M. (1980). *A divorce dictionary: A book for you and your children.* Boston: Little, Brown.

Goldstein, S., & Solnit, A. J. (1984). *Divorce and your child.* New Haven: Yale University Press.

Majid, K., & Screibman, W. (1980). *Divorce is . . . a kid's coloring book.* Gretna, LA: Pelican.

Stein, S. B. (1979). *On divorce: An open family book for parents and children together.* New York: Walker.

Salk, L. (1978). *What every child would like parents to know about divorce.* New York: Harper and Row.

NATIONAL
ASSOCIATION OF
SCHOOL
PSYCHOLOGISTS

Fact Sheet

School Dropouts:
Reasons and Responses

1. *Prevalence*

It is difficult to estimate accurately the number of school dropouts because of widely varying definitions and methods for counting dropouts. Various surveys have differed in how long students remained truant before being considered a dropout, which age and grade groups were included, whether special groups (for example, special education, G.E.D.) were included, and whether steps were taken to eliminate students who moved or to include students who dropped out over the summer.

Considering the above complications, the best overall estimate is that 15 to 30% of students in the U.S. drop out before graduating from high school. This is an improvement over the turn-of-the-century rate of 90% and distressing when compared to the Japanese dropout rate of only 7%.

2. *What are the personal and societal consequences of school dropout?*

The negative repercussions for students who drop out of school are significant, and include:

—High unemployment rates
—Low income and lifetime earnings
—Low cognitive growth

The indirect repercussions for society are even more significant:

—Lowered tax revenues
—High overall unemployment
—High welfare payments
—Increased crime

It is estimated that billions of dollars per year are spent in the U.S. to solve problems directly or indirectly associated with school dropout.

3. *Are there characteristics of students that can be identified early which may predict the potential for school dropout?*

Yes, there are a number of factors that tend to cluster together which can be grouped into six categories:

A. Demographic factors

—Ethnic minorities (other than Asian)
—Males more than females
—Lives in urban, rather than suburban or rural, setting

B. Social and family factors

—Low socioeconomic status
—From single-parent families
—Low educational/motivational support at home

C. Personality factors

—Low self-concept
—Tendency to blame problems on factors other than self
—Low need for self-improvement

D. Early transition into adulthood

—Experience a teen pregnancy
—Married
—Have a job

E. Deviant behavior

—Become institutionalized or incarcerated
—Involved in delinquent acts
—Use drugs

F. In-school factors

—Low academic achievement and grades
—Low IQ
—Reading problems
—Retained one or more times
—Older than grade peers
—Behavior problems in school
—Poor attendance rate
—Poor social skills

It should be apparent that many of these factors are highly related to each other and may not act individually to influence dropping out of school.

4. *Are there characteristics of schools that may influence dropout rates which have the potential for correction?*

Yes. These factors are, again, highly related to each other and may act in concert or individually to influence student decision-making. They include:

—Weak administrative leadership

—Low levels of empowerment experienced by staff

—Low rates of time actually engaged in instruction

—Ability grouping of students

—Misuse of standardized tests

—Overcrowding in schools

—Low attendance rates

—High failure rates

—Poor discipline standards and disorder

—Increased performance standards without additional support/staff resources

5. *How early can school dropout be predicted?*

Fairly accurate prediction can be achieved, especially for boys, as early as the seventh grade. Seventh graders, who show some of the characteristics in the categories above, are aggressive and tend to associate with older children who have already dropped out or who are themselves at-risk for dropping out.

6. *What can schools, parents, and professionals do to reduce or prevent school dropout?*

Most dropout programs used in schools today are preventive programs designed to identify dropout-prone students early and keep them in school. Other programs are re-entry programs for students who have already dropped out.

Dropout prevention programs usually have a number of components that may include combinations of the following approaches:

• Instructional and Academic Approaches

—Individualized instruction

—Flexible curriculum and school hours

—Basic skills and school social skills instruction

—Small class sizes and low student/teacher ratios

—Alternative education programs and settings

• Employment and Economic Incentives

—Vocational education tracks

—Employment preparation and job training

—Job search services

—Community work experiences

—Financial incentives to stay in school

• Personal and Affective Approaches

—Counseling for personal development and self-esteem building

—Peer support mentors and tutors (or at-risk students as tutors)

—Staff training to act as mentors and supporters

- Social Services Approaches

    —Health care and family planning
    —Prenatal guidance, parent support, and childcare
    —Family intervention/involvement
    —Parent training

Most comprehensive programs recruit support from community businesses and social agencies. No systematic evaluations have been conducted to determine which combinations of approaches are most effective. The best evidence suggests that both work experience and classroom training should be provided for the most success.

Given the long list of possible causes of and influences on school dropout, programs should be designed to meet the needs of specific groups.

Fact Sheet

Summarizing the Important Elements of Early Childhood Primary Prevention Programs for Emotional and Behavioral Problems

Primary Prevention programs are programs that deliver services to an entire group of individuals (e.g., children) in order to prevent specific problems *before they have a chance to occur.*

Primary prevention programs for infants and preschoolers have demonstrated their effectiveness both in decreasing children's long-term mental health problems and in decreasing later financial burdens for families, communities, and society. When discussing the impact of primary prevention on children's emotional and behavioral problems, it is important to discuss successful programs *and the components/activities* that make those programs successful. This fact sheet will summarize the effective components of American and Canadian primary prevention programs focusing on infants and preschoolers as summarized by the Ontario Ministry of Community and Social Services in its 1989 technical report, *Better Beginnings, Better Futures*.

Primary Prevention Programs

Relative to programs focusing on children's emotional and behavioral problems, primary prevention programs should have at least three goals:

- Reduce the incidence of serious, long-term emotional and behavioral problems in children;
- Promote the optimal social, emotional, behavioral and cognitive development in those children at highest risk for such problems; and
- Strengthen the ability of communities to respond effectively to the social and economic needs of children and their families.

In addition such programs should follow four objectives:

- To provide all children with a favorable environment in which to develop;
- To assist the family in support of the child, by a) providing opportunities for parent(s) to enhance their competencies and confidence in their role as parent(s), and b) reducing stressful family environments, thereby strengthening the family;
- To promote cooperative efforts between any new program and existing community services and resources whose mandate involves children and families; and

- To provide a context for long-term research which evaluates the effectiveness of primary prevention with children.

Infant Programs

After evaluating a number of primary prevention programs for infants, the following program design and program components were identified as present in "good programs":

1. *Program Design*

    a. High Risk. The program should be provided in a circumscribed geographic area with a concentration of risk indicators.

    b. Accessibility. To avoid stigmatization, the program should be open to all pregnant women within a high risk community.

    c. Appeal. The program should reach and appeal to those at highest risk (e.g., poor, teenage, no family support).

    d. Community involvement. The program should involve the community, where possible, in all phases of development and implementation: delineating needs, recruiting participants, designing and implementing the program.

    e. Developmental approach. The program should empody a developmental approach in design, planning and implementation, recognizing the stages of the family life cycle and child development.

    f. Focus. The program should focus on promoting the optimum development of the child (e.g., physical, socio-emotional, cognitive, communicative) and promoting the continued development of the parents.

    g. Continuity. The program should provide temporal continuity and be delivered primarily through the family, beginning early in pregnancy and continuing through infancy to school age.

    h. Flexibility. The program design should be flexible and have the capability to respond to the changing needs of the child, family and community.

    i. Sensitivity. The services should be delivered in a manner that is sensitive to the social and cultural diversity of families.

2. *Program Components*

    a. Health care. There should be an emphasis on both maternal and child health including regular pre-natal care from the first trimester, nutrition counseling, life style counseling; regular infant health assessment, screening and counselling regarding infant feeding, health hazards and safety.

    b. Home visits. Home visits which begin with the prenatal period and continue through the first two years are valuable not only for the teaching of parenting skills and for counselling but also as an outreach mechanism.

    c. Good quality alternate child care. (e.g., day care, relief care). This type of care, if implemented so it does not interfere with the development of emotional ties within the family, can facilitate parental employment or schooling or access to better invironmental stimulation for the young child.

    d. Family support. This type of program component should focus on: parents' basic needs (e.g., housing, food, employment), socio-emotional needs (transition issues, crises) and educational needs (as individuals or as a couple); development of problem-solving skills;

enhancement of parental self-esteem, empowerment and the development of natural support systems.

    e. Linkages. The facilitation of access to other needed health, social, educational, recreational resources and the establishment of a collaborative network of service providers are important considerations in programming for infants and their families.

Effective infant programs evidenced a number of short-term and long-term effects. Short-term positive effects included:

CHILDREN:

- better physical health (less chronic illness; fewer disabilities);
- better nutrition provided by parents;
- fewer low birth weight babies;
- fewer feeding problems;
- fewer accidents and less need for emergency hospital use;
- less abuse by parents.

PARENTS:

- better networks of social support;
- greater confidence;
- improvement in parenting skills;
- less decline in the quality of marital relationships;
- better parent-child interactions;
- less abuse of children;
- longer spacing between pregnancies;
- more frequent, appropriate use of other services.

Long-term positive effects include:

CHILDREN:

- less hostility, impulsiveness and distractibility in school;
- less delinquency;
- better attitudes toward school;
- better socio-emotional functioning in school;
- higher rates of pro-social attitudes and cooperativeness;

PARENTS:

- more registration in school by mothers;
- more high school completion by mothers;
- higher rates of employment in the family.

In addition, programs with the greatest impact had:

- multiple components (e.g., home visits, parent-support groups, plus day care or nursery school), and were of a
- long-duration (e.g., two to five years).

Almost all good programs began pre-natally. And, home visits were a major component of most of the programs.

Pre-school Programs

After evaluating a number of primary prevention programs for preschool-aged children, the following components were identified as present in "good programs:"

1. *Program Design*

   - Available for a minimum of two years.
   - A 'holistic' approach to the child and family.
   - Flexible and open to change to meet the child and family's needs as they become apparent.
   - Emphasizing health and education, rather than pathology.
   - Well-developed curricula, with clearly stated goals, carefully implemented and thoroughly evaluated. The content of the program is not as important as how it is done.
   - An emphasis on meeting the developmental needs of the preschool child, including programming to encourage independence, self-esteem, effective problem-solving skills, attention and task persistence.
   - Community needs assessment and cooperation of the community in program design and development.
   - Planning, in collaboration with existing resources in the community, to avoid overlapping services and to promote collaboration.
   - Integrated with other helping resources and services in health, housing, education, social assistance and employment.
   - Continuity from infant programs to preschool programs, and from preschool programs to primary school programs.
   - A reasonably complex and well-designed evaluation.

2. *Program Components*

   - A child-parent drop-in center, available on the same premises and linked to the program so parents can be comfortable coming with their other younger children or with their preschoolers when they are not in their designated time in the program.
   - Parent support and the opportunity for time away from the children.
   - Responsiveness to the needs of 'special' children, and the ability to integrate them into the program (with consultation from appropriate outside agencies).
   - Promotion of family involvement without requiring it. Family involvement must be seen as non-threatening.
   - Relevance of programs for economically disadvantaged families, e.g., employment support and literacy, as well as parent/child training.

3. *Program Implementation*

   - Open year round, and involving an outdoor summer program.
   - A flexibly arranged full and half day program.
   - Qualified staff, experienced in their areas of input to the children.
   - Staff knowledge of the community.
   - Encouragement of staff participation in management.

- Adequate preparation time for staff.
- Ratios of staff to pupil not to exceed five children to one staff in the day care or preschool setting.
- Fostering parent involvement within the management of the program.

Effect preschool programs evidenced a number of short-term and long-term effects. Short-term positive effects included:

CHILDREN

- IQ gains;
- Greater school readiness;
- More self-esteem;
- Higher achievement motivation;
- Improved social behavior.

PARENTS:

- Less anxiety and depression;
- Fewer somatic complaints;
- More happiness;
- Improved child-rearing practices;
- More appropriate use of health and social services.

Long-term positive effects include:

CHILDREN:

- Fewer special education placements;
- Less retention in grade;
- Higher employment rates, average earnings, personal savings, and job satisfaction;
- Lower crime rates, arrests, juvenile court appearances, months on probation, and fines;
- Lower rates of teen pregnancies;
- More medical and dental examinations, speech, language and developmental assessments, vision and hearing screenings, nutritional evaluations;
- Especially positive outcomes if they were physically handicapped.

In addition, the following other results were identified:

1. Goals for parents is one of the strongest predictors of the child's success in public school.
2. Programs generated appropriate use of other educational, health and social services.
3. Programs were especially beneficial for children with physical handicaps or developmental delays.
4. Two-year programs were more effective.
5. There does not appear to be an "ideal" curriculum mode.
6. The curriculum needs to be high quality, developmentally appropriate and well-rounded.
7. Staff development and administration are important in successful programs.

Community Involvement

All of the primary prevention programs significantly involved the community. The following elements of successful community involvement were identified:

- A "bottom-up" approach to program planning and implementation that includes community participants in the identification of needs and goals.
- The community context, including culture and values, must be an important aspect of planning and implementation for programs to be effective.
- Programs must be flexible and responsive to community needs.
- Leadership training and support are essential for meaningful and effective community involvement.
- Coordination of services increases comprehensiveness, continuity and effectiveness of programs.
- Building on community strengths and resources aids in the development of healthy communities.
- Changes in community environments or institutions can sustain short term gains over a longer period of time.
- The enhancement of social networks and the resulting reduction in isolation can have positive and measurable effects on individuals "at risk."
- Primary prevention programs and research should be translated into the languages spoken in the communities where the programs are located.

In addition, the following guidelines for community involvement were specified:

1. Respond to what people want for their children by understanding the conditions of family and community life.
2. Adopt an "ecological" perspective, i.e., see the child in the context of the family, and the family in the context of its social network and community environment.
3. Identify and capitalize on the strengths of the children, families and community.
4. Promote a sense of community by fostering mutual aid, affiliation and involvement in community life.
5. Promote empowerment by creating community processes that foster competence, control and involvement.
6. Provide flexibility and diversity in programming as needed to adapt to community environments.
7. Coordinate with other groups and services to enhance the quality and continuity of programming.
8. Facilitate access to other services.
9. Identify how institutions can adapt to provide optimal support to children and families.
10. Provide ongoing evaluation to identify and document the intended and unintended impact on the child, family, social network and community environment.

Summary

After reviewing prevention programs for economically disadvantaged young children, with special emphasis on community involvement and research, twelve common themes emerge.

1. **Children's functioning must be understood within an environmental context.**

   This view has evolved over the last decade from programs which focused solely on the child, or the child and mother, to programs which view children in the context of their family (however it is structured) and the family in the context of the community.

2. **There is no magic age of development at which prevention works best.**

   To be most effective, prevention programs must address the needs of children and their families throughout their developmental cycle, with special attention to the critical transition periods.

3. **Primary prevention programs must be comprehensive.**

   There exists, in the field of primary prevention, a myth that single, simple, relatively inexpensive, one-shot programs can produce long-term positive outcomes for economically disadvantaged children. Such myths are illusory. In order for prevention programs to produce positive outcomes for a significant number of children, and for those outcomes to last, programs must address a number of important risk factors.

4. **Successful programs must be flexible in both program components and services to participants.**

   The best prevention programs provide program components carefully tailored to community conditions. Additionally, programs are flexible so that families with greater needs receive greater services. In these two ways, prevention programs provide multiple program and service responses to meet the needs of children and their families within the context of their communities.

5. **The best prevention programs coordinate with community resources and link with its agencies/institutions.**

   In order to improve conditions and provide the best possible continuity of services, the best programs are not stand-alone programs. They are well-coordinated in the community at all levels. This also implies sensitive attention to the cultural and ethnic composition of each community.

6. **Parent involvement has the potential to improve the quality and effectiveness of programs.**

   Parent involvement helps to strengthen the family and consolidate gains made through the program. However, implementation of parent involvement needs to be planned according to community and family goals.

7. **The coordinated primary prevention initiative should build on existing resources.**

   Because many communities are actively involved in developing and offering prevention programs, it is important to build on these programs. There are a wealth of programs, and these programs should be priorities in research demonstration projects.

8. **Universal accessibility is important.**

   In order to avoid stigmatizing children or arbitrarily excluding children through restrictive program criteria, universal accessibility within a given community is important. Universal accessibility also involves a broader population of children and families, which enriches the development of the program.

9. **Good prevention programs require high caliber staff.**

   Staff must be given adequate remuneration, receive management support, training, and good supervision in order to develop and become knowledgeable about the children, families and communities in which they work. The importance of this factor cannot be over-stated.

10. **A limited number of program components are associated with successful prevention programs.**

    The components, identified in the literature and program review, associated with successful prevention programs, should be considered.

11. **Good primary prevention requires cooperation and collaboration both at the corporate and local levels.**

    It is clear that prevention of emotional and behavioral problems is associated with prevention of negative health problems and educational difficulties, and program models for prevention of emotional and behavioral problems cross inter-sectoral boundaries of service delivery (e.g., pre-natal classes, affective education). Thus, good primary prevention programs require the cooperation and collaboration of those responsible for public health, community health, education, housing and recreation as well as social services.

12. **Good primary prevention research should show short-term, as well as long-term positive outcomes.**

    The research review conclusively shows that it is not necessary to wait 10 years or more to establish the advantages of primary prevention. The research indicates that to measure the FULL VALUE of primary prevention, it is important to follow program participants longitudinally. Nonetheless, there should be BOTH short-term and long-term psycho-social and social/mental health service outcomes with good primary prevention programs for young children.

Fact Sheet

School Grade Retention

1. *What is grade retention?*

Retention (nonpromotion) is the practice of requiring a child to repeat a particular grade or requiring a child of appropriate age to delay entry into kindergarten or first grade. Retention is usually tried when students have not progressed up to the academic expectations for the grade placement or when children are considered socially or emotionally "immature" for their grade placements.

2. *How prevalent is retention?*

The rate of retention has not been well-documented, but the best estimate suggests that 15% to 19% of public school students are retained at some point in their education. Every year, over 2,000,000 American school children are retained in the same grade.

3. *How expensive is retention?*

Lorrie A. Shepard of the University of Colorado, Boulder, and Mary Lee Smith, Arizona State University, estimate the national school retention rate at 6% — about two students in every class of 30. Assuming an even more conservative retention rate of 4%, Marshall Smith of Stanford University estimates the cost at $5.76 billion a year.

4. *What does the research show about the effectiveness of retention as an intervention for academic and social/developmental problems?*

- Most low achievers do not "catch up" when they are retained. In fact, they are more likely to fall further behind. Some children show gains during the retention year, but they often cannot be distinguished from their promoted peers within two or three years.

- Retention is generally unsuccessful even at kindergarten or first grade. Retention appears to have more negative effects on older children, but there is no strong evidence to support it as an effective intervention for kindergarten or first grade students either. "Transition" kindergarten or "pre-first" classes are another form of retention with no proven efficacy.

- Many children who eventually drop out of school were retained one or more times. Multiple retentions and retentions in later grades increase the likelihood of school dropout.

- "Immature" children do not generally benefit from another year to grow. There is no evidence that children will mature faster or have a better adjustment if retained. They are more likely not to benefit emotionally from retention, and they show lower self-concepts, more adjustment problems, and more negative attitudes toward school than promoted peers.

373

- In some special cases, retention has the potential for being effective. Students with good self-concepts and peer relations who have the skills to catch up quickly may benefit from retention. In addition, children who have missed a significant number of days due to illness or family moves may benefit if the causes of excessive absences have been corrected. However, there is no way for school officials to accurately predict which individual students will ultimately benefit from retention, so alternatives should still be seriously considered whenever possible.

5. *In light of strong evidence that retention is not a viable intervention to solve student academic and social/emotional problems, why do schools still support the practice?*

- "Tradition"—retention has been in use since the beginning of organized public schooling.
- Teachers (or schools) believe some students "are just not ready" developmentally and do not consider the possibility of altering teaching practices or curricula to benefit the child who is struggling.
- Teachers (or schools) often are aware only of immediate results and do not realize that temporary gains following retention usually "wash out" in a year or two.
- A strong focus among education leaders and parents on increasing academic standards and accountability in American schools has forced schools to "push" children through a pre-established sequence of skills with little flexibility. There also has been a push to teach skills at earlier and earlier ages.

6. *Are there effective alternatives to retention that can help underachieving or maladjusted students?*

It seems clear that retention and promotion alone rarely can be considered interventions by themselves. There are a number of alternatives that have been positively supported by research. Many of these choices will require greater flexibility among schools and parents, but in the long run, will be less emotionally and academically costly to children and less financially costly to school systems. Some ideas include:

- **tutoring** by adults and/or peers within and outside of schools
- structured **summer school** remediation
- **enhanced teaching strategies,** such as, mastery learning, team teaching, direct instruction, individualized instruction, cooperative learning, progress monitoring and reinforcement
  The teaching skills listed above can be learned by teachers through inservice training and by consulting with resource persons who are available in most public schools today:
    —school psychologists
    —school social workers
    —school nurses
    —guidance counselors
    —special education teachers
    —reading specialists
    —school administrators

Many of these professionals work as part of problem-solving teams in schools.

- **catching the problem early**—if a child is not keeping up, look for ways to solve the problems *before they grow unmanageable (using strategies such as the ones above)*
- **parent involvement**—parents should be encouraged and supported in efforts to act as "teachers" for their children, monitor and help their children with homework and organizational skills, observe or even assist teachers in classrooms, and play a role in school decision-making and extracurricular functions

NATIONAL
ASSOCIATION OF
SCHOOL
PSYCHOLOGISTS

Fact Sheet

Multicultural and Minority Issues in Education

1. *Statistics*

By the year 2000, one-third of the U.S. population will consist of individuals from minority groups.

By the year 2000, 40% of the U.S. *student population* will be children from minority groups.

Currently, much higher percentages of minority children than majority children drop out of school prior to graduation.

Minority professionals are highly under-represented in regular education, special education, and school psychology.

These statistics suggest an ever-increasing need for the development of *cultural competence* among educators, children, and parents to facilitate positive attitudes and expectations toward the academic and social development of children appropriate for their cultural backgrounds.

2. *What is cultural competence?*

Cultural competence is the ability to interact effectively with people from all different cultural groups, with the following results:

—increased personal satisfaction

—positive interpersonal interactions

—task effectiveness

This definition goes beyond learning ethnic-specific information and suggests the need to be "culturally sensitive" to all aspects of the person, including ethnicity, socioeconomic status, gender, setting, etc.

3. *What are the negative consequences of a lack of cultural competence among educators?*

- Wider gaps in communication and cooperation between schools and minority children and their parents.

- Inaccurate, inappropriate, and stereotypical attitudes and expectations toward minority children that negatively affect their social and academic development.

- Lack of sensitivity to our awareness of the diverse learning styles and needs of culturally different children.

377

4. What are the positive consequences of biculturalism among children?

- Four patterns of adjustment to a mainstream culture among cultural minorities have been identified:

    —abandoning the native culture in favor of the mainstream culture

    —embracing completely the native culture and having little contact with the mainstream culture

    —having no strong identification with either culture

    —retaining important aspects of the native culture while integrating the traditions and norms of the mainstream culture (biculturalism)

    The fourth pattern above, **biculturalism** (a subset of cultural competence), has been associated with the best psychological adjustment among individuals entering the mainstream culture.

5. What factors determine the degree to which children can adjust biculturally?

- Individual factors

    —the child's developmental age—younger children have fewer adjustment problems than older children

    —the child's self-esteem—high self-esteem makes adjustment easier

    —the child's facility with native and English languages

- Family factors

    —the parents' adjustment—the child's pattern of adjustment may parallel that of the parents or parental attitudes may push the child in the opposite direction (for example, the parents may embrace the native culture while the child quickly assimilates the new culture to avoid alienation)

    —the parents' facility with English—this determines the degree to which parents get along in the mainstream culture and provide bicultural role models for their children

    —the role of extended family—this is an important support system and preserver of the native culture

- Ecological factors

    —the receptivity of the environment—school environments that provide experiences necessary to function in both (or many) cultures facilitate biculturalism in minority children

    —contact and socialization with both cultures

6. What can be done in schools to foster the adjustment of cultural and ethnic minority children and enhance the cultural competence of children, educators, and parents?

- **For children**—develop multicultural competence programs as part of the curriculum. Children can learn about the customs, art, music, dress, attitudes, and philosophies of other cultures while sharing their own. These programs would not replace but would enhance traditional curricula to instill an understanding of the strength and value of cultural diversity.

- **For parents**—encourage the continuation of their strong ethnic identification; bilingualism;

acceptance of children's mainstream *and* native culture friends; contact with extended family; affiliation with religious organizations, mainstream, and native community organizations; and subscription to mainstream and native publications.

- **For school personnel**—encourage the development of their own cultural, ethnic, and personal identity. Then train staff in cultural sensitivity through knowledge of cultural differences in heritage, history, traditions, customs, and languages of the many cultural minority groups in the U.S. The ability to teach multicultural education and respond appropriately to minority children should naturally follow. Knowledge about differences in the way children from other cultures respond to various learning methods and environments will help teachers meet the individual needs of their cultural minority students.

    Also, the greater the cultural competence demonstrated by school staff, the more parents will feel welcomed and encouraged to enhance their own cultural competence.

- For the community—help families identify community support groups for the native culture or help families develop their own support groups. Community organizations and parent groups should have access to multicultural education and awareness.

For more information

Barona, A., & Garcia, E. E. (1990). *Children at risk: Poverty, minority status, and other issues in educational equity.* Washington, D.C.: National Association of School Psychologists.

Nixon, J. (1985). *A teacher's guide to multicultural education.* Oxford: Basil Blackwell.

<u>Fact Sheet</u>

Children's Self-Esteem

1. *What is self-esteem?*

Self-esteem may be defined as:
"The evaluation which the individual makes and customarily maintains with regard to himself; it expresses an attitude of approval or disapproval and indicates the extent to which an individual believes himself to be capable, significant, successful, and worthy." (Coopersmith, 1967)

2. *What is the strongest indicator of a child's self-esteem?*

One indication of children's level of self-esteem is the number of positive or negative statements they tend to make about themselves or others. Children with low self-esteem tend to make many negative comments about their own behavior or attributes and also may be hypercritical of others. These negative self-statements may be observed in natural settings or recorded by personality tests, such as the *Piers-Harris Self-Concept Scale for Children.*

Many other behaviors may accompany poor self-esteem in children. These include:

—Verbal or physical bullying
—Withdrawal
—Reluctance to try new things
—Overdone attempts to draw attention to self, bragging
—Significant defensiveness

3. *What are the negative consequences of low self-esteem in children?*

Poor self-esteem in children has been shown to be related to:

—depression
—suicide
—drug and alcohol experimentation (greater likelihood of being influenced by user peers)
—poor peer relations
—lowered academic achievement

4. *What positive consequences are associated with high self-esteem in children?*

High levels of self-esteem in children are related to:

—good social skills

—better overall adjustment

—greater independence

—good peer acceptance

—less deviant behavior

—better academic achievement

5. *What can be done in schools to enhance student self-esteem?*

- Improve academic skills—many child suffer low self-esteem because they perceive themselves as academic failures. Simply remediating their academic deficits (often in reading) can enhance their self-esteem. Many methods can be used to help these students academically. Examples are:

    —peer tutoring

    —individualized instruction

    —home-school reinforcement

    —progress monitoring and reinforcement

- **Training positive self-talk**—getting children to say nice things about themselves can actually raise their self-esteem. School psychologists can work with students individually or consult with teachers who in turn train the children to use more positive self-talk. This involves:

    —enhancing students' self-monitoring of their positive behaviors and attributes

    —enhancing their "vocabulary" of positive self-statements

    —reinforcing them for using the positive self-statements in natural settings.

    —teachers can model praise behavior by praising themselves when they do a "good job" and teach children to praise themselves and others.

- Teaching children to set realistic goals and to evaluate their progress realistically—many children with low self-esteem have expectations for their own behavior which are unrealistically high and often set themselves up to perceive failure. Teaching them to set reasonable short-term goals and reward themselves for small steps toward their goals can greatly enhance self-esteem.

- School-wide programs with the characteristics above may prevent many self-esteem problems in students before they occur.

6. *What can be done at home to enhance children's self-esteem?*

- **Parent involvement** in programs to enhance self-esteem is critical. Parents can be taught skills in parent training groups and individual training/counseling sessions that will increase their childrens' ability to love and accept themselves. These essential skills include:

    —learning to discipline *behavior*, rather than attacking a child's basic nature (for example, saying, "I don't like it when you leave your clothes on the floor" instead of saying, "You are so stupid. All you ever do is make a mess.")

    —Emphasizing a child's good behavior more than bad behavior and attending to and rewarding the good behavior whenever possible

    —Defining limits and rules very clearly (with the child's help) and enforcing them consistently

    —Respecting a child's feelings and ideas

    —Having reasonable expectations for children

—Giving children responsibilities appropriate to their developmental levels
—Spending time with their children to show support and caring

NATIONAL
ASSOCIATION OF
SCHOOL
PSYCHOLOGISTS

Fact Sheet

Issues, Concerns, and Guidelines for Selection and Evaluation of Child Sexual Abuse Prevention Programs*

Introduction

Child Sexual Abuse Prevention Programs (CSAP) are in their infancy (Conte, Rosen, Saperstein, & Shermack, 1985; NCPCA, 1986). The over 500 CSAP materials and programs currently available on the market are as diverse in their content and presentation as they are diverse in their appropriateness and value. Unfortunately, many if not most of these programs have been developed hurriedly and without sufficient validation research (Repucci & Haugaard, 1989; Wurtele, 1987). Many programs have known and unknown unintended effects (Conte, Rosen, Saperstein, 1986; Kleemeier & Webb, 1986; Tharinger, Krivacska, Laye-McDonough, Jamison, Vincent & Hedlund, 1988), and many more are designed in apparent ignorance of what we know about child development, learning theory and primary prevention program development (NCPCA, 1986; Wurtele, 1987).

These guidelines are based on Emory Cowen's primary prevention program development model (1984), a five step process:

1. Identification of the generative base of knowledge (i.e., the knowledge base needed to develop a viable program);
2. Development of guiding program concepts;
3. Development of program technology (i.e., program design);
4. Implementation;
5. Evaluation.

These guidelines are intended to assist school psychologists and other educators in asking the right questions when identifying, reviewing, and selecting CSAP programs. Given the experimental nature of CSAP programs (NCPCA, 1986; Reppucci & Haugaard, 1989; Wurtele, 1987), there is likely no program currently in existence which conforms to all of these guidelines. Nevertheless, these guidelines represent our current state of knowledge. The information provided below is obviously only a brief summary of what is currently known and being discussed in the child abuse prevention literature and should be viewed as representative, not exhaustive. It will be the responsibility of local educators and school districts to modify programs or add other components in order to ensure that CSAP efforts are consistent with current research and theory.

* Authored by James Krivacska. NASP Children's Services Committee is solely responsible for the content of this document.

Summary of Issues and Proposed Guidelines

I. Generative Base of Knowledge

At least 4 areas can be considered to make up the generative base of knowledge for CSAP programs: child development theory, prevention program theory and practice, concept learning theory, and child sexual abuse dynamics theory.

Guideline 1: *The program recognizes the young child's security, safety and intimacy needs within the context of family and culture, and acknowledges diversity found in families regarding the expression of intimacy and affection as well as parental child roles and relationships.*

Child Development Theory—The three critical aspects of child development theory for CSAP programs involve the emotional, cognitive and sexual development of children. Emotional needs of children include security and safety, particularly with respect to parent-child relationships (Elkind, 1976; Gilbert, 1988; Kraizer, 1986). To develop into confident and competent adolescents and adults, children need to form attachments and to feel emotionally and physically safe and secure, particularly in their preschool years (Bowlby, 1973, 1983). The current focus of many programs on teaching young children about incest raises serious concerns about the potential impact of such messages on parent-child relationships (Gilbert, 1988; Kraizer, 1986; Tharinger, et al., 1988). Programs which include such instruction must be carefully reviewed and children's interpretations of program content carefully monitored for misconceptions (Wurtele, 1987). Research is needed to identify ways of reaching children who are or will be abused by family members, while not raising undue concern among the remaining population. Programs must also recognize cultural diversity in the form of expression of intimacy and affection within families (Gilbert, Berrick, Le Prohn, & Nyman, 1989).

Guideline 2: *The program presents concepts and information in a manner consistent with the developmental levels of the children to whom it is directed and is designed only for children who will benefit from its instruction (approximately 1st or 2nd grade and older)*

Cognitively, younger children are less able to process and assimilate abstract constructs and concepts. In particular, pre-school children lack the cognitive structures needed to relate to instruction beyond the most concrete level, and have great difficulty with a future perspective (Elkind, 1976; Gilbert, 1988; NCPCA, 1986; Trudell & Whatley, 1988). Even early elementary school aged children may appear more sophisticated than they really are (Elkind, 1981), and their ability to incorporate and utilize prevention strategies must not be overestimated (NCPCA, 1986). For both of these younger groups of children there is a tendency to overgeneralize any concepts they learn due to limited discrimination ability (Elkind, 1976). The primary line of defense for these two groups remains adult supervision (Gilbert, 1988; NCPCA, 1986; Woods & Rhodes, 1986). Older children may be better able to grasp some of the abstract concepts contained in CSAP programs. However, they still require concrete behavioral responses upon which they can draw in abusive situations (NCPCA, 1986; Wurtele, 1987).

Guideline 3: *Prior to discussion of sexual abuse, the program provides age-appropriate sex education including, at minimum, labeling of body parts and their functions. The program distinguishes between sexually abusive contacts and age-appropriate childhood sexual experiences and feelings.*

Children have long been recognized by psychologists as sexual beings. For fear of being rejected as sex education programs, many CSAP programs attempt to divorce themselves from sexual references (Finkelhor, 1984; Reppucci & Haugaard, 1989). From the Kinsey research in the 1940's to more recent investigations, up to 50% of all children will experience some form of sexual interaction with peers while growing up (Kinsey, Pomeroy & Martin, 1948; Kinsey, Pomeroy, Martin, & Gebhard, 1953). Additionally, children are known to have sexual thoughts and feelings (Martinson, 1981). When information normalizing these experiences and feelings for children is lacking, there is great risk that the child's first formal and adult validated experience with sexuality will be within the negative and frightening context of sexual abuse (Finkelhor, 1986; Tharinger, et al., 1988; Trudell & Whatley, 1988; Wood & Rhodes, 1986).

How children view peer sexual play and their own sexual thoughts and feelings after exposure to sex abuse prevention programs is unknown, but represents an area of considerable concern for the future development of a healthy sexuality (Finkelhor, 1986). Additionally, programs should not assume that all children in the program audience (particularly younger children) are necessarily aware of the differences between the sexes. Prevention of child sexual abuse should include acknowledgement of what is an appropriate and healthy sexuality (Anderson, 1986; Trudell & Whatley, 1988) and program concepts should be presented within the context of a comprehensive sex education curricula (Brassard, Tyler, & Kehle, 1983; Finkelhor, 1986).

Guideline 4: *The program promotes skill acquisition through the use of modeling, behavioral rehearsal and feedback rather than relying upon knowledge acquisition as the primary method of sexual abuse prevention training. Additionally, the program enhances children's overall competency by promoting the development of social problem solving skills, and avoids the use of scare tactics.*

Prevention Program Theory and Practice—Twenty-five years of primary prevention program development directed at a broad range of social problems (from drug abuse to teen pregnancy) have provided some clues as to what types of programmatic interventions work. One clear result of that research has been that knowledge-based prevention programs (which assume behavioral change will result from increased knowledge) are largely unsuccessful. Thus, increases in knowledge do not automatically lead to behavioral change (Leventhal, 1987). What has emerged is the need for behavioral skill development and rehearsal in which target behaviors are taught through modeling, rehearsal and feedback (NCPCA, 1986; Reppucci & Haugaard, 1989; Wurtele, 1987).

Additionally, recent research has begun to show that development of social problem solving skills increases confidence and self-esteem and may serve as a form of inoculation against many social problems typically encountered by youth growing up (Bloom, 1986; Spivack & Shure, 1974). A particularly susceptible group of children has been identified as those who are perceived as vulnerable by child abusers (Finkelhor, 1984). Programs which reduce a child's vulnerability may help prevent abuse. For example, children who suffer from poor self-esteem have been found to have difficulty learning prevention skills associated with even the more concrete and easily definable situation of stranger abduction (Fryer, Kraizer & Miyoski, 1987). Finally, research has shown that prevention programs which heighten program recipient's levels of fear by stressing potential negative personal dangers tend to make the target group feel more vulnerable and less able to resist the target problem (Kleinot & Rogers, 1982), and are to be avoided (Finkelhor, 1986).

Guideline 5: *The program clearly defines all concepts, identifies the critical attributes of each, and presents the concepts consistent with research on concept learning. The program enhances discrimination learning through the presentation of both examples and non-examples of the concept.*

Concept Learning Theory—Concepts may be introduced to children by first clearly defining the concept to be learned, identifying the critical attributes which permits discrimination of the concept from similar or related concepts, and presenting the concepts using a sequenced learning approach (Merrill & Tennyson, 1977). Such an approach includes presentation of the concept and its defining attributes, the presentation of a series of examples of the concept along with nonexamples, a systematic review and application of the critical attributes to the examples to rehearse discrimination skills, and systematic evaluation of the child's ability to appropriately discriminate examples on his/her own.

For example, Fryer, et al. (1987) defined the concept of stranger as "people you don't know" in their stranger abduction prevention program for children. The concept was further elaborated, within the context of prevention, by adding the critical attribute of the presence of a caretaking adult known to the child. Thus, children were given a concept (stranger) and a critical attribute (presence of a known caretaker) to guide them in their discrimination of potentially dangerous from non-dangerous situations. Using Merrill and Tennyson's model, children would next be presented with examples of strangers to avoid (e.g., a stranger approaching a child who is alone on the street and asking for directions) and examples of appropriate stranger interactions (e.g., a non-example of a stranger in line at the supermarket who remarks to a child accompanied by her mother, that her dress is very pretty) to aid them in developing discrimination skills.

When concepts are not adequately defined and the critical attributes not clearly formulated and stated, overgeneralization by the child will most likely occur. Children, in fact, learn new concepts by first formulating a prototype of the best example of the concept they find, and then comparing that example against all new examples to make a determination. In the absence of counter-examples, the prototype used may be too broad and all-inclusive resulting in overgeneralization (Tennyson & Cocchiarella, 1986; Tennyson, Youngers & Suebonthi, 1983).

Guideline 6: *The program avoids placing responsibility on children either for sexual abuse or its prevention. Children are encouraged to report abuse. However, their need to think about reporting for awhile if they are not ready to make the report at the present time is acknowledged and supported. Children are taught there are people whom they may tell when they are ready.*

Child Sexual Abuse Dynamics—Most CSAP programs rely on the assumption that by increasing children's knowledge of sexual abuse, as well as by empowering them to refuse sexually abusive advances, sexual abuse can be prevented (Reppucci & Haugaard, 1989). Other dynamics, however, are involved and have been identified as contributing to sexual abuse (Finkelhor, 1984). Emotionally insecure or needy children, children with close trusting relationships with potential offenders, and children who have been coerced or who have not been educated about sexuality are children at risk for sexual abuse (Finkelhor, 1984; Tharinger, et al., 1988).

Simple provision of information and mandates to resist sexual advances will be inadequate. The great danger of ignorance of these other contributing factors is the assumption that children will be able to prevent abuse after exposure to these programs, negating the importance of other efforts to prevent abuse (Finkelhor, 1986; Reppucci & Haugaard, 1989; Tharinger, et al., 1988; Trudell & Whatley, 1988). Additionally, promulgation of the view that abuse is not the child's fault and that the child should report the abuse may prove confusing to a child in a CSAP program audience who has been abused and who may not feel capable of reporting the abuse because of the presence of one or more of the above factors. Such children might now feel guilty about their inability to report the abuse (NCPCA, 1986; Trudell & Whatley, 1988; Wood & Rhodes, 1986; Wurtele, 1987) resulting in an increase in their self-perceived powerlessness (Swift & Levin, 1987).

II. Guiding Program Concepts

Guideline 7: **The program has a clearly defined purpose and goals which are based upon a sound and identifiable philosophy or theory. The purpose, goals, and program implementation are consistent with the current generative base of knowledge in child development, concept learning, prevention theory and child sexual abuse dynamics.**

Drawing from the generative base of knowledge, program developers need to identify the overall purpose and theoretical basis for the program, as well as the specific program goals (Cowen, 1984). From these goals the guiding program concepts to be taught to the target population can be developed. The guiding program concepts must logically flow from the program goals, which in turn must relate to the overall program purpose. All three, purpose, goals and concepts, must be consistent with the underlying theoretical base for the program as well as be consistent with the generative base of knowledge (Cowen, 1984).

Guideline 8: **The program is supported by research evidence as to its validity for the populations for which it is to be implemented. That research relies upon assessment of behavioral change rather than consumer satisfaction surveys and knowledge gain assessments.**

Programs which do not adhere to these principles of program design will lack program integrity, will be difficult to translate into a coherent program design and will be very difficult to implement and evaluate effectively (Carnine, Kameenui & Maggs, 1982). As noted earlier, program concepts should be clearly defined. Program concepts which lack clarity and comprehensiveness may lead to misunderstanding or overgeneralization by children (Wood & Rhodes, 1986). Program promoters should be willing to provide validation research demonstrating the effectiveness of the program. Such research should go beyond consumer satisfaction and knowledge gains given the limited usefulness of such information in evaluating program effectiveness (NCPCA, 1986; Tharinger, et al., 1988).

Guideline 9: **The program recognizes the importance of adults placing limits upon children's activities, desires and behaviors. It avoids promoting children's belief in "rights" which are both abstract and beyond their ability to fully appreciate and which will be contradicted by real life experiences. The program avoids reliance on concepts which lack empirical support or which run counter to current cultural norms.**

Program concepts must be carefully thought out and be consistent with children's everyday experiences. A frequently used concept (body ownership) is constantly contradicted in a child's everyday experiences (being made to take a bath, receive medical treatment, or even finishing one's vegetables) (Finkelhor, 1986; Tharinger & Krivacska, 1988). Other concepts, often incorporated in CSAP programs, suggest the existence of an innate intuition in children about appropriate and inappropriate behavior (usually expressed by such phrases as "trust your feelings"). The existence of such intuition has never been empirically supported (Tharinger, et al., 1988).

Mainstream cultural values in both national and local contexts must be considered (Finkelhor, 1986; Gilbert, 1988; Wurtele, 1987). Programs which label or infer that spanking is abusive run counter to a socially endorsed form of punishment. While NASP and many other professional organizations have taken a stand against corporal punishment, such efforts must be directed at society and parents, not focused indirectly through children with the expectation that they will somehow change parental behavior.

Similarly, many programs label the buttocks as a private part of the body. Since there is no consensus for labelling the buttocks as a private part of the body, programs using this designation may unduly confuse and alarm many children. Much physical contact, particularly with young children, includes contact with the buttocks (e.g., in the act of picking up and holding a child). Parents frequently pat their child on the buttocks as an expression of affection.

Guideline 10: *The program's guiding concepts stress age-appropriate promotion of normal childhood sexuality, self-esteem and social competency. It avoids use of the touch continuum because of its ambiguous and abstract nature and instead relies upon direct and unambiguous labeling of what touch is appropriate and what touch should be resisted and/or reported.*

Many programs rely on the touch continuum, a concept popularized some ten years ago and which attempts to discriminate between touches by labeling them "good" or "bad" (some programs include a third category called "confusing"). Programs based on the touch continuum have proliferated with such modifications as OK-touch, Not-OK touch; Yes-touch, No-touch, etc. (Tharinger, et al., 1988; Wurtele, 1987). These concepts are rarely well defined and present enormous problems for young children (i.e., approximately 7 years old and younger) when it comes to making discriminations among them (Gilbert, et al., 1989; NCPCA, 1986; Woods & Rhodes, 1986).

Young children, for example, will have a difficult time reconciling the concept that bad touch can come from good people (family, friends, etc.) (Kraizer, 1986; Woods & Rhodes, 1986). They will be confused by the fact that some good touch can feel bad (application of medicine to a wound, vaccinations, etc.) and that some bad touch can feel good (genital stimulation) (Finkelhor, 1986; Wurtele, 1987). Additionally, most sexual abuse starts with touch that feels good and is appropriate (Kraizer, 1986; Woods & Rhodes, 1986). Consistent with the issue of emerging childhood sexuality as discussed earlier, there is also concern about the long term impact on the development of a healthy sexuality arising from repeated association of the concept of bad touch with the genitals (Tharinger, et al., 1988; Trudell & Whatley, 1988). Peer sex explorations and masturbation raise additional problems for a child trying to conceptually navigate the touch continuum (Finkelhor, 1986; Wurtele, 1988).

Appropriate program concepts include promotion within children of an awareness and acceptance of their whole body including the sexual organs, and an age-appropriate awareness and acceptance of their own sexuality (Trudell, 1988; Tharinger, et al., 1988). Sexual abuse is conceptualized as abuse, or more appropriately misuse, of the child's sexuality for the purposes of adult gratification. Thus, children are given a context within which to place masturbation and peer sex exploration in particular, a context which is quite apart from sexual abuse (Krivacska, 1990). A second critical concept is the promotion of social competency and self-esteem. Self-esteem and perceived competency may be related to the ability to implement prevention strategies (Fryer, Kraizer & Miyoshi, 1987), a view supported by research in other areas of prevention programming (Kleinot & Rogers, 1982). For adolescents, concepts related to love and affection, sexuality, individual rights (including body rights) and responsibilities can form the core of a prevention effort designed to reduce the likelihood of adolescents developing abusive behavior patterns as adults.

III. Technology Development and Program Design

Guideline 11: *The program helps children develop an accurate mental prototype of the concept to be learned through exercises in generalization and discrimination using clear and unambiguous examples of the concept.*

Guideline 12: *The program provides children with feedback on classification errors (classifying abusive behavior as non-abusive or non-abusive behavior as abusive).*

Translation of the program concepts into a program design requires careful attention to the integration of program purpose and intent with current knowledge about teaching and learning (NCPCA,

1986). As discussed earlier, we know a great deal about how children learn as well as about their ability to handle abstract concepts. Many of the concepts being taught will require children to make difficult discriminations of adult behavior. The previously cited work on concept learning stresses the importance of helping children learn a concept through the development of an accurate mental prototype using clear and unambiguous examples of the concept. The ability to further discriminate the concept emerges through generalization and discrimination exercises using a series of examples, some of which fit the criteria for the concept while others deviate from the criteria in one or more critical attributes. Feedback on performance is constantly provided to the child (See Merrill & Tennyson).

Assessment of how well children are learning discriminations must be made constantly (NCPCA, 1986; Reppucci & Haugaard, 1989). Research which shows that children increase their knowledge about abuse and how to respond to it after exposure to CSAP programs nevertheless also shows that significant portions of the prevention concepts were not learned (Conte, et al., 1985; Finkelhor, 1986; Wolfe, MacPherson, Blount & Wolfe, 1986) and that young children learn significantly less than older children (Finkelhor, 1986; Wurtele, 1987).

Guideline 13: *The program identifies the criterion level of learning to which all children receive instruction. Instruction continues until each child attains the criterion.*

Given the risks associated with a child mistaking appropriate physical contact as abusive, a mastery learning approach should be taken to ensure that each child has adequately learned how to make correct discriminations and how to respond to an abusive situation. Training to the attainment of a predetermined criterion has already been reported in the literature on prevention of child abuse (Poche, Brouwer & Swearingen, 1981). Such training may involve the use of verbal simulations. Wurtele and her associates have developed a series of discrimination exercises called "What If" Situations Test which they use as an evaluation tool. Students are provided with scenarios which they must first identify as abusive or non-abusive and provide the appropriate response (Wurtele, et al., 1986; Wurtele, et al., 1988). Programs should include discrimination of peer sex exploration and masturbation from sexual abuse.

Guideline 14: *The program presents empowerment as a model to help children develop a sense of self-worth, self-esteem and competency through acquisition of social problem solving skills, rather than as a model which places children's right and parental rights in conflict.*

Many programs are based upon an empowerment model (borrowed from rape prevention programs) which emphasize children's rights and attempt to increase children's power in relation to adults (Butler, 1986; Finkelhor, 1984). Reliance on an empowerment model that sets up children's rights in conflict with parental rights carries great risks for children who cannot be expected to change parental behavior (Melton, 1983; Tharinger, et al., 1988; Trudell & Whatley, 1988). Research shows that children suffering from poor self-esteem (Fryer, et al., 1987) or who have an external locus of control (Nelson, 1985; cited in Hazzard & Angert, 1986), may have difficulty learning prevention concepts, suggesting the need for a reformulation of the empowerment model away from a children's rights perspective. Empowerment models which seek to increase a child's self-esteem, self-confidence and perceived self-competence however, may help make children appear less vulnerable, reducing the likelihood they will be abused.

Guideline 15: *The program uses clear and explicit labels for the parts of the body and communicates to children an openness to talking about sex and sexuality so as to encourage children to feel comfortable talking with adults about sex, particularly sexual abuse.*

As discussed earlier, children need clear and explicit information upon which they can rely. Terms such as "private parts," and "the parts of the body covered by the bathing suit" tend to confuse children and send conflicting messages (Tharinger, et al., 1988; Trudell & Whatley, 1988). Many programs do not give children the language they will need to make an accurate and unambiguous report of abuse. Furthermore, despite the overt message that it is okay to talk about abuse, children are given a covert message that it's still not okay to talk about the private parts of the body (Wurtele, 1987). Additionally, such euphemisms include parts of the body which are not considered "private parts" (buttocks, hips, back, and for girls who wear one piece bathing suits, the upper torso of the body).

Guideline 16: *The program provides children with a repertoire of alternative actions from which the child may choose the one most appropriate for a given situation.*

Since little is understood about the initiation of children into abuse (Reppucci & Haugaard, 1989), diverting abuse, or the attributional styles of abused children, prevention strategies presented to children should include a repertoire of behaviors the child can use (Woods & Rhodes, 1986). This will recognize the diversity among children (Finkelhor, 1986). Some children may be comfortable with saying no, others with just running away, and still others with going along until they get an opportunity to report the abuse.

IV. Implementation

Guideline 17: *The program provides for follow-up and booster sessions in recognition of learning deterioration effects over time.*

Educators are well aware of the concept of the learning curve and the decreased retention of learned material that takes place over time. Consequently, any prevention program should provide for follow-up and booster sessions to increase retention of program concepts and skills (NCPCA, 1986; Reppucci & Haugaard, 1989; Woods & Rhodes, 1986). Follow-up serves a second important function by providing an opportunity to clear up misconceptions children may have about learned concepts. Consequently, it has been generally recognized by prevention specialists that one-shot or short duration programs are the least effective (Reppucci & Haugaard, 1989; Wood & Rhodes, 1986) given the complex cognitive tasks being required by these programs.

Guideline 18: *The program recognizes that prevention programs may increase the number of abuse disclosures. Staff are trained to respond appropriately to abuse allegations, and to assist children who have disclosed when they return to their classroom. Staff are also trained that, because of possible uncertainty or confusion about appropriate touch, some reports may represent a child seeking clarification as to the appropriateness of certain behavior rather than a report of abuse.*

The program should provide for comprehensive training of program presenters and implementors (NCPCA, 1986). Such training should include instruction regarding the program concepts (discussed under the implementation section). Presenters and potential recipients of a child's report of abuse should also be trained in how to respond to abuse disclosures (NCPCA, 1986). The school or agency in which the program is to be presented must be prepared for an increase in the number of abuse disclosures subsequent to program presentation (Tharinger, et al., 1988). How staff should respond to a child who has disclosed abuse and who subsequently returns to the classroom should also be covered (Finkelhor, 1986). Finally, since it is likely that some children will have difficulty with some of the concepts being introduced in CSAP programs, teachers and other personnel must be aware that a child may, at times, be seeking clarification of the appropriateness of certain touch rather than be making an abuse report. Thus, not every child who expresses concern about touch or who asks a question about touch has been abused. Kraizer (1986) gives the example of a young child who misinterpreted the message that he should not allow anyone to touch his private parts, and that his buttocks were a private part of his body. The child subsequently misconstrued the affectionate pat of his father on his buttocks as he was going up to bed as a violation of his private parts. Clarification of what is abusive touch, not a child abuse report, is the appropriate response of staff in this situation.

Guideline 19: *The program provides for parental participation, full and complete disclosure of all program materials and context prior to program presentation, and presents accurate information regarding both the potential positive and negative effects of the program. Parents are given the opportunity to withdraw their child from the program.*

Parent participation and education should be an integral part of prevention efforts (Brassard, 1983; Wood & Rhodes, 1986). Such parent involvement may first help to secure parental support for the program, and second may encourage parental follow-up at home of program concepts (Finkelhor, 1986). All parents should be given full access to program materials and content. They should also be made aware of any potential negative effects to watch for that may indicate that their child has misunderstood program concepts or that their child has been abused. Many program promoters are reluctant to discuss potential negative effects with parents for fear that parents will withdraw their child from the program. Denial of information about potential negative effects is a violation of the concept of informed consent and the American Psychological Association Ethical Principles regarding research with human subjects (APA, 1981). CSAP programs are still experimental and their effects are not well understood (Finkelhor, 1986). Consequently, parents should be allowed to withdraw their child from the program though possible effects of that action on the child should be discussed with the parent first.

Guideline 20: *The program provides training materials which are sufficiently clear and detailed so as to permit accurate and consistent presentation of the program content.*

Guideline 21: *The program monitors implementation to identify and correct unplanned deviations from the program model, content or form.*

Deviation from program guidelines has emerged as a concern relative to child sexual abuse prevention programs (Conte, et al., 1985; Conte, et al., 1986; Tharinger, et al., 1988; Wood & Rhodes, 1986). The key to successful program implementation is monitoring to ensure that the program is implemented in a manner consistent with its design (Maher & Bennett, 1984; Wurtele, 1987). Deviation from program design typically occurs due to inadequate training of or misunderstanding about program concepts by program presenters. When a program is new, problems in implementation may arise that were not anticipated and a mechanism for uncovering and reporting those problems to program managers is necessary to maintain program integrity.

It has sometimes been argued that implementors need to be able to vary program design based on the particular needs of the target group. This is true when there are recognized and validated alternative approaches to implementing a program. These do not exist for CSAP programs as yet (Reppucci & Haugaard, 1989), and deviations from program design made by presenters are based primarily in the presenter's subjective view of the audience and program. Evaluations are significantly impaired when undocumented deviations occur (Conte, et al., 1985; Wood & Rhodes, 1986; Wurtele, 1987). CSAP

393

programs have not been sufficiently researched and validated to permit individual deviations. Any deviations that may be felt to be necessary should be approved and acknowledged by all those responsible for the program, and the effects of the deviation should be monitored.

Guideline 22: *The program monitors for misunderstanding or confusion of program concepts on the part of the children during instruction.*

Unintended consequences have been documented to occur subsequent to CSAP program presentations (Garbarino, 1987; Gardner, 1987; Gilbert, 1988; Kleemeier & Webb, 1986; Kraizer, 1986; Wolfe, et al., 1986). These effects have taken various forms including emotional reactions of heightened fear and anxiety (e.g., Garbarino, 1987), behavioral manifestations of anxiety or withdrawal from certain types of adult-child contact (e.g., Kleemeier & Webb, 1986; Kraizer, 1986), and false allegations of abuse (Gardner, 1987). Unintended consequences may also be more subtle, such as the often observed effect of children refusing "unwanted" hugs and kisses from relatives (Reppucci & Haugaard, 1989). This result is frequently attributed to children's heightened awareness of "body rights." However, given the problem with the vagueness of this concept, the alternative explanation that children may be misinterpreting adult behavior, or associating such behavior with bad touch, must be ruled out first.

Monitoring for unintended consequences requires systematic investigation of how children are processing the information they are getting from CSAP programs. Children should be periodically interviewed using an open-ended format to assess how they are assimilating and utilizing program concepts (Hazzard & Angert, 1986; NCPCA, 1986). Since no program is immune from negative or unintended effects (Rolf, 1985), misconceptions should be anticipated and should be explicitly clarified.

V. Evaluation

Guideline 23: *The program provides for a systematic evaluation of program effectiveness using sound evaluation methodology. Such evaluation includes assessment of knowledge gains, behavioral change and unintended effects. Evaluation of behavioral change employs the use of role plays or written/verbal simulations.*

Guideline 24: *The program systematically assesses for the presence of negative effects across a number of domains including cognitive, affective and behavioral. Additional instruction is provided to correct identified negative effects. Where a consistent pattern of negative effects is observed, program modifications are made to avoid those effects in the future.*

Evaluation of any prevention program entails a systematic collection and analysis of data predicated upon evaluation questions which are identified prior to program implementation (Maher & Bennett, 1984). Assessment should include multiple measures and, whenever possible, adhere to sound evaluation research methodology to ensure the validity of the results. In schools, the most common method will probably continue to be pre-post test evaluations of program effectiveness. Ideally, control groups should be used; however, use of such groups is not always feasible (NCPCA, 1986).

Assessment must go beyond measurement of how much the students, staff, and parents liked the program, and must do more than assess increases in knowledge arising from participation in the program (Finkelhor, 1986). Ultimately, the only true measure of program success will be a reduction in the incidence of child sexual abuse. In the interim, however, measurement of behavioral skills must be an integral part of program evaluation. The latter can be accomplished with the use of role-play scenarios to assess student's ability to discriminate safe from non-safe situations and demonstrate the prevention skills (Fryer, et al., 1987; Hazzard & Angert, 1986; Miltenberger & Thiesse-Duffy, 1988; Poche, Brouwer, Swearingen, 1981; Poche, Yoder & Miltenberger, 1988; Saslawsky & Wurtele, 1986; Wurtele, Kast, & Kondrick, 1988; Wurtele, Marrs & Miller-Perrin, 1987; Wurtele, Saslawsky, Miller, Marrs

& Bretcher, 1986). Systematic assessment should be included for negative effects including increased fear or apprehension, behavioral changes, and misconception of program concepts (Hazzard & Angert, 1986; NCPCA, 1986; Tharinger, et al., 1988).

Summary

Although some have argued that prevention of child sexual abuse is not feasible (Melton, in press), there is emerging evidence from the research in child sexual abuse prevention which, when combined with what is known about child development and prevention theory and practice, suggests a less pessimistic view. Nevertheless, the dynamics of child sexual abuse are poorly understood. The impact of child sexual abuse prevention programs on children is even less understood, particularly in the area of childhood sexuality. As with all new research, desire for immediate gains must be tempered with a respect for the unknown. The development of child sexual abuse prevention programs which significantly impact on the incidence of sexual abuse will require cautious program development. As with any scientific investigation, those wishing to implement child sexual abuse prevention programs must start with what is currently known and then slowly build upon that knowledge through close attention to issues of evaluation, program effectiveness and program effects.

These efforts are necessary and should be encouraged as one component of an overall program of child sexual abuse prevention. To be truly comprehensive, the programs must also be directed at parents, perpetrators and those societal factors which promote, support or permit sexual abuse to occur. School psychologists can utilize their knowledge of psychology, child development, learning, research and evaluation to further these efforts. These guidelines represent an attempt to present, in a concise and cogent form, the current state of knowledge regarding sexual abuse prevention programs from which school psychologists may inform and educate teachers, administrators, school board members, parents and the public in general.

References

American Psychological Association (1981). Ethical Principles of Psychologists. *American Psychologist, 36,* 633–638.

Anderson, C. (1986). A history of the touch continuum. In M. Nelson & K. Clark (Eds.), *The educator's guide to preventing child sexual abuse.* Santa Cruz, CA: Network Pub.

Bloom, B. L. (1986). Primary prevention: An overview. In J. T. Barter & S. W. Talbott (Eds.), *Primary prevention in psychiatry: State of the art.* Washington, D.C.: American Psychiatric Press, Inc.

Bowlby, J. (1973). *Attachment and Loss.* New York: Basic Books.

Bowlby, J. (1983). Attachment and loss: Retrospect and prospect. *Annual Progress in Child Psychiatry and Development, 69,* 29–47.

Brassard, M. R., Tyler, A. H., & Kehle, T. J. (1983). School programs to prevent intrafamilial child sexual abuse. *Child Abuse & Neglect, 7,* 241–245.

Carnine, D., Kameenui, E., & Maggs, A. (1982). Components of analytic assistance: Statement saying, concept training, and strategy training. *Journal of Educational Research, 75,* 374–377.

Conte, J. R., Rosen, C., & Saperstein, L. (1986). An analysis of programs to prevent the sexual victimization of children. *Journal of Primary Prevention, 6*(3), 141–155.

Conte, J. R., Rosen, C., Saperstein, L. & Shermack, R. (1985). Evaluation of a program to prevent the sexual victimization of young children. *Child Abuse & Neglect, 9,* 319–328.

Cowen, E. L. (1984). A general structural model for primary prevention program development in mental health. *The Personnel and Guidance Journal, 62*(8), 485–490.

Elkind, D. (1976). *Child development and education: A piagetian perspective.* New York: Oxford Univ. Press.

Elkind, D. (1981). Recent research in cognitive and language development. In L. T. Benjamin, Jr. (Ed.), *The G. Stanley Hall Lecture Series, Vol. 1,* pp. 61–80. Washington, DC: American Psychological Association.

Finkelhor, D. (1984). *Child sexual abuse; New theory and research.* New York: Free Press.

Finkelhor, D. (1986). *A source book on child sexual abuse.* Beverly Hills: Sage Publications.

Fryer, G. E., Kraizer, S. K., & Miyoshi, T. (1987). Measuring actual reduction of risk to child abuse: A new approach. Child Abuse & Neglect, 11, 173–179.

Garbarino, J. (1987). Children's response to a sexual abuse prevention program: A study of the *Spiderman* comic. *Child Abuse & Neglect, 11,* 143–148.

Gardner, R. (1987). *The parental alienation syndrome and the differentiation between fabricated and genuine child sex abuse.* Cresskill, NJ: Creative Therapeutics.

Gilbert, N. (1988). Teaching children to prevent sexual abuse. *The Public Interest, 93*(Fall), 3–15.

Gilbert, N., Berrick, J. D., Le Prohn, N., & Nyman, N. (1989). *Protecting young children from sexual abuse: Does preschool training work?* Lexington, MA: Lexington Books.

Hazzard, A., & Angert, L. (1986, August). Child sexual abuse prevention: Previous research and future directions. Paper presented at the American Psychological Association meeting. Washington, D.C.

Kinsey, A. C., Pomeroy, W. B., & Martin, C. E. (1948). *Sexual behavior in the human male.* Philadelphia: W. B. Saunders.

Kinsey, A. C., Pomeroy, W. B., Martin, C. E., Gebhard, P. (1953). *Sexual behavior in the human female.* Philadelphia: W. B. Saunders.

Kleemeier, C., & Webb, C. (1986). Evaluation of a school based prevention program. Paper presented at the American Psychological Association Convention, Washington, D.C. (August, 1986).

Kleinot, M. C., & Rogers, R. W. (1982). Identifying effective components of alcohol misuse prevention programs. *Journal of Studies on Alcohol, 43,* 802–811.

Kraizer, S. K. (1986). Rethinking prevention. *Child Abuse & Neglect, 10,* 259–261.

Krivacska, J. J. (1990). *Designing child sexual abuse prevention programs: Current approaches and a proposal for the prevention, reduction and identification of sexual misuse.* Springfield, Ill: C. C. Thomas.

Leventhal, J. M. (1987). Programs to prevent sexual abuse: What outcomes should be measured? *Child Abuse & Neglect, 10,* 169–171.

Maher, C. A. & Bennett, R. E. (1984). Planning and Evaluating special education services. Englewood Cliffs, NJ: Prentice Hall.

Martinson, F. M. (1981). Eroticism in infancy and childhood. In L. L. Constantine & F. M. Martinson (Eds.), *Children and Sex: New Findings, New Perspectives* (pp. 23–35). Boston: Little, Brown & Co.

Melton, G. B. (1983). *Child advocacy: Psychological Issues and interventions.* New York: Plenum Press.

Merrill, M. D., & Tennyson, R. D. (1977). *Teaching concepts: An instructional guide.* Englewood Cliffs, NJ: Educational Technology Publications.

Miltenberger, R. G. & Thiesse-Duffy, E. (1988). Evaluation of home-based programs for teaching personal safety skills to children. *Journal of Applied Behavior Analysis, 21,* 81–87.

National Committee for Prevention of Child Abuse (1986). *Guidelines for Child Sexual Abuse Prevention Programs.* Chicago: NCPCA.

Poche, C., Brouwer, R., & Swearingen, M. (1981). Teaching self-protection to young children. Journal of Applied Behavior Analysis, 14, 169–176.

Poche, C., Yoder, P., & Miltenberger, R. (1988). teaching self-protection to children using television techniques. *Journal of Applied Behavioral Analysis, 21*(3), 253–261.

Reppucci, N. D., & Haugaard, J. J. (1989). Prevention of child sexual abuse: Myth or reality. *American Psychologist, 44,* 1266–1275.

Rolf, J. E. (1985). Evolving adaptive theories and methods for prevention research with children. *Journal of Consulting and Clinical Psychology, 53,* 631–646.

Spivack, G., & Shure, M. B. (1974). *Social adjustment of young children: A cognitive approach to solving real-life problems.* San Francisco: Jossey-Bass.

Swift, C., & Levin, G. (1987). Empowerment: An emerging mental health technology. *Journal of Primary Prevention, 8,* 71–93.

Tennyson, R. D. & Cocchiarella, M. J. (1986). An empirically based instructional design theory for teaching concepts. Review of Educational Research, 56, 40–71.

Tennyson, R. D., Youngers, J. & Suebonthi, P. (1983). Concept learning by children using instructional presentation forms for prototype formation and classification-skill development. *Journal of Educational Psychology, 75,* 280–291.

Tharinger, D. J., & Krivacska, J. J. (1988, April). *Child sexual abuse prevention programs: The role of school psychologists*. Paper presented at the National Association of School Psychologists Annual Conference, Chicago, Il.

Tharinger, D. J., Krivacska, J. J., Laye-McDonough, M., Jamison, L., Vincent, G. G., & Hedlund, A. D. (1988). Prevention of Child Sexual Abuse: An analysis of issues, educational programs and research findings. *School Psychology Review, 17*(4), 614–634.

Trudell, B., & Whatley, M. H. (1988). School sexual abuse prevention: Unintended consequences and dilemmas. *Child abuse & Neglect, 12,* 103–115.

Wolfe, D. A., MacPherson, T., Blount, R., & Wolfe, V. V. (1986). Evaluation of brief interventions of educating school children in awareness of physical and sexual abuse. *Child Abuse & Neglect, 10,* 85–92.

Woods, S. P., & Rhodes, C. (1986, August). *Sexual abuse prevention programs for children: a critical review.* Paper presented at the American Psychological Association Convention, Washington, D.C.

Wurtele, S. K. (1987). School-based sexual abuse prevention programs: A review. *Child Abuse & Neglect, 11,* 483–495.

Wurtele, S. K. (1988, August). *Harmful effects of sexual abuse prevention programs? Results and implications.* Paper presented at the 96th Annual Convention of the American Psychological Association, Atlanta, Georgia.

Wurtele, S. K., Kast, L. C., & Kondrick, P. A. (1988, August). *Development of an Instrument to Evaluate Sexual Abuse Prevention Programs.* Paper presented at the American Psychological Association Convention, Atlanta, Georgia.

Wurtele, S. K., Saslawsky, D. A., Miller, C. L., Marrs, S. R., & Britcher, J. C. (1986). Teaching personal safety skills for potential prevention of sexual abuse: A comparison of treatments. *Journal of Consulting and Clinical Psychology, 54,* 688–692.

Subject Index

Adolescent HIV/AIDS (pg. 245)
Adopted Children (pg. 253)
Adopted Children at School (pg. 339)
Anger Control Problems (pg. 75)
Anorexia and Bulimia (pg. 181)
Anxiety (pg. 185)
Assertiveness (pg. 79)
Asthma (pg. 263)
Attention Deficit Hyperactivity Disorder (pg. 129)
Attention Deficit Hyperactivity Disorder—Fact Sheet (pg. 347)

Bullying (pg. 189)
Bullying—Fact Sheet (pg. 351)

Cancer (pg. 267)
Career and Career Decision-Making (pg. 3)
Cheating (pg. 137)
Childcare (pg. 95)
Chronic Illness (pg. 271)
Communicable Diseases (pg. 7)
Competition (pg. 81)
Creativity (pg. 11)

Delinquency (pg. 195)
Dependency (pg. 15)
Depression (pg. 199)
Disasters—How to Respond (pg. 273)
Different Cultural Backgrounds (pg. 19)
Divorce (pg. 285)
Divorce and Our Children (pg. 359)
Divorce—Access and Visitation Arrangements (pg. 287)
Dropouts: Reasons and Responses (pg. 361)
Drug Abuse (pg. 203)
Dysfunctional Families (pg. 291)

Early Childhood Primary Prevention Programs for Emotional and Behavioral Problems (pg. 365)
Encopresis (pg. 207)
Enuresis (pg. 209)

Family Size (pg. 99)
Fears and Phobias (pg. 211)
Firesetting (pg. 213)
Foster Homes (pg. 293)

Gifted Children: Special Needs and Considerations (pg. 141)
Giftedness (pg. 145)
Grade Retention (pg. 373)
Grades (pg. 147)

Head Injury (pg. 215)
Hearing (pg. 21)
Holidays—Coping with Loss (pg. 295)
Homework (pg. 151)
Homosexuality (pg. 25)
Hospitalization (pg. 299)
Household Chores (pg. 103)
Humor (pg. 27)

Increasing Academic Learning Time (pg. 153)

Language Development (pg. 31)
Limited English Proficiency (pg. 157)

Maladaptive Habits (pg. 35)
Masturbation (pg. 37)
Medication (pg. 105)
Moving (pg. 303)
Multicultural and Minority Issues (pg. 377)

Nailbiting (pg. 39)

Obesity (pg. 41)
Obsessive Compulsive Disorder (pg. 217)
Organization (pg. 161)

Peer-Influenced Academic Interventions in the Classroom (pg. 163)
Peer Relations (pg. 85)
Perception of Time (pg. 45)
Physical Abuse (pg. 221)
Prejudice (pg. 47)
Prematurity (pg. 49)

Reactions to Death (pg. 307)
Reading (pg. 167)
Religion (pg. 51)
Responsibility (pg. 53)
Retention (pg. 171)
Running Away (pg. 225)

School Entry Decisions (pg. 175)
Seizures (pg. 309)
Self-Control (pg. 89)
Self-Esteem (pg. 381)
Sexual Abuse (pg. 227)
Sexual Interest (pg. 57)
Sexual Abuse Prevention Programs (pg. 385)
Shyness (pg. 59)
Siblings (pg. 107)
Siblings of the Handicapped (pg. 313)
Single-Parent Homes (pg. 315)
Sleepwalking (pg. 61)
Stealing (pg. 231)
Stepfamilies (pg. 319)
Stress (pg. 63)
Study Skills (pg. 177)

Suicide (pg. 233)
Suicide Intervention (pg. 235)
Surviving the Holidays (pg. 113)

Television (pg. 115)
Temper Tantrums (pg. 119)
Temperament (pg. 65)
Thumbsucking (pg. 69)
Tourette Syndrome (pg. 239)
Transition Planning for Handicapped Students (pg. 323)

War—Responding to Operation Desert Storm (pg. 329)
Working Parents (pg. 123)